SHAKESPEARE SURVEY

ADVISORY BOARD

SHAKESPEARE SURVEY

AN ANNUAL SURVEY OF

SHAKESPEARE STUDIES AND PRODUCTION

45

EDITED BY

STANLEY WELLS

CAMBRIDGE
UNIVERSITY PRESS

PUBLISHED BY THE PRESS SYNDICATE OF THE UNIVERSITY OF CAMBRIDGE
The Pitt Building, Trumpington Street, Cambridge, United Kingdom

CAMBRIDGE UNIVERSITY PRESS
The Edinburgh Building, Cambridge CB2 2RU, UK
40 West 20th Street, New York NY 10011- 4211, USA
477 Williamstown Road, Port Melbourne, VIC 3207, Australia
Ruiz de Alarcón 13, 28014 Madrid, Spain
Dock House, The Waterfront, Cape Town 8001, South Africa

http://www.cambridge.org

First published 1993
First paperback edition 2002

A catalogue record for this book is available from the British Library

ISBN 0 521 42055 5 hardback
ISBN 0 521 52384 2 paperback

Shakespeare Survey was first published in 1948. Its first
eighteen volumes were edited by Allardyce Nicoll.
Kenneth Muir edited volumes 19 to 33.
Stanley Wells edited volumes 34 to 52.
The current editor is Peter Holland.

EDITOR'S NOTE

Volume 46 of *Shakespeare Survey*, which will be at press by the time this volume appears, will have as its theme 'Shakespeare and Sexuality', and will include papers from the 1992 International Shakespeare Conference. Volume 47 will concentrate on 'Playing Places for Shakespeare'.

Submissions should be addressed to the Editor at The Shakespeare Institute, Church Street, Stratford-upon-Avon, Warwickshire CV37 6HP, to arrive at the latest by 1 September 1993 for Volume 47. Pressures on space are heavy; priority is given to articles related to the theme of a particular volume. Please either enclose postage (overseas, in International Reply coupons) or send a copy you do not wish to be returned. All articles submitted are read by the Editor and at least one member of the Editorial Board, whose indispensable assistance the Editor gratefully acknowledges.

Unless otherwise indicated, Shakespeare quotations and references are keyed to the modern-spelling Complete Oxford Shakespeare (1986).

Review copies of books should be addressed to the Editor, as above. In attempting to survey the ever-increasing bulk of Shakespeare publications our reviewers inevitably have to exercise some selection. We are pleased to receive offprints of articles which help to draw our reviewers' attention to relevant material. With this volume David Lindley takes over as reviewer of Critical Studies and Martin Wiggins as reviewer of Shakespeare's Life, Times, and Stage; they replace respectively R. S. White and Richard Dutton, whose services are gratefully acknowledged.

S. W. W.

CONTRIBUTORS

MURRAY BIGGS, *Yale University*
LAWRENCE DANSON, *Princeton University*
MARY EDMOND, *London*
R. A. FOAKES, *University of California, Los Angeles*
GRAHAM HOLDERNESS, *University of Hertfordshire*
PETER HOLLAND, *Trinity Hall, Cambridge*
DAVID LINDLEY, *University of Leeds*
KENNETH MUIR, *Liverpool*
ELLEN J. O'BRIEN, *Guilford College, Greensboro*
NIKY RATHBONE, *Birmingham Shakespeare Library*
PAUL N. SIEGEL, *Long Island University*
LESLIE THOMSON, *University of Toronto*
R. S. WHITE, *University of Western Australia*
MARTIN WIGGINS, *The Shakespeare Institute, University of Birmingham*
H. R. WOUDHUYSEN, *University College, London*

CONTENTS

ILLUSTRATIONS

THE RECEPTION OF HAMLET

R. A. FOAKES

No! I am not Prince Hamlet, nor was meant to
  be;
Am an attendant lord, one that will do
To swell a progress, start a scene or two,
Advise the prince; no doubt, an easy tool,
Deferential, glad to be of use,
Politic, cautious, and meticulous;
Full of high sentence, but a bit obtuse;
At times, indeed, almost ridiculous –
Almost, at times, the Fool.
  T. S. Eliot, 'The Love Song of J. Alfred Prufrock'

Prufrock[1] speaks for much of the twentieth century in his inability to conceive of being Hamlet the *Prince*. By 1917, when this poem was published, Hamlet the prince had been deflected into a Prufrock figure, ever failing to make decisions: 'There will be time to murder and create . . . And time yet for a hundred indecisions'; and in the end Prufrock will not dare to 'Disturb the universe'.[2] Although our first impression from the poem is of someone like Polonius, and although Prufrock denies he is Prince Hamlet, reminding us of a royal authority figure, there is no prince in the poem, but only, as the centre of attention and of self-consciousness, Prufrock, who presents himself as an embodiment of what had become known as Hamletism. Perhaps no other character's name in Shakespeare's plays, and few in any other author's works, have been converted into a noun expressive of an attitude to life or 'philosophy', as we say, and a verb (to Hamletize). Adjectives like Falstaffian, and nouns like Micawberism, relate to the idiosyncrasies of these characters, whereas Hamletism has a wider resonance, representing a body of ideas abstracted from a character already extrapolated from the play *Hamlet*.

Hamletism as a term had become established by the 1840s, and came to have a range of meanings, all interconnected, and developed from an image of Hamlet as well-intentioned but ineffectual, full of talk but unable to achieve anything, addicted to melancholy, and sickened by the world around him, – in short, the Hamlet of the first and third soliloquies: Hamlet contemplating self-slaughter, speaking of death as a kind of sleep, or confronting death as he examines the skulls in the graveyard scene. It was used by Herman Melville in his novel *Pierre* (subtitled *The Ambiguities*, 1852) to express the idea of a 'nobly-striving but ever-shipwrecked character';[3] and as the term became widely current later in the century, it carried gloomier connotations, especially in France after the production of the play by William Macready there in 1844; this was described by Théophile Gautier in his *History of*

---

[1] T. S. Eliot, *Collected Poems 1909–1962* (London, 1963), p. 17. This essay ties in with my article 'King Lear and the Displacement of Hamlet', *Huntington Library Quarterly*, 50 (1987), 263–78, and with my forthcoming book, *Hamlet versus Lear: Cultural Politics and Shakespeare's Art*.

[2] Eliot, *Poems*, p. 14.

[3] Herman Melville, *Pierre*, edited by Harrison Hayford, Hershel Parker and G. Thomas Tanselle (Evanston and Chicago, 1971), pp. 135–6.

Dramatic Art in France (1859), with especial emphasis on the graveyard scene, in which, after he threw down the skull of Yorick, Macready drew out a fine cambric handkerchief and wiped his fingers with disgust.[4] The image of a refined, over-sensitive figure was fixed in the French imagination in a series of lithographs by Delacroix, which Baudelaire hung on his walls; for one early composition, that of Hamlet with the gravediggers, Delacroix used a female friend as a model for Hamlet drawn as a beardless youth, delicate, pallid, and with 'white feminine hands and tapering fingers, an exquisite nature, but without energy'.[5] Hamletism came to embody for the Symbolist poets an idea of an effeminate man whose natural bent was for contemplation, and who was unsuited for action; they thus saw in Hamlet 'not action impeded by morbid melancholy or reflection, as had their elders, the Romantics, but rather the image of mundane action thwarting their pursuit of the ideal'.[6] Whether Hamlet was seen as typifying someone required to act but failing to do so, or as typifying a man prevented by the need to act from dedicating himself to the pursuit of the ideal, the idea of failure attached itself to him. For Jules Laforgue in particular, Hamlet summed up the *fin de siècle* mood of pessimism, *ennui* and despair which he dramatized in his poetry. As Thomas Mann's fictional hero Tonio Kröger travelled to Denmark in search of his alter ego, Hamlet, so Laforgue went to Elsinore so that he could stand by that sea whose monotonous waves assuredly inspired in Hamlet this 'epitaph on the history of humanity: "Words, words, words"'.[7]

Laforgue in turn had a major impact on T. S. Eliot, whose Prufrock resembles some of the figures in Laforgue's *Complaintes*. Gautier had seen Hamlet as raising the question whether the universe is nothing more than the nightmare of a sick god ('L'univers n'est-il que le cauchemar d'un dieu malade . . . ?'),[8] and the defeatism of intellectuals whose time always seemed to be out of joint came to be identified with Hamlet

and Hamletism. The term was sufficiently current in England by 1905 for the *Daily Chronicle* to advise its readers to 'forget Hamletism and all its ills'.[9] In D. H. Lawrence's *Women in Love* (1920), Birkin rejects love, weary, as he says, with 'the life that belongs to death – our kind of love', and sums up his negative mood to Ursula in the boating episode by saying, 'One shouldn't talk when one is tired and wretched – One Hamletises, and it seems a lie.'[10] In denying that he is Prince Hamlet, Prufrock, who comes across as a sort of connoisseur of oblivion, may nevertheless be seen as Hamletizing. Such an idea of Hamlet is a far cry from the heroic Hamlet portrayed on the eighteenth-century stage, or Ophelia's image of him as 'The courtier's, soldier's, scholar's eye, tongue, sword,' or Horatio's 'Goodnight, sweet prince.' I want to trace how and why this shift took place, and comment in a preliminary way on its significance for interpreting Hamlet now.

Although there have been vigorous stage Hamlets since David Garrick played the role with 'uncommon spirit',[11] the theatrical tradition of cutting out the ending of the play,

---

4 Théophile Gautier, *Histoire de la littérature dramatique en France depuis vingt-cinq ans* (6 vols., Paris, 1858), vol. 3, p. 324; see also René Taupin, 'The Myth of Hamlet in France in Mallarmé's Generation', *MLQ*, 14 (1953), 432–47, citing p. 434.

5 Helen Phelps Bailey, *Hamlet in France from Voltaire to Laforgue* (Geneva, 1964), p. 138.

6 Bailey, p. 152.

7 Albert Sonnenfeld, 'Hamlet the German and Jules Laforgue', *Yale French Studies*, 33 (1964), 92–100, citing p. 9.

8 Gautier, 3.324.

9 Cited in *A Supplement to the Oxford English Dictionary*, ed. R. W. Burchfield, vol. 2 (Oxford, 1976), under 'Hamletism', p. 20.

10 *Women in Love*, edited by David Farmer, Lindeth Vasey, and John Worthen (Cambridge, 1986), pp. 186–7.

11 Review in the *London Chronicle*, 17–19 December 1771, cited in *Shakespeare, The Critical Heritage*, ed. Brian Vickers, vol. 5 (London, 1979), p. 46. Garrick cut out 898 lines of the 1002 in Act 5 to rescue this 'noble play' from 'all the rubbish of the 5th act' (Vickers, 5.11).

dispensing with minor characters like Fortinbras, and even Horatio sometimes, no doubt contributed to the remarkable change that took place towards the end of the eighteenth century. The conflation of the Second Quarto and Folio texts in printed editions from Theobald's (1733) onwards also fostered misconceptions in critical assessments of the play, and helped to establish the idea of Hamlet as delaying his revenge for no good reason, and as continually deferring action.[12] Furthermore, the ideal of a prince embodied in the Renaissance conception of the courtier as a man of action lost its meaning in the wake of the French Revolution, in an age that saw the emergence of mass industrial societies, and the rise of individualism in the nineteenth century. So it should not surprise us that Hamlet begins to be appropriated into a new image at the end of the eighteenth century. He sheds his role as prince and courtier, and becomes privatized, as in Goethe's famous *Wilhelm Meister's Apprenticeship* (1796); in this novel, Wilhelm interprets Hamlet in relation to himself: 'A lovely, pure, noble and most moral nature, without the strength of nerve which forms a hero, sinks beneath a burden which it cannot bear and must not cast away.'[13] Incapable of heroism, Hamlet is conceived as a soul unfit for the performance of a great action. The sensitive, melancholy figure, shrinking from involvement, projected in Goethe's novel passes into the ineffectual dreamer who seemed to typify intellectuals who were incapable of translating their revolutionary ideals into action. This is seen in Ferdinand Freiligrath's famous poem of 1844 beginning 'Germany is Hamlet' ('Deutschland ist Hamlet'), and portraying a Hamlet whose 'boldest act is only thinking'; Freiligrath ends by identifying himself with Hamlet as a 'poor old dreamer'.[14]

Hamlet could thus be absorbed into the German consciousness in two ways, as identified by the observant scholar Gervinus in 1849, either as an idealist, unequal to the real world; or as embittered by its deficiencies and his inability to change things.[15] So in Germany, as in France, Hamlet came to be seen as a contemplative in pursuit of ideals, but trapped in a world demanding action, or as a noble figure capable of action, but embittered and rendered ineffectual by his disgust with the world around him. Both perspectives contributed to a sense of Hamlet as settling for what Kierkegaard in *Either/Or* identified as the aesthetic choice, i.e. neutrality, or refusing to act, out of a sense of the futility of all endeavour.[16] Although the Furness Variorum edition (1877) was, after the Franco-Prussian war and the German victories of 1870, dedicated to the 'GERMAN SHAKE-SPEARE SOCIETY OF WEIMAR REPRESENTATIVE OF A PEOPLE WHOSE RECENT HISTORY HAS PROVED ONCE FOR ALL THAT GERMANY IS NOT HAMLET',[17] the familiar Hamlet returned in the influential formulation by Nietzsche in *The Birth of Tragedy*, as someone afflicted with a disgust so powerful that it becomes a disease, a nausea towards life and a world he cannot face.[18]

In Russia Hamlet became the exemplar of what Turgenev called the superfluous man. In his *Diary of a Superfluous Man* (1850), Turgenev imagines a thirty-year-old man (age of Hamlet) who keeps a diary in the last few weeks of a life that is meaningless, a life that, as he says, has almost driven him out of his mind with *ennui*. He fails in his pursuit of love and dies in the spring as everything else comes to life; he has

---

[12] See the Introduction by G. R. Hibbard in his edition of *Hamlet* (Oxford, 1987), pp. 22–7.

[13] Cited in Ruby Cohn, *Modern Shakespeare Offshoots* (Princeton, 1976), pp. 118–19.

[14] Cited in *Hamlet*, A New Variorum Edition of Shakespeare, edited H. H. Furness, 2 vols. (Philadelphia, 1877; reprinted New York, 1963), vol. 2, pp. 376–8.

[15] Cited in *Hamlet*, ed. Furness, vol. 2, pp. 300–1.

[16] Søren Kierkegaard, *Either/Or*, translated Howard V. Hong and Edna H. Hong, 2 vols. (Princeton, 1976), vol. 2, pp. 166–9; Bailey, p. 153.

[17] *Hamlet*, ed. Furness, 1877; the dedication was removed from later reprints, and does not appear in that of 1905.

[18] Frederick Nietzsche, *The Birth of Tragedy* (1872), translated Walter Kaufman (New York, 1967), p. 60.

derived pleasure only from the contemplation of his own unhappiness.[19] This followed a short story, 'Hamlet of Shshtchigry District' (1849), in which Turgenev listens to the life-story of a strange man educated in Germany (again like Hamlet), who lives bored on his family estate, and sees himself as insignificant and useless; he refuses to name himself, only saying, 'call me the Hamlet of Shshtchigry county. There are lots of such Hamlets in every county.'[20] In his well-known essay of 1860 comparing Hamlet and Don Quixote, Turgenev depicted Hamlet as representative of persons who are thoughtful and discriminating, but 'useless in the practical sense, in as much as their very gifts immobilize them'; for him Hamlet personified scepticism.[21] Hamlet also lies behind Dostoevsky's *Notes from Underground* (1864), with its central figure, apparently a civil servant, for whom 'not only too much consciousness, but any sort of consciousness is a disease', and who finds the 'result of consciousness is to make all actions impossible', so that he cannot take the revenge he desires.[22]

Later still Chekhov created Layevsky in his story *The Duel* (1891), described by another character as 'a failure, a superfluous man, a neurotic, a victim of the age'.[23] In refusing to take responsibility for the life of lies he leads, Layevsky says, 'I'm as bad as Hamlet'. This story was, in a way, a response to Turgenev, who is blamed in the course of it for 'inventing failures',[24] and it ends with Layevsky, the Hamlet figure, living in poverty, and working off his debts, so taking on responsibilities. He is thus to some extent redeemed; but the image of Hamlet as a failure haunted Chekhov, who had created in *Ivanov* (1887–9) a central figure who neglects his wife, talks endlessly, and does nothing: he says, 'I do nothing and think of nothing, but I'm tired, body and soul ... I'm bored here too', and he sees himself as 'a kind of Hamlet': 'Wherever I go I carry misery, indifference, boredom, discontent, and disgust with life.'[25] Ivanov ends by shooting himself, carrying out the suicide merely contemplated by Hamlet. He is different from the figures in

Turgenev and Dostoevsky in that he blames himself, not society, for what he is. Yet through all these responses to the character of Hamlet runs the burden of Hamletism, the image of Hamlet as disgusted, consumed by ennui, sensitive and over-conscious, and unable to do anything about it.

In France Hamlet was mythologized well into the twentieth century as a dreamer who opts for an ideal of pure being, and finds 'his vocation thwarted, his pure world violated, by the necessity to act', or who suffers from *taedium vitae* and is averse to action.[26] Hamletism in fact took several forms, but as René Taupin summed it up, it expresses 'the lure of nothingness, the delightful contemplation of ruins, sadism and masochism, the desire for and the inability to love, sarcasm and humour turned against oneself'[27] – this was what was

[19] Ivan Turgenev, *The Diary of a Superfluous Man* (1850; translated Isabel Hapgood, *Novels and Stories of Ivan Turgenieff*, 6 vols. (New York, 1904), vol. 3; subject to ennui in his meaningless life, he finds pleasure in the contemplation of his own unhappiness (p. 71). Turgenev does not mention Hamlet in this story, but Chekhov links Layevsky in *The Duel* with both the 'superfluous man' and with Hamlet. See also Grigori Kozintsev, *Shakespeare Time and Conscience* (translated Joyce Vining, New York, 1966), pp. 126–7.

[20] 'Hamlet of Shshtchigry District' (1849), translated Hapgood, *Novels and Stories*, vol. 2 (New York, 1903), pp. 146–90, citing p. 190.

[21] *Hamlet and Don Quixote* (1860), translated Robert Nichols (Edinburgh, 1930), p. 26.

[22] Fyodor Dostoevsky, 'Notes from the Underground', translated David Magarshack, *Great Short Works of Fyodor Dostoevsky* (New York, 1968), pp. 267, 276.

[23] Anton Chekhov, 'The Duel', in *The Oxford Chekhov*, translated Ronald Hingley, 9 vols. (London, 1965–80), vol. 5, pp. 150, 144.

[24] Chekhov, 'The Duel', vol. 5, p. 147.

[25] Anton Chekhov, 'Ivanov' (1887–9), *The Oxford Chekhov*, tr. Ronald Hingley, vol. 2 (London, 1967), 2.6, p. 193; 4.10, p. 225.

[26] Peter Brooks, 'The Rest is Silence: Hamlet as Decadent', in *Jules Laforgue Essays on a Poet's Life and Work*, ed. Warren Ramsey (Carbondale, 1969), pp. 93–110, citing p. 97; Taupin, 'The Myth of Hamlet', p. 439.

[27] Taupin, p. 442.

read into Shakespeare in the 1880s and remained a mordant presence in the consciousness of French intellectuals. As late as 1950, in the wake of two world wars, Paul Valéry imagined the figure of Hamlet brooding over millions of ghosts in the graveyard of Europe:[28]

Today, from an immense platform at Elsinore which stretches from Basel to Cologne, and which reaches the sands of Nieuport, the marshes of the Somme, the hilltops of Champagne and the granite of Alsace, our European Hamlet contemplates millions of spectres. But he is an intellectual Hamlet; he reflects upon the life and death of human truths ... He is overwhelmed by the accumulation of discoveries and knowledge we have piled up; he is incapable of coping with this unlimited activity. He muses on the boredom of repeating the past; he muses on the folly of always wanting to be an innovator ...

It is a vision of bleakness in which Hamlet becomes himself a giant spectre or ghost symbolizing the European intellectual brooding over desolation and not knowing what to do with all the skulls around him.[29] Valéry's metaphor transforms the graveyard scene so that Europe itself becomes a vast cemetery in which Hamlet picks over the skulls of great artists and thinkers of the past, Leonardo, Leibniz, Kant and Hegel, whose work has led to nothing. This is the culmination of the French obsession with Hamlet holding a skull, an obsession that goes back to Delacroix's painting of a 'delicate and wan' figure, 'with white and feminine hands, an exquisite but weak nature', and a 'somewhat irresolute air', as Baudelaire described the picture.[30]

In England Hamlet was privatized initially by the Romantics, as by Coleridge, who saw him as a figure overwhelmed by the activity of his mind, so that 'he is a man living in meditation, called upon to act by every motive human & divine, but the great purpose of life defeated by continually resolving to do, yet doing nothing but resolve'.[31] His famous remark, 'I have a smack of Hamlet myself,'[32] absorbs the character into Coleridge's own persona, abstracting him from the play, and

giving him the independent life that before long led to the idea of 'Hamletism'. Even the radical William Hazlitt found himself able only to echo Coleridge in his essay on the play, broadening Coleridge's identification of Hamlet with himself into 'It is *we* who are Hamlet. The play has a prophetic truth, which is above that of history.'[33] Hazlitt extends the privatization of Hamlet, who, as a man 'whose powers of action have been eaten up by thought', turns into an embodiment of each of us, or at any rate of 'whoever has become thoughtful and melancholy through his own mishaps or those of others ... he who has felt his mind sink within him, and sadness cling to his heart like a malady, who has had his hopes blighted ... whose powers of action have been eaten up by thought'.[34] But the private Hamlet was soon returned to the public and political arena, as by Emerson, who gave currency to an image of Hamlet as typifying the 1830s in his essay on 'The American Scholar' (1837), in which he defines his age as one of introversion: 'We, it seems, are critical. We are embarrassed with second thoughts. We cannot enjoy any thing for hankering to know whereof the pleasure consists.' He saw his age as 'infected with Hamlet's unhappiness' and 'sicklied o'er with the pale cast of thought', so that Hamlet is identified with the nineteenth-century intellectual for whom 'action, this way or that, is profoundly insignificant'.[35]

---

28 Paul Valéry, 'Variété', in *Oeuvres Complètes* (Paris, 1950), vol. 4, pp. 20–1, as translated by René Taupin, p. 446.

29 Valéry, vol. 4, p. 21: 'Et moi, se dit-il, moi, l'intellect européen, que vais-je devenir?' See also Bailey, *Hamlet in France*, p. 154.

30 Taupin, 'The Myth of Hamlet', p. 434.

31 Samuel Taylor Coleridge, *Lectures 1808–1819: On Literature*, ed. R. A. Foakes, 2 vols. (Princeton, 1987), vol. 1, p. 390.

32 Coleridge, *Table-Talk*, 24 June 1827.

33 William Hazlitt, *Characters of Shakespeare's Plays*, in *The Complete Works of William Hazlitt*, ed. P. P. Howe, 21 vols. (London, 1930–4), vol. 4, p. 232.

34 Hazlitt, vol. 4, p. 232.

35 'The American Scholar', *Collected Works of Ralph Waldo Emerson*, vol. 1 (Cambridge, Mass., 1971), p. 66.

Lowell (1850) generalized in a somewhat different way, but to much the same effect, saying men of Hamlet's 'type are forever analysing their own emotions and motives. They cannot do anything because they always see two ways of doing it.'[36]

Matthew Arnold (1853) in his gloomy way also identified Hamlet with the problems of the age, the modern world, in which 'the calm, the cheerfulness, the disinterested objectivity' of the ancient Greeks have disappeared, and the 'dialogue of the mind with itself has commenced; modern problems have represented themselves; we hear already the doubts, we witness the discouragement, of Hamlet and Faust [i.e. Goethe's *Faust*]'.[37] Later in the nineteenth century, Edward Dowden applauded what Schlegel and Coleridge had said, and repeated Emerson's comment, 'action, this way or that, is profoundly insignificant to Hamlet'; but he wanted to locate what he called Hamlet's 'malady' in his heart as well as his head, in his sensibility as well as his intellect.[38] A. C. Bradley (1904) effected this shift by finding the immediate cause for Hamlet's inaction in a disgust for life brought on by his discovery of his mother's lustfulness; and so the malady of Hamlet turned into a neurosis, a morbid condition of melancholy, the paralysing pressure of which, from 'the psychological point of view', became the centre of the tragedy.[39]

Ernest Jones extended this psychoanalysis in 1923, and later in his book *Hamlet and Oedipus* (1949), arguing that Hamlet cannot kill Claudius because he is repressing an unconscious desire to have displaced his own father himself, and in Hamlet, 'as in every victim of a powerful unconscious conflict the Will to Death is fundamentally stronger than the Will to Life'.[40] This view, anticipated in Chekhov's embodiment of Hamletism, the suicidal Layevsky, is reflected in James Joyce's *Ulysses* in Stephen Daedalus' image of Hamlet/Shakespeare as a 'deathsman of the soul', who causes the 'bloody shambles' of Act 5; and it was taken over into academic cricitism in the influential essay by Wilson

Knight (1930, 1947), called 'The Embassy of Death', in which Hamlet, as the ambassador of death, affects others like a 'blighting disease' by his passivity and negation;[41] but the most subtle expression of this kind of reading is found in Freud's *Civilization and its Discontents* (1930). Here, in a sweeping view of the evolution of civilization as a struggle between 'Eros and Death, the instinct of life and the instinct of destruction', the price of advance in civilization is seen as 'a loss of happiness through heightening the sense of guilt', and this is manifested as anxiety or malaise. Although Freud does not comment specifically on the play, it was in his mind, for he cites in this connection the line, 'Thus conscience does make cowards of us all.'[42]

I have jumped rapidly from Coleridge lecturing in 1811 to the twentieth century, but I have said enough, I hope, to show how Hamlet, converted into a projection at first of the troubled minds of individual Romantics, and so democratized, became available as a representative embodiment of the failings of a class, of a group of intellectuals, of a nation, of Europe in Valéry's despairing vision, and even of the world. Hamlet could thus be identified with an attitude or philosophic stance as Hamletism, and incorporated into an image of 'Man'

---

[36] James Russell Lowell, 'On *Hamlet*', *c.*1850, in Williamson, p. 84.

[37] Matthew Arnold, Preface to *Poems* (1853), in *The Poems of Matthew Arnold*, ed. Kenneth Allott (London, 1965), p. 591.

[38] Edward Dowden, *Shakespeare's Mind and Art* (1875; 3rd edn, London, 1886), pp. 132, 134. Dowden refers to Hamlet's 'malady' on p. 160.

[39] A. C. Bradley, *Shakespearean Tragedy* (London, 1905), pp. 117–27, citing p. 127.

[40] Ernest Jones, *Essays in Applied Psycho-analysis* (1923), in C. C. H. Williamson, *Readings in the Character of Hamlet 1661–1947* (London, 1950), p. 435; see also *Hamlet and Oedipus* (New York, 1949; reprinted 1976).

[41] G. Wilson Knight, *The Wheel of Fire* (1930, revised 1949; New York, 1957), p. 32.

[42] Sigmund Freud, *Civilization and its Discontents* (1930, tr. James Strachey, New York, 1961), pp. 69, 81 and n.

with a capital 'M', the whole of mankind. The growth of Hamletism is traceable mainly in the works of men of letters, essayists, poets, novelists and dramatists, who were writing for a general readership. But ideas of Hamlet and Hamletism to which they gave wide currency affected the academic criticism that has burgeoned with the professionalization of university English departments since the 1930s. The most influential academic essays of the twentieth century have continued to offer us, with whatever qualifications, an image of Hamlet infected if not overwhelmed by Hamletism. An example is J. Dover Wilson's *What Happens in Hamlet* (1935, 9 impressions by 1962), in which we are told that 'From the very beginning Shakespeare has been playing variations upon the Hamlet theme . . . suggesting that sense of frustration, futility and human inadequacy which is the burden of the whole symphony'; and Shakespeare 'never lets us forget that he [Hamlet] is a failure, or that he has failed through weakness of character'.[43] Another is Maynard Mack's 'The World of Hamlet' (1951–2). In this important essay the play is presented as a 'paradigm of the life of man', 'Man in his aspect of bafflement', envisaged as 'moving in darkness on a rampart between two worlds';[44] Hamlet's inability to act is linked to the overlapping meanings of words like 'act', 'play', and 'show', and in a world of seeming Hamlet raises questions about the nature of reality when to act is to play or to pretend. Hamlet confronts a condition not of his own making, and cannot do anything about it; so he seems to embody for Mack 'an emphasis on human weakness, the instability of human purpose, the subjection of humanity to fortune – all that we might call the aspect of failure in man'.[45] Mack avoids committing himself to a psychology, or finding a neurosis in Hamlet, and his analysis is primarily moral and metaphysical, but his conclusions are in many ways in line with those of Dover Wilson and earlier critics.

There have been alternative voices, notably Peter Alexander, who tried to restore a notion of Hamlet as 'the ideal prince',[46] referring to Shakespeare's sources in Saxo and Belleforest, but although he claimed that Hamlet unites 'heroic passions of antiquity with the meditative wisdom of later ages', the best he could do for a modern equivalent was to link him somewhat oddly with Raymond Chandler's hero, Philip Marlowe, citing his famous comment, 'down these mean streets a man must go who is not himself mean, who is neither tarnished nor afraid',[47] and diminishing the Prince into a tough but humane private eye. Yet this is perhaps the best analogy for the heroic anyone has come up with in an age when, as Joseph Wood Krutch argued years ago in *The Modern Temper* (1929), the idea of the hero has lost most of its force.[48] George Hunter also tried to rescue the Prince in an essay affirming 'The Heroism of Hamlet' (1963) as that of an individual who 'keeps facing up to and maintaining some control over the flux of action he stirs around him', a heroism depending less on 'acting or even knowing than on being',[49] but again this is a

---

43 J. Dover Wilson, *What Happens in Hamlet* (1935; 3rd edn, 1951, reprinted Cambridge, 1962), pp. 261, 268, 274.

44 Maynard Mack, 'The World of Hamlet', *Yale Review*, NS 41 (1951–2), 502–23, citing pp. 503, 507.

45 Mack, p. 515.

46 Peter Alexander, *Hamlet Father and Son* (Oxford, 1955), p. 166.

47 Alexander, pp. 184, 174.

48 Joseph Wood Krutch, *The Modern Temper* (New York, 1929): Krutch thought Hamlet showed 'greatness of spirit', and died 'not as a failure, but as a success' (p. 131), while now we 'can believe in Oswald [Alving in Ibsen's *Ghosts*], but we cannot believe in Hamlet' (p. 132). His was a rare voice in continuing to see Hamlet as heroic, and he seemed unaware of the process by which Hamlet had come to embody something not unlike the diseased consciousness of Oswald.

49 G. K. Hunter, 'The Heroism of Hamlet', in *Hamlet*, edited J. R. Brown and Bernard Harris (Stratford-upon-Avon Studies 5, London, 1963), 90–109, citing pp. 104, 105; see also, for versions of a strong Hamlet, Joseph Summers, *Dreams of Love and Power* (Oxford, 1984), pp. 45–67; Andrew Gurr, *Hamlet and the Distracted Globe* (Edinburgh, 1978).

sadly diminished and slimmed down concept of heroism, consisting rather in a stance towards events than in doing anything. And Laurence Olivier, fresh from his energetic triumph in the film of *Henry V*, presented in his movie of *Hamlet* (1947) an image of a golden-haired courtier, wearing braid on his shoulder suggestive of a military officer, so that he seemed to Harry Levin to coalesce with the image of the swashbuckling Douglas Fairbanks;[50] but this image was contradicted by much else in the film, notably by the voiceover at the beginning saying, 'This is the story of a man who could not make up his mind.'

Hamlet as indecisive, a neurotic nauseated by sex or the world, a nihilist in love with death, above all a failure: these have remained the dominant images. At the same time, an extraordinary shift has taken place since Goethe, Schlegel and Coleridge deconstructed the Prince and turned him into a private reflection of each of us, a common man, or, in Hazlitt's words, 'as little of the hero as a man can well be'.[51] For the privatized Hamlet, abstracted from the play and turned into a projection of each of us as individuals ('It is *we* who are Hamlet'; 'I have a smack of Hamlet myself') was gradually restored to the public arena, though still largely withdrawn from the play as an autonomous figure. Indeed, once set free from the play, Hamlet was not easily put back into it. Numerous academic critics have, of course, written on the play, often treating it as self-contained, as a text to be confined within its own boundaries, having no wider relevance; they have argued interminably about whether Claudius committed incest, whether the Ghost comes from Heaven, Hell or Purgatory, whether Claudius sees the play within the play, and why Hamlet doesn't stab the King when he is praying and at his mercy. But many, too, have made the character the centre of their attention, and have found in the play 'a study in indecision',[52] seeing Hamlet as neurotic or morally trapped, or they have rapped him over the knuckles as showing a 'desire to escape from the

complexities of adult living', and seen him as 'unable to break out of the closed circle of loathing and self-contempt'.[53] And at its best, as in Maynard Mack's essay, academic criticism has had a strong intertextual relationship with the writings on Hamlet by artists, poets, novelists, directors and intellectuals; and the reception of Hamlet by these is what I have been mainly concerned with.

So let me return to the shift that brought back Hamlet from the private to the public world in the nineteenth and twentieth centuries. This shift took two forms.[54] One was overtly political, as in Freiligrath's identification of Hamlet with young German intellectuals unable to bring about the desired revolution, or in Valéry's despairing vision of Europe after World War 2 as the spectre of Hamlet presiding over a civilization diminished to an anthill. From a right-wing point of view, Hamlet seemed to represent the failure of a 'great nature confronted with a low environment',[55] or, in a harsher aspect, a 'spirit of disintegration', as a man 'isolated, self-nauseated, labouring in a sense of physical corruption',[56] a representative of what W. B. Yeats[57] called 'this filthy modern tide' ('The

---

[50] Harry Levin, *The Question of Hamlet* (New York, 1959), p. 131.

[51] Hazlitt, vol. 4, p. 233.

[52] Allardyce Nicoll, *Studies in Shakespeare* (London, 1927), p. 80.

[53] L. C. Knights, *An Approach to Hamlet* (London, 1960), pp. 90–1; *Explorations* (London, 1946, reprinted 1958), p. 70.

[54] I am leaving out of account here the treatment of Hamlet in the Soviet Union and eastern Europe, where efforts were made to reconstruct Hamlet as a courageous and heroic character; see, for instance, Eleanor Rowe, *Hamlet a Window on Russia* (New York, 1976).

[55] E. K. Chambers, 'Hamlet' (1894), cited in Williamson, *Readings in the Character of Hamlet*, p. 186.

[56] D. H. Lawrence, *Twilight in Italy*, 1916; New York, 1958, p. 88; Lawrence was describing Enrico Persevalli's performance in the role.

[57] W. B. Yeats, 'The Statues', in *Collected Poems* (1933, 2nd edn, London, 1950), pp. 375–6.

Statues', 1938), or of 'the reaction from the great aristocratic to the great democratic principle' deplored by D. H. Lawrence.[58] From a left-wing point of view, though Hamlet was momentarily rescued in the middle of World War 2 by Max Plowman, who identified him in 1942 as 'self-conscious man encompassed by a world of violence . . . our world is in fact the world of Hamlet, a world that has suffered injury and cries out for justice',[59] Hamlet is more likely to be seen, in Charles Marowitz's words, as 'the supreme prototype of the conscience-stricken but paralysed liberal, one of the most lethal and obnoxious characters in modern times'.[60]

By the 1960s, in any case, a larger disillusion had set in; we had Jan Kott's influential vision of *Shakespeare our Contemporary* (English version, 1964), written by someone who, as Peter Brook said in his foreword, 'assumes without question that every one of his readers will at some point or other have been woken by the police in the middle of the night'.[61] Hamlet was necessarily politicized in the context of the cold war. In 1965 there was a notable production of the play by the Royal Shakespeare Theatre, directed by the young Peter Hall, and people, mostly young themselves, stood in line for hours to get tickets. Hamlet was played by a tall adolescent David Warner, dressed like a student, and wearing the ankle-length scarf then fashionable; he was gauche, gangling, anti-romantic, there was nothing to suggest a prince, and, as the conservative *Financial Times* reported, Hamlet appeared 'a beatnik, not only in his dress and appearance, but in his behaviour as well';[62] the term 'beatnik' was introduced in 1958 with reference to the 'beat generation' who rejected bourgeois values in America; Webster coyly defines it as 'a person who rejects the mores of established society (as by dressing and behaving unconventionally) and indulges in exotic philosophizing and self-expression'.[63] Hamlet the beatnik caught the imagination of audiences then, and it is worth noting Peter Hall's address to the cast of his

production; Hall was a Cambridge graduate and had read the critics, and after referring to Granville-Barker, Brecht and Jan Kott, he said[64]

Shakespeare himself was entering a dark valley — a place of cynicism, tragedy, and disgust . . . For our decade, in my view, the play will be about the problems of commitment in life and in politics, and also about the disillusionment that produces an apathy of the will . . . There is a sense of what-the-hell-anyway, over us looms the mushroom cloud. And politics are a game and a lie, whether in our own country or in the East–West dialogue, which goes on interminably, without anything very real being said . . . [at the end] you are left with Fortinbras, the perfect military ruler . . . I would not particularly like to live in a Denmark ruled by Fortinbras.

In the world of the H-bomb cynicism seemed the only stance: what possibility was there of commitment? There have been other political readings since Peter Hall's production, though the play seemed for some time to lose its contemporary relevance after 1970, in England

---

[58] D. H. Lawrence, *Twilight in Italy*, p. 69.

[59] Max Plowman, *The Right to Live* (1942), cited in Williamson, p. 717.

[60] Charles Marowitz, *The Marowitz Shakespeare* (New York, 1978), p. 13.

[61] Jan Kott, *Shakespeare our Contemporary* (translated Boleslaw Taborski (London, 1964), p. ix; Peter Brook's foreword was not included in the American edition, which has instead a foreword by Martin Esslin, who writes, strangely in view of Kott's readings, 'it is one of the roots of Shakespeare's universality that his work seems free of any definite ideological position' (p. xvii).

[62] *Financial Times*, 20 August 1965, B. A. Young reviewing. Alan Brien, in the *Sunday Telegraph*, 25 August, saw Warner's Hamlet as a 'lanky, seedy overgrown student out of a Russian novel'.

[63] *Webster's Ninth New College Dictionary* (Springfield, Mass., 1986). According to the Supplement to the *Oxford English Dictionary*, the word was introduced, after 'sputnik', in 1958, in reference to the 'beat generation', seen as new barbarians rebelling against American bourgeois values.

[64] Peter Hall's talk to his company of actors, as reported in *The Observer*, 15 August 1965.

at any rate; it was not produced by the Royal Shakespeare Theatre between 1970 and 1980 except in a modern-dress version in the small Other Place, seating only 120. Here, at any rate, it seemed that Hamlet was marginalized, and when the play was revived in 1980 in a production devised in metadramatic terms, played on a stage within a stage, receding into a rehearsal and props room, Sheridan Morley, reviewing it in *Punch*, could see little point in the production, or in 'doing Hamlet here and now'.[65]

It is striking that Hamlet has usually been seen in political terms either as a 'great nature' rendered ineffectual or nauseated by a democratic society in which action seems useless, an image related to the Coleridgean view of him as required to act but failing to do so; or alternatively, as a conscience-stricken intellectual who recoils from violence and is thus unable to take action, an image corresponding to the Symbolists' view of him as thwarted in his pursuit of the ideal by involvement in the world of action. These are two familiar and related but different faces of Hamletism; and academic criticism that evades a directly political emphasis by transposing discussion on to a philosophical plane, and treating Hamlet as an embodiment of 'failure in man', is in fact reinforcing the political version of the character as typifying ineffectuality, the inability to act, or what J. L. Calderwood has recently called the '*via negativa*'.[66]

A second way in which Hamlet has been returned to the public arena is in relation to what Peter Hall called 'commitment in life'. Here I recall the better academic criticism; Maynard Mack pointed out the centrality of showing, acting, playing, in Hamlet – if to act is to play or pretend, what is the nature of an act? Who are the guilty creatures sitting at a play? It was traditional for a long time for critics to echo one another in finding Hamlet's delay to be the central issue in the play, which is the academic way of talking about indecision or inability to act; and the notion of delay was often formulated in terms like those of Harold

Jenkins in the Arden edition (1982), who thinks of the play as about 'a man with a deed to do who for most of the time conspicuously fails to do it'.[67] It is another way of rapping Hamlet's knuckles, as someone who fails to carry out a 'duty' imposed by the Ghost of his father. But recent critics have understood Hamlet's delay in subtler and more convincing terms, as a dramatic device which allows the dramatist to 'question the nature of the act of revenge'.[68] Pursuing this line of enquiry, we may begin to see another, deeper relevance of *Hamlet* which accounts for the continuing interest in the play, marked by no fewer than three major editions in the last decade or so,[69] and three productions in London and Stratford in 1989.

It may seem, at first sight, a long way from Coleridge and Hazlitt ('We are all Hamlet') to Prufrock ('I am not Prince Hamlet'), but if we have lost the prince, we have gained something too. For beyond the political versions of Hamlet as a figure for the irresolute intellectual, inhibited from action, we may glimpse a deeper concern with commitment, with the nature, usefulness, and indeed the possibility of action in a world we can't comprehend – our democratic world, in which the structures of power have become almost as remote and inscrutable as those of Kafka, as the Irangate affair and the trial of Colonel North show. In the best-known literary response to *Hamlet* in recent times, Tom Stoppard's *Rosencrantz and Guil-*

---

[65] Sheridan Morley in *Punch*, 16 July 1980.

[66] J. L. Calderwood, *To Be and Not to Be: Negation and Metadrama in Hamlet* (New York, 1983), p. 189: 'Hamlet is extraordinarily given to the *via negativa*. Here, perhaps, more than anywhere else in his work, Shakespeare specializes in nonbeing and inaction, in forms of verbal suicide, in junctures and caesurae, in unnamings and unspeakings.'

[67] William Shakespeare, *Hamlet*, edited Harold Jenkins (Arden edn, London, 1982), p. 140.

[68] R. N. Alexander, *Poison, Play and Duel* (London, 1971), pp. 2–6 and especially p. 10.

[69] Besides the Arden edition (1982), those by Philip Edwards (Cambridge, 1985), and G. R. Hibbard (Oxford, 1987).

denstern are Dead (1966), we lose sight of Hamlet through much of the play. Instead of seeing with Hamlet as observer, we see all through the eyes of Rosencrantz and Guildenstern, who don't understand what is going on. 'We are little men', they say, 'we don't understand the ins and outs of the matter.'[70] From the point of view of Rosencrantz and Guildenstern, *Hamlet* is all action, this is all they see, uncomprehendingly. But there is one moment when they have an opportunity to intervene, when they are with Hamlet on the boat travelling to England. They open Claudius' letter to find it contains orders for the immediate execution of Hamlet on his arrival there. After debating what to do about the letter, Guildenstern concludes, 'All in all I think we'd be well advised to leave well alone'; they are the ones who cannot act. As Rosencrantz says, 'We don't question, we don't doubt. We perform.'[71] They perform their assigned roles, and when faced with a genuine moral and political problem, they leave well alone; they treat life as a game. But action is a serious matter for Hamlet, who overhears their conversation, and sends them to their deaths instead. In *Rosencrantz and Guildenstern are Dead*, Shakespeare's play is glimpsed from time to time in a series of incomprehensible brief actions, and perhaps this is why Stoppard later boiled Hamlet down to his fifteen-minute version, reducing it to a chain of events, and so revealing it as farce; for speeding up the play in this way (as Marowitz and Joseph Papp also have done) empties all significance from the plot as such, as if to show that its power lies not in the events, but in the play's investigation of the problem of doing anything significant in a world that preaches morality and is evidently corrupt; as Papp said in the preface to his 'unravelling and reweaving' of the play, '*Hamlet* is a crisis-ridden play, and if ever humanity was in a crisis, it is now.'[72]

In *Shakespeare our Contemporary* Jan Kott wrote of Hamlet in specific relation to two productions in Poland, one in Cracow in 1956, the other in Warsaw in 1959. In these the play was presented as a 'drama of political crime', with Hamlet as a rebel, passionate and brutal. In the first production the text was, in Kott's words, 'deprived of the great soliloquies'.[73] In other words, the emphasis was on action, violence and political intrigue. In order to key the play into his own political world, the director omitted what for many academic commentators are central, the major soliloquies, which is why so many are disconcerted or refuse to believe the evidence when faced with the probability that Shakespeare revised the play by removing the whole of the last major soliloquy, 'How all occasions do inform against me.' The Polish treatment of the play is at the opposite extreme from that of Stoppard, a Czech writing in conservative Britain. Effectively, Stoppard expanded material from the soliloquies into the endless ramblings of Rosencrantz and Guildenstern, and telescoped the action so as to reduce it to nonsense, inscrutability, or mere performance. What Stoppard has done parallels what many academic critics do in commenting on the play in purely philosophical, moral, psychological, or metaphysical terms, as though these can stand alone, and the play can be treated entirely as an exploration of the grounds for any meaningful action at all. The play is such an exploration, certainly, but it is more than this. For Sir Philip Sidney 'the ending end of all earthly knowledge is virtuous action';[74] but what place is there for virtuous action in the world of policy and diplomacy, built on deceptions, concealment, hypocrisy? In

---

[70] Tom Stoppard, *Rosencrantz and Guildenstern are Dead* (London, 1967), p. 82.

[71] Stoppard, pp. 80, 78.

[72] Tom Stoppard, *Dogg's Hamlet, Cahoot's Macbeth* (London, 1980); Charles Marowitz reduced *Hamlet* to a 28-minute collage (London, 1968), and see Joseph Papp, *William Shakespeare's 'Naked' Hamlet A Production Handbook* (Toronto, 1969), citing pp. 30, 31.

[73] Kott, pp. 51, 52.

[74] Sir Philip Sidney, 'An Apologie for Poetry', in *Miscellaneous Prose*, ed. Katherine Duncan-Jones and Jan van Dorsten (Oxford, 1973), p. 83.

order to challenge the power of Claudius, Hamlet is forced to adopt his methods, and taint himself, and this constitutes the overt structure of the play. It is, in the end, inescapably political, as the novelists, artists, poets and essayists have eloquently shown us over two centuries.

The idea of Hamletism as an attitude to life, a 'philosophy' as we casually put it, developed after the Romantics freed Hamlet the character from the play into an independent existence as a figure embodying nobility, or at least good intentions, but disabled from action by a sense of inadequacy, of failure, or a diseased consciousness capable only of seeing the world as possessed utterly by things rank and gross in nature. Hamletism gained currency as a term to describe not only individuals, but the failings of intellectuals, political parties or nations, and so was restored to the public arena in its use by poets like Freiligrath, Valéry or Yeats, novelists like Joseph Conrad,[75] D. H. Lawrence, and James Joyce, and directors like Peter Hall, to characterize the condition of Germany, or Europe, or the world, or the decline of the aristocracy in the face of democracy, and above all to symbolize modern man. As the idea of Hamletism prospered, so it came to affect the way the play was regarded, and the most widely accepted critical readings of it have for a long time presented us with a version of Shakespeare's drama re-infected, so to speak, with the virus of Hamletism, and seen in its totality as a vision of failure in Man. Since about 1800 Hamlet has become a representative of modern anxieties, and has been democratized into a figure symbolizing the dismay of ordinary people in the lonely crowd of modern societies at their inability to change what they see as wrong in their environment. It is perhaps not too much to conclude that in this period Hamletism has been more potent and influential not only than Hamlet the prince, but also than *Hamlet* the play.

Whether the attitude is cynical, a throwing up of the hands, as in Stoppard's play; or authoritarian, as in the criticism of those who rap Hamlet over the knuckles for not carrying out his 'task' or 'duty'; or radical, as in the work of those who, like Peter Hall, have been concerned with commitment in life and politics, Hamlet can be made to fit. But the dominant image that recurs again and again has been that of failure, of Hamlet pinioned and ineffectual, or, in Seamus Heaney's words in *North* (1975), 'dithering, blathering'. But if Hamlet is a failure, what would success mean for him? If Hamlet has come to typify the emergence of the bourgeois subject with his self-consciousness and claim to interiority ('I have that within which passeth show'), to a privacy of inner life, success might seem to lie in an evasion of politics altogether, but Hamlet the prince could not merely dither and blather. If Hamlet is a failure in not carrying out his 'task', success would lie in resolute and tough action, no questions asked, and would convert him readily into a right-wing Colonel North, or into a kind of Arnold Schwarzenegger as terminator, and even perhaps into Mel Gibson in Franco Zeffirelli's film, and again this would hardly do justice to the play. Failure and success are narrow and inadequate terms, in my view, and to recover a fuller sense of the play, we need to put Hamlet back into it as fully as we can, given that princes are now mainly decorative. Let me offer by way of conclusion the briefest of sketches of how that might be. In the play Hamlet belongs in two worlds. One is the world he identifies with through his father, who appears, the Ghost in armour, pretty much as Hamlet has projected his image, the great warrior with martial stalk, deified as the god who gives 'commandments'. The old world he

---

[75] The pervasive influence of *Hamlet* on *Lord Jim* is analysed in the context of Hamletism by Eloise Hay in '*Lord Jim* and le Hamletisme', in *L'Epoque Conradienne: première partie des Actes du Colloque de Marseille, 13–17 septembre 1990*, pp. 9–27; a revised English version is to be published in 1992 by Stanford University Press in a volume in honour of Thomas C. Moser.

represents is one of violence, in which quarrels are settled by war or combat. Hamlet's nostalgia is for hierarchy, order, command, a simple world where the sword is law. But he has been educated at college to think, to use words rather than weapons, and his appropriate place is in the new world of diplomacy represented by Claudius and his court. The play shows us Hamlet's reluctant adaptation to that world, the modern political world of deceit, spying, equivocation and plotting; and he is successful in outfoxing Claudius at the end. Hamlet demonizes Claudius, just as he hero-worships his father, but, in the light of modern experience, there is not much to choose finally between the worlds of old Hamlet and Claudius: both use violence to achieve their ends, one openly, the other covertly. Hamlet's last gesture is to vote for Fortinbras, who, as Peter Hall said, will make a good military dictator; and the play does not decide between a corrupt government by consent on the one hand, and on the other, a military government by force. Such a reading would, of course, need to be fleshed out, and it would be a contemporary interpretation; but then I take it as axiomatic that no other kind is possible. At least it might help to release the play from the burden of Hamletism.

'HAMLET, REVENGE!': THE USES AND ABUSES OF HISTORICAL CRITICISM

PAUL N. SIEGEL

For more than two centuries critics of *Hamlet* were in agreement that Hamlet is morally obligated to take revenge on Claudius. It is only in our time that many historical critics have asserted that Elizabethans would not have readily accepted the ghost's injunction as a command that Hamlet must in all conscience obey and that we, if we are to be true to Shakespeare, must respond in the same manner. It is rare that there has been so sharp a reversal of general critical opinion.

It is fascinating to survey the major historical criticism on the subject of Hamlet's revenge and on such ancillary matters as the reasons for Hamlet's delay, the nature of the ghost, and the significance of the play's conclusion. The fray on the critical battlefield has its peculiar interest, as we observe interpretations advanced and disputed, errors made and refuted. For historical criticism is, of course, no magic talisman. Critics using the historical method can go wildly wrong, just as critics who rely only on their acumen can have insights that are corroborated by historical scholarship. But, in spite of the confusion of the fray, something approaching a substantial body of opinion has emerged from it – there can never be total assent – that has superseded the previous predominant body of opinion.

So convinced were the critics of the nineteenth century that Hamlet has a duty to kill Claudius that the favourite critical question was 'Why does Hamlet delay?' Like the ghost of the earlier *Hamlet* that was Shakespeare's source,

which, said Thomas Lodge, cried like an oyster-wife, 'Hamlet, revenge!', they called repeatedly for him to take action. Men who spent their lives in their studies, where the greatest violence they committed was the slitting open of envelopes with paper knives, charged him with being an irresolute intellectual or with being of too delicate a sensibility to do the thing he had to do.

E. E. Stoll in his *Hamlet: An Historical and Comparative Study* vehemently attacked these critics for having detached Hamlet from the play and the play from the drama of Shakespeare's time. '[T]he history of *Hamlet* criticism', he exclaimed, is 'a blot on the intellectual record of the race'.[1] For him Hamlet was neither the man of feeling of Henry Mackenzie and Goethe nor the man of thought of Schlegel and Coleridge. He was the avenger hero of Elizabethan drama, a man of action.

However, the delay which so exercised critics and caused them to construct so many fine-spun theories of his character also offered difficulties for Stoll. He regarded the hero's references to his delay as a dramatic device to remind the audience that 'the main business in hand, though retarded, is not lost to view'. 'Mere exhortation, not damaging revelation of a character, is the function of self-reproaches in the old Latin dramatist [Seneca] . . . creator of the revenge-play type . . . [T]hose far from

---

[1] Elmer Edgar Stoll, *Hamlet: An Historical and Comparative Study* (New York, 1968, 1st edn, 1919), p. 14.

weak or spiritless ladies, Medea and Clytemnestra . . . chide and scold themselves only to spur themselves on.'[2]

But when Hamlet asks if the ghost has not come to chide him that, 'lapsed in time and passion', he has delayed 'th'important acting of your dread command' (3.4.98–9), he is not reproaching himself in soliloquy but addressing the ghost, and the accuracy of his description of his apathy is corroborated by the ghost's statement that it has indeed come to 'whet' Hamlet's 'almost blunted purpose'. Awe-stricken question and stern reply underscore that Hamlet's self-castigations are not without warrant: the ghost would have no need to re-appear if Hamlet did not need to be roused to do its 'dread command'.

If Stoll, however, rejected the Hamlet of earlier critics, substituting his own problematic explanation of his delay, he accepted their idea of his 'sacred duty' and explained it as a convention of revenge tragedy. '[T]he vendetta was not established in Elizabethan England', he said, but a play is a play, not life. It is governed by its conventions, which can be inferred from a study of the drama of the time. The 'revenge convention' is 'stage morals', and the revenger is not to be judged by the moral canons of real life.[3]

Earlier critics, in accepting the idea of Hamlet's 'sacred duty', often sounded as if they actually approved of murderous revenge. The moral Doctor Johnson found poetic justice to be violated because the revenge demanded by the ghost 'is not obtained but by the death of him that was required to take it'.[4] If Shakespeare had not killed Hamlet at the same time that he had Hamlet kill Claudius, poetic justice would have been served. The moral lesson that Johnson demanded does not include, it would seem, the idea that vengeful murder is wrong and should be punished.

So too Coleridge stated that Hamlet is 'called upon to act by every motive human and divine'.[5] By every motive human and divine! One would think that Coleridge, a pillar of political and religious orthodoxy after a youthful radical fling, had never heard of the law against murder and the commandment 'Thou shalt not kill.'

Undoubtedly, Johnson and Coleridge in life would each have called the law down upon his father's slayer rather than have murdered him. They wrote as they did because they had entered so deeply into Shakespeare's play that they forgot for the moment the principles of their own morality. But this is that confusion between literature and life which Stoll condemned even though in this instance they did not judge the hero by their own moral canons but twisted the canons to fit the play.

Later historical critics, however, concerned with the study of attitudes towards revenge prevalent in Elizabethan society, did not divorce literature and life as completely as Stoll did. They assumed that the Elizabethan audience brought these attitudes with it to the theatre and that its response to the plays was affected by them. We shall see a little later how far this assumption is correct and how far Stoll is correct.

Fredson Bowers did not deal with *Hamlet* in his *Elizabethan Revenge Tragedy*, a revision of his doctoral dissertation, saying in his preface that to have written on this greatest of all revenge tragedies would have 'thrown completely out of balance the scale and proportions of my more general survey'.[6] The consequence, however, is that it is like a production of *Hamlet* without the Prince. Nevertheless his study is very useful for the understanding of Shakespeare's play.

Bowers, following Lily B. Campbell's article 'Theories of Revenge in Renaissance

---

[2] Stoll, p. 17.
[3] Stoll, p. 55.
[4] *Shakespeare Criticism: A Selection, 1623–1840*, ed. D. Nichol Smith (Oxford, 1961), p. 122.
[5] *Four Centuries of Shakespearian Criticism*, ed. Frank Kermode (New York, 1965), p. 436.
[6] Fredson Thayer Bowers, *Elizabethan Revenge Tragedy, 1587–1642* (Princeton, 1940), p. vii.

England',[7] found that Elizabethan homilists and political theorists insistently repeated that vengeance belonged only to the Lord or to the ministers of the state through whom He effected justice. In doing so, they were upholding the authority of the newly centralized state of the Tudors. '[Y]et there was a very real tradition existing in favor of revenge under certain circumstances . . .'[8] This tradition, it could be added, may be compared with the 'unwritten law' in accordance with which juries in some parts of the United States would, until recently and perhaps even now, not convict a man who killed his wife's lover on coming upon them while they were engaged in sexual intercourse: it goes against the official code, but it is to be reckoned with, nevertheless, as affecting the responses of members of the audience in one case and of jurors in the other case.

The contradiction between the official code and the undercurrent of feeling derived from feudal tradition caused the audience to have mixed feelings towards the revenger in the revenge plays. It began by sympathizing with the avenger but found its sympathy alienated, as in the pursuit of his revenge he plunged into crime after crime. Yet it 'hoped for his success, but only on condition that he did not survive. Thus his death was accepted as expiation for the violent motives which had forced him to override the rules of God . . .'[9]

In an article published fifteen years after his book, Bowers sought to analyse *Hamlet* in the light of his study of Elizabethan revenge tragedy and its background of contemporary thought. Hamlet, he concluded, is waiting for the opportunity to kill Claudius as God's 'minister', the unsinning agent who effects public justice, rather than as God's 'scourge', who takes private revenge, fulfilling God's purpose in punishing the criminal but only through himself committing a crime and bringing punishment in turn on himself.[10]

The trouble with this thesis is the trouble with so many other theses on Hamlet: it attributes to him thoughts which Hamlet himself

does not express or imply. Nowhere does Hamlet wonder if he will be able to carry out the ghost's command in a manner acceptable to heaven. On the killing of Polonius, he says (3.4.176) that he has been punished in accordance with his role as 'scourge and minister'. He regards himself at this moment as being both, and indeed, as Paul Jorgensen pointed out, the two words do not necessarily have the distinct meanings that Bowers assigns to them, often being used by the Elizabethans interchangeably.[11]

In *Hamlet and Revenge*, a learned study informed for the most part by critical good sense, Eleanor Prosser declared that the Elizabethan spectator of *Hamlet* – indeed, of the revenge plays generally – was 'trapped in an ethical dilemma – a dilemma, to put it simply, between what he believed and what he felt'.[12] He felt sympathy for the victim of injustice, but he believed that revenge was wrong.

Previous generations of critics who had the idea that Hamlet was morally obligated to take revenge, she pointed out, were uneasily aware of the indications that in obeying the command of the ghost he was embarking on an evil course. The anonymous author of *Some Remarks on the Tragedy of Hamlet* (1736), the first extended criticism of *Hamlet*, said, 'To put the Usurper to Death . . . was highly requisite' but 'to desire to destroy a Man's Soul' was really going too far: Hamlet should have been content with Claudius suffering the tortures of purgatory, not the eternal ones of hell.[13] So too Johnson was horrified that Hamlet,

---

[7] Lily B. Campbell, 'Theories of Revenge in Renaissance England', *Modern Philology*, 28 (1931), 281–96.

[8] Bowers, p. 40.

[9] Bowers, p. 184.

[10] Bowers, 'Hamlet as Minister and Scourge', *PMLA*, 70 (1955), 745.

[11] *Clio*, 3 (1973), 126, cited in *Hamlet*, ed. Harold Jenkins (New York, 1982), p. 523.

[12] Eleanor Prosser, *Hamlet and Revenge* (Stanford, 1967), p. 4.

[13] Quoted by Prosser, p. 245.

'represented as a virtuous character', sought to kill Claudius at a moment when Claudius was sure to go to hell.[14] This was also the view of others in the eighteenth century, but they explained it and other such things as Hamlet's cruelty to Ophelia and his callousness concerning the death of Polonius as the faults in a Shakespeare who was conceived of as being great at his best but highly uneven. 'We are to lament that the hero, who is intended as amiable, should be such an apparent heap of inconsistency', said Francis Gentleman in 1770.[15]

The Bardolaters of the nineteenth century, rather than criticizing Shakespeare, sought to explain away Hamlet's conduct. Thus Hazlitt, echoing Coleridge,[16] said that Hamlet's 'refinement of malice' in deferring revenge until a time when the king will assuredly be damned is 'only an excuse for his own want of resolution'.[17] So too Lamb said of Hamlet's 'vulgar scorn at Polonius' and of the 'asperity' with which he treats Ophelia that these are offensive on the stage, where the actor is concerned only with the immediate effect, but that in the study, where we can contemplate and fully appreciate 'the shy, negligent, retiring Hamlet', we 'explain . . . these temporary deformities in the character' of the gentle hero as the products of a mind 'unhinged' for the moment by his situation.[18] 'Given the play as Shakespeare wrote it', Prosser commented tartly, 'no actor could portray the Hamlet envisioned by the Romantics: the reflective thinker of pensive sadness, free from all taints of violence or cruelty, shrinking from action.'[19]

Prosser, like Stoll, therefore, used historical scholarship to criticize previous Hamlets. But, where Stoll used his scholarship to explain the truth of the traditional belief in Hamlet's 'sacred duty', she used hers to clear away the scholarship that in her view 'has mistakenly led us to distrust our own responses': 'Only when we cease searching for explanations outside the play, whether in pagan codes or theatrical conventions, can we respond directly to the play itself', finding in so doing that 'the command to

murder is as malign as we sense it to be, and Hamlet himself is to blame for his descent into savagery'.[20]

As against Stoll's observation about 'stage morals', Prosser stated: 'No one has ever interpreted the "willing suspension of disbelief" to mean that an audience leaves all of its accumulated knowledge, all of its ethical beliefs, all of its religious faith, at the box office.'[21] Yet, it might be said in response, Johnson and Coleridge seem to have forgotten their ethical beliefs and religious faith in discussing Hamlet's revenge. To be sure, even they boggle, if not at the idea of retaliatory murder, then at the idea of the murderer seeking eternal damnation for his victim. Perhaps we can say that although we do not check our beliefs and attitudes at the box office when we enter a theatre, our beliefs and attitudes are like our overcoats when we are unable to check them in the theatre's cloakroom: carried along by the drama, we may almost forget them as they lie heavily on our laps, but we are never entirely successful in doing so.

Prosser's great virtue was that, while insisting on Hamlet's 'descent into savagery', she was aware of the ambivalence of feeling that

---

[14] *Samuel Johnson on Shakespeare*, ed. W. K. Wimsatt, Jr (New York, 1960), p. 111.

[15] Quoted by Prosser, p. 245.

[16] *Coleridge's Writings on Shakespeare*, ed. Terence Hawkes (New York, 1959), p. 163.

[17] Smith, *Shakespeare Criticism*, p. 290.

[18] Smith, p. 199.

[19] Prosser, *Hamlet and Revenge*, p. 248. Among those besides Bowers and Prosser who do not regard Hamlet's revenge as a moral duty are Harold C. Goddard, *The Meaning of Shakespeare* (Chicago, 1951), vol. 1, pp. 333–6; Paul N. Siegel, *Shakespearean Tragedy and the Elizabethan Compromise* (Lanham, Md., 1983, 1st edn, 1957), pp. 101–3; Harold S. Wilson, *On the Design of Shakespearean Tragedy* (Toronto, 1957), pp. 41–5; John Vyvyan, *The Shakespearean Ethic* (London, 1959); Irving Ribner, *Patterns in Shakespearean Tragedy* (London, 1960), p. 67; L. C. Knights, *An Approach to 'Hamlet'* (Stanford, 1961), pp. 45–6.

[20] Prosser, *Hamlet and Revenge*, pp. 249, 248.

[21] Prosser, p. 34.

Hamlet excited; yet she herself diminished that ambivalence of feeling in dismissing as non-existent the feudal tradition of revenge traced by Bowers. But such statements as Thomas Lodge's 'Be . . . in thy revenges bolde, but not too bloody' or Bacon's 'The most tolerable sort of revenge is for those wrongs which there is no law to punish'[22] indicate a grudging acknowledgement of a tradition that, although officially condemned, was not forgotten.

However, Prosser was much more nearly correct than Stoll, who was entirely unaware of Elizabethan attitudes towards revenge. The Hamlet who says (3.2.398–400) that he could 'drink hot blood, / And do such bitter business as the day / Would quake to look on' is a revenger who stands swaying dizzily on the brink of moral destruction.

On the other hand, she did not emphasize sufficiently the heroic aspects of Hamlet's character perceived by Stoll. From the perfect courtier ('The courtier's, soldier's, scholar's, eye, tongue, sword' – 3.1.152–3), who constantly reminds us of what he used to be by his courage and energy in thrusting aside his alarmed companions to follow the ghost and in being the first to board the pirate ship, by his philosophical meditation, by his love of the drama, and by his skill with the sword, Hamlet has become that Elizabethan object of dread, the malcontent, bitter, cynical, and caustic.[23] As G. Wilson Knight, a neo-romantic critic who scorned historical scholarship, said in one of his flashes of insight, he is a 'princely hero' who has been transformed into 'the incarnation of cynicism'.[24]

Knight attributed Hamlet's delay in taking revenge to his deep depression. He cannot move himself to do anything because he has discovered life to be meaningless so that no action is worth doing.[25] Perhaps the first to assert this was Lamb, who wrote, 'His very melancholy, and . . . dejection of spirits . . . produced an irresoluteness and wavering of purpose . . .'[26] To be sure, this was only one of a number of reasons for Hamlet's delay that

Lamb gave, including the rather astounding one, considering Hamlet's obsessive disgust at the thought of Gertrude's sexual relations with Claudius and his fear that he will be impelled to kill her, that 'the usurper was his mother's husband'.

But the critic who wrote at length on this subject, to whom Knight was undoubtedly indebted, was A. C. Bradley. Bradley found Hamlet to be an idealist disillusioned by his mother's shallowness and his uncle's perfidy and plunged into a state of melancholia that is manifested by his morbid cynicism and that inhibits his action. His analysis has proved influential.[27]

Both Stoll and Prosser, however, took issue with him. Stoll, in an amazing lapse for a great scholar who was ordinarily so able to summon instances from Elizabethan drama to prove his points, stated: '[T]here is no necessary or frequent connection between Elizabethan melancholy and procrastination. It is not to be found

---

[22] Quoted by Bowers, *Elizabethan Revenge Tragedy*, pp. 35, 36.

[23] Stoll was the first to see Hamlet ('Shakespeare, Marston and the Malcontent Type', *Modern Philology*, 3 [1906], 281–303) as a 'brooding, jeering Malcontent', but for him the Elizabethan malcontent was a purely literary type. The Elizabethan malcontent, however, as Donne, Marston, Nashe, and Lodge attest, was a real-life person who, like Hamlet, customarily wore black and affected a careless disorder of dress, the sign of his anti-social misanthropy. Cf. Siegel, pp. 100 and 200 n. 2.

[24] G. Wilson Knight, *The Wheel of Fire: Interpretations of Shakespearean Tragedy* (New York, 1962, 1st edn, 1930), p. 40.

[25] Knight, p. 23.

[26] Quoted by Paul S. Conklin, *A History of Hamlet Criticism, 1601–1862* (New York, 1947), p. 130.

[27] Among those besides G. Wilson Knight who have accepted it are Joseph Quincy Adams, ed., *Hamlet* (Boston, 1929), pp. 225–6; J. Dover Wilson, *What Happens in Hamlet* (Cambridge, 1956, 1st edn, 1935), p. 43; Oscar James Campbell, ed., *The Living Shakespeare* (New York, 1949), p. 745; Siegel, *Shakespearean Tragedy*, pp. 100–1, 113; Charles A. Hallett and Elaine S. Hallett, *The Revenger's Madness: A Study in Revenge Tragedy Motifs* (Lincoln, Neb., 1980), pp. 187–8.

in any other melancholy character on the Elizabethan stage – not in Marston's Malevole or Shakespeare's own Jaques, Don John, or Antonio, Merchant of Venice.'[28] He forgot the much more apropos examples, the grief-stricken revengers such as Hieronimo, the Antonio of *Antonio's Revenge*, and Titus Andronicus, who are oppressed by melancholia and temporary insanity that impedes their action. Yet as early as 1902 the drama historian Ashley H. Thorndike had said: 'Hamlet, overpowered with the burden of his task, struggles to its accomplishment through the same weaknesses and delays [as Hieronimo and Antonio of *Antonio's Revenge*.]'[29]

Stoll was intent on showing that there was no real delay because he was put off by those who regarded Hamlet's inability to act, except in fits and starts, as a 'damaging revelation of character'.[30] Oddly, though, even as he was denying that Hamlet delayed, he spoke of Hamlet's 'collapses into apathy or indifference after excitement' as a sign of his melancholy and noted that Hieronimo, although similarly melancholy, was of 'heroic character'.[31] This is the key that Stoll failed to turn. Hamlet's 'collapses into apathy or indifference' (the dulness of spirit for which he castigates himself), like the debilitating grief and temporary madness of Hieronimo and Titus, prevent him from acting with sustained purposefulness, but these collapses are not signs of weakness of character. Revenge is so heavy a burden and the revenger is in so terrible a situation that even strong men falter.

Prosser did not deal much with the subject of Hamlet's delay, but she referred in a footnote to Bertram Joseph's *Conscience and the King* and John W. Draper's *The 'Hamlet' of Shakespeare's Audience* 'for convincing cases against the assumption of Bradley and others that melancholy was considered a normal cause for inactivity, procrastination, and weakness'.[32] However, Lawrence Babb, a later and more thorough student of Elizabethan writing on melancholy, found that, although this is true of the normally morose person born under the influence of Saturn, it is not true of the man of 'unnatural melancholy', whose immoderate grief, which is due to some special circumstance that changes his natural disposition, incapacitates him. Such a person is subject to incessant brooding and an inability to act, but has abrupt shifts of mood and sometimes erupts into sudden, rash activity. He concluded that 'A. C. Bradley . . . is . . . substantially right' about Hamlet.[33]

Hamlet, therefore, is like the other malcontent revengers who, weighed down by their melancholia, are temporarily unable to fulfil their missions. He himself speaks (2.2.608) of 'my weakness and my melancholy' which, he fears, make him particularly susceptible to the wiles of the devil, with 'weakness' referring to the mental and emotional fatigue that is the result of his obsessive brooding.

Thus a student of Elizabethan intellectual history corrected earlier scholars and confirmed the perception of a fine critic. Bradley did not have to read what Elizabethans wrote about melancholy, for the pseudo-science of Elizabethan psychology was, after all, seeking to cope with empirical phenomena such as the indecisiveness of those suffering from depression that we are still able to observe.[34] Nor did Shakespeare and the authors of other revenge plays have to read treatises on melancholy to be affected by the widely known psychological

---

[28] Stoll, *Hamlet*, p. 72.

[29] Ashley H. Thorndike, '*Hamlet* and Contemporary Revenge Plays', *PMLA*, 17 (1902), 204.

[30] Stoll, *Hamlet*, p. 16.

[31] Stoll, *Hamlet*, pp. 72–3.

[32] Prosser, p. 128 n.

[33] Lawrence Babb, *The Elizabethan Malady* (East Lansing, Mich., 1951), p. 107 n.

[34] Adams cites (pp. 225–6) Kraft-Ebing and other turn-of-the-century psychiatrists on the inability of a person suffering from severe depression to make a decision. For a statement to the same effect by a contemporary psychiatrist, see Demitri F. Papolos, M.D., and Janice Papolos, *Overcoming Depression* (New York, 1987), p. 4.

doctrine of their times, just as writers today who make use of the concepts of repressions, Oedipus complexes, and inferiority complexes need not have read Freud and Adler.

Although Bradley's discussion of Hamlet's melancholy anticipated historical scholars' findings on the Elizabethan view of melancholy, he did not anticipate historical scholars' findings on Elizabethan attitudes towards revenge. He accepted as axiomatic the romantic critics' assumption that Hamlet has a moral obligation to kill Claudius. Not perceiving the Elizabethan audience's ambivalence about Hamlet's dedication to revenge, he did not appreciate that this ambivalence was compounded by Hamlet's depression. For this depression was the sickness of soul of a malcontent whose baleful cynicism made him a threat to society. His inability to act was a sign of his soul sickness, but if he were to take revenge it would entail his damnation. Either way – obeying the ghost's call for revenge or failing to act because of a debilitating disgust with life – was a path towards Hamlet's destruction.

Another question related to the question of how we are to respond to the ghost's call for revenge is that of how we are to regard the ghost itself. From the late eighteenth century on, it ceased being presented on the stage as a terrifying visitation and became a majestic figure before whom Hamlet kneels in reverence, ready to do its bidding. This was also how it was regarded by critics. J. Dover Wilson, however, examining the Elizabethan literature on ghosts, restored the terror of the *Hamlet* ghost. He found that ghosts could be regarded as hallucinations, devils, angels, or (by Catholics) souls from purgatory. The ghost in *Hamlet*, displaying bewilderingly diverse indications of what it was, was watched by the Elizabethan audience with doubt and uncertainty. This doubt and uncertainty, said Wilson, was never resolved.[35]

Following Wilson, there was a many-sided debate on this subject. Roy W. Battenhouse, whose enormous erudition in theology is matched only by his misapplied ingenuity in applying this erudition to Shakespeare, took on Monsignor I. J. Semper, who had contended that the ghost came from purgatory to urge Hamlet to perform a morally justified deed. Battenhouse argued that the ghost is too vindictive to be a soul from purgatory who, according to Catholic belief, was, although it had to do penance for its sins, a spirit of grace. In doing so, he dismissed the ghost's use of Catholic vocabulary in referring to his death without the proper rites as an 'isolated gobbet of sacramental language' and found it to have come not from a Catholic purgatory but a paganesque after-world.[36]

Robert H. West found that the objections Semper and Battenhouse each raised against the arguments of the other were correct. The ghost, a compound of the purgatorial spirit of Catholicism, the Senecan revenge ghost, and the earth-bound ghost of popular folk-lore, is all the more awesomely mysterious for its theological inconsistency.[37]

Sister Miriam Joseph for the most part reaffirmed what Semper had said without attempting to refute the arguments that Battenhouse had made in opposition to it. She did try, however, to justify the idea of a purgatorial spirit calling for revenge. One not well versed in Thomist doctrine may be forgiven for believing that the ghost's call for revenge is a violation of the commandment 'Thou shalt not kill', but this, according to her, is really not so. Sister Miriam Joseph explained it all. Saint Thomas had cited God's command to Moses to kill those who had worshipped the golden calf as a special exception to this commandment. The ghost's call for revenge is another such exception, a 'special command from God brought by a good spirit'.[38]

[35] J. Dover Wilson, pp. 184–5.

[36] Roy W. Battenhouse, 'The Ghost in *Hamlet*: A Catholic "Linchpin"?', *Studies in Philology*, 48 (1951), 162.

[37] Robert H. West, 'King Hamlet's Ambiguous Ghost', *PMLA*, 70 (1955), 1107–17.

[38] Sister Miriam Joseph, 'Discerning the Ghost in *Hamlet*', *PMLA*, 76 (1961), 501.

It is easy enough, to be sure, to find theological warrant for such special exceptions – all churches at all times have, for instance, condoned mass murder through the doctrine of the 'just war' – but the question is: what reason is there to believe that Elizabethans would have found such an exception in *Hamlet*? The ghost does not say that it bears such a command from God, and Sister Miriam did not present any evidence that divine authority stands behind the ghost's call for revenge. Instead, she met the objection that the ghost, since it commands Hamlet to do what is evil, cannot be a good spirit with the statement that, since the ghost is a good spirit, what it commands cannot be evil. She assumed, that is, what she had to prove – and she said nothing, moreover, of the ghost's failure, on appearing to Hamlet immediately after the prayer scene, to admonish him for his unChristian desire to ensure the damnation of Claudius. One can only exclaim: 'Good God! Is *this* a good ghost?'

West, returning to the subject a decade later and summing up the debate at this point, stated: 'No scholar, so far as I know, has published a detailed argument supporting the theory that the Ghost is actually a devil working to lure Hamlet into deadly sin; but anyone who cared to assert it from specifically pneumatological evidence might make as good a case as Battenhouse, Semper, and Sister Miriam Joseph make for their views.'[39] Shakespearian scholarship, however, like nature, abhors a vacuum, and even as West's book appeared, Eleanor Prosser's book was in press. She declared that while the Elizabethan audience initially was nervously uncertain about the nature of the ghost, it must have finally been convinced that it was the devil intent on tricking Hamlet into believing that it is the ghost of his father and gaining his soul. This was also to be the view of Arthur McGee in his bizarre *The Elizabethan Hamlet*, in which, unlike Prosser, he found the devil to have been successful in effecting Hamlet's damnation. But more of McGee later.

The moral ambiguity of the ghost would seem, however, to have been preserved until the end. The ghost returns not only to renew its call for revenge but to defend Gertrude from Hamlet's tirade. Its concern for her, reminiscent of the elder Hamlet's solicitude for her in life, serves to humanize the ghost. Hamlet says in one breath that its appearance would rouse the very stones to action and in the next breath that the continuance of its piteous gaze upon him will divert him from his stern purpose (3.4.127–30). The audience's uncertainty and ambivalence of feeling go deeper than Prosser recognized.[40]

We come, then, to the final point ancillary to the question of whether Hamlet is morally obligated to kill Claudius, the significance of the play's conclusion. Bradley, although he affirmed that Shakespeare 'practically confined his view to the world of non-theological observation and thought', seems to have been the first to suggest that there is a sense of providence effecting its will in the last act. At the end of the play, he says, there is a 'feeling, on Hamlet's part, of his being in the hands of Providence'. This is not Hamlet's feeling alone but that of the sensitive reader. 'It appears probable' that Hamlet's capture by the pirate 'thieves of mercy' (4.6.21) is meant to 'impress the imagination as the very reverse of accidental'. The 'effect is to strengthen in the spectator the feeling that . . . [Hamlet's] task will surely be accomplished, because it is the purpose of a power against which both he and

---

[39] Robert H. West, *Shakespeare and the Outer Mystery* (Lexington, Ky, 1968), p. 61.

[40] Other critics who have seen the ghost as an ambiguous figure are Lily B. Campbell, *Shakespeare's Tragic Heroes, Slaves of Passion* (New York, 1952, 1st edn, 1930), p. 128; J. Dover Wilson, pp. 84–5; John Erskine Hankins, *The Character of Hamlet and Other Essays* (Chapel Hill, NC, 1941), p. 134; Siegel, pp. 103–5; Vyvyan, pp. 31–2; Ribner, p. 72; Virgil K. Whitaker, *The Mirror up to Nature: The Technique of Shakespeare's Tragedies* (San Marino, Ca., 1965), p. 193; Nigel Alexander, *Poison, Play, and Duel: A Study of Hamlet* (Lincoln, Neb., 1971), pp. 32–3; Hallett and Hallett, p. 185.

his enemy are impotent'. Horatio's words about Hamlet's soul being carried by angels to its rest are an 'intimation' of a 'vaster life of which it ["the limited world of ordinary experience"] is but a partial appearance'.[41]

Roland M. Frye found theological warrant for Bradley's perception:

Calvin's words [describe] the perils from which Hamlet has emerged . . . : 'If a man light among thieves . . ., . . . if having been tossed with the waves, he attain to the haven, . . . all these chances . . . the reason of the flesh doth ascribe to fortune. But whosoever is taught by the mouth of Christ . . . will firmly believe that all chances are governed by the secret counsel of God' . . . Having passed through experiences like those which Calvin hypothesizes, Hamlet has come to sense in what would seem quite inconsequential details that 'even in that was heaven ordinant' and to declare . . . 'There's a divinity that shapes our ends'.[42]

Eleanor Prosser agreed that 'Hamlet now rests serene in the faith that Providence has a plan' and rejects 'his intention of usurping God's function', but, oddly enough, did not find that Hamlet's faith in a plan of divine providence was confirmed by the conclusion of the play. She cited Horatio's statement that he will speak

> Of accidental judgements, casual slaughters,
> Of death put on by cunning and forced cause:
> And, in this upshot, purposes mistook
> Fall'n on th'inventors' heads. (5.2.336–9)

She commented: 'There is no word here of righteous revenge, of just punishment of the wicked, of a divine command. There is no suggestion that Horatio attributed everything to the necessary workings of Providence. His is a statement of awful chaos . . . Hamlet's soul is ultimately saved, but in spite of, not because of, his revenge.'[43]

It is certainly true that there is no suggestion here of a divine command to take revenge, but there is more than a suggestion of a divine providence that brings a just punishment of the wicked. 'Accidental judgments', said George

Lyman Kittredge, a master of Elizabethan English, means 'judgments of God brought about by means apparently accidental', and 'casual slaughters' 'merely repeats the idea'.[44] Kittredge's gloss on Horatio's words is in accord with the words of Calvin – 'all chances are governed by the secret counsel of God' – quoted by Frye in defence of the idea that a sense of divine providence is suggested in the last act of *Hamlet*.[45] It would seem, furthermore, to be borne out by the stage action, which is emblematic of retributive justice. Hamlet, in killing Claudius and Laertes with the sword of their plot against him, is enacting the words of Buckingham in *Richard III*, who says (5.1.23–4) that God causes 'the swords of wicked men / To turn their own points in their masters' bosoms'. In forcing the poisoned wine between Claudius' lips, he is enacting Macbeth's words (1.7.10–12), 'This even-handed justice / Commends th'ingredients of our poisoned chalice / To our own lips'. Far from 'awful chaos', we are witnessing the work of divine justice.

Divine providence did, then, finally use Hamlet as its agent but without his acquiring the guilt of the malcontent avenger. His killing

---

[41] A. C. Bradley, *Shakespearean Tragedy* (London, 1904), pp. 25, 173.

[42] Roland Mushat Frye, *Shakespeare and Christian Doctrine* (Princeton, 1963), pp. 231–2.

[43] Prosser, p. 237.

[44] *The Complete Works of Shakespeare*, ed. Irving Ribner and George Lyman Kittredge (Waltham, Mass., 1971, 1st Kittredge edn, 1936), p. 1101.

[45] It was a commonplace among the homilists and moralists of the day that divine providence uses coincidences and seeming accidents in rendering punishments on earth. Cf. Henry Hitch Adams, *English Domestic or Homiletic Tragedy* (New York, 1943), p. 18. Adams notes that the homilists and moralists were much more explicit in explaining these coincidences and seeming accidents as the work of divine providence than were the dramatists, who nevertheless made suggestive use of these commonly recognized means through which it operated. That Shakespeare does not specifically mention God does not mean that he is not suggestively alluding to divine providence.

of Claudius is not premeditated murder but virtually self-defence in the duel that Claudius has been waging against him through his tool Laertes. The ambivalence of the audience is resolved by its perception that Hamlet has done God's work without having incurred his just wrath.[46]

Since Prosser, there have been two books that have sought to bring together for the study of *Hamlet* what can be learned about Elizabethan attitudes towards revenge and revenge tragedy, *The Renaissance Hamlet* by Roland M. Frye and *The Elizabethan Hamlet* by Arthur McGee. Before we take these up, however, it might be well to discuss Peter Mercer's *Hamlet and the Acting of Revenge*, which states that its primary concern is with 'discovering significant form' in *Hamlet* and the other revenge tragedies rather than with studying their 'engagement with revenge as a problem of *ethics*'. Mercer accepts as a given the 'Christian moral framework' that historical scholarship has found to be present in the revenge tragedies, but he claims to find complexities that transcend the *Hamlet* of the historical scholars.[47]

One instance of such a complexity is the ghost, 'an object of pity, as well as terror', and yet 'the awful implications of his demand remain, for all that, the same [as in the other revenge tragedies]'. Another instance is the transformation of the structure of the revenge tragedy effected in *Hamlet*'s conclusion: 'Hamlet is brought, finally, to the achievement of his revenge, but in a way which extraordinarily leaves him free of its guilt.'[48]

Mercer does not do justice to the historical critics, of whose work he makes use. He is particularly harsh on Eleanor Prosser: 'She is certain that the audience believed wholeheartedly and unanimously that revenge, on or off the stage, was "illegal, blasphemous, immoral, irrational, unnatural, and unhealthy, not to mention unsafe ... it was also thoroughly un-English"'.[49]

But the subject of the clause quoted by Mercer is not 'the audience' but 'Elizabethan moralists'.[50] Prosser was summarizing these moralists, the expounders of the official morality, whose writing she was reviewing prior to seeking to surmise the response of the audience to the revenge plays. Her conclusion concerning this response was, as we have seen, 'the average spectator at a revenge play was probably trapped in an ethical dilemma – a dilemma, to put it most simply, between what he believed and what he felt'. This is far from an expression of certainty concerning the wholehearted and unanimous condemnation of revenge by the audience.

Similarly, Bowers' description of the audience's mixed feelings toward the revenger can be scarcely said to attribute to it, as Mercer says he does, a 'naïve directness'.[51] So too, as we have seen, the ambiguity of the ghost had been written about by J. Dover Wilson and Robert H. West and the regeneration and guiltlessness of Hamlet at the conclusion had been written about by Prosser and others. Ambiguity and complexity were not Mercer's novel discoveries.

Frye's *The Renaissance Hamlet* is an immensely learned book that supplements and reinforces what previous scholars had said, but it does not break very much new ground. Concerning Elizabethan attitudes towards revenge, it says that they were 'far less unified and considerably more ambiguous in 1600 than

---

[46] Among other critics who have seen the workings of divine providence in the conclusion of *Hamlet* are S. F. Johnson, 'The Regeneration of Hamlet', *Shakespeare Quarterly*, 3 (1952), 204; Siegel, pp. 113–5; John Holloway, *The Story of the Night: Studies in Shakespeare's Major Tragedies* (London, 1961), pp. 35–6; Frank Kermode, 'Introduction to *Hamlet*', *The Complete Signet Classic Shakespeare* (New York, 1972), p. 1140; R. Broude, 'Revenge and Revenge Tragedy in Renaissance England', *Renaissance Quarterly*, 28 (1975), 56.

[47] Peter Mercer, *Hamlet and the Acting of Revenge* (Iowa City, 1987), pp. 4–5.

[48] Mercer, pp. 6–7, 26, 247.

[49] Mercer, p. 4.

[50] Prosser, p. 10.

[51] Mercer, p. 5.

some literary historians and critics have recognized'. Concerning the ghost, it says that it 'is not finally identified in the familiar terms of Elizabethan pneumatology'. Concerning the conclusion, it says: 'The Prince has resolved his own conscience, and he now shows no sign of that satanic rage to see Claudius suffer in hell which he had earlier expressed. Once he is prepared in mind to act, he waits calmly for providence to provide his cue and the propitious moment.'[52]

McGee's The Elizabethan Hamlet is an entirely different kind of book. Its publisher, Yale University Press, describes it on the jacket as 'provocative', and it is indeed that but at the sacrifice of good sense. Beginning with the sound enough thesis that the revenge play, whose usual setting is Italy or an Italianized Spain or France, reflected the audience's anti-Catholicism, McGee goes on to argue that Hamlet is led to damnation by the devil pretending to be a ghost from a non-existent purgatory, that Horatio is a sycophant and probably homosexual, and that Gertrude, 'a seasoned toper', dies tipsy. To cap it all, McGee assures us that the Elizabethan audience would have inferred that Ophelia had committed incest with Polonius and Laertes.[53] Alas, poor Ophelia!

McGee's method may be illustrated by what he has to say about the play's conclusion. The Anglican Church, he states, forbade gambling and denied Christian burial to the participants of a duel. 'Yet Hamlet has agreed to fight Laertes in a fencing match that is likely to develop into a duel, and wager is also involved – both courses of action which would lead to damnation if they ended in death'.[54] It might be pointed out in response that Hamlet has no idea that the fencing match will become a deadly duel, that he is not responsible for Claudius' wager, and that, using McGee's reasoning, Sir Andrew Aguecheek is a Christian hero in refusing to fight a duel, although, to be sure, he shows a certain weakness in finally permitting Sir Toby to persuade him to challenge Sebas-

tian. Sebastian, for his part, is distinctly un-Christian when, on being slapped in the face by Sir Andrew, he does not turn the other cheek but instead bloodies Sir Andrew's head, going even beyond the Old Testament's 'an eye for an eye'.

So too McGee comments, 'Before he [Laertes] dies he "exchanges forgiveness" with Hamlet . . . Laertes has misused the little time left to him in order to repent and make his peace with God. Only Christ can forgive sins . . . In the same way Hamlet's apparently pious "Heaven make thee free of it!" . . . is downright blasphemous, for . . . how can he speak on God's behalf?'[55] McGee cites various Elizabethan theological works in the course of his book, but he here forgets the familiar words of the Lord's Prayer, 'Forgive us our trespasses, as we forgive those who trespass against us.'

Finally, McGee says that Horatio's words 'Now cracks a noble heart. Good night, sweet prince, / And flights of angels sing thee to thy rest' (5.2.312–13) are derived from the Catholic burial service. 'Thus it is doubtful whether they would have roused much sympathy from an Elizabethan audience because they were to prepare Hamlet's soul to enter Purgatory [which the audience regarded as a false Catholic belief] . . .' Here he could have profited from Frye, who devotes seven pages to the numerous Elizabethan references to singing angels carrying souls to heaven, including quotations from Luther and Calvin.[56]

The use of the historical method in criticism is, therefore, not foolproof. But, despite abuses in its use, it has contributed to a growing weight of opinion, well summarized in Frye's book, that has corrected opinions of the past.

---

[52] Roland Mushat Frye, The Renaissance Hamlet: Issues and Responses in 1600 (Princeton, 1984), pp. 11, 167, 268.

[53] Arthur McGee, The Elizabethan Hamlet (New Haven, 1987), pp. 175, 171, 195–6.

[54] McGee, p. 165.

[55] McGee, pp. 271–2.

[56] Frye, The Renaissance Hamlet, pp. 271–7.

Hamlet, both a Renaissance courtier and an Elizabethan malcontent, is a complex, artistically integrated figure, not the 'apparent heap of inconsistency' of Francis Gentleman and other eighteenth-century critics. He is not the 'lovely, pure, noble, and most moral nature, without the strength of nerve which forms a hero' of Goethe[57] or the 'shy, negligent, retiring Hamlet' of Lamb. Nor is he the uncomplicated hero of the early historical scholar Stoll. He is not merely a man of feeling or of thought or of action; he is all three.

Nor does the revenge that Hamlet seeks, called for by a morally ambiguous ghost, arouse a simple and uncomplicated response. Hamlet's delay is not caused by a flaw of character, nor is it a creation of critics. It rises from the hero's paralysing depression that prevents him from taking the revenge towards which the Elizabethan audience had mixed feelings. That Hamlet is a bitter malcontent disgusted with life only compounds the ambivalence of feeling of the audience. This ambivalence is resolved only at the play's conclusion.

While many will not agree with one point or another of this paradigm of modern *Hamlet* criticism, in its general outline, whatever the quarrels about details, it has superseded the nineteenth-century paradigm.

---

[57] Johann Wolfgang Goethe, 'The Character of Hamlet', *Interpreting Hamlet*, ed. Russell E. Leavenworth (San Francisco, 1960), p. 44.

REVISION BY EXCISION: REWRITING GERTRUDE

ELLEN J. O'BRIEN

From 1755 until 1900 (and not infrequently from 1900 to World War II) actors playing Gertrude found in their scripts a significantly different role than those in either the First Folio or Second Quarto texts. That Gertrude's role was both radically and nearly consistently cut throughout the era will scarcely be startling news to anyone acquainted with the performance practices of the nineteenth century. But the consequences of such cutting may be. Close comparison of Gertrude's role as it appears in the Folio and Second Quarto texts with the role as it emerges from the standard nineteenth-century version reveals the potential for subtle but powerful revision inherent – though often nearly invisible – in cutting.

To grasp the significance of this, we must understand that the Shakespearian actor grounds decisions about the role in the patterns of thought, speech, and action inherent in the text. Cuts, or conversely, added lines and stage directions, can create patterns at odds with those of the original texts. Many actors, when asked to play a cut role, will attempt to act the implications of the full version, to play the role as it was written rather than as it was cut.[1] Yet since the editions of *Hamlet* most commonly used as nineteenth-century promptbooks regularly omitted lines, added stage directions, and, on occasion, revised lines, the actors had no choice but to respond to a very different set of performance signals.[2] In Gertrude's case, these editions destroyed many of the verbal patterns of the role and eviscerated patterns of visual

imagery established by the Folio and Second Quarto texts. The result was a very different Gertrude.

Before we can see the impact of the nineteenth-

---

[1] The significance of this distinction was brought home to me in an experiment which Bernice Kliman and I conducted at the 1982 Folger/NEH Institute on Shakespeare in Performance. In order to explore the impact of cuts on performance, we asked two actors to perform several different cut versions of the first Polonius/Ophelia scene. After several rounds of this, one of the actors pointed out that in each case, they were still attempting to act the implications of the full version without the missing words.

I am deeply indebted to Bernard Beckerman and Cary Mazer, who directed that Institute, for introducing me to the fundamental issues of text and performance. My debt is equally great to Michael Warren, for his criticism of this manuscript at two different stages, and to Shakespeare Santa Cruz: particularly to Michael Edwards, Paul Whitworth, and Audrey Stanley – for enabling me to work with those issues in rehearsal – and to Kate Rickman, the Shakespeare Santa Cruz Gertrude, whose questions in rehearsal instigated my thinking on the subject.

[2] I have taken the number of listings for each edition in William P. Halstead, *Shakespeare as Spoken*, 14 vols. (Ann Arbor, 1977), vols. 11 and 13, and Charles H. Shattuck, *The Shakespeare Promptbooks: A Descriptive Catalogue* (Urbana, 1965) as a rough indicator of the most commonly used editions; by this measure, the French edition was by far the most popular. Like the Oxberry, Cumberland, Lacy, Irving, Modern Standard Drama, Inchbald, Booth-Hinton and Booth-Winter editions, French did not print lines cut. Indeed, of the nineteenth-century editions I have examined, only the Memorial Theatre Edition of 1880 prints lines usually cut, setting them off by using smaller type.

century cuts, we must examine the patterning of the original texts. As Steven Urkowitz has demonstrated, the First Quarto, Second Quarto, and Folio texts each give Gertrude a different textual pattern. Nevertheless, while the First Quarto is too distinctive to be treated with the others, the Folio and Second Quarto texts do share a subtle but consistent complex of textual patterns in Gertrude's language and the stage directions affecting her. Most striking is the marked shift in these patterns which occurs around the closet scene – suggesting that Gertrude's encounter with Hamlet in that scene has some lasting effect and that the role is therefore dynamic rather than static. The verbal patterns are too complex to be explored within the limits of this paper, but the simpler patterns of visual imagery created by stage directions explicit and implicit in the text offer a manageable example.[3]

For Gertrude almost nothing beyond entrances and exits is made explicit in the stage directions of the Folio or Second Quarto texts. Nevertheless, these do create an intriguing visual pattern which, up to the closet scene, establishes an association between Claudius and Gertrude and then, in succeeding scenes, seriously undercuts that association. Before the closet scene, Gertrude always enters with Claudius; in that scene she enters with Polonius, here strongly associated with the King through their collusion in arranging this encounter between Hamlet and his mother.[4] However, her first entrance after the closet scene (4.5) is made with Horatio and a gentleman (in the Folio, Horatio only): a telling switch.[5] While the gentleman may be regarded as neutral, Horatio is clearly aligned with Hamlet, visually associating Gertrude with Hamlet as Polonius associates her with Claudius in the closet scene. Indeed, this may be the reason for Horatio's somewhat odd inclusion in the scene. Although neither the Folio nor the Second Quarto offers any equivalent to the First Quarto scene which establishes a specific alliance between Gertrude, Horatio, and Hamlet, the visual image here carries for-

ward at least some of its suggestion. In 4.7 Gertrude enters alone to announce Ophelia's death, and while her first line may be a response to Claudius (particularly if he speaks the Folio's 'How sweet Queen?' rather than the Second Quarto's impersonal 'but stay, what noise?') the rest of her speeches are almost certainly directed to Laertes, not Claudius. After the closet scene, Gertrude enters with Claudius only in 5.1 and 5.2 – for the funeral and the fencing match – both large court entrances on formal occasions which would almost automatically assign her a place with the King. When given any choice in the matter, she seems to remain separate from him.

---

[3] I discuss the verbal patterns at length in 'Unheard is not Unseen: Stage Images for Shakespeare's Silent Presences', presented at the Seminar on Stage Images, World Shakespeare Congress, West Berlin, 2 April 1986.

[4] Since the Folio and Quarto stage directions give only mass entrances, entering 'with' someone does not necessarily mean more than entering at the same time. However, simultaneous but separate entrances in Shakespeare can be implied by dialogue or made explicit by including a phrase like 'at several doors' in the stage directions. In the absence of such evidence to the contrary, I have assumed that the King and Queen are, in fact, entering together.

[5] Although the Second Quarto gives an entrance for Gertrude in 4.1, only a singular 'exit' appears at the end of 3.4, and for Gertrude to exit with Hamlet and immediately return with Claudius (as the Second Quarto's entrance suggests) would violate the so-called 'law of reentry'. 'As C. M. Haines has pointed out, most of the exceptions [to this law] occur in battle scenes . . . The other exceptions are in large measure suspect': Bernard Beckerman, *Shakespeare at the Globe: 1599–1609* (New York, 1962), p. 176. I therefore follow the Folio, in which the King enters to her (as he does in the First Quarto), and discuss no entrance for Gertrude in 4.1; this seems to me a continuation of 3.4 rather than a separate scene.

The significance of the Second Quarto gentleman's disappearance in the Folio is cogently argued in Steven Urkowitz, 'Five Women Eleven Ways: Changing Images of Shakespearean Characters in the Earliest Texts', *Images of Shakespeare: Proceedings of the Third Congress of the International Shakespeare Association, 1986*, ed. Werner Habicht, D. J. Palmer, and Roger Pringle (Newark, Delaware, 1988), p. 302.

Exits are more ambiguous, but suggest a parallel pattern. In every exit before the end of the play-within-the-play, Claudius either leaves with Gertrude or makes verbal provision for her exit. Here, however, he issues only a general 'Away' (3.2.257) not specifically addressed to Gertrude. The context and Gertrude's 'How fares my lord?' (3.2.255) certainly suggest that she exits in his wake, yet he, for the first time, does nothing to determine this. This loosening of corporate identity on the King's part functions as an ironic anticipation of Gertrude's behaviour following the closet scene. Her exits in those scenes fall into two patterns. In 4.1 and 4.7, Claudius not only asks Gertrude to come with him but does so twice, repeating 'come' or 'let's follow' within a few lines. Repetition of this kind occurs nowhere in Claudius' exit lines to other characters, though a similar double command to Gertrude does occur in 4.5 when he tells her twice to release Laertes. It seems clear that Gertrude does not let go of Laertes on the first command, and the double exit lines in 4.1 and 4.7 suggest a parallel response. Gertrude may well hesitate to follow her husband at first command after the revelations of the closet scene.[6]

Gertrude's remaining exits, in 4.5 and 5.1, are not made specific: both the Folio and the Second Quarto simply indicate mass exits ('Exeunt') at the end of the scene. Since no other provision is made for the Queen, this might logically be expected to include her, yet such an exit works in opposition to the substance of these scenes as well as the pattern of her other exits. At the time of the exit in 4.5, Claudius is completely focused on the rebellious Laertes, having said nothing to or about Gertrude since telling her to let Laertes speak his piece before Ophelia's entrance. Moreover, if Claudius' exit line – 'I pray you go with me' (4.5.217) – were to include Gertrude as well as Laertes, the Queen would almost become one of the conspirators in the plot against her son, particularly since the line is immediately preceded by a veiled threat to Hamlet: '. . . where

th'offence is, let the great axe fall' (4.5.216). Given what Claudius is about to discuss with Laertes, he could hardly want Gertrude to go with them. In performance, Gertrude frequently follows Ophelia out earlier in the scene, leaving the conspirators to exit together – as they will re-enter in 4.7. Indeed, in the nineteenth century, Gertrude's early exit was so regular a practice that it was printed in many of the standard editions, and it is not unusual today. The absence from both the Folio and the Second Quarto of stage directions for Gertrude at several points where stage business is clearly implied (including her exit before the nunnery scene) makes it tempting to believe that such an exit was intended but not recorded.[7] The First Quarto almost requires it: while no separate exit is indicated for the Queen (only 'exeunt om.' at the end of the scene), the stage direction which follows immediately, 'Enter Horatio and the Queene' (H2v line 4, 5) suggests strongly that she has exited before Laertes and Claudius. With only a few exceptions, Shakespeare's characters do not exit at the end of one scene and immediately re-enter in the first lines of the next.[8] Yet even if Gertrude remains on stage until the end, the dialogue invites visual emphasis on the association of the two men. Gertrude

---

[6] A similar double exit line to Gertrude occurs in 1.2 immediately after Gertrude has made her appeal to Hamlet to remain in Denmark and he has agreed to stay. Here the Queen's preoccupation with Hamlet may cause a lack of response to the first 'Madam, come', prompting Claudius to pull her away from her son with the later 'Come away.' This interpretation made an effective moment in the 1985 Shakespeare Santa Cruz *Hamlet*.

[7] An even more striking omission occurs in the absence of a stage direction marking Gertrude's death when the deaths of Laertes, Hamlet and Claudius are all specifically noted in the stage directions of both the First Quarto and the Folio. (The Second Quarto is more even-handed, specifically marking deaths for no one.) Nineteenth-century Gertrudes frequently died off-stage.

[8] Bernard Beckerman, *Shakespeare at the Globe: 1599–1609* (New York, 1962), p. 176.

might simply be left behind, forgotten – or deliberately excluded – in the heat of the exchange between Laertes and the King. Whenever her exit occurs, the textual patterning suggests an image associating Claudius and Laertes while isolating Gertrude from them.

The closing lines of the funeral scene suggest a similar effect, for Claudius is once again focused on a volatile Laertes, turning to Gertrude only to say 'Good Gertrude set some watch over your son' (5.1.293) – a line which may well prompt her exit before Claudius delivers the final lines of the scene to Laertes. Here, too, a final image of the two conspirators is likely.

What emerges from the original stage directions, then, is a visual pattern which not only undercuts the initial visual association of Claudius and Gertrude after the closet scene, but simultaneously focuses our eyes on the developing bond between Claudius and Laertes. In addition, the later scenes establish a parallel association between Gertrude and Hamlet. This is initiated by the closet scene's pact of secrecy between mother and son and is extended visually by Gertrude's entrance with Horatio, a visual link to Hamlet, at the opening of 4.5. But it is most powerfully embodied in the implicit stage imagery of the moments preceding Gertrude's death. The proffering of her napkin all but requires proximity to Hamlet, and her subsequent offer to wipe his face strongly suggests intimacy as well as proximity. This visual association is corroborated by the focus of Gertrude's dialogue. Her first words in the scene, although prompted by Claudius' 'Our son shall win', hardly seem addressed to the King, for they focus entirely on Hamlet: 'He's fat and scant of breath . . .' (5.2.239; 240). The only other words she addresses to Claudius are a flat rejection of his order not to drink: 'I will, my lord, I pray you pardon me' (5.2.244). Her remaining lines are directed exclusively to Hamlet. At the same moment that Gertrude and Hamlet are drawn into visual association, the private exchange

between Claudius and Laertes necessitates at least a momentary visual association of the two conspirators.

LAERTES   My lord, I'll hit him now.
CLAUDIUS   I do not think't.   (5.2.248–9)

Thus, the demands of the dialogue call for a stage picture which pairs Gertrude with Hamlet and Claudius with Laertes, echoing and reinforcing the pattern of exits and entrances in Acts 4 and 5.

This pattern has frequently been obscured by the tradition of a Gertrude who dotes on Claudius, yet the patterning of Gertrude's language suggests no such obsession. To begin with, we have the striking fact that Gertrude never speaks Claudius' name; before the play-within-the-play she never addresses him even by title and refers to him only once (as 'Denmark' 1.2.69), although others speak of the King frequently. He, on the other hand, refers to the Queen often and uses her name thirteen times, four times with the epithet 'dear', 'sweet' or 'good' attached to it.[9] Moreover, up to this point she never speaks to Claudius without first being spoken to by him. The King doesn't seem to be much on Gertrude's mind. In striking contrast, Hamlet's name occurs in Gertrude's speech fifteen times, twelve in direct address, and four with precisely those epithets Claudius attaches to her name: 'dear', 'sweet' and 'good'. The intensity of attachment Claudius manifests for her is thus paralleled not in her language to or about Claudius but in what she says to and about her son. Indeed, prior to the closet scene she says nothing that isn't at least indirectly related to Hamlet, taking no part in Claudius' discussion of other matters – not even their marriage. In light of all of this, the tradition of a Gertrude who dotes on Claudius seems very

---

[9] My word counts are based on Marvin Spevack, *The Harvard Concordance to Shakespeare* (Cambridge, Mass., 1973) with minor corrections.

much at odds with her textual patterning. Instead, she appears preoccupied from the first with Hamlet. It is Claudius who finds Gertrude 'so conjunctive to [his] life and soul / That, as the star moves not but in his sphere, [he] could not but by her' (4.7.14–16) – not vice versa. The preoccupations of her language suggest that, if pushed to a choice, Gertrude is more disposed to ally herself with Hamlet than with Claudius.

The patterning of her entrances and exits suggests that, after the closet scene, she has, consciously or unconsciously, made that choice. The association between Gertrude and Claudius established prior to that scene is broken in the succeeding scenes, as Gertrude is paired with Hamlet and Claudius with Laertes. (As I noted earlier, Gertrude's verbal patterns also shift at this point in the play, underscoring the strength of the shift and pinpointing its location.) While I would not argue that Gertrude is now actively in league with Hamlet, as she is in the First Quarto, the visual patterning of the play moves her toward him and away from Claudius.

Yet nineteenth-century texts and performances suggested no such thing. Apparently insignificant alterations actually created radical revisions in the visual patterns of the play: maintaining the pre-closet scene association of Gertrude and Claudius to the final scene, while eliminating the post-closet scene association of Claudius and Laertes. Far more damaging – indeed, fatal – is the fact that the standard cuts of the nineteenth century completely obliterated the association of Hamlet and Gertrude by paring away so much of the defining context for the entrance/exit pattern that neither actor nor audience could be expected to discern their underlying significance. Thus, for nearly two hundred years, actors playing Gertrude worked from a text which implied a very different character – a woman ultimately unaffected by her closet scene encounter with Hamlet.

This is not to say that nineteenth-century performance practice disregarded the implications of visual association. We have already seen that Gertrude's awkward presence at the end of 4.5 was frequently dealt with by making explicit her potential early exit with Ophelia. There, the adjustment reinforced the patterning of the role. But all too frequently, awareness of visual implications led to alterations which obscured that patterning by making the association of Gertrude and Claudius a constant in the play. At the end of the funeral scene, nineteenth-century productions apparently sensed the implications of Gertrude's presence with the conspirators, though they responded with less unanimity to this than to the similar problem in 4.5. Only the Oxberry edition printed an exit for Gertrude before Claudius' ambiguous closing couplet: 'An hour of quiet shortly shall we see; / Till then, in patience our proceeding be' (5.1.295–6). The printed stage directions of other standard editions either explicitly or implicitly kept the King and Queen together in the closing moments of the scene. Yet in performance, there seems to have been discomfort with combining this image and these lines. A number of promptbooks write in the Oxberry's early exit, and one 1864 promptbook keeps Gertrude onstage but has her walk to the right of Ophelia's grave while the King and Laertes remain to the left as the curtain falls. But more often the promptbooks cut the couplet, closing the scene on the King's 'This grave shall have a living monument' and eliminating the closing image of the two conspirators. Similarly, in 4.1, 4.5, and 4.7, Claudius' repeated exit lines to Gertrude, with their implication of hesitation, were nearly always cut, thus reinforcing the impression of stability in the Gertrude/Claudius visual association.

Perhaps the most devastating cut occurred in the closet scene itself, eliminating both Hamlet's appeal to the Queen not to reveal that his madness is feigned and her vow to do so. Here we have the most direct manifestation of an association between Gertrude and her son, yet with overwhelming consistency, the acting editions and promptbooks of the day cut the final twenty-eight lines of the Folio text (along with the Second Quarto's additional nine lines), ending the scene with Hamlet's couplet: 'I must be cruel only to be kind: / Thus bad begins, and worse remains behind' (3.4.162–3). Indeed, the cut seems to be almost universal: of the 182 nineteenth-century promptbooks collated in *Shakespeare as Spoken*, all but six cut this entire block.[10] The first appearance of the block cut seems to be in the Woodfall edition of 1767 after which it became almost immediately universal. But editors and performers had begun chiselling away at the scene much earlier. Gertrude's vow itself (3.4.181–3) disappeared in the 1755 Witford edition, perhaps under Garrick's influence. After 1755 the vow appears only in reprints of the 1743 Knapton edition (1756, 1758, 1759, 1760) and the Hitch edition of 1759. Even the 1763 Hawes edition, which largely follows Knapton, cuts the vow. It does not reappear until the late nineteenth century – and even then in a mere handful of texts, only one of which appears to be a promptbook. For all practical purposes, Gertrude is not heard promising to keep Hamlet's secret from 1755 to 1900. Moreover, since nearly all the standard acting editions did not even print the excised lines, many actors probably never knew such a vow existed, creating a serious distortion in the textual patterns from which they might work.

In many cases, this led to stage business which not only ignored but specifically reversed the pattern of association between Hamlet and Gertrude initiated by the closet scene. In a mid-century promptbook, Hamlet's final 'good night' led to the following business:

Queen goes to door, clasps her hand in grief, turns to throw herself upon Hamlet's neck. He shrinks from her. She sighs heavily and exits overwhelmed with grief. (Folger: *Hamlet* 29)

Although I have yet to find stage directions of this kind actually printed in nineteenth-century editions, the number of times that similar business is written into contemporaneous promptbooks suggests a powerful tradition. For Kemble, Forrest, Booth and their imitators, the image was elaborated to include an attempt

by Gertrude to bless her son from which he recoiled.[11] Although Booth was quite tender with Gertrude earlier in the scene, placing his arms 'shieldingly' about her, allowing her to sob 'on his heart' as she declares her heart 'cleft in twain' and stroking her hair as he bids her 'good night', he returned at the end to an image of the traditional revulsion and separation, not only recoiling from her but 'check[ing] the motion' to bless him.[12] Henry Irving, in the 1870s, appears to have been the first nineteenth-century Hamlet to close the encounter with his mother on an image of reconciliation. Frequently, Hamlet delivered the closing couplet after Gertrude had left the stage, depriving her of whatever sympathy there might be in 'I must be cruel only to be kind' (3.4.162) and focusing the scene's closing image on an isolated Hamlet.

Other nineteenth-century cuts stripped away the signals that Gertrude had been profoundly affected by the closet-scene exchange. The succeeding scene, in which Gertrude tries to shield Hamlet by asserting his madness (and by engaging in several rhetorical manipulations too complicated to discuss here), was cut in its entirety from about twenty per cent of the books, although it was printed in the majority

---

[10] I have not included every one of Halstead's nineteenth-century listings in my count. Where cuts listed are not clearly derived either from promptbooks (which reflect performance practice) or from the printed texts (which are the raw material from which performers derive their sense of the play), I have ignored the listing. This includes role-books, study books, and other books of dubious provenance. While Halstead acknowledges errors in his collations (some of which I have been able to correct) and I make no claim to absolute accuracy or exhaustiveness, the general patterns are overwhelmingly clear.

[11] John A. Mills, *Hamlet on Stage: The Great Tradition* (Westport, Connecticut, 1985), p. 66. New York Public Library Promptbooks: *NCP.342977; *NCP.342926; *NCP.

[12] William Winter, ed., *Edwin Booth's Prompt-Book of Hamlet* (Penn, 1909), annotated copy in the New York Public Library Theatre Collection. Also in New York Public Library Theatre Collection promptbook *NCP.

of the most commonly used acting editions. However, even those printed editions (and all but three promptbooks) cut two crucial lines which suggest Gertrude's efforts to protect Hamlet. The Second Quarto's 'Bestow this place on us a little while' (K1r, line 11) is the first order Gertrude has issued in the play which does not reiterate an earlier order by Claudius; its effect is to delay the revelation of Hamlet's killing and, by removing Rosencrantz and Guildenstern, to deliver it privately to Claudius. '... a weeps for what is done' (4.1.26), Gertrude's first self-initiated lie,[13] also shields Hamlet by making him appear more remorseful than anything in his own language would indicate. Neither of these lines appears in the standard editions and both are cut from all but a handful of the nineteenth-century books.[14] Gertrude's only explicit expression of guilt after the closet scene is heard at the opening of the mad scene: 'To my sick soul, as sin's true nature is, / Each toy seems prologue to some great amiss. / So full of artless jealously is guilt, / It spills itself in fearing to be spilt' (4.5.17–20). These lines do not appear in a single eighteenth-century book, and though Macready apparently restored them in 1842, they appear in only about twenty-two books before 1900. Thus little overt evidence remains in the nineteenth-century books to indicate that the closet scene had had any impact whatsoever on Gertrude.

With the most obvious indications of an association between Gertrude and Hamlet excised, it is not surprising that the more subtle should also be allowed to slip away. At times, however, the excisions seem amazingly systematic, as though the violation of the pattern had created intuitive recognition of it, prompting the removal of its remaining pieces. The best example of this occurs in the lines surrounding Gertrude's drinking of the poison (5.2). The conscious motive for cutting at this point may simply have been to reduce Gertrude's role to the minimum, but the effect is to weaken, indeed virtually eliminate, her association with Hamlet and her dissociation from

Claudius. Like the cuts discussed above, these begin to appear in the mid-eighteenth century and become standard by the 1770s. Yet in this case, we have not only cuts, but overt revision. Lines 239 to 248 of the scene usually read as follows in nineteenth-century editions (stage directions are taken from the Modern Standard Drama edition and are typical):

KING Our son shall win.
QUEEN The Queen carouses to thy fortune, Hamlet.
  (*The Queen drinks, and returns the cup to Francisco.*)
HAMLET Good madam!
KING (*Aside to the Queen.*) Gertrude, do not drink.
QUEEN I have my lord: – I pray you pardon me.
KING (*Turning aside from the Queen.*) It is the poisoned cup: it is too late.
LAERTES I'll hit him now.

The changes here are small but of great significance. The line which invites physical proximity of mother and son – 'Here, Hamlet, take my napkin. Rub thy brows'[15] appears in only five nineteenth-century books; that which suggests physical intimacy – 'Come, let me wipe thy face' – in only three. Missing with nearly equal frequency is Hamlet's 'I dare not drink yet, madam, by and by' – a line which strongly suggests that she makes a direct offer of the poisoned cup. Nothing remains to invite the stage image associating Gertrude with Hamlet which is so powerfully implicit in the Folio and Second Quarto. At the same time, the revision of Gertrude's response to Claudius' order not to drink – from 'I will' to 'I have' –

---

13 'Mad as the sea and wind ...' only follows Hamlet's instructions; 'He weeps for what is done' seems to be Gertrude's own invention and thus an important step in her alienation from Claudius.

14 Although I have found no evidence that the full scene was cut before 1856, the first of these lines disappeared for all practical purposes in 1755 when it was cut in the Witford edition and the second was rarely seen (or heard) after Garrick excised it in 1773.

15 This is the Second Quarto reading; the Folio reads, 'Heer's a Napkin, rub thy brows.' Although the language is less intimate, the same physical proximity is implied.

makes her speech to Claudius apologetic rather than defiant. She seems less estranged from Claudius' authority than excessively thirsty. The motivation for this revision may have been the difficulty of making credible Claudius' failure to stop Gertrude from drinking if she is still at his side – as the cut scene (and a good many promptbook notations) would suggest that she is. Its effect, however, is to deal a final blow to the controlling patterns of Gertrude's role, making her relationships at the end of the play quite different from those implicit in the Folio and Second Quarto texts.

Ironically, though no nineteenth-century promptbook I have consulted indicates that the Queen moves away from Claudius during this exchange and several make clear that she does not, the awkwardness of this arrangement is recognized in a number of attempts to mitigate it. This is most obvious in several of the Booth books which record something like the following. 'While the Queen drinks, Osric and others approach the King' as though to provide him with a distraction from her act. Then 'suddenly observing the Queen', Claudius cries 'Gertrude do not drink.'[16] The Queen, of course, can only apologize by then.

One further set of cuts in this exchange deserves attention. Laertes says not 'My lord, I'll hit him now' but only 'I'll hit him now', as though to himself, and the King's response 'I do not think't' is entirely omitted, suggesting that the visual association of the conspirators, like the association of Gertrude and Hamlet, is eliminated.[17] A cut of this kind appears in about ninety per cent of the nineteenth-century books. Thus Gertrude remains visually associated with Claudius to the end, apparently unaffected by her closet scene exchange with Hamlet.

This complex of nineteenth-century cuts eviscerated the textual patterns which give coherence – and even interest – to Gertrude's role – an effect which would be all the more striking had we space to examine her verbal patterns along with the visual. There too we find a complex of textual patterns, all of which shift markedly after the closet scene and call for a corresponding change in Gertrude's behaviour. Although the post-closet-scene Gertrude may be many things, this patterning suggests that she cannot be unchanged. By obliterating those patterns, nineteenth-century cutting made of Gertrude an unresponsive, mindless figure, momentarily distraught by Hamlet's closet scene harangue, but ultimately unaffected by it.

It is hardly surprising that all these changes should have emerged in the mid-eighteenth century, become nearly universal between 1770 and 1800, and endured to the late nineteenth century. The Restoration introduction of changeable scenery necessitated cuts to make time for scene changes, and the habits of editing and performance tended to preserve cuts once they were made. Both editors and performers relied largely on previous editions rather than the Folio or Second Quarto in preparing new editions and promptbooks.[18] Moreover, since many editions purported to give the play 'as performed' by the major actors of the day, cuts were not only tolerated but expected. Similarly, actors performing in an age of tradition mastered their roles by learning the stage business of their predecessors. An innovation might be praised and imitated if audiences accepted it (as was Kemble's rejection of Gertrude's blessing), but could bring devastating

---

16 Many details of this and other Booth stage business are handwritten into a copy of Winter, *Edwin Booth's Promptbook of 'Hamlet'* in the New York Public Library Theatre Collection. The first page is inscribed: 'Some of Edwin Booth's business in Hamlet, observed and noted by Edward Tuckerman Mason, from 1862 to 1891.'

17 That visual association is also missing in the Second Quarto where Laertes says 'Ile hit you now my Lord', addressing the line to Hamlet, and the King's response is absent. The Hamlet/Gertrude association, however, remains more or less intact.

18 Indeed, Halstead's diagram of the derivation of editions of *Hamlet* suggests that no edition between 1676 (Smock Alley) and 1925 (H. K. Ayliff) was directly derived from the Second Quarto or First Folio. William Poel's 1900 production used the First Quarto.

criticism if rejected. Mills cites the story of 'an old critic who, in the reign of George II, refused to see any great merit in the performance of a new Hamlet, declaring, "He did not upset the chair, sir [upon seeing the Ghost in Gertrude's closet]. Now Mr. Betterton always upset the chair."'[19] Re-introducing previously cut material was equally risky. When Henry Irving restored 'Now might I do it pat', many of the critics objected to the speech as 'rather revolting'.[20] In such a milieu, cuts became quickly and thoroughly entrenched.

Yet the re-written Gertrude survived the changing performance practices of the first half of the twentieth century with startling frequency. Although the block cut (3.4.165–91) surrounding her closet scene vow is rare after 1925, the vow itself is missing from fully half the pre-World War II books.[21] Indeed, despite a gradual restoration of Gertrude's text beginning around the turn of the century, it is only after World War II that the cuts which devastated Gertrude's role in the preceding century become the exception rather than the rule. Nearly all those cuts appear in about fifty per cent of the books dated between 1900 and the war. Even after World War II, Olivier's 1948 film, the Globe Theatre Version published by

French in 1951, a 1959 CBS television production, and Nicol Williamson's 1969 film preserve all of the crucial cuts – including the vow – and hence the nineteenth-century Gertrude.[22] Given the impact of film and television and the wide circulation of an edition (as compared to a promptbook) – and particularly the impact of the Olivier film – these four have an influence far greater than their numbers would suggest. For many people who know *Hamlet* through these sources, the distorting lenses of the preceding age have still not been cast aside. Though her public appearances have become less frequent, the nineteenth-century Gertrude is not dead yet.

---

[19] Mills, *'Hamlet' on Stage*, p. 15.

[20] Mills, *'Hamlet' on Stage*, p. 167.

[21] Halstead lists the block cut only for W. Bridges Adams' promptbook, dated 1933 but apparently used for 1929 and 1930 productions.

[22] Although the Olivier film does not make the block cut, it comes close, cutting the vow and everything else except a few lines on the journey to England and the scene's closing lines on Polonius. Despite a radically cut and reconstructed script, there are moments when we seem to see Gertrude's growing alienation from Claudius, but the subtext from which it springs has been all but eradicated.

GAZING AT HAMLET, OR THE DANISH CABARET

LAWRENCE DANSON

'A was a man. Take him for all in all, / I shall not look upon his like again' (1.2.186–7).[1] Among all the doubts, fears, uncertainties attendant on his father's death, there's this for Hamlet to contend with too, this hinted anxiety about keeping up the old gender-roles. Where once men were men, and women – hanging upon them as if increase of appetite did grow where it did feed – women, there now rules an ambiguous queen-king: bidding Claudius farewell for England, Hamlet calls him 'dear mother', because 'Father and mother is man and wife, man and wife is one flesh, and so my mother' (4.3.51–4). And Hamlet himself? In this essay I want to look at some moments in *Hamlet*'s cultural history when the Prince's own sex or gender (the slippage between those terms is part of that history) have been defined in unusual ways. Apart from their occasional bizarrerie, they interest me because they suggest that *Hamlet*, that great drama of patriarchal piety and misogynistic rage, has had under certain circumstances the power to shake the most firmly-planted binary representations.

Or perhaps those representations were ripe for shaking from the start? Several recent critics, including Thomas Laqueur and Stephen Greenblatt, have drawn attention to a possibility latent, at least, within Renaissance ideas about sexual anatomy.[2] Ian Maclean concisely reports the basic case:

In Aristotelian and Galenic terms, woman is less fully developed than man. Because of lack of heat in generation, her sexual organs have remained internal, she is incomplete, colder and moister in dominant humours, and unable to 'concoct' perfect semen from blood. Two axioms are implied here: that the hottest created thing is the most perfect, and that a direct comparison can be made between the genitalia of man and woman in function, number and form.[3]

Like the egg and the chicken, a woman in this scheme is a man *in potentia*, as nature herself, striving toward perfection, strives to make all things male. This is heady stuff, though Maclean himself, like the classical and Renaissance writers he surveys, goes cautiously: he notes that there are few attested cases of sex change in the Renaissance, that they are considered inconclusive by the physiologists who treat them 'with great circumspection', and that all involve women changing into men (38–9). Still, a little of such instability goes a long way, and Stephen Orgel's bold extrapolation from the evidence may conveniently introduce my essay about Hamlet's vicissitudes in the sex-gender system: 'The frightening part of the teleology [that leads from female to male] for the Renaissance mind . . . is precisely the fantasy of its reversal, the conviction that men can

---

[1] *Hamlet* quotations are from *William Shakespeare: The Complete Works*, ed. Stanley Wells, Gary Taylor, John Jowett, and William Montgomery (Oxford, 1986).

[2] Laqueur, 'Orgasm, Generation, and the Politics of Reproductive Biology', *Representations*, 14 (1986), 1–41; Greenblatt, *Shakespearean Negotiations* (Berkeley, 1988), pp. 66–93 ('Fiction and Friction').

[3] *The Renaissance Notion of Woman* (Cambridge, 1980), p. 31.

turn into – or be turned into – women; or perhaps more exactly, can be turned *back* into women, losing the strength that enabled the male potential to be realized in the first place.'[4]

I

Jacqueline Rose has asked 'How far the woman has been at the center, not only of the internal drama, but also of the critical drama – the controversy about meaning and language – which [*Hamlet*] has provoked?'[5] In her argument, T. S. Eliot's dissatisfaction with the form of *Hamlet*, and Eliot's and Freud's invocation of the Mona Lisa to characterize the play, bespeak a male-centred desire for clarity and order which is threatened by the female – literally, threatened by Gertrude, but figuratively also by 'woman' as that which is inimical to the male desire for clarity and order. Rose is perhaps too hard on one of the men in the case: Eliot does not, as she claims, blame Gertrude for failing to measure up as an 'objective correlative'; even he knew that the problem lies in the male fantasist, not in the object of his fantasy. But Rose's point is suggestive: a woman has occasionally figured at the centre of *Hamlet*, and on some of those occasions the 'woman' was Hamlet.[6]

Beginning in the late eighteenth century, Hamlet's rougher, more murderous edges were smoothed away. His delay, no longer a matter of craft or madness, was softened by the pale cast of thought. In this introspective Hamlet two conflicting nineteenth-century representations of gender meet in one line: Hamlet the thinker is partly bred out of the stereotype of the Romantic hero, voyaging through strange seas of thought; but merely thinking on the event is passive, and passivity – in the commonplace binary scheme, more potent in the nineteenth century than it had been in the seventeenth – was conventionally aligned with femininity, so that the Romantic Hamlet could also be seen as a womanly Hamlet. Goethe's

influential description, with its strikingly gendered metaphors, may stand for the many it spawned: 'Here is an oak-tree planted in a costly vase, which should have received into its bosom only lovely flowers; the roots spread out, the jar is shivered to pieces. A beautiful, pure, noble, and most moral nature, without the strength of nerve which makes the hero, sinks beneath a burden which it can neither bear nor throw off . . .'[7] The phallic roots of the oak-tree Hamlet shatter his precious but fragile containing form. Ophelia, with her flowers, might (especially in nineteenth-century productions) fit such a container; but Goethe's male hero is in self-conflict with the virtues, conventionally gendered female, of loveliness, purity, and superior morality. This Hamlet cannot contain himself: either he will self-destruct as his masculine-defining qualities (like the physical apparatus of male sex in the Renaissance scheme) grow outwards, or he will become his own metonym, Goethe's precious container rather than the thing contained.

The feminized Romantic Hamlet appears by explicit allusion in Hazlitt's description (1817): his character 'is made up of undulating lines; it has [like Perdita] the yielding flexibility of "a

---

4 'Nobody's Perfect: Or Why Did the English Stage Take Boys for Women?' *South Atlantic Quarterly*, 88 (1989), 7–29; p. 14.

5 'Sexuality in the Reading of Shakespeare's *Hamlet* and *Measure for Measure*', in John Drakakis, ed., *Alternative Shakespeares* (London, 1985), pp. 95–118; p. 95.

6 David Leverenz, 'The Woman in Hamlet: An Interpersonal View' (in Murray M. Schwartz and Coppélia Kahn, eds., *Representing Shakespeare: New Psychoanalytic Essays* (Baltimore, 1980), pp. 110–28) claims that Hamlet's tragedy is that his feminine qualities are repressed by a patriarchal world that equates woman with weakness. Patricia Parker discusses 'the feminization of the verbal body' and the link between Hamlet's 'delay and womanish wordiness', in *Literary Fat Ladies: Rhetoric, Gender, Property* (London, 1989), pp. 22–3.

7 *Wilhelm Meister* (1795), quoted in the translation ('slightly varied') by Carlyle, in the Variorum *Hamlet*, vol. 2, p. 273.

wave o' th' sea".[8] Hamlet's association with the feminine becomes clearer in the more extravagant flights of Victorian character-criticism. As critics fill the margins of the play-text they domesticate Hamlet – literally, they move him into the traditionally female space of the home; and in that space his masculine attire merely usurps his nature. John Weiss's (1876) fantasy is most touching in this regard, and worth quoting at length. Hamlet with Ophelia becomes David Copperfield with Dora, a man attracted to a softly nurturing, lethean world of escape from his masculine social role:

His love for Ophelia was the most mastering impulse of his life; it stretched like a broad, rich domain, down to which he came from the shadowy places of his private thoughts to fling himself in the unchecked sunshine and revel in the limpid path of feeling. How often had he gone to let her smile strip off the shadow of this thought, and expose him to untroubled nature! The moisture of her eyes refreshed his questioning; her phrases answered it beyond philosophy; a maidenly submission of her hand renewed his confidence; an unspoken sympathy of her reserve, that flowed into the slightest hints and permissions of her body, nominated him as lover and disenfranchised him as thinker; and a sunshower seemed to pelt through him to drift his vapors off.[9]

Weiss dwells with almost voyeuristic pleasure on those 'hints and permissions of [Ophelia's] body'. In the 'broad, rich domain' where Hamlet 'revel[s] in the limpid bath of feeling', Hamlet's own shape virtually dissolves into that of the woman who refreshes him. The dreamy scene of escape from a world where thinking and feeling are rigidly divided between male and female gives eloquent evidence of the burden of Victorian masculinity. In Weiss's fantasy, not only Ophelia but Hamlet too becomes a Victorian 'angel in the house', 'disenfranchised . . . as thinker' – a consummation devoutly to be wished.

Goethe, Hazlitt, and Weiss are all quoted in the Variorum edition. But the full truth was not announced until after the publication of that treasure-trove of psychologized, domesticated

Hamlets. Indeed it was announced in a book dedicated to its editor, Horace Howard Furness, and published, like it, by Lippincott of Philadelphia; and for all its looniness it may be seen as a fitting culmination of Furness's work. The book is called *The Mystery of Hamlet*, by Edward P. Vining (1881). In it Vining goes the illogical next step from gender-stereotype to sexual fact: Hamlet is not only a 'womanly man' but 'in very deed a woman, desperately striving to fill a place for which she was by nature unfitted . . .' (59):

if we imagine that the poet here portrayed a woman incapable of accomplishing the revenge which the perturbed spirit of her father had imposed upon her, driven to the borders of distraction by unbearable burdens, suffering from a hopeless love that she might never reveal, tortured by jealousy, sorely sensitive to all a woman's natural faults, and incensed far more at the sacrifice of personal purity made by her mother in marrying again so speedily, than even by the murder of her father; shrinking from the mortal struggle with the king, fearing bloodshed, and viewing the possibility of her own death with a shuddering horror, and hence anxious to find some escape, some easier method of fulfilling her duty; that which before seemed at variance with all ordinary modes of thinking now becomes an exhibition of the deepest human feeling. (75)

---

8 *Characters of Shakespeare's Plays*, in *The Complete Works of William Hazlitt*, ed. P. P. Howe (London, 1930), vol. 4, p. 237. Hazlitt objects to the acting of the part both by Kemble and Kean: the one 'plays it like a man in armour, with a determined inveteracy of purpose, in one undeviating straight line', the other is full of 'sharp angles and abrupt starts . . . too strong and pointed'; neither catches Hamlet as he is, 'full of weakness and melancholy', a character of 'natural grace and refined susceptibility'.

Susan J. Wolfson's essay 'Feminizing Keats' (in *Critical Essays on John Keats*, ed. Hermione de Almeida (Boston, 1990), pp. 317–56) provides a fascinating account of the ambiguous ways in which the language of femininity was attached to another Romantic figure. Her discussion of Keats amplifies by implication some of the brief suggestions I am making here about Hamlet's image in Romantic iconography.

9 *Wit, Humor, and Shakespeare* (Boston, 1876), p. 177, quoted in the Variorum *Hamlet*, vol. 2, p. 193.

Contemplating his portrait of a woman trapped in a man's social body, Vining asks, 'Shall human pity ever sound the depths of woe that engulfed this unhappy life?' (91).

A critic who seriously proposes that Hamlet is a woman will seem either mad or, with the right theory behind him, very modern. In fact Vining was just quintessentially the nineteenth-century literary amateur, with a penchant for autodidactic intellectual extravagance. After *The Mystery of Hamlet*, he wrote his 787-page masterpiece, *An Inglorious Columbus; or, Evidence that Hwui Shan and a Party of Buddhist Monks from Afghanistan Discovered America in the 5th Century A.D.* (New York, 1885); then, with more professional seemliness – he was by trade a railway man – he wrote *The Necessity for a Classification of Freight* in 1886, and in 1906 his religious treatise, *Jacob, or Israel's New Name*. (In 1890 he edited *Hamlet* for The Bankside Shakespeare.) Along the way, at the age of thirty-nine, he received the Master of Arts from Yale, and at the age of sixty-one, the Doctor of Laws from William Jewell College. Vining's solution to the mystery of Hamlet is worth remembering for several reasons. His fantasy of a female Hamlet, however idiosyncratic, is also a cultural product; his ideas about gender – what constitutes a real woman, what a real man – are recognizably not his alone. And those ideas can interestingly be compared both to some Renaissance ideas and to some modern ideas. Furthermore, Vining's little book has had a surprisingly vigorous afterlife. It comes up one June day in 1906 in the library in Dublin, where John Eglinton tells Stephen Dedalus 'that an actress played Hamlet for the fourhundredandeighth time last night in Dublin. Vining held that the prince was a woman.'[10] In Ernest Jones's *Hamlet and Oedipus*, Vining is preserved in a footnote, paired with the critic who proved that Hamlet was overweight.[11] But as Jones's Freudian theory bore cinematic fruit in Olivier's 1948 film – to which I will return – so too Vining's theory was once magnificently justified on screen. And to that, too, I will return.

But Vining first – who disarmingly sneaks up on his radical thesis by seeming to propose only the Romantic commonplace that 'the charms of Hamlet's mind are essentially feminine in their nature' (47). Vining is explicit about what constitutes the 'essentially feminine'. For instance, 'Gentleness, and more or less dependence upon others, are inherent qualities of the feminine nature, and Hamlet possessed both' (47). He also possessed other, more disturbing feminine qualities. Woman, for instance, 'with less strength to accomplish her desires by straightforward action', uses instead shrewdness, subtlety, indirection, and dissimulation; thus Hamlet's feigned madness and his use of the play-within-a-play 'are stratagems that a woman might attempt, and that are far more in keeping with a feminine than with a masculine nature' (47). Vining cites the authority of the great psychologist Dr Henry Maudsley, who also found that Hamlet 'was by nature something of a dissimulator, – that faculty having been born in him ...' Maudsley's clinical observations (quoted by Vining) provide an etiology for the development of feminine traits in men: 'we not uncommonly observe the character of the mother, with her emotional impulses and subtle but scarce conscious shifts, in the individual when young, while the calm deliberation and conscious determination of the father come out more plainly as he grows older' (48).[12] Thus for the Victorian psychologist, as for Renaissance Galenic theorists, femininity is a stage in the teleological development of

---

[10] James Joyce, *Ulysses* (New York, 1934, 1961), p. 198.

[11] Jones, *Hamlet and Oedipus* (1949), (New York, 1954), p. 27, n 17.

[12] On Dr Maudsley, see Elaine Showalter, *The Female Malady: Women, Madness, and English Culture, 1830–1980* (New York, 1985), and (on a matter related to the subject of my essay) her treatment of Ophelia in the Victorian iconography of female insanity, 'Representing Ophelia: Women, Madness, and the Responsibilities of Feminist Criticism', in Patricia Parker and Geoffrey Hartman, eds., *Shakespeare and the Question of Theory* (New York and London, 1985), pp. 77–94.

masculinity; and Dr Maudsley's female-minded dissimulating Hamlet is a case of arrested gender development.

But Vining goes further; his amassing of supposedly essential female traits prepares the way for his – and, as he traces it, Shakespeare's – transition from a merely female-minded Hamlet to Hamlet as a woman in perfect fact. Hamlet's fear of death is a female trait. His 'impulsiveness' is another; so is his 'love of obtaining the advantage in a wordy warfare, which induces him to tantalize and mock at Polonius and Osric' (54); also his use of '"pretty oathes"' and 'his fear of breaking into tears' (55). Like a woman, Hamlet is 'small and delicate' (as we know because he contrasts himself disparagingly with Hercules), but also 'at least moderately plump'. He has 'a woman's daintiness and sensitiveness to weather and perfumes' (because he notices that 'the air bites shrewdly' and because he is revolted by the smell of Yorick's skull). He suffers from hysteria, the female malady (77–8). Even his misogyny proves he is a woman: '. . . such is the abhorrence which he expresses of [women's] frailties and weaknesses that it irresistibly suggests the question, Is not this more like the bitterness of one woman against the failings of another, than like the half compassion, "more in sorrow than in anger", with which a man regards a feminine weakness?' Hamlet's indictment of Ophelia in the nunnery-scene is so ungentlemanly that only a woman could have done it: 'Did ever a noble youth so abuse and insult a lovely gentle girl?' (57).

If Vining is clear about the fact that women dislike other women, he is equally clear about the fact that men like women: 'The Creator has implanted in humanity a subtle attraction toward the opposite sex, which in a man, and particularly a man of Hamlet's age, invests all womankind with a tender charm' (55). Hamlet is different – not only doesn't he like women, he does like men: 'In Hamlet . . . we find an entire inversion of what should have been expected. His admiration is expended upon men

and masculine perfection alone' (55). Now, 'inversion' (so innocently slipped into the preceding extract) was to become a common term for same-sex attraction during the 1890s, the period during which homosexuality came increasingly to be seen not as an aberration of conduct but as an identity. The word 'homosexuality' itself, coined by a Swiss doctor in 1869, also did not enter English until the 1890s.[13] In Vining's day, 'the Love that dare not speak its name' actually had no legitimizing name to speak: the available words of legal condemnation, like 'sodomy', 'buggery', and their cognates, refer to actions that express a wilful departure from the supposed norms of a man's 'essential' sexual identity; the creation (or rediscovery) of an idea of male sexuality which could be expressed appropriately in the acts to which those words refer was only in progress at the time Vining was solving Hamlet's mystery.

Still, Vining's occlusion of any third possibility, beyond men-love-women and women-love-men, suggests a notable blindness. Vining's fellow American, Walt Whitman, had already provided a role-model and a defining term, 'adhesiveness', for writers struggling to define a specifically gay consciousness.[14] Only a few years after Vining's book, in 1889, Oscar Wilde published 'The Portrait of Mr W. H.', his playful 'neoplatonic' solution to the mystery of Shakespeare's sonnets. At Wilde's first trial, Mr Carson (for the defence) asked Wilde, 'I believe you have written an article to show that Shakespeare's sonnets were suggestive of unnatural vice?' Wilde's reply must count among his very best paradoxes: 'On the contrary I have written an article to show that they are not. I objected to such a perversion being put upon Shakespeare.'[15]

---

[13] Jeffrey Weeks, *Coming Out: Homosexual Politics in Britain from the Nineteenth Century to the Present* (London, 1977), p. 3.

[14] Weeks, pp. 53–4.

[15] *The Trials of Oscar Wilde*, ed. H. Montgomery Hyde (London, 1948) p. 130. I expand on these matters in 'Oscar Wilde, W. H., and the Unspoken Name of Love', *ELH* 58 (1991), 979–1000.

The idea of a love between men which is not 'unnatural', not a 'perversion' was, in 1895, a paradox *almost* (but, as Wilde's reply shows, not quite) beyond the reach of linguistic possibility.

Vining's assumption, therefore, that a man who likes other men is by definition a woman, was culturally the easier conclusion to reach than the conclusion that he was gay. But it also suggests that some versions of nineteenth-century misogyny (like Vining's) are displaced versions of homophobia – by which I mean not only hatred of gays, but fear of being gay, thus being femininized. In any event, it allows Vining to play safely with the wonderful notion that Hamlet's true love is not Ophelia but Horatio: 'His eulogy of Horatio in the third act is characterized by a warmth of fondness and admiration far greater than is natural between friends of the same sex' (65). Vining notices that Hamlet's line, in the folio text, about 'disprized love' is missing from the first quarto and appears in the second quarto as 'despized love'. As a textual theorist, Vining is very modern: he finds that the variation reflects Shakespeare's own revision of his texts, and that it makes a critical point:

Horatio did not despise the affection of Hamlet, but he can have had but the dimmest apprehension of the depth of Hamlet's whole-hearted love and never suspected the true cause of the latter's confidence in him. Hence Hamlet could not but have felt that his love was and must ever remain 'disprized'. (65)

With the sad story of Hamlet's love for Horatio at its heart, the Victorian tragedy of Hamlet, Princess of Denmark, is now complete: We learn that on the day of old Hamlet's combat with old Fortinbras, Gertrude gave birth to a daughter; that fearing old Hamlet's death, and a dynastic crisis, she gave out the false information that a royal son had been born; and that, 'This step once hastily taken could not be recalled . . . There could be no retreat, no change: the part once taken must be played through to the end' (83). And that end for Vining's version of the Romantic feminized Hamlet is inevitably tragic: 'Hamlet must die, for the "cursed spite" under which he was born was such that for his woes there could be no other end than death' (95).

Vining calls Hamlet a woman, but it would be more accurate to say that Vining's Hamlet is a man emasculated by another man's competitive scrutiny. Reading the opening pages of his sober-seeming analysis, segueing then into the more bizarre passages of his revisionary tale, we never quite give up the idea of the man-Hamlet; that idea is constantly worked on, transformed: the woman-Hamlet literally depends on it. (Hence the problem of pronouns, as when I say, he is a woman.) Discovering the female Hamlet is an operation of power: as you peer into Hamlet, can you see that this trait or that is really a feminine trait? Can you see that he's only trying to pass? Can you find him out? When you have, you can, like Vining, submit him to your pity: you can turn the nineteenth century's great symbol of intellectual power into an object of sexual pleasure, a woman. You can simultaneously unfix the restrictive binary of sexual identity while reaffirming the hierarchy which puts the male spectator on top.

II

In late nineteenth-century America, the feminized Hamlet was pathetic – fearful, jealous, sexually repressed. What would she look like under different cultural conditions, to other subjectivities, feminine as well as masculine? I can give one reasonably factual answer to the question. In 1920, Vining's *The Mystery of Hamlet* (mixed up with bits of Saxo and Belleforest) provided the scenario for a silent film, made in Germany, directed by a Dane, Svend Gade, and starring the most famous European actress of the time, Gade's Danish wife, Asta Nielsen (1883–1972).[16] One approaches Vining's

---

[16] In her autobiography *Den Tiende Muse* (Copenhagen, 1946), vol. 2, p. 145, Nielsen says that she formed her own company, 'Art Film', to produce *Hamlet* in 1920.

text with a mixture of humour and curiosity, as a kind of critical freak. Asta Nielsen's *Hamlet*, by contrast, abashes condescension: however inauspicious its origins in Vining's 'theory', however strange the very idea of a *silent* Hamlet (of whatever gender), Nielsen's is a powerful performance in one of the great productions of Weimar cinema. Watching the Nielsen-Gade *Hamlet* in 1991, it is still possible to agree with the reviewer who wrote seventy years ago in *The New York Times*, 'It does not need to apologize to any production that has come from a foreign or domestic studio since the invention of motion pictures. It holds a secure place in the class with the best.'[17]

There is a long tradition of actresses playing Hamlet, to which Nielsen, however unique her posture, belongs; it stretches from Sarah Siddons in 1775 to (at least) Diane Venora for The New York Shakespeare Festival in 1983.[18] Bernard Grebanier's *Then Came Each Actor* gives a reasonably thorough survey of the tradition, although its condescending tone is as revealing as its hodge-podge of information.[19] Grebanier thinks that 'the inexplicable obsession which has driven some women to assume men's roles' may be connected to the belief that Hamlet is 'a kind of milk-sop too sensitive to act', a misconception which may have 'encouraged the dears to think of him, quite incorrectly, as a sister under the skin' (253). Since his chapter about women playing Hamlet deals with 'Shakespearean curiosa' it is (he says) 'as fitting a place as any, without any insult intended to the ladies, to append [a description of the *Dog Hamlet*] given in the early nineteenth century, when well-trained dogs were much in demand upon the "boards"' (263). Grebanier's academic version of good-old-boyishness, with its updated comparison of walking dogs and preaching women, is excessive enough to suggest that the phenomenon of female Hamlets – women usurping the central role in our central drama of patriarchy – causes him a degree of anxiety. To tactics such as his, 'the dears' might reply that acting well is the best revenge.

The actress who played Hamlet 'for the fourhundredandeighth time last night in Dublin' (as Stephen hears in *Ulysses*) was Mrs Bandmann-Palmer, the longest-playing (408 was less than half her total) of several *fin de siècle* female Hamlets. Sarah Bernhardt's was the most famous. Bernhardt had played travesty roles in her youth; now, in middle age, she drew on the stage's transvestite tradition to provide her with starring roles in what she called her 'three *Hamlets*': Rostand's *L'Aiglon*, Musset's *Lorenzaccio*, and the thing itself. Her justification was that 'These roles portray youths of twenty or twenty-one, with the

---

The American version (a print is in the Film Library at the Museum of Modern Art, New York) calls itself an 'Asta Films' production, and is dated 1921. Direction and Design, Svend Gade; Scenario, Erwin Gephard; Photography, Kurt Courant and Axel Graatkjer; with Eduard von Winterstein as Claudius, Helena Makowska as Gertrude. An opening card says that the film is based on ancient legend and on 'the contention of the eminent American Shakespearean scholar, Edward P. Vining (Hon. M.A. Yale)'.

17 *N.Y. Times*, 9 November 1921. The critic in *Variety* (11 November 1921) was less impressed. 'Miss Nielsen's abilities are exceptional, but they are not the type to enrapture the American public. Almost emaciated, she has command and distinction of movement. Her facial pantomime is of considerable range, but dead whites and blacks have to be used to overcome her physical deficiencies.' (Her *what?*) There is a sympathetic discussion of the film in Robert Hamilton Ball, *Shakespeare on Silent Film* (London, 1968), pp. 272–8. Robert A. Duffy discusses Gade's cinematography but not Nielsen's performance in 'Gade, Olivier, Richardson: Visual Strategy in *Hamlet* Adaptations', *Literature/Film Quarterly* 4 (1976), pp. 141–52. See also Bernice Kliman, '*Hamlet*': *Film, Television, and Audio Performance* (Rutherford, N.J., 1988).

18 Diane Venora is unique in having gone, as she matured, from playing Hamlet to playing Ophelia (again at Joseph Papp's New York Shakespeare Festival, in the 1990 production starring and directed by Kevin Kline). According to Frank Rich in *The New York Times* (2 December 1982), Venora's Hamlet resembled Bernhardt's in that 'we are simply asked to forget that a woman (and a beautiful one) happens to be playing a prince'.

19 New York, 1975.

minds of men of forty.'[20] When an actor has experience enough to play such parts, he no longer looks the part; but an actress of forty (or maybe fifty-five) has in every sense the appropriate stature. Bernhardt's age is relevant: although the heyday in the blood is not necessarily tame in one's fifties, there was little of the risqué in Bernhardt's potentially transgressive casting. Admirers of her five-hour production, in Paris in May 1899 and a month later in London, praised her suppression of 'the feminine element': 'If it were not for the high pitch of the voice and its occasional thinness, you would never imagine that this Hamlet was a woman. And even this slight reminder of the fact disappears after the first few minutes, when you get accustomed to it . . . In no other respect could I discover the slightest trace of the woman . . .'[21] Others were not so impressed. Max Beerbohm, in the *Saturday Review*, took a leaf from Vining's book to agree that 'Hamlet, in the complexity of his nature, had traces of femininity. Gentleness and a lack of executive ability are female qualities . . .' But Shakespeare's Hamlet was no woman, and Bernhardt's Hamlet was no man: 'The only compliment one can conscientiously pay her is that her Hamlet was, from first to last, *très grande dame*.'[22]

With Asta Nielsen's performance it would be otherwise. Her screen persona was already indelibly inscribed with the sexually transgressive. During the War her image had served as pin-up on both sides of the line. Guillaume Apollinaire's ecstatic description, which unintentionally calls to mind Pater's description of the Mona Lisa, catches her sexually protean quality: 'She is all! She is the vision of the drinker and the dream of the lonely man. She laughs like a girl completely happy, and her eye knows of things so tender and shy that one could not speak of them.'[23] The spice of androgyny helped make Nielsen this perfect Weimar icon. Even before the War she had appeared in transvestite roles: a photo in her autobiography, *Den Tiende Muse*, shows her in masculine

evening dress in the Danish film *Ungdom og Galskab* (*Youth and Madness*), from 1912–13; in 1916 there was *Das Liebes ABC* (*The Alphabet of Love*) in which 'disguised as a young man, [she] takes a male friend through the night clubs and dives of a metropolis to introduce him to the facts of life'.[24] When her roles were not explicitly androgynous, they still tended toward the sexually ambiguous or transgressive: *Miss Julie* (1921), Mary Magdalen in *I.N.R.I.* (1923), Lulu in Wedekind's *Erdgeist* (1923),[25] *Hedda Gabler* (1924). Her Hamlet, a woman but no lady, belongs in this gallery.

I suspect that Nielsen and Gade discovered Vining's book through the reference to it in Ernest Jones's *Das Problem des Hamlet und der Oedipus-Komplex* [1911], the original version of the book published in 1949 as *Hamlet and Oedipus*.[26] *Why* they decided to use it is the more interesting question. Possibly they were attracted to *Hamlet* as a kind of political joke: Germany's greatest post-war film star, a Dane, plays the greatest English tragic hero, a Dane. Also, Nielsen was attempting to establish herself as an actress of 'art' roles – and what could be more arty than *Hamlet*? She could become

20 Quoted by Elaine Aston, *Sarah Bernhardt: A French Actress on the English Stage* (Oxford, 1989), p. 115; I am indebted to her account.

21 Theodore Stanton, 'Sara Bernhardt as Hamlet', *The Critic* 35 (1899), p. 638. Thanks to Professor Deborah Barker for bringing this review to my attention.

22 'Hamlet, Princess of Denmark', 17 June 1899, rpt. in *Around Theatres* (New York, 1954), pp. 36, 37.

23 Apollinaire is quoted without further attribution (and in slightly different translations) both by Siegfried Kracauer, *From Caligari to Hitler: A Psychoanalytic History of the German Film* (Princeton, 1947), p. 26, and by Herbert G. Luft, 'Asta Nielsen: The Once Celebrated "Duse of the Screen" is Living in Retirement in Copenhagen', *Films in Review* 7 (1956), 19–26; p. 21.

24 Luft, p. 21.

25 Nielsen here played the role more famously associated with Louise Brooks, who played it in G. W. Pabst's *Lulu* (1928).

26 *Das Problem des Hamlet und der Oedipus-Komplex* (Leipzig, 1911; rpt. New York, 1970), in which Vining's theory is described on p. 5 and in a footnote on p. 39.

the Bernhardt of motion pictures by doing *Hamlet*, but she could not do it *à la* Bernhardt, who was drawing on a long stage tradition of transvestite performance. Cinema conventions, by contrast, tend to enforce a continuity, and in the case of stars like Nielsen a virtual identity, between performer and role. So the actress playing Hamlet on film could not, like Bernhardt, try to erase her sex. She could, however, make the suppression of her sexuality part of the diegesis; she could make *Hamlet* the story of an actress playing Hamlet disguised as a man. It was the story Vining had already written, but significantly revised for a German audience of the 1920s.

Vining's female Hamlet had been a male fantasy, clearly addressed to other men; Nielsen's, by contrast, was addressed both to women and men, but with the possibility of different readings. According to Patrice Petro (to whose recent study *Joyless Streets: Women and Melodramatic Representation in Weimar Germany* I am indebted), Nielsen was 'from the start [an] indisputable [favorite] with female audiences'; her presence 'ensured that a film would appeal to the female audience'.[27] That appeal was implicit in the Nielsen screen persona, with its combination of independence and vulnerability, its powerful but often repressed and exploited sexuality. Her two most famous roles in contemporary social dramas were as prostitutes – Auguste in *Die freudlose Gasse* (*Joyless Streets*, 1925), and Maria in *Dirnentragödie* (*Tragedy of the Whore*, 1927); both roles are marked by the pathos of a woman's sexual and economic exploitation. In Nielsen's polymorphous sexuality a viewer could read the strong image of a conceivable freedom from gender restrictions, crossed with the pathos of that freedom's bafflement by actual social conditions.

Weimar Germany's famous gender crisis – the world's most glamorous such crisis, thanks to Kander and Ebb's *Cabaret* – was visible in contemporary magazine articles decrying *die Vermännlichung der Frau* (the masculinization of

women). Patrice Petro in *Joyless Streets* compares the iconography of these illustrated magazines to the iconography of Weimar cinema. '*Nun Aber Genug!*' ('Enough already!') says the headline to an article from the *Berliner Illustrirte Zeitung* from 1925: the page shows two photographic portrait busts, a man and a woman, both with short cropped hair, tie and jacket; the drawing below shows them in matching unisex dressing gown and pyjamas. From *Die Dame* of 1926 there is a fashion article, *Variationen über den Smoking*, with a cartoon of a shocked waiter and an amused hotel pageboy looking at an identically dressed pair of swells – except that her evening suit has skirt instead of trousers.[28]

Petro's discussion of the German New Woman-in-man's-clothing draws on Atina Grossman's study of the Sex Reform movement. Grossman characterizes the New Woman as 'A much abused and conflated image of flapper, young stenotypist, and working mother'; her appropriation of masculine roles and prerogatives threatened not only the conservative demand for traditional gender distinctions but the radical demands of the Sex Reform movement as well.[29] The movement's aim was to 'redomesticate' the New Woman as the answer to a host of perceived social problems ('the decline in the birthrate, the high incidence of abortions, the rise in the marriage age, and the increasing number of married women and mothers in the waged labor force'

---

[27] (Princeton, 1989), p. 159. Petro cites the sociological study of cinema attendance done in 1914 by Emilie Altenloh. Altenloh is also cited by Miriam Hansen, 'Early Silent Cinema: Whose Public Sphere?' *New German Critique* 29 (1983), pp. 147–84, who draws attention to the gender politics of Nielsen's androgynous roles. Luft also claims that Nielsen provided 'an emotional release for women' (p. 21).

[28] Petro, pp. 106, 112, 113.

[29] 'The New Woman and the Rationalization of Sexuality in Weimar Germany', in Ann Snitow, Christine Stansell, Sharon Thompson, eds., *Powers of Desire: The Politics of Sexuality* (New York, 1983), pp. 153–71; pp. 156.

[157]). Central to its aims was a cure for female sexual frigidity by the promotion of mutual orgasm: through happier sexuality it would recuperate the liberated, or masculinized, woman for the patriarchal family. Asta Nielsen would have been a hard case for the sex reformers. Though she could be almost all things to all people she was not the image of a procreative, sexually satisfied *hausfrau*. Grossman describes the iconography that identifies 'the new deviants' of the Sex Reform movement – women, that is, 'unfit for marriage': 'short, dark hair; dressed in a unisex shift; distinctly unmaternal – the image not only of the prostitute but of the Jewess and the lesbian' (167). It is also in its details the image of Asta Nielsen's Hamlet, a new deviant in an ancient setting.

But the description leaves out the most important Nielsen feature: the eyes, the 'immense blazing eyes'[30] that dominate Nielsen's pale, startlingly luminous face and have power to control the entire screen. Petro contrasts Nielsen's 'intense, dramatically focused gaze' to 'the unfocused, almost mirrorlike gaze' of screen actresses in the next generation in Germany and Hollywood: 'Nielsen . . . belong[s] to a period of filmmaking when a focused and highly motivated female gaze was imbued with a pathos so intense that [her] performances became emblematic of an era, and a premonition of things to come' (160). In *Hamlet*, we first see those weirdly illuminated, searching eyes at work after some awkward opening sequences – battle, king's wounding, queen's delivery, false report of baby's sex, Hamlet's early childhood – that promise the spectator little beyond a superior laugh. Then the *mise-en-scène* becomes a classroom at the University of Wittenberg. First day of term, and all the high-spirited guys are in attendance – Laertes, Fortinbras, Horatio, Hamlet. Horatio has shoulder-length wavy blond hair – a more conventionally female style than Hamlet's short black hair with fringe brushed to one side over her forehead. They are seated side by side;

Hamlet's books drop; Hamlet and Horatio both stoop, bang heads, recover – and Hamlet gazes with frank desire at the unwitting Horatio.

Of course there's nothing like it in Shakespeare, not only because Shakespeare never wrote the scene but because the gaze belongs both to male and female, both to Shakespeare's Hamlet and his Ophelia; it is encoded with the active intensity of the one character and the thwarted yearning of the other. The female Hamlet's gaze, here and elsewhere in the film, is overdetermined also in terms of audience identification. Hamlet's gaze holds and directs the audience's; we share her visual desire. Here, Hamlet solicits the audience's eroticizing scrutiny of Horatio as, elsewhere, she will of Ophelia. At the same time, however, and precisely because of the way the camera records the commanding intensity of her gaze, Hamlet him/herself is the object of the audience's erotic interest: the visually less exciting Horatio is no match for her; his blank surface intensifies her gaze, as a mirror does sunlight, and reflects its erotic charge back on her. The female Hamlet allows an unusual division of labour between the camera, which peruses Hamlet, and Hamlet in the diegesis, who is the active looker, simultaneously the object and director of the look.

The complexity of the viewing situation appears in a subsequent Wittenberg scene where Hamlet meets Laertes, his noisy, boorish upstairs neighbour in the dorm. A group of flirtatious girls has gathered beneath their windows. The feckless Laertes borrows money from Hamlet and invites Hamlet to join him downstairs with the girls. Hamlet refuses; and in close-up the camera watches Hamlet's eyes, gazing now not at the scene outside but into a distance over the audience's shoulder, a space for her impossible longing. The object of her

---

[30] The phrase is from Lotte Eisner, *The Haunted Screen: Expressionism in the German Cinema and the Influence of Max Reinhardt*, trans. Roger Greaves (Berkeley, 1969, first French pub. 1952), p. 261, and is accidentally repeated verbatim by Petro, p. 167.

fantasy is neither Laertes nor the girls, but by the same token the fantasy is marked, by her costume and gaze, as potentially polymorphous. Her look designates her both as desiring and desirable, whether viewed with a male or a female subjectivity. As normatively male subject, the spectator is indulged in a voyeuristic fantasy: a woman, unaware of his presence, exposes herself as sexual being to his controlling gaze. Nielsen's masquerade of masculinity – her unisex black tunic over black hose – works not to disguise her sexuality but to invite the intrusive look; it tantalizes with what it pretends to hide. Male anxiety about masculine women is defused, and indeed converted to erotic energy, because the costume is a source of vulnerability – the audience is invited to see *through* the costume, sometimes by a literal slipping at the cleavage – rather than of strength. As normatively female subject, the spectator has the pleasure of identifying with a frankly desiring woman, one whose transgressive mobility is figured both in sexual and economic terms (she moves among the men as a first among equals); simultaneously, anxiety over the usurpation of male prerogatives is defused as Hamlet's male pose becomes a source of pathos, the sign of her/his inability to join either Laertes or the girls outside – becomes, indeed, its own punishment.

Throughout, the film keeps a balance between empowering and disabling its masculinized heroine. The female Hamlet in Weimar, unlike the female Hamlet in late nineteenth-century America, is a lively, inventive, controlling presence. The script revises Vining (and Shakespeare) by removing the Ghost: this Hamlet will not be upscreened by any protoplasmic patriarch. After his offscreen death, old Hamlet is present only metonymically in the form of his own tomb, at which Hamlet grieves with long, almost erotic intensity, her arms virtually embracing the stone sarcophagus. Most visibly, the qualities of liveliness, inventiveness, and control can be read in Nielsen's lithe body and expressive face. Unlike a later

film Hamlet – Olivier's, to which I will shortly turn – Nielsen seldom hides her gaze either from the other characters or from the viewing audience: the eyes are alert, searching; they invite us to join her in actively exploring those ignorant others – the rest of the cast of characters – whose less purposive looks make them all, in effect, characters within a narrative of her controlling. Mary Ann Doane says in the course of her attempt to 'theorize the female spectator', that 'There is always a certain excessiveness, a difficulty associated with women who appropriate the gaze, who insist upon looking'.[31] Nielsen's female Hamlet, perusing Horatio with as much intensity as she does Ophelia and acting the detective role more fully than Shakespeare's Hamlet, is (in Doane's phrase) 'the site of an excessive and dangerous desire'.[32]

The one character who knows Hamlet's secret, her mother Gertrude, is seldom allowed very close visual contact with Hamlet. The one character she would *like* to have know her secret, Horatio, is too dim and, later, too infatuated with Ophelia to know that there's a secret to be found out. Feigning madness, Hamlet is examined, at Polonius' direction, by a comically inept doctor. The doctor feels Hamlet's head, then puts his ear to her chest, but recognizes nothing: the scene, absurd as it is, increases the spectator's sense of privileged participation in the erotically charged secret of Hamlet's sex. Borrowing and revising a trick from Shakespearian comedy, the actress playing a young man woos another woman, Ophelia (both because Hamlet wants to hoist Polonius with his own petard and because she wants to alienate Ophelia's affections from Horatio).

---

[31] 'Film and the Masquerade: Theorizing the Female Spectator', *Screen*, 23 (1982), 74–87; p. 83.

[32] Doane, 84. On Hamlet as detective: instead of a Ghost to give away the game, this female Hamlet must herself explore the cistern in the castle dungeon where Claudius keeps the writhing snakes with which, in this version, he killed old Hamlet.

The scene, with Hamlet nibbling Ophelia's fingers, is played for laughs at Ophelia's expense, but the laughs do not obscure the transgressive eroticism. Making love to Ophelia, gazing at Horatio, soliciting the gaze both of men and women in her offscreen audience, Nielsen's Hamlet makes figurative androgyny into actual bisexuality, and realizes a possibility only deeply latent either in Shakespeare's play or Vining's 'theory'.

Nielsen's Hamlet, then, is a fuller appropriation, even subversion, than Vining's. Up to a point, she is a figure of woman transcending woman's social role. Simultaneously, however, she is also a cautionary figure of the lonely fate presumably awaiting the masculinized woman; her bisexuality is a source of pathos and circumscription. The woman playing a man making love to a woman is allowed that scope only on the terms that she is really pining for a man. Unfulfilment with either man or woman is the cost of her bisexuality. For all its bold – its characteristically Weimar – polymorphous indulgence, the Nielsen *Hamlet* still works to gratify male heterosexual fantasy. Its infamous final scene shows Horatio cradling his dead friend Hamlet in his arms. Horatio strokes Hamlet, beginning at the head; his hand reaches Hamlet's chest; and in the greatest scene of *anagnorisis* Shakespeare never wrote, the mystery of Hamlet is solved by a man's discovery of a woman's anatomical secret.[33] But in Freud's Germany as in Shakespeare's England, the discovery of sexual difference may also be man's threat, the sign of a possible loss or reversion he dreads. Horatio peruses Hamlet as in the more familiar version Hamlet did Ophelia, with 'a sigh so piteous and profound / That it did seem to shatter all his bulk / And end his being' (2.1.95–7).

III

Nielsen's silent, female, German-Danish *Hamlet*, for all its many virtues, stands out as an oddity even in the strange history of *Hamlet* productions. As a coda to it and a brief conclusion, I want to turn to a more central document, the film of *Hamlet* made in 1948 with Laurence Olivier as director and star. I can't claim that Olivier was directly influenced by Nielsen's film, but he probably knew of it. He knew about Ernest Jones's Oedipal theory; and Jones knew about Vining; and the makers of the Weimar *Hamlet* seem to have known about Vining via Jones. But even without that web of relations, Olivier's film is implicated, as Nielsen's is, in the question posed by Jacqueline Rose, How far has the woman been at the centre of *Hamlet*?

Let me begin with a scene – it is 2.1 in the printed text – which intricately involves questions of spectatorship and gender. On the Shakespearian page it begins with Polonius instructing Reynaldo to dangle a 'bait of falsehood' to catch the 'carp of truth' (61) and continues with Ophelia's account of Hamlet's appearance in her closet, 'with a look so piteous in purport / As if he had been loosèd out of hell / To speak of horrors' (83–5). This is our first sight of Ophelia, the first time the play acknowledges her existence, and through her narration it also becomes, in the mind's eye, our first representation of Hamlet since he declared his intention 'To put an antic disposition on' (1.5.173). The whole scene comes in such a questionable shape that it may stand as the play's quintessentially indeterminate scene. Is Ophelia honest, or is she an unreliable narrator? The Hamlet she describes is a clinical picture of melancholic distraction: is it real or feigned? If real, why? Is it 'the very ecstasy of love'? Or grief for a father murdered and a mother whored? If feigned, for whose benefit? Ophelia's? Or is she the bait to take a bigger fish?

But everyone knows the options. I want to ask a different kind of question: Who in this

---

[33] Professor Susan Wolfson reminds me that at this moment in Nielsen's *Hamlet* a German audience would recall Siegfried's discovery of Brunhilde's sex when he takes off her armour.

scene is the observer, who observed? We *hear* that Hamlet took Ophelia by the wrist, went to arm's length, and fell to such perusal of her face as if he would draw it; then he gazed at her until he found his way out of doors without the help of eyes, and to the last bent their light on Ophelia. On stage we *see* Ophelia being looked at by Polonius with the intensity of a jealous father and a suspicious state counsellor. In her narration Ophelia is the object of Hamlet's gaze, and in the present scene the object of Polonius': she is ringed round by the looks, not only piteous in purport, of men. As such, she may, at this complex moment of on- and off-stage viewing, 'be said to connote *to-be-looked-at-ness*', to borrow Laura Mulvey's controversial, influential, and now much-modified description of the conventional role of women in classic cinema.[34]

Yet many *readers* of the play – and I suspect many viewers in their retrospective experience of the play – will have at least as vivid an image of Hamlet as they do of Ophelia. On stage, too, Polonius' intense regard of Ophelia is motivated by his desire to see Hamlet through her narration. In this scene of specular interrogation, Hamlet, gazing on the enigma of Woman (for in Ophelia he sees superimposed the image of Gertrude too, both of them named Frailty) becomes himself the enigma for Polonius' speculation. With his clothes and wits in disarray, an ambiguous document for others to read, Hamlet plays a part similar to the one Ophelia will play in her own madness. Turning his gaze silently, mysteriously, dangerously on Ophelia, Hamlet directs everyone else's gaze at himself, becoming the elusive object of their desire for controlling knowledge. Hamlet's delay – his failure to drop the other shoe after the one he drops in 2.1 – manifests itself as a passive-aggressive tease, a threatening allure. God has given him one face and he makes himself another; and now the court must regard him with the kind of anxious regard he gives to Ophelia and Gertrude.

Olivier's filmed version literally puts Hamlet in visual place of Ophelia by flattening, in effect, the distance between on-stage narration and off-stage action. The sequence opens on a close-up of Jean Simmons' Ophelia, with her voice-over recounting the scene with Hamlet that we now see mimed in visual present tense; there is no Polonius to look at Ophelia as she narrates the incident. An iris shot focuses our attention on Ophelia's eyes, and then (as the scene opens out again) Hamlet enters her room with his look so piteous in purport. For a few moments the camera looks equally at Hamlet and Ophelia in close mid-shot; but when Hamlet falls to perusal of Ophelia's face, Simmons turns her back to the offscreen spectator and her look directs ours to Hamlet.

Olivier's directorial choice to make Hamlet rather than Ophelia the object of the audience's gaze involves more than the cinematographic prejudice against a talking head. It's true that throughout the production Olivier tried to avoid static shots of long speeches. Deep focus photography and voice-overs give Hamlet mobility during soliloquies. Shooting continuously, without cuts, while the voice comes either from the speaker directly or disembodied from an unlocalized space of psychic authority, this camera can record a moving speaker even where Shakespeare's text requires only a speaking speaker. According to Olivier's cameraman Desmond Dickinson, deep focus achieved 'extremely natural and realistic photography, with perfect focusing and no distortion'.[35] But in cinema, 'natural' and 'realistic' are conventional values; they are, conventionally, achieved

---

[34] *Visual and Other Pleasures* (London, 1989). The particular essay, 'Visual Pleasure and Narrative Cinema', first appeared in *Screen* in 1975. There is a helpful discussion in Robert Lapsley and Michael Westlake, *Film Theory: An Introduction* (Manchester, 1988). A revisionary account is by Paul Willemen, 'Voyeurism, the Look, and Dwoskin', in Philip Rosen, ed., *Narrative, Apparatus, Ideology: A Film Theory Reader* (New York, 1986), pp. 210–18.

[35] In Brenda Cross, ed., *The Film Hamlet: A Record of its Performance* (London, 1948), p. 29.

precisely with the montage that Olivier's cinematography avoids. In fact, for most viewers, Olivier's *mise en scène*, with its nearly expressionistic settings recorded in deep focus by a travelling camera, will appear the very opposite of 'natural' or 'realistic'.[36] The effect of Olivier's restless camera, with its swooping gaze going up and down stairs and in and out of archways and rooms, is to keep the viewer insistently aware of the camera's presence. The classic Hollywood cinema tends to efface the camera through cutting and editing, and gives the spectator the pleasure of seeming to control the scene; Olivier's camera, by contrast, is a virtual actor, the uneffaced controller of our gaze. It is moreover a gendered camera, a distinctively male actor, watching (in 2.1 and elsewhere) a Hamlet/Olivier cinematically coded (again, in 2.1 and elsewhere) for a conventionally female 'to-be-looked-at-ness'.

The camera's gender is the effect of its intrusiveness, its habit of penetrating into spaces, often arched or colonnaded, that it reciprocally inscribes as female. The famous visual bridge from battlement to court (1.1 to 1.2) makes the point early on, as the camera travels down the tunnel-like stairs, pauses to observe a book on a chair, tracks to one of the archways that will metonymically figure Ophelia, and finally (with the climax of William Walton's music) enters the Queen's bedroom to reveal the labial curtains of its enormous bed. No interior space can exclude this camera, not even the interior space of the body. Here it relies on metonymy to investigate the genitalia of Ophelia and Gertrude. In the case of Hamlet himself, the camera's curiosity is upwardly displaced: during the 'To be or not to be' soliloquy, it bores through the back of Hamlet's head, exposing (for one brief bizarre moment) the organic brain beneath the skull. The brain is the conventionally masculine site for Hamlet's interiority; in other ways, however, and in other scenes, the camera turns its gaze on Hamlet with feminizing penetration.

Reviewing the film in 1948, *The New York Times* characterized Olivier's Hamlet as 'a solid and virile young man';[37] my purpose is not to 'out' this manly man, but to suggest that Olivier's performance continues the Romantic tendency toward a feminized Hamlet. Indeed there are ways in which Olivier's Hamlet, more than Nielsen's, culminates the oak tree-in-a-costly-vase tradition, of which Vining's *The Mystery of Hamlet* is a slightly irregular offshoot. Olivier has claimed that he originally wanted only to direct, not star in, his production because he felt himself better suited to 'stronger character roles' than to 'the lyrical, poetical role of Hamlet'.[38] To fit himself to that role, and (he says) 'to avoid the possibility of Hamlet later being identified with me' (15), he dyed his hair the bright blond colour that contrasts so sharply with Nielsen's dark Hamlet, and which in Hollywood films of the 1940s is the studio starlet's colour-of-choice. And by comparison with Nielsen's Hamlet, with her unabashed gaze, Olivier's Hamlet is languidly passive, an object to be seen by the aggressive camera.

He is shown to us first during the court scene of 1.2: Claudius has dispatched the business of marriage and funeral, and dealt with Laertes' request to go to Paris, when the camera finally reveals Hamlet slumped despondently in his chair. His first two enigmatic lines ('A little more than kin and less than kind', 'Not so, my lord, I am too much i'th' sun' (65, 67) are cut, so that Claudius and Gertrude address a silent, apparently passive figure with downcast eyes. This is the Hamlet who carries 'the stamp of one defect', that 'vicious mole of nature' to

---

36 Dale Silviria, *Laurence Olivier and the Art of Filmmaking* (Rutherford, New Jersey, 1985), pp. 24–5, says that Olivier's photography 'violates the psychological realism of classic Hollywood film editing . . . the self-conscious quality of the traveling camera emphasizes . . . the viewer's act of observation. It emphasizes the viewer's role as witness.'

37 Quoted in Robert L. Daniels, *Laurence Olivier: Theatre and Cinema* (San Diego, 1980), p. 105.

38 In his contribution to Cross, p. 15.

which Olivier's voice-over in the opening se-quence gives a name: 'a man who could not make up his mind'. Between that diagnosis of Hamlet's dram of indecisiveness and the Freud-Jones diagnosis of unresolved Oedipal conflict there is considerable slippage: Olivier has said that he was impressed with Jones's analysis of Hamlet's problem, but in the movie it has been generalized to 'such a kind of gaingiving as would perhaps trouble a woman' (5.2.161–2). Fear of death, Vining said, is an 'essentially feminine trait'; and the inability to make up one's mind (he might as well have said) is another.

But of course we no longer believe in, or at least we're suspicious of, 'essential' anythings. In the 1989–90 season, The Mabou Mines com-pany directed by Lee Breuer presented its play *Lear*, sans *King*, with *all* the roles gender-reversed.[39] Race, ethnicity, and class were simi-larly submitted to experimental deconstruction: the scene was the American deep South, Lear's castle a sort of God's Little Acre shack, and the heath a ruined miniature golf course. In the cultural context of such a production it seems worthwhile to call attention to earlier experi-ments in cross-gendering Shakespeare, from

Vining through Nielsen to Olivier. One might speculate (elsewhere) why *King Lear* is current-ly of more interest than *Hamlet* to critics and performers concerned with questioning tradi-tional gender constructions. Man, Hamlet says, delights not him; and (because Rosencrantz and Guildenstern smirk at the innuendo they hear) he adds, 'nor woman neither' (2.2.310): the three versions of *Hamlet* I've looked at suggest that his displeasure with the conventional distribution of gender roles has been widely felt, if sometimes strangely manifested, but that even in the mimic world of theatre the attempt to dismantle rigid distinctions between mascu-line and feminine records mainly the fear that gives life to the hope. Horatio's sweet prince, gazed at by man and woman as, delighting in neither, he gazes at both, remains a sign of that melancholy fact.[40]

---

[39] Mabou Mines's *Lear*, adapted and directed by Lee Breuer, at The Triplex Theater (New York), 9 January–11 February 1990, with Ruth Maleczech as Lear.

[40] I would like to thank Mary Ann Jensen, curator of the Theatre Collection, Princeton University Library, for her help in locating material and even translating from the Danish.

'HE'S GOING TO HIS MOTHER'S CLOSET': HAMLET AND GERTRUDE ON SCREEN

MURRAY BIGGS

It is now almost a truism that the universality of videotape has made Shakespeare accessible as never before; or more to the point, has made certain productions of Shakespeare endlessly repeatable at the flick of an armchair switch. The availability of this or that acted version of a Shakespeare play is thus for the first time simply a technological achievement. There is no use lamenting this fact, even if we wish to; wiser rather to assess its likely influence, for better or worse, on Shakespeare criticism and appreciation, both learned and popular: a larger issue than can be attempted here.

This essay considers those four modern productions of *Hamlet* that are easily the most visible, because the most easily viewable. They are, first, the black-and-white film made in 1947, which Laurence Olivier produced, directed, adapted, and starred in; second, the colour film of 1969, with Nicol Williamson, directed by Tony Richardson; third, the BBC television version of 1980, with Derek Jacobi, directed by Rodney Bennett; and, as a brief coda, the most obviously 'popular' of the four, Franco Zeffirelli's 135-minute colour film of 1990, which is set fair to guide young viewers of the play in particular as the same film-maker's *Romeo and Juliet* (1967–8) did their parents. This *Hamlet*, more than any other on stage or screen, is likely to define and even precede their understanding of Shakespeare's text. *The New York Times* proclaimed it 'a drama that speaks easily and directly to our own age . . . Mel Gibson may not be a Hamlet

for the ages, but he is a serious and compelling Hamlet for today'.[1] All four of these productions, however, seem bound not only to stimulate but to determine the current afterlife of Shakespeare's work to an extent that no mere reading of it, however powerful or persuasive, can or will.

I shall concentrate on one scene of the play, Act 3, Scene 4. There are three reasons for this circumscription. The first may be expressed by G. R. Hibbard's observation in his Oxford edition that the closet scene constitutes the play's 'emotional centre'.[2] Though in both structure and theme it recapitulates much of the nunnery scene (3.1) – the protagonist's earlier confrontation with female 'frailty' – Hibbard is surely right to describe it as he does. Zeffirelli puts it more globally: '[It is] the most beautifully written scene in world theatre.'[3] Second, the scene is itself conceived through the eye of a camera. Its people are unusually *observed*. Polonius begins as hidden ear, presumably spied on by the Ghost, who succeeds him as 'voyeur' in the dramatic action, while we the ultimate audience eavesdrop and leer at all these players as they enact their more-than-dreams of passion. Third, the climactic encounter between Hamlet and Gertrude expresses the

[1] Caryn James, *The New York Times*, 19 December 1990, pp. C15, 21.
[2] Ed. G. R. Hibbard, *Hamlet* (Oxford, 1987), p. 276.
[3] Interview with Steve Grant, *Time Out*, 17–24 April 1991, p. 16.

dynamics of the war of love as that genre has since become enshrined in the history of film itself.

Laurence Olivier, as everyone knows, was much interested in a Freudian investigation of Hamlet's relations with his mother. In his poem *King Claudius*, C. P. Cavafy wittily pretends of the closet scene that Hamlet simply 'went / to his mother to discuss / certain family affairs'. Needless to say, it is the latent meanings of 'affairs' that have most engaged modern Hamlets. Not that Olivier was the first of them to romanticize the queen. John Barrymore, for example, according to John Gielgud, 'cut the play outrageously so that he could, for instance, play the closet scene all out for sentiment, with the emphasis on the "Oedipus complex" – sobbing on Gertrude's bosom'.[4] One can of course achieve the same suggestion of erotic complicity without cutting a line.

Olivier had played Hamlet on stage, in both England and Denmark, some ten years before the film. He and his director then, Tyrone Guthrie, got the idea of an Oedipal Hamlet from the mouth next to the horse's own, Freud's biographer Ernest Jones, whom the actor found 'very entertaining'.[5] What the entertainment came out to in the film may be glimpsed from two moments that more or less frame the closet scene itself. The more obvious one comes second, at the end of the prince's confrontation with his uncle (4.3), where a lingering close shot tells us that the young man is fixated on his mother. That 'one flesh' of father and mother (line 49) is unusually savoury.[6] More subtle is the implication that Olivier casts on the short soliloquy at the end of 3.2, en route to his mother's chamber. His Ghost-bound resolution not to lose his 'nature' and to eschew 'unnatural' behaviour presumably means, on the surface, that he must not kill his mother; 'I will speak daggers to her but use none' (line 357). Olivier's covert interpretation enters at a deeper level of meaning. Analogously: the play is *explicit* about incest between a mother and her brother-in-law. It is

implicit, say Jones and Olivier, about incest between mother and son, or at least about the son's half-acknowledged desire for his mother. The daggers that Olivier's Hamlet muses upon are therefore ambiguously phallic, and Shakespeare's allusion to the Roman emperor Nero (line 355) becomes extra-suggestive, since there was incest as well as murder in that royal family too. (Agrippina, Nero's mother by her first husband, poisoned her second, and then incestuously married her uncle, the emperor Claudius, whose name Shakespeare was the one to give to Hamlet's stepfather-uncle. Nero adored his mother, though he finally did away with her, fearing her insane fury that he had become his own man.)

Olivier's ending of 3.2 at line 357, 'I will speak daggers to her but use none', plants extra weight on the thought. Indeed the whole soliloquy is mesmerized. Hamlet moves slowly up a spiral staircase toward his design, as it were, like a ghost, and the camera closes in on him at the beginning of 3.4 to show that his triple iteration of 'Mother' is unconscious. He enters a circular chamber, one corner of the royal bed visible in the camera frame. He offers to expose his mother's 'inmost part' by pointing toward her his dagger rather than the more obvious 'sword' bared at 3.3.88, or the 'rapier' of her own official recollection (4.1.10); and he turns the same dagger against his rival, the usurper of his mother's bed, as he assumes it to be, discarding his weapon on the corpse when it has failed its mark. 'Oh me, what hast thou done?' she has asked him, at line 25. Olivier's entranced response, 'Nay I know not', seems a dreamy speculation on the prospect of life closer to mother if stepfather is out of the way.

The closet scene offers Gertrude little room

---

[4] John Gielgud, *An Actor and his Time* (Penguin Books, Harmondsworth, 1981), p. 66.

[5] Laurence Olivier, *On Acting* (New York, 1986), p. 79.

[6] Quotations from *Hamlet* are from the edition by Philip Edwards (Cambridge, 1985), which prints a conflated text, earmarking the Folio's cuts by square brackets.

for manoeuvre. Already compromised by allowing the meeting to be bugged, she squanders her only chance of influencing it by raising a false alarm; after that she is powerless. The fact that Hamlet has five times her number of lines (174 against 36) itself indicates the extent of his suzerainty over her. But individual actresses may find moments of initiative, as does Eileen Herlie (elsewhere disarmingly weepy) when she tenders the blessing her son (conditionally!) begs of her at line 173 by kissing him impulsively on the lips. He has, one might say, asked for it by looking her face up and down in Hollywood's best pre-osculatory style. Indeed he gives her even clearer signals at line 213, while alluding to some inconvenient guts, when he becomes the one to launch into the fully impassioned embrace that closes their encounter. Olivier's casting of a woman thirteen years his junior (though she scarcely looks that young) further equalizes the relationship of mother and son. The scene ends with his parting view of her, as she moves across the screen with the whole bed as background, sitting lonely and downcast upon it to a very slow fade of lights. And what a bed it is! Even the Burtons would have been lost in its quadruple spaces. Does it naughtily suggest a solution to the Oedipal dilemma? Gertrude has room to accommodate both father and son at once, and perhaps even the third man too. In any event, the camera lingers over this motif at the beginning and end of the film itself. There it sits, centre-screen, its tapering curtains drawn in open invitation.

Of an interest at least equal to the Freudianism of Olivier's *Hamlet*, and less often discussed, is the star's own acting style. A mobile camera is likely to probe a dramatic character more inwardly than can the stationary and more distant eye of a live audience, and Olivier's performances do not always stand up to the closer scrutiny of film. From the first (his 1936 Orlando), and with the partial exception of his aptly debilitated Lear (1983), Olivier's Shakespearian screen roles never quite left the stage

and their physical proportions there. It is surely no great heresy to suggest that throughout his film career, and not just the Shakespeare repertory, Olivier remained an essentially bravura actor. Extraordinary though his gifts were, they were physical rather than primarily intellectual; broad strokes of passion and display rather than nuances of emotion; the exterior more than the inward man.

A few years before his death, the actor himself wrote of his Shakespeare films: 'In the end I judge the film of *Hamlet* as a rattling good story, inside and outside Hamlet's mind, told cinematically; and that makes it my favourite Shakespeare film. My acting performance was thrilling enough [to me], but not, perhaps, as satisfying as Richard III.'[7] Put that beside his statement nearly forty years earlier that he was not his own first choice for the title role in the film of *Hamlet*. 'For myself, I feel that my style of acting is more suited to stronger character roles, such as Hotspur and Henry V, rather than to the lyrical, poetical role of Hamlet.'[8] Perhaps – who can ever know? – there was a certain disingenuousness about his claim to prefer not to act as well as direct Hamlet, but we may well agree that he *was* more suited to roles like Hotspur and Henry V (and, supremely, to Richard III) than to 'the lyrical, poetical role of Hamlet'.

It is instructive, too, to set Olivier's own account of the role as 'lyrical' and 'poetical' against his later recall of what actually happened in 3.4 in the film: 'Eileen Herlie . . . and I revelled in the closet scene, which, confident of the camera, we played as big as in Drury Lane' (one of London's very largest theatres).[9] It is as if the 'lyrical, poetical' gives the nod – not necessarily conscious – toward Gielgud, acknowledges what Hamlet supposedly should be; but Olivier's own natural, revelling con-

---

[7] Olivier, *On Acting*, p. 296.
[8] Ed. Brenda Cross, *The Film 'Hamlet': A Record of its Production* (London, 1948), p. 15.
[9] Olivier, *On Acting*, p. 291.

fidence is what we actually get. Not that the 'lyrical, poetical' is necessarily what we should be most looking for in any Hamlet, least of all in the closet scene; but Olivier's penchant for large effects, always more strident on screen than stage, must work against the complexity of characterization called for in this, the play's 'emotional centre'.

Putting it more precisely, we can I think say that the actor projects an understanding of his lines that is somewhat general. This is ironical, in light of his concern to make the film-script intelligible in detail to a non-Shakespearian audience, a concern evidenced by the text editor's discreet substitutions. (Among other examples in the closet scene, 'leave their tinct' (line 91) becomes 'lose their stain', 'enseamèd' (92) 'lascivious', 'tithe' (97) 'worth', 'rule' (99) 'throne', 'capable' (126) 'sensitive', and 'ecstasy' (139–40) 'madness'.) Olivier seems to confuse 'correct' verse speaking with the conveyance of semantic meaning, as if the first guaranteed the second. Like most actors of his generation, he attributes to 'verse' certain undefined and mysterious powers which both confer intellectual authority on the initiated actor/speaker and require a certain deference in return. Thus Olivier tells us that he 'used only actors who could speak the verse, either from experience or from their natural talent – like Stanley Holloway, who was the gravedigger'.[10] But the gravedigger *has* no verse, except in song. Again, the director writes of 'the obvious advantage, for a film in verse, that deep focus photography enabled us to shoot unusually long scenes'.[11] But there is small connection between the use of verse and the length of a scene. Shakespeare wrote scenes long and short, some in verse, some in prose. Olivier's thinking about 'verse' is automatic.

And it shows throughout his speaking of Hamlet. Though (as always) lacking Gielgud's famous suppleness, the voice is technically accomplished (its elocution a little too drama-school-clean to our ears, perhaps), and the speaker moves confidently through the main

'beats' of Shakespeare's text. But that is where it stops. Olivier gets on a roll, as actors say, and plays the general shape of the scene or the speech at the expense of its verbal particulars. The reading is impressively smooth, but not inflected in the kind of detail that shows the actor aware of, and intending, the character's meaning word by word. Thus the long speech beginning at line 53 of 3.4 ('Look here upon this picture') is essentially rhetorical, a fact more troubling in the screen's intimate spaces than perhaps at Drury Lane. The actor builds his tirade to line 76 ('What devil was't . . . ?'), when he moves away from Gertrude to complete an attack on her that is almost impersonally declamatory, in voice and gesture, rather than directed moment-by-moment by a particular son against a particular mother. He fails to point, for example, the biting contrast between 'matron' and 'youth' in lines 83–4. At lines 141–2 he misses the force of the comparison between Hamlet's pulse and its music and his mother's; and he glides over the crucial moral hiatus between her trespass and his 'madness' (145–7). Both Nicol Williamson and especially Derek Jacobi explore such meanings more thoroughly.

In fairness to Olivier I should add that, listening to a sound recording of John Gielgud's Hamlet, one may be struck by the same inclination to let the 'verse' do most of the work, as if its technical mastery were mostly enough. Neither actor differentiates all the local implications of meaning within their broad swathes of verse. Gielgud tends to 'sing' the lines, with ample vibrato to boot. His rendering of lines 40–51 of the closet scene for example ('Such an act . . . thought-sick at the act') is stronger in general rhetorical design than in personal disgust, at least until the last line. This Hamlet's voice is eager, even enthusiastic, rather than repelled; 'Heaven's face doth glow' more in

---

[10] Olivier, *On Acting*, p. 291.
[11] Cross, *The Film 'Hamlet'*, p. 12.

good health than in shame. Gielgud himself has written that in Shakespeare 'rhythm and sound can often be as important as they are in singing',[12] an admirable doctrine that should not be applied uncritically, without full regard to the semantic and psychological context. Shakespeare is not always equally lyrical. Gielgud seems to exaggerate the playwright's musicality when claiming that 'in some of the great Shakespearian speeches, Cleopatra's mourning over the body of Antony, for instance, it is more important to find the richness and pattern of the sound ... than to stress the meaning or the sense'.[13] Of his own Antony, he reminds us: 'I remember thinking that I could not learn the words because there were whole speeches I did not understand and there was no time to discuss or analyse them.'[14]

Critics typically stress the differences in acting style between Gielgud and Olivier. Certainly Olivier was more expressive physically; Gielgud sometimes gave an impression of laziness. But as history closes in around these two mid-century luminaries, we can more easily perceive what twinned them: as actors they were both essentially romantic. And here we may simply be registering a period, the days before 1960, the year in which Peter Hall and his cadre of Cambridge graduates took over the Shakespeare theatre in Stratford-upon-Avon and brought to bear on the texts the kind of intellectual analysis and deliberate debunking that they had become used to in English tutorials inspired by Richards and Leavis. Some would argue that Hall's Royal Shakespeare Company spelt the death not only of Shakespeare's (or Wilson Knight's) 'music', but of knowledgeable verse-speaking generally, through, for example, its players' slow pacing and artificial disruption of the verse line. This is not the place to enter into that dispute in any detail; but if actors since 1960 have tended to turn Shakespeare's verse into prose, the fault is neither better nor worse than its opposite, which is to regard the verse as a cure-all for difficult meanings, a substitute for conveying the actual

sense (the prose *equivalent*) in all its complex detail. Gielgud wrote of his trust in 'the sweep of a whole speech, concentrating on the commas, full-stops and semi-colons. If I kept to them and breathed with them, like an inexperienced swimmer, the verse seemed to hold me up and even disclose its meaning.'[15] This old-order faith in the power of verse to charm sense has not entirely passed. As recently as 1991, Tim Luscombe, directing *The Merchant of Venice* for the English Shakespeare Company, declared: 'With Shakespeare, if you get the verse right, you get the sense right.'[16] Of course actors should get the verse right: that is, they should understand scansion, rhythm, caesura, enjambement, and so on. But the idea that these skills in themselves confer the understanding of meaning should be laid to rest once and for all. To borrow from Peter Porter on poetry at large: 'The meaning of the music will never, in any easy sense, be the meaning of the words.'[17]

Between Olivier's Hamlet (1947) and Nicol Williamson's (1969) there is a gap of more than a generation. The later version would hardly have been thinkable without the whole new order established by Peter Hall. Gielgud's universalizing dictum – 'the man who essays [Hamlet] must obviously be equipped with certain essential qualities – grace of person and

---

[12] John Gielgud, *Stage Directions* (London and New York, 1963), p. 25. Since he wrote this, Gielgud may have changed his mind. In an interview recorded in about 1982 for London Weekend Television's 'Tribute to Sir Laurence Olivier', edited by Melvyn Bragg, Gielgud remarked that he had recently re-viewed himself as Henry IV in *Chimes at Midnight* (1966), and was shocked: 'I was like an old operatic diva, singing.'

[13] Gielgud, *Stage Directions*, p. 14.

[14] Gielgud, *An Actor and his Time*, p. 74.

[15] Gielgud, *An Actor and his Time*, p. 74.

[16] Tim Luscombe, English Shakespeare Company 'Background Notes', available from company (London, 1991), unpaginated.

[17] Peter Porter, 'The Recording Angels: Music and Meaning in the Voices of Poetry', British Academy Warton Lecture 1991, *TLS*, 15 March 1991, p. 4.

princely bearing . . .'[18] – seems not only less than obvious to us; it is blatantly contradicted by such major Hamlets of the 1960s as David Warner, directed by Hall himself on the Stratford stage, and Nicol Williamson, first at the Round House in London and then on film. Indeed Williamson's performance (directed by Tony Richardson) can be read as an aggressive counterblast to the Hamlets of both Gielgud and Olivier; nothing lyrical, poetical, or declamatory about him. Ironically, although the film is closely based on the stage performance, and was made at the same site, the actor is much less stagey than Olivier. His whole interpretation follows a close scrutiny of the lines and the character's intimate exchanges with other characters, most notably the two women. The director puts close-up to work.

Williamson's gifts as an actor, whatever his role, are precisely those that were not conspicuous in Olivier: an intense, sometimes agonized inwardness, and an ability to express his character's intellectual and emotional self-awareness in the heat of the moment of experiencing it.

If there is a subtext to Williamson's Hamlet, it is not an incestuous one, except perhaps at one moment: 'And when you are desirous to be blessed, / I'll blessing beg of you' (lines 172–3). Both mother and son have broken down, and are comforting each other on the bed. The camera shows Hamlet's eyes beginning to wonder – this is clearly the first he has thought of it – whether their embrace has gone on too long. If Claudius entered now, he might *really* wonder; after all, she at least, as he knows well enough and we have seen for ourselves, is a committed sensualist. Hamlet detaches himself, gets up, and begins to leave; the scene is cut so as to end six lines later.

Williamson is a Hamlet's Hamlet, a very precise thinker indeed. He can both explain and be explained. The soliloquy ending 3.2 to which Olivier gives such weight is here reduced to two lines, 356–7: 'Let me be cruel, not unnatural: / I will speak daggers to her but use

none'. So far from playing Oedipus and intimating forbidden desire, this thinker takes off his glasses and addresses the lines to fellow-student Horatio as if he had solved a painful moral syllogism.

The key to this Hamlet's revulsion from his mother is moral shock. In place of Olivier's somewhat stiff heroics we have wounded idealism, trembling with incredulity and indignation. 'Ha! have you eyes?' (line 67) waits for an answer; the question is not simply rhetorical; the other disputant in this moral debate may just possibly have a counter-argument. 'You cannot call it love, for at your age / The heyday in the blood is tame, it's humble' (lines 68–9) is aggressive, yet meant to persuade; surely, he seems to insist, you accept my reasoning. This unworldly Hamlet has clearly not read the temperature of Judy Parfitt's Gertrude right, though she is visibly younger than, say, Congreve's wrinkled Lady Wishfor't, whose ardour was unabated. But even if, as the chaste son would prefer to think it should have, his mother's lustful blood had cooled, she might well have 'loved' Claudius as Claudius asserts he loves her (4.7.13–16).

Such a Hamlet is ripe for tears; never far away, they break out at line 91 ('Nay, but to live . . .') – his mother is already crying – and he sits on the bed to recover himself. She joins him on 'Oh speak to me no more' (line 94), as if accepting her moral responsibility; and together, for the rest of the scene, they experience the therapy of confessional weeping. By 'Mother, for love of grace' (line 145) his cheeks are streaming; he cannot bear to look at her, and shields one side of his face. At 'Confess yourself to heaven' (line 150) he falls back on the bed, which by the time her heart is cleft in twain (line 157) is awash with tears. The scene ends with her still prostrate, sobbing.

This emotional outpouring, convincing though in close reach of the camera, prevents

---

[18] John Gielgud, *Stage Directions*, p. 59.

Williamson's raisonneur from seeming too cerebral, or rather shows how deeply felt his moral convictions are. His Hamlet probes more searchingly than Olivier's the issue of whether it is Claudius he has killed, and what it would mean. He must claw at a fabric before he can bring himself to ask, with evident difficulty, 'is it the king?' (line 26). The unwilling killer bitterly regrets that it is Polonius, perhaps because it must further divide him from Ophelia.

At least in the closet scene, Williamson's Hamlet is emotionally persuasive. Its weakest moment here is directorial. As in earlier scenes, the Ghost is presented simply by a bright light shining in the observer's face signalling 'overwrought'. In this scene of the film, the Ghost has nothing to say. We neither see him nor hear him, only Hamlet's reaction. Gertrude's 'Alas he's mad!' (line 105) is thus all too one-sidedly credible, as well as a complete revelation to her. Richardson's modern evasion of the play's frank Elizabethan supernaturalism is a clue to his slant on the work as a whole. He is as much a rationalist as Williamson's protagonist. The production cuts away both romantic and spiritual traditions. Thus Williamson – balding, bearded, unceremoniously dressed, pouting in a clipped, almost whining leftover of his native Scottish accent – not only debunks and overturns Olivier's melancholy blond nineteenth-century Teutonic nobleman. He is also a professional student. 'To be or not to be' dissects the issue of suicide as a Russell-like problem of philosophy rather than as a dilemma in the speaker's own life; no vision here of those 'more things in heaven and earth, Horatio, / Than are dreamt of in your philosophy' (1.5.166–7). This student, too, is specifically a radical of the late 1960s at war with the old guard, fully represented here by a Claudius (Anthony Hopkins) who is a self-indulgent, anti-intellectual boor.

Tony Richardson's stance in his version of *Hamlet* is ultimately, then, a political one. The film was made for Woodfall Films, a company that he had founded with Karel Reisz and John Osborne to make low-budget, socially active pictures like *A Taste of Honey*, *The Loneliness of the Long-Distance Runner*, and *Saturday Night and Sunday Morning*. These were the angry young men of British film in the sixties. Richardson had directed the spearhead work of the movement, Osborne's *Look Back in Anger*, both at the Royal Court Theatre (which he co-founded) and on film; he had been married to the activist Vanessa Redgrave; and he brought the critical eye of the Oxford graduate to his austere directing of *Hamlet* at the Round House, a converted railway shed in North London, which he chose, he said, because it made a social statement.[19] His use of the pop singer Marianne Faithfull as Ophelia gave the statement an extra punch. A generation later, we inevitably see his work at a distance. Gratingly original though it was in its day, this *Hamlet* too has dated. Nicol Williamson is riveting for a time, but his one-track style cannot sustain a role of such length and demanding such variety: even though the text is cut back to two hours. John Bayley noted of *Antony and Cleopatra* that it 'has room in its five acts for almost every human strangeness', and of *Hamlet* that it 'is almost the same'.[20] The Williamson–Richardson interpretation makes the strange all too familiar. It is at its strongest in Hamlet's rapier-thrust confrontations with Polonius and Rosencrantz and Guildenstern in 2.2. These debates, of course, are written in *prose*, the natural language of rational discourse. This Hamlet could never be mistaken for mad.

Eleven years later Rodney Bennett directed *Hamlet* for the BBC television series initiated by Cedric Messina. In keeping with the policy of the series, this production made only minor cuts in the text and ran for three hours and forty minutes. It therefore had the advantage of pre-

---

[19] Interview with Sheridan Morley in *The Times* (London), quoted by Roger Manvell, *Shakespeare and the Film* (London, 1971), p. 127.

[20] John Bayley, 'Hamlet as a Film', *National Review*, 131 (December 1948), 603–6; p. 605.

serving, necessarily, the play's own eclecticism, what Bayley calls its 'incredibly rich and varied texture', indeed its 'glut of material'.[21] This version was eclectic in the sense, too, that like Messina's productions generally it aimed at a broad audience and hedged its interpretative bets to the middle of the road. Indeed the director's own hand is held behind his back. New to Shakespeare, Bennett came to this play, he said, without a 'theory' about it.[22] Although Olivier's film is therefore more dynamically directed and makes for more exciting cinema, the BBC's policy of simply, as it were, photographing the text does allow the viewer his or her own interpretative freedom.

The closet scene nicely exemplifies the production as a whole. Only about thirty-five lines (sixteen per cent) are cut, and the omission of nearly a third of those is sanctioned by the Folio itself. The relatively full text allows that naturally flexible actor, Derek Jacobi, to add his own eclecticism to the scene. He is by turns innocent, lyrical, violent, tearful, zealous, mad. His director could not imagine any other actor capable of playing the role 'in such a total way'.[23] Above all, Jacobi parlays his Cambridge degree into a fresh analysis of the text. The little, reflective pause he puts between 'adders' and 'fanged' in line 204 ('and my two schoolfellows, / Whom I will trust as I will adders fanged') is typical of this actor's prying out of every possible implication through vocal nuance.

Jacobi establishes a kind of innocence for the character when his mother cries, 'What wilt thou do? thou wilt not murder me?' (line 21). He takes a moment to realize why she is anxious; his sword is still out, and pointing vaguely at her. He withdraws it hurriedly, almost apologetically, as if actually using daggers on his mother was the last thing on his mind. This moment of embarrassment prepares the moral diatribe that follows. His elegy for old Hamlet (lines 55–63) is delivered largo, with all the tenderness at his vocal command; but there is an abrupt switch to harsh presto for Claudius, whose description (lines 63–71) is energized with bullying gestures. He pursues his mother about the room for the rest of the speech. At 'flaming youth' (line 84) he throws her onto the bed, where he briefly (and with their lower halves off camera) simulates sex with her at 'compulsive ardour' (line 86) and in the passage beginning at 'enseamèd bed' (line 92). This is not accomplished without anguish.

Jacobi takes a long pause before responding to his mother's charge of 'ecstasy' (lines 139–40), as if gathering together all his recent memories of madness, including the 'antic disposition', and the 'ecstasy' of line 74. His reply when it comes is coldly rational, peeling the 'skin and film' off 'the ulcerous place' of her soul (line 148). His 'live the purer with the other half' (line 159) sounds to her like forgiveness; she hugs and kisses him impulsively, but is forced to freeze on his next line, 'go not to my uncle's bed'. Like the king himself, it seems, she was hoping to have her cake and eat it too.

'For this same lord' (line 173) registers a shocked reminder of Polonius, quite forgotten since his killing. 'One word more' (line 181) brings another abrupt change, as Jacobi extends his strikingly supple voice still further to produce an eight-line parody of Patrick Stewart's thin-toned Claudius, the 'bloat king' at his reechy tricks. At the thought of the 'knavery' to which his old school-chums marshal him (line 206), he chuckles with what sounds like genuine madness (elsewhere in the production Jacobi brings his character daringly close to the real thing); and his scheme 'to have the engineer / Hoist with his own petar' (lines 207–8) echoes with associations of the mad scientist. He weeps briefly over the 'foolish prating knave' (line 216) – innocence again – but his final, prosaic 'Good night' shows that he is still in control. It

21 Bayley, 'Hamlet', p. 605.
22 Quoted in The BBC TV Shakespeare, *Hamlet* (London, 1980), p. 22.
23 BBC *Hamlet*, p. 17.

is a performance of commanding range and richness, almost but not quite excessive, and lights up the scene's full complexity.

Jacobi is aided by Claire Bloom's unusually spirited Gertrude. Like Judy Parfitt in Richardson's film, and looking rather like her, she adjusts her appearance before the encounter, nicely establishing who means to be boss, and how; and she actually slaps her naughty boy's face for his cheekiness at line 15, 'You are the queen, your husband's brother's wife'. Indeed she stays defiant until his unanswerable comparison of the two pictures beginning at line 53.

Patrick Allen's Ghost, too, makes a telling contribution to the scene. Philip Edwards in his edition (p. 179) reminds us that the First Quarto stage direction for line 101 reads 'Enter the ghost in his night gowne'. We have previously seen Hamlet's dead father in full armour on the ramparts, and it seems entirely plausible that he would change into something more comfortable to haunt his wife's boudoir. Almost all productions, however, keep him stuck in that suit of mail around the clock, and this one is no exception; yet here it helps to underline the difference between father and son. This old man is a crisp and prematurely retired army officer, who probably *would* sleep in his battledress, and would like and expect nothing more than to have his son follow him into the service. Yet a military career is the last thing promised by Jacobi's Hamlet, loose of voice and limb alike; indeed the vocal and physical discrepancy between the generations is for the younger Hamlet a potent source of additional guilt.

It is a weakness of the BBC production that the Ghost is presented only from Hamlet's point of view. The camera ought also to show us, as it does under both Olivier's and Zeffirelli's direction, that from Gertrude's perspective there is nothing to see; it is what she says, at line 132. The queen is not simply deprived of her senses here, or lying about what she does or does not see. It is her moral obliquity that

obscures her vision, just as Hamlet's enhanced sensibility enables his.[24]

With Mel Gibson's Hamlet, as befits the actor whom his director hails as 'a red-blooded male',[25] we return to the Olivier tradition of manly physicality. This is an active prince undone by surrounding circumstances. As always, Zeffirelli aims at visual rather than textual seduction of his audience. The closet scene is cut by about 100 lines (almost half), though a few lines referring to Rosencrantz and Guildenstern are sensibly inserted before Hamlet's taking leave for England. Gibson is not at peace, in the film generally, with Hamlet's introspection, and compensates with vocal and facial melodrama. But 3.4 begins with a new Hamlet: cocky and mocking. 'Is it the king?' (line 26) is actually sarcastic; and 'Ay lady, 'twas my word' (line 30) continues the raillery at Gertrude's expense. An 'actorly' Hamlet is unusual here, and in principle playable.

But the drive of the scene in this version depends on Glenn Close's queen. 'To think of Gertrude as a blonde / is difficult', reflected Norman MacCaig in his poem, 'Folio'. Well, not any more; the honey-haired Close makes an entirely plausible paramour. Her Hamlet is a mother's boy if ever there was one (blue-eyed besides); the director, in an incomparable locution, calls him 'tied to his mother's titties'; and indeed the Ghost interrupts a mock-coitus, blunting an aberrant purpose in favour of the more filial one. 'These words like daggers enter in my ears', she protests at line 95, but all the same kisses her boy tempestuously. Zeffirelli makes no bones about translating the Oedipal theme into a full-blown, vulgarized, traditional screen romance between coevals, in which the

---

[24] See Stanley Wells's discussion of the Ghost's appearance in this scene in 'Staging Shakespeare's Ghosts', in *The Arts of Performance in Elizabethan and Early Stuart Drama*, ed. Murray Biggs et al. (Edinburgh, 1991), pp. 50–69; pp. 64–5.

[25] Steve Grant interview, p. 16.

viewer is less aware of Shakespeare's mother and son than of the Hollywood stars who have transformed them into other types altogether. Gibson recommends his father's medallion to her on 'the other half' (line 159), as if almost to say 'like father like son'; she hides it from Claudius as this scene segues into the next.

Here then we have the four most accessible twentieth-century Hamlets, observed in the microcosm of their most significant scene; four Hamlets largely different from each other, each of its own more local time, yet each contributing to the continuing modern debate about the character and his play: Laurence Olivier directing himself as a traditional prince turned inward to Freudian neurotic-depressive; Nicol Williamson the cynical academic, more at home in rationalist Wittenberg than spooky Elsinore; Derek Jacobi the most contemporary,

occasionally mannered and excessive (a *post-modern*, in short), Hamlet the manic actor interwoven with Jacobi the actor's actor, impulsive and self-revealing in both his roles, his own and the character's; and Mel Gibson, Hamlet as film/video kitsch for the nineties, what the *Times* dubbed 'a fast-food Hamlet'.[26] Harry Levin described *Hamlet* as 'the most problematic play ever written by Shakespeare or by any other playwright'.[27] Its performance, necessarily linear on stage or screen, is bound to simplify its problems, or at least address only some of them; and the virtue of considering more than one rendering, especially in conjunction, is that we can step closer to its simultaneous complexity.

---

[26] Geoff Brown, *The Times* (London), 18 April 1991, p. 17.

[27] Harry Levin, review in *Shakespeare Quarterly*, 6, no. 1, (1956), 105.

SHAKESPEARE REWOUND

GRAHAM HOLDERNESS

This paper proposes to argue that certain relatively little-known screen adaptations[1] of Shakespeare's plays can be shown to exemplify and embody constructive explorations of certain key issues widely recognized as central to the problems of contemporary Shakespeare interpretation. The film-texts in question are marginal to the point of invisibility, either because of their institutional origin and technological medium, or because normative criticism has yet to find a means of reconciling their 'alternative' character with the apparatus of critical analysis and interpretation. The formative context of this argument is shaped by the conviction that there now exists a canonical apparatus of 'Shakespeare on film', authorized by a legitimating body of criticism and scholarship.

The 'Shakespeare-on-film' canon could already be seen in the process of construction in those critical studies which still at present constitute the standard literature in the field: the late Roger Manvell's *Shakespeare and the Film* (1971, revised 1979), Charles Eckert's edited collection *Focus on Shakespearean Films* (1972) and Jack Jorgens's *Shakespeare on Film* (1977).[2] Ground-breaking, pioneering, vitally necessary and perennially useful studies, these books together conspire to privilege a particular canon of great films of great plays by great directors – Olivier, Welles, Kozintsev, Kurosawa, Brook; with a supporting team of somewhat lesser but notable directors in Reinhardt, Mankiewicz, Zeffirelli, Polanski; and a substitute bench of praiseworthy parvenues such as Tony Richard-

son, Peter Hall, Stuart Burge, Renato Castellani.

The methodology of such canonical appropriation entails three principal strategies. One is the assumption that there were no genuinely filmic adaptations of Shakespeare before the invention of sound technology.[3] The second is

---

[1] The productions to be discussed are:

Hamlet (1979), produced and directed by Celestino Coronado. A Royal College of Art production, in association with the Design Department of North London Polytechnic. Hamlet, the Ghost and Laertes, Anthony and David Meyer; Ophelia and Gertrude, Helen Mirren; Claudius, Barry Stanton; Polonius, Quentin Crisp.

Hamlet (1987), adapted and directed for the stage by Roland Kenyon with Cambridge Experimental Theatre. Video production by Cambridgeshire College of Arts and Technology Audio-Visual Unit. Directed by Rod Macdonald. Edited by Richard Spaul and Rod Macdonald. Gertrude, Melanie Revill; Claudius, Richard Spaul; Ophelia, Tricia Hitchcock; Polonius, Alan Wilson.

The Tempest (1980), directed by Derek Jarman. Produced by Guy Ford and Mordecai Schreiber. Edited by Richard Melling. Designed by Yolande Sonnabend. Prospero, Heathcote Williams; Miranda, Toyah Wilcox; Ferdinand, David Meyer; Caliban, Jack Birkett ('the Incredible Orlando'); Ariel, Karl Johnson.

[2] Roger Manvell, *Shakespeare and the Film* (New York, 1971, revised 1979); Charles Eckert (ed.), *Focus on Shakespearean Films* (New Jersey, 1972); Jack Jorgens, *Shakespeare on Film* (Bloomington and London, 1977).

[3] See Manvell, *Shakespeare and the Film*, p. 21: 'It was better to wait until Shakespeare's plays could be filmed with speech'; and Jorgens, *Shakespeare on Film*, who speaks of 'one- and two-reelers struggling to render great poetic drama in dumb show' (p. 1). Robert Hamilton

an 'auteur' theory of film production, which permits the authorizing signature of the 'great' (invariably male) director to act as proxy for the 'great' (irrefutably male) dramatist. The third is a positioning of all discussion on the matrix of a putative relation, or system of relations, between the film and some conception of 'the Shakespeare text'.

The body of normative criticism helping to hold this structure in place has recently been augmented by Anthony Davies's *Filming Shakespeare's Plays*,[4] which consolidates in fine style what is now clearly visible as the Great Tradition of Shakespeare-on-film. This book studies the work of four great directors (Olivier, Welles, Brook, Kurosawa), and their great films of the four great tragedies (plus Welles's virtually-tragic *Chimes at Midnight*, and that exception to all rules, Olivier's non-tragic but inexplicably great *Henry V*). Davies confidently affirms, in the closing words of the book, that his subject is the work of 'the world's greatest dramatist'; and his selective focus closes the circle of greatness in a hermetically sealed ellipsis firmly excluding alternative possibilities which might challenge the basis of the structural totality.

Davies draws his theoretical problematic from André Bazin, distinguishing between theatre and cinema, live performance and film, in terms of a hierarchized configuration of cultural levels. A theatre audience can be assumed to possess a certain degree of cultural competence, so that a staged version of a classic play is received as one version among several of a familiar original. A cinema audience is more prone to accept (as in Bazin's theory) what it sees at face value, and thus to mistake the simulacrum of a filmic interpretation for the original itself: cinema spectators are 'less able to set a particular presentation of a play in context' (Davies, p. 3). In the case of filmed Shakespeare, the cinema runs the risk of undermining and supplanting the 'original' by presenting the spectator with an apparently independent 'fixed text'.

The model of relationship between text and film adaptation at work in this study is hierarchical and élitist in its cultural politics. Topping the hierarchy are the Shakespeare texts 'themselves'. In the theatre, dramatic adaptation takes place in a context of informed cultural competence, so that the level of collateral damage to the cultural hierarchy is minimized. In the cinema and on television, the plays enter a dimension of potential contamination by exposure to the limited intelligibility threshold of the average spectator, who is likely to confuse Roman Polanski's *Macbeth* with Shakespeare's 'true originall copie'. Davies approaches each film adaptation as a more or less responsible translation into an appropriately cinematic language of one of a limited range of permissible interpretations of Shakespeare's original play. The director's control over the film's 'vision' is assumed to be absolute. If that directorial authority can be shown as weak or insecure (as in the case of Welles's *Macbeth*), then the film becomes disunified, incoherent, an artistic failure. The job of the critic within this theoretical apparatus is a straightforward one: it is the duty of painstaking formal analysis devoted to interpretation of the film-texts, in relation to the fixed parameters of the Shakespearian text, the aesthetic and technical character of cinema, and the directorial vision.

I am not arguing that Davies's book is not a good and useful study;[5] only that it provides symptomatic evidence that there is now firmly established a 'Shakespeare-on-film' canon which can be used to underpin the authority of

---

Ball's *Shakespeare on Silent Film: A Strange Eventful History* (London, 1968) of course covers the silent era, though it is (remarkably) by no means free from the assumption that Shakespeare without the spoken word is not truly 'Shakespeare'.

[4] Anthony Davies, *Filming Shakespeare's Plays* (Cambridge, 1988), p. 152.

[5] But see John Collick's review of Davies in *Critical Survey*, 2:1 (1990), pp. 108–11. It will be evident to what extent my own arguments converge with those of John Collick, to whose work I am much indebted.

a hegemonic critical discourse. If such a cultural apparatus does exist, then the work of deconstructing it must also begin. Here I want simply to essay a general reconsideration, provisionally sustained by the specific examples discussed here, of that basic theoretical problem, the relation between film and 'Shakespearian text'.

It should be evident by now that the 'Shakespeare-on-film' apparatus has the power to produce its own notion of Shakespearian textuality, which can then be invoked as a validating guarantee of authenticity in adaptation. Here the privileging of the four great tragedies, deriving from a long critical tradition consolidated at strategic historical points by the Romantic critics, A. C. Bradley and G. Wilson Knight, carries with it the full charge of liberal-humanist (and some Christian-humanist) values – universality, spiritual liberation and enlightenment through suffering, sacrifice, and redemption. To sustain such a universalizing capacity, both plays and films need the traditional resources attributed to Shakespeare by post-Romantic criticism – coherent narrative, intelligible character, meaningful action, significant imagery, organic aesthetic form. The critical apparatus of Shakespeare-on-film systematically invokes these criteria in application to the film-texts, thereby reproducing the films as narrative, character, action, imagery, organic form.

The film-texts themselves, drawing as they do on a certain history of film conventions and a certain history of theatre, frequently work to endorse this methodology, shaping their own reconstructions of the Shakespearian theatrical narrative along lines prescribed by contingent contemporary cultural priorities. Olivier's Freudian reading of *Hamlet* produces a film-text that resembles an analyst's report more than it does an imaginative exploration of the unconscious: the introspective character of the Prince, the Expressionist castle, the extravagantly Oedipal gestures, are comprehensively controlled by a unifying narrative which marshals all filmic elements into coherence,

order, symmetry – exemplified nowhere better than the shot which positions Hamlet standing over the slain body of Claudius, surrounded by a perfect circle of guards whose extended pikes constellate the victorious revenger as the centre of a ring, the hub of a wheel, the still point of a turning world. This film treatment is hardly, in any truly Freudian sense, the stuff that dreams are made of, and it does not answer readily to the preoccupations of modern psychoanalysis.

Kozintsev's Marxist reading of *King Lear* discomposes the Shakespearian theatrical narrative only in order to produce what is basically a Romantic, almost nineteenth-century narrative of exploitation, poverty, endurance, spiritual discovery. Lear's lunatic ravings about the inequalities of rich and poor become in the Soviet treatment gentle, irrefutably rational statements of self-evident fact. The cyclical collapses of society into ruin and disaster are balanced by the foregrounding of a romantic narrative in which Edgar falls only to rise as the hero of an epic human resistance. Even Peter Brook's *Lear*, acknowledged by many critics for its liberty of adaptation, its avant-garde techniques and its repudiation of ideological consolations, substitutes for a putative narrative of sacrifice and redemption another narrative, still coherent even in its affirmations of incoherence, yet rational in its revelations of unreason. Even those films that push the formal dissonances of this narrative medium to extreme limits – Welles's *Othello*, Brook's *Lear*, Kurosawa's *Castle of the Spider's Web* – are operating within parameters prescribed by an authoritative critical apparatus, by the hegemonic sway of realism over the medium of cinema, and by the dominance of naturalism in the theatre.

Returning from these grand, coherent tragic narratives (in which meaningful actions are performed by intelligible characters within the significant imagery of an organic aesthetic form) to 'the Shakespeare text' as we encounter it in the 1990s, we find a significant displacement. Contemporary criticism can no longer provide us with any support for the concept of a stable, coherent text on the basis of which such exercises in filmic textualization could effectively be accomplished. The modern Shakespeare text is in virtually all its critical and scholarly manifestations remarkably unstable, self-contradictory, fissured, labile, permeated by a radical indecideability. For deconstruction, the text's ostensible coherence is there to be systematically discompounded. For Marxist and cultural-materialist criticism, the ideology of the text is there to be rubbed against the grain, demystified and exposed. For feminism the text's patriarchal inflections are there to be combated by an overtly ideological re-reading. For New Historicism the text's spurious individuality is to be challenged by its absorption into a general context of discursive practice. For psychoanalytic approaches the latent sub-text will reveal more meaning than the mechanism of repression that is its surface meaning. For postmodern readings the text is alive only in so far as it resists ideological closure and meta-narrative authority, making its resources available for irresponsible play. For theatre studies the text appears in so many radically incompatible manifestations in different stage productions that any notion of a central coherence begins to look like a convenient fiction. For film studies traditional literary-critical methods may well seem to produce a fictitious coherence belied by a method of reading which focuses on specifically filmic language – film narrative, editing, etc. For textual bibliography, the 'plays' traditionally stabilized in idealized compilation texts are splitting apart into variant and equally valid textualizations.

What would be the nature of a filmed Shakespeare which answered to these contemporary definitions of Shakespearian textuality, as an alternative to that Great Tradition of 'Shakespeare-on Film' which sustains outmoded nineteenth and early twentieth-century models of narrative, character, action, imagery, and form? One answer is to point to a particular tradition of 'underground' film adaptations which seems to me to deserve far more attention (and cele-

bration) than has hitherto been the case, and which seems to me capable of bearing some of these interpretative responsibilities. Another answer would be to contemplate various avenues of lost possibility in the intertwined histories of theatre, film and Shakespearian adaptation. John Collick in *Shakespeare, Cinema and Society*[6] has traced certain historical inter-relations between developments in the nineteenth-century theatre (such as the substitution for verbal drama of a visual and musical language of theatre, enforced by the Patent Laws) and the origins of silent film (Collick, pp. 33–57). From this configuration arose the Symbolist theatre of Appia and Craig, in which the elements of visual design and music grew correspondingly in importance relative to the authority of the verbal text. Such a theatre is predisposed towards the deconstruction of dramatic literature and interpretative traditions that are fundamentally rooted in verbal language. As is also, in a different way, the theatre of Antonin Artaud,[7] with its revolutionary demand for a new language of theatre, replacing verbal narrative and dialogue with physical gesture and interaction, visual design, non-verbal vocalization. Both the 'theatre of light' fostered by Appia and Craig, and Artaud's 'theatre of cruelty' are resistant to conventional notions of character, to linear narrative, to the logocentric authority of a world controlled and ordered by and in written or spoken language.

Theatrical work inspired by these models is necessarily avant-garde and deconstructionist in relation to canonical authority and textual authenticity – Charles Marowitz's collage versions of Shakespeare for instance exemplify the influence of Artaud.[8] Artaud has also been extremely important in the theatre work of

---

[6] John Collick, *Shakespeare, Cinema and Society* (Manchester, 1989).

[7] Antonin Artaud, *The Theatre and its Double* (1964), trans. Victor Corti (London, 1970).

[8] Charles Marowitz, *The Marowitz Shakespeare* (London, 1978).

Peter Brook, though that influence is scarcely visible in Brook's screen version of *King Lear*. For examples of filmed Shakespeare based on theatrical influences of this type we need to look beyond the confines of the Great Tradition of Shakespeare-on-film. It is equally important however to recognize that the art of film, so widely and routinely employed as a medium of naturalistic representation, has become so only as a consequence of specific cultural and institutional applications of the technology; and that in its infancy film art manifested itself as a means of creating illusion, as well as a means of representing reality. The experimental cinema of George Melies, like the Symbolist theatre of Appia and Craig and the physical theatre-language of Artaud, offered a genuine though eventually defeated alternative, surfacing later in the Surrealist cinema of Luis Bunuel and Jean-Luc Godard, to the ultimate victory of naturalism in film. Here the grotesque and irrational symbolism of Freudian 'dreamwork' is presented directly, without normative mediation, to the spectator. Melies, as John Collick has observed, 'continually set out to destroy the orthodox logic of narrative-based drama. Instead he built a multitude of strictly enclosed images that, like dreams or hallucinations, possessed their own transgressive rationale' (Collick, p. 74).

There are then within the histories of theatre and film, as well as within the methodologies of contemporary post-structuralist criticism, resources for the production of an alternative 'Shakespeare-on-film'. I will now turn to some brief descriptive analyses of several adaptations exemplifying this underground movement in practice. Since some of my examples, being productions of *Hamlet*, don't in terms of content escape from the territory of the Great Tradition, I will by way of a preliminary positioning glance at some antecedents from Craig and Melies, tracing a continuity to Coronado and the Cambridge Experimental Theatre. I will close with a discussion of Derek Jarman's *The Tempest*, which should in my

view have already put this kind of Shakespeare cinema on both the cultural map and the theoretical agenda.

In 1912 Edward Gordon Craig was invited to Russia to work with Stanislavsky on the Moscow Art Theatre's production of *Hamlet*. The history of this production, which was not in anyone's view a success, is that of a struggle between competing and incompatible theoretical approaches to drama, particularly those of Stanislavsky and Craig. Craig, who believed the theatre was choked with words, wanted to replace them wherever possible by the visual eloquence of design, *mise-en-scène*, gesture and music. In the MAT *Hamlet* Craig tried to eliminate the boundaries between all the various aspects of the performance: plot, characterization, scenery and lighting. Linear narrative should be subdued to the synchronic Expressionism of spectacle and design; character too became of minimal importance, with the actors conceived as 'marionettes' to be manipulated within the designer's plan. One of Craig's bright ideas, firmly rejected by Stanislavsky, but documented in one of Craig's production sketches, was that the figure of Hamlet should at all times be accompanied by a companion figure, a 'Daemon death' symbolizing the protagonist's relationship with fate. Craig described having dreamed of a 'bright golden figure' who approaches Hamlet during his 'To be or not to be' soliloquy, and thereafter never leaves his side. In keeping with Expressionist methods, the divided inner consciousness of the hero, normally contained within the dramatic speech and within the brooding introspection of the character, is extrapolated into exterior symbolism.[9]

To a literary-critical reading such an idea will appear extravagantly unnecessary. To certain kinds of theatrical approach (though not Stanislavsky's) it may seem a possible avenue of exploration. For a film-maker willing to

---

[9] Lawrence Senelick, *Craig's Moscow Hamlet* (London, 1962), p. 68.

experiment with Expressionist, Symbolist or Surrealist techniques, who is confronted with a classic dramatic moment (such as Hamlet's famous soliloquy) that is obdurately fixed in the non-visual media of verbal dialogue and interiorized thought, such a possibility could well appear as a breakthrough. George Melies had already in 1907 made his one-reel fantasy of *Hamlet*, in which the entire action becomes a series of encounters between a demented Hamlet and various 'apparitions'. The other characters of the play are transformed into hallucinatory presences which assail Hamlet, but are represented in the film's fantasy medium as external to the Prince's mind.

He attempts to grasp them in vain, and he falls to brooding. Now is shown the scene in which he meets the Ghost of his father and is told to take vengeance on the reigning monarch, his uncle; but not content with this, Hamlet's fate tantalises him further by sending into his presence the ghost of his departed sweetheart, Ophelia. He attempts to embrace her as she throws flowers to him from a garland on her brow, but his efforts are futile; and when he sees the apparition fall to the ground he, too, swoons away, and is thus found by several courtiers.[10]

The 'apparition' of Ophelia in Melies's film is clearly related to the 'daemon death' of Craig's *Hamlet* design. In each case a theatrical or filmic medium of an Expressionist, Symbolist or Surrealist kind is able to dispense with both narrative and character as traditionally understood, and to operate on an aesthetic plane where the binary oppositions between truth and reality, interior and exterior, reality and fantasy begin to break down.

In Celestino Coronado's *Hamlet* (1979) this device of visual doubling is taken much further. The film opens with a whispered voice-over rendering of some lines from the 'To be or not to be' soliloquy, accompanied by intermittently flashing, distorted images. There is a strange noise of wind without any visual climatic accompaniment (there is no castle, no battlements). A miniature figure momentarily

appears, naked and crucified, to the accompaniment of an Artaudian 'primal scream'. Hamlet lies on a bed which could be an operating table, or a slab in a morgue, partially covered by a sheet. His face, pointed towards the camera, is inverted, so that a tight close-up shot frames grotesquely distorted features. The miniature figure again appears, montaged over Hamlet's face, again punctuated by the Artaudian scream. The Ghost then appears at the head of the bed, Hamlet's face propped at an angle towards the camera, the body grotesquely foreshortened. The Ghost is naked, standing in a posture of crucifixion, pain and anger expressed graphically through visible muscular tension. The figure that initially appeared as a figment of imagination, a mote to trouble the mind's eye, now stands fully incarnated beside Hamlet. And the two figures are virtually identical.

The Ghost and Hamlet in this film are played by twins, Anthony and David Meyer. The reassuring binary oppositions which conventionally divide the living from the dead, father and son, real presence and imaginary fantasy, immediately break down. In this opening scene the Ghost has his natural colour, while the face of the living prince is by a stark reversal chalky-white. As the Ghost delivers his temptation, his face leans towards Hamlet until their lips virtually touch: the Ghost's searing communication is breathed, inspired directly into the Prince's passive and receptive body, and the faces form a mirror-image, a disconcerting doubleness that confuses the dividing line between self and other. In the 'nunnery' scene, as Hamlet speaks with Ophelia, the Ghost stands behind him, then leaps onto him and from behind grapples his throat. The vocal line passes from the gentle Prince to the ferocious and vindictive Ghost, who finally pushes Hamlet aside to become the Prince himself. The physical combat is re-enacted in the final scene,

[10] Gaston Melies, quoted in Ball, *Shakespeare on Silent Film*, p. 34.

when the twins interchangeably play Hamlet and Laertes.

Gertrude and Ophelia are also played by the same actress, Helen Mirren, a doubling which presents some intriguing displacements in the female roles. Ophelia is played as a 'dumb blonde', erotically passive and slow of wit. Gertrude is played as a mature and powerful woman, confident in her overt sensuality. But the two can pass into one another and exchange identities. In the nunnery scene already described, the Hamlet/Ghost figure uses a red grease-paintstick (which is both phallic and cosmetic, erotic and violent) to inscribe marks of violation on Ophelia's throat (compare 'I will speak daggers to her, but use none'). This is simultaneously Hamlet taking his revenge on Ophelia as woman, and the Ghost wreaking a fevered sensual assault on Gertrude his treacherous wife. At first Ophelia/Gertrude swoons in helpless sensual passivity as the male figure vents on her body his lust and anger. Then, in a startling reversal, she recovers her poise, and emerges from the 'status-game' having defeated the Ghost/Hamlet (who in turn falls helplessly away) with a smile of frank sensual power.

Coronado's *Hamlet* escapes attention in all the critical literature on the subject of Shakespeare-on-film (though his subsequent 1984 production of *A Midsummer Night's Dream* in collaboration with Lindsay Kemp is discussed by Collick (pp. 103–5)). *Hamlet* was produced in 1979 at the Royal College of Art, London, by professional actors working with staff and students of the Department of Design, North London Polytechnic. The contingent institutional context was thus one of public-sector higher education. The informing theatrical context was that of small-scale, avant-garde experimental theatre, with a clear theoretical link to Artaud, a visual context familiar with Surrealism and the 'theatre of light', and a background in the kind of intensive improvisation and experiment appropriate rather to the studio of a drama school or a theatre department than to a film studio.

Patently low-budget, studio-based, even in some ways amateurish, this film seems to me quite extraordinarily resourceful in the inventive openness of its explorations into possible relations between text and performance. Here we have a film treatment attuned to the intellectual sophistication and imaginative complexity of the post-structuralist, post-modern Shakespeare text. When Hamlet delivers the 'too, too sullied flesh' soliloquy, the camera dissolves his face into a cubist montage of diverging faces: the too, too sullied flesh is literally seen melting, as it does in no other film production of *Hamlet*. Ophelia's drowning is a disturbing collage of dismembered features – ears, nose, eyes, teeth and tongue – glimpsed under water, poetically split and separated as they so often are in the fetishistic poetry of the play. When Hamlet in the 'closet scene' urges his mother to 'look but upon this picture', what they see is the grotesque, corpulent body of Claudius, hammering one bloodstained hand repeatedly onto a cluster of nails. Is the image a wish-fulfilment fantasy of Hamlet's? Gertrude's perverse fantasy of sexual gratification through violence? Or a representation of the King, tortured by remorse into self-mutilation? The experimental medium of the film allows all these possibilities of meaning, together with many others, to circulate abundantly through the spectator's consciousness in a condition of radical indecideability very close to a deconstructionist reading.

In 1987 the Audio-Visual Unit of Cambridgeshire College of Arts and Technology (now Anglia Polytechnic University) produced a videotape version of another avant-garde, studio adaptation of *Hamlet* performed by Cambridge Experimental Theatre. Roland Kenyon's deconstructive reworking of *Hamlet* is staged in an empty studio by a small ensemble of two men and two women. There are no props, not even a skull. The 'text' is cut, transposed, and re-aligned with a Marowitzean disregard for the principles of textual integrity, classical narrative and inferred authorial intention. The production is, for a start, a *Hamlet* without the Prince of Denmark: the four actors are cast as Gertrude, Claudius, Ophelia and Polonius, and the lines of the dispossessed prince are re-distributed between them. The great individuated hero of Romantic tradition is abolished at a stroke, and with him disappear all the modern bourgeois myths of subjectivity. 'Character' is fractured, fragmented, dissipated and re-born as dramatic interaction and social interdependence.

In support of these explorations Cambridge Experimental Theatre invoked post-structuralist literary theory, the psychology of personality and the nature of 'subjectivity' in Renaissance culture. In the performance, individuality is minimalized by neutral uniformity of costume, mask-like face-painting and the simultaneous fragmenting and re-orchestration of the verbal text − collective choric delivery, broken and interrupted cadences, emotional tones rubbing against the grain of patent sense-meaning. And although the production displays an emphatic and particularizing concern with verbal communication (akin, as I suggest below, to some of the more formalistic techniques of language-analysis employed in deconstructionist criticism) its primary medium is physical: an attempt at devising an eloquence of the body, of visual gesture constructing significant compositions of physical space.

The filming of this production was by no means a straightforward transmission of stage performance to screen. Interacting with the avant-garde techniques of performance employed in the production are a range of deconstructive devices available to the medium of video − freeze-frame, dissolve, silhouette, montage, multi-layered sound and vision mixing. The Shakespearian text is deconstructed twice over, in the course of its passage through stage and onto screen. The video is designed specifically for educational use − it is supplied with a supplementary 'guide', containing both explanatory discussions and practical exercises − and in these terms it has certain advantages over the various feature films, TV productions and other available material. It can be used to challenge traditional notions and to provoke debate about some central issues of both text and performance. Aligned with the received play-text, it can broach a number of contentious issues relating to the passage of text into performance: the sacrosanctity of text, the limits of adaptation, the relative autonomy of performance, the signifying potentialities of verbal communication and physical gesture. Its defamiliarizing approach to the most familiar of plays can be used to interrogate deeply rooted assumptions about naturalism, character, narrative. And as an instance of exploratory and creative rapprochement between separate media, it can be used to foreground and call into question not only traditional representations of Shakespeare on the screen, but the nature of filmic representation itself.

It was clearly part of the producers' intentions that the project should be something more than metadrama: that it should accomplish a strategic cultural intervention, should do more than foreground its own deconstructive devices. Nigel Wheale in the supplementary 'guide' links the methodology of the performance to the originating conditions of *Hamlet's* production:

the Renaissance audience was less interested in the deep ('fully rounded') characterization of individual roles, but rather would have attended more to the impersonal and communal issues being debated within the drama: questions focussing on the nature of monarchy, the function of religious institutions and belief, and particularly on questions concerning the organization and conduct of the family. These were controversies centering on personal conduct and property rights which were very pressing in the early modern period. This is to argue that Renaissance drama was overtly didactic in ways which are no longer directly obvious to us. The Cambridge Experimental Theatre production, through its formalizing of verse, action and staging, through the role-sharing, and the intervention of video effects, actively impersonalizes the issues of the drama.[11]

---

[11] *Hamlet: A Guide*, Cambridge Experimental Theatre/ Cambridgeshire College of Arts and Technology Audio-Visual Unit (1987), p. 7.

In practice the production does not quite do this. Earlier examples of avant-garde 'deconstructive' productions of *Hamlet*, such as Charles Marowitz's collage, or the Coronado film (not sufficiently recognized here as a precedent) were much more interpretative, polemical, in the broadest sense political, than this one: much more disposed to provoke and precipitate contestation and debate about 'issues' – power, individualism, gender, sexuality. Both these latter adaptations worked against conventional concepts and techniques of representation: but both also managed simultaneously to hew new meanings from the play and to throw it into meaningful juxtaposition with contemporary issues and problems. The methods of Cambridge Experimental Theatre's production are rather those of the more formalistic tendencies of deconstruction: concentrating attention exclusively on the signifying practices of language (whether word or image). It was for instance intended that the fragmentation of the role of Hamlet and its dispersal across gender differences would lead to an interrogation of sexual politics in both play and contemporary context (see *Hamlet: A Guide*, pp. 8–9). Yet the rendering uniform by costume and make-up of the actors, and the emphasis on stylized gesture and movement, effectively neutralizes gender as it destroys individuality: sexual difference is suppressed rather than subverted.

Derek Jarman's version of *The Tempest* (1980) shows the underground spring of alternative-Shakespeare-on-film temporarily surfacing in the form of art-house cinema. Like Coronado's balletic adaptation of *A Midsummer Night's Dream* (1984), Jarman's film did not go on general release, but occupied the minority space of the London avant-garde. *The Tempest* was subsequently broadcast on Channel 4 television. The experimental quality of Jarman's film resides far less in the dimension of technology than the examples so far discussed, despite the fact that in general his films are technically very adventurous. The deconstructionist effects of *The Tempest* operate rather at the levels of textual adaptation and dramatic interpretation; casting, setting, *mise-en-scène*, costume; and sexual politics.

As in Coronado's *Hamlet*, the Shakespearian text (of which there is of course in the case of *The Tempest* only one version, that of 1623) is very freely adapted and cut, with roughly one third of it employed in the film, and with the text that remains often radically transposed and reorganized. Some transpositions force the poetry to operate differently in an altered context. Benedictory lines from the Masque in Act 4 are spoken early in the film by Ariel to Miranda, from his position on the child-woman's rocking-horse. The peculiar intimacy, sexless yet erotically playful, created here between the naïve girl and the restless, cynical yet affectionate spirit/slave, marks a clear contrast with the formal betrothal ceremony from which Shakespeare's lines were drawn. Tenderness in this film occurs between alienated individuals, not in the collective social rituals which endorse sexual 'normality'. The speech from the play-text in which Prospero renounces his necromantic power closes on 'by my so potent art', with Prospero gazing into the magic glass through which he is able to see the courtiers held in his enchantment. This Prospero has no intention of giving up his art or his power. Often the dramatic verse operates in the film, in the manner of the 'theatre of light', as a commentary on the visual spectacle, rather than as a substantive means of advancing narrative or developing character; the poetry is, in a sense, 'set to vision' as words can be set to music.

Jarman's principal thematic interests lie in the conception of Prospero as magician, and in the nature of the 'island' world dramatized by the play, with its strange mixed company of inhabitants. Jarman saw the magic in the play not as a symbol for something else (Christian benevolence or political despotism) but substantively as a form of knowledge, a science. Jarman seems more inclined than most of us to take the occult seriously; but his concern in the film is rather with the kind of exploratory and experimental humane science that magic was in the Renaissance. His earlier film *Jubilee*, a synoptic comparison of the ages of two Queen Eliza-beths, features John Dee as a central figure in Renaissance humanism, whose philosophical 'magic' offered a synthesis of science and art. Jarman contrasted this spirit of liberal enquiry, characteristic of the Elizabethan age and of the period of his own formative development (the nineteen sixties and seventies) with the repres-sive view of the occult characteristic of James I, and with the political, cultural and sexual rep-ression of the nineteen eighties. Heathcote Williams, who plays Prospero in the film, is not an actor but an occultist, a writer and magician who (evidently) believes himself to be possessed of necromantic powers. He is also a strikingly young Prospero (the character is generally assumed by tradition to be at least as old as Michael Hordern appears always to have been), so the powers he exercises seem to have little to do with either patriarchal authority or avuncu-lar benevolence. Through the obsessive studies in which he is engaged for most of the film are expressed energies of restless physical quickness, an unappeasable curiosity, an enormous hungry vitality and a craving moral appetite to make the world a better place. The treachery, rebel-liousness, opposition he encounters at every point seem to him petty irritations obstructing a project of general improvement, rather than deeply wounding personal grievances. There is room in the film of course to question Pros-pero's régime – Caliban, Ariel, Ferdinand are there to focus such interrogation – but in terms of the film's general interpretation, the presen-tation of Prospero is a positive celebration of the liberal intellectual struggling against a climate of ignorance and repression. The medium of surrealist or fantasy film can also be held, as it has from George Melies onwards, to be a kind of magic capable of attaining through estrangement a new and different knowledge of the world.

Jarman is a product of the freedom and spirit of enquiry which characterised the English cultural scene in the 1960s and 1970s. His film – and his

representation of magic as an intellectual and imaginative faculty of the utmost significance – is a stand against the puritanism and conservatism which have developed here in the last decade.[12]

It is of course arguable that Jarman has side-stepped the very issues of power and authority that preoccupy modern discussions of this play. But his *Tempest* is no longer a treatment of colonialism. In the film neither Prospero's own domestic empire, nor the courtly community of Milan and Naples, can be held to represent any normative social collectivity. There is very little concrete sense of a 'real world', some-where else, by reference to which the micro-cosm of the island could be orientated. The entire population of the island seems literally shipwrecked, utterly alienated from all norms and conventions of social behaviour. Prospero's aspiration seems therefore to be that of bringing an alienated, expatriate community into social cohesion, rather than that of imposing any abstract concept of justice, restoring any rules of equity, rights of legitimacy or structures of authority. This effect is achieved partly by the setting of the film, which alternates between an exterior location, shot through a derealizing blue filter, on a windswept beach in North-East England; and the dilapidated, Gothic interior of Stoneleigh Abbey, a Tudor mansion in the Midlands, in the half-ruined eighteenth-century wing of which the film's interior se-quences are played. The confusion of historical period is exploited through both setting and costume: in rooms of faded Regency splen-dour, lit only by candles, carpeted by straw and accumulated leaves, characters are dressed in a bizarre mixture of historical costume designs. Prospero is dressed in a Romantic style resem-bling young Werther on one of his most suffer-ing days; while his daughter (the punk singer Toyah Wilcox) bursts the seams of a tight

---

12 David L. Hirst, *Text and Performance: The Tempest* (London, 1984), pp. 54–5.

Regency décolleté. Caliban (the brilliant and grotesque blind mime actor Jack Birkett) wears the uniform of a nineteenth-century butler; Ariel the white boiler-suit of a nuclear technician.

These carefully juxtaposed stylistic inconsistencies are exploited to extreme and stunning effect in Jarman's version of the betrothal masque, which in this adaptation closes the film. Both the courtiers and the co-conspirators of Caliban – who are presented here as farcically comic and quite incredibly ineffectual – are fixed in Prospero's power, and form (in the case of the courtiers) comatose, or (in the case of Caliban, Trinculo and Stephano) enthralled spectators of the entertainment. Jarman replaced the formal masque and attendant ceremonies with a clumsy but good-natured hornpipe executed by extremely camp sailors; followed by the entrance of a single goddess, in the form of cabaret singer Elizabeth Welch, who delivers a delightful 'soul' rendering of 'Stormy Weather'. The entire displaced community of the film – the betrothed couple, who sit on a chaise longue under a shower of confetti; the 'liberated' mariners, who form a swaying, appreciative audience for the singer; Caliban and his co-conspirators, lulled into enraptured submission by the delights of music – are drawn together in a filmic concord which (paradoxically in logic, though perhaps natural in film) depends on the rapprochement of diversity, the yoking together of opposites, the celebration of difference.

'In Shakespeare', wrote Peter Brook in 1968[13]

It is through ... unreconciled opposition ... through an atonal screech of absolutely unsympathetic keys that we get the disturbing and the unforgettable impressions of his plays. It is because the contradictions are so strong that they burn on us so deeply.

Shakespeare's plays were written to be performed continuously ... their cinematic structure of alternating short scenes, plot intercut with subplot, were all part of a total shape. This shape is only revealed dynamically, that is, in the uninterrupted sequence of these scenes, and without this their effect and power are lessened as much as would be a film that was projected with breaks and musical interludes between each reel. The Elizabethan stage was ... a neutral open platform – just a place with some doors – so it enabled the dramatist effortlessly to whip the spectator through an unlimited succession of illusions ... it also allowed him free passage from the world of action to the world of inner impressions.

In an ideal relation with a true actor on a bare stage we would continually be passing from long shot to close, tracking or jumping in and out – and the planes often overlap. The power of Shakespeare's plays is that they present man simultaneously in all his aspects ...

Here Brook can be seen reading Elizabethan drama cinematically, finding in the technical language of film a modern equivalent for his historical view of how Shakespeare's plays were designed to be performed. He was also, obviously, beginning to think about the problems of filming Shakespearian drama, since his own *King Lear* was in the making by the end of 1968. Brook's insistence here on the need for a 'free passage' from 'the world of action' to 'the world of inner impressions' is one of the bases for the aesthetic shape of that film. It is perhaps equally significant, given the ambitious aesthetic programme expounded here, that *King Lear* does not go further in the direction of an exploration of that theoretical acknowledgement of overdetermination – how to render in cinematic terms, in other words, the 'overlapping planes' of the Shakespeare text. In 1965 Brook proposed that the correct way to gather and grasp these overlapping planes would be to make a film of a Shakespeare play designed to be projected onto three separate screens, each of which would represent a different visual image.

---

[13] Peter Brook, *The Empty Space* (1968) (Harmondsworth, 1972), pp. 96–8.

Another method is of course that of formal montage, developed in Welles's *Othello*. But perhaps the most successful attempts to capture that elusive, shifting complexity of the Shakespeare text are to be found in the deconstructive experiments of 'underground' cinema. Here at least is a recoverable body of cultural production which seems to offer some degree of filmic equivalent to the modern theoretically activated Shakespearian text.

FREUD'S HAMLET

KENNETH MUIR

Hamlet receives two commands from the Ghost: to kill Claudius, and not to harm Gertrude. As he cannot do the first without causing agony to his mother, he is given an apparently impossible task. It is therefore arguable – and it has been argued powerfully – that Hamlet did not really delay in carrying out his task. As soon as the guilt of Claudius is proclaimed publicly by Laertes, and Gertrude has declared that she has been poisoned by the cup intended for her son, Hamlet immediately executes justice on his uncle, while he himself is dying from the poisoned rapier. His mission has been accomplished, despite the fates of Rosencrantz, Guildenstern, Polonius and Ophelia, without deadly sin, and without harming his mother.

Nevertheless, most critics insist that Hamlet did delay,[1] referring both to the Ghost's accusation of his 'almost blunted purpose', to Hamlet's refusal to kill the King at his prayers, and to his frequent self-accusations.[2] Freud, followed by Jones, put forward one of the most popular explanations of the delay, that Hamlet was in love with his mother and that he was inhibited from killing his rival. This theory of Oedipus Complex has had a remarkable success, especially in the theatre, where we often see Gertrude's closet transformed into a bedroom, and where we see the relationship between Hamlet and his mother erotically charged.

It was outside Freud's terms of reference to consider the way in which Shakespeare was hemmed in by theatrical restraints. He had to provide suitable parts for his fellows; and, in rewriting a play which had been popular for a dozen years, his main purpose would be to play variations on an old theme. He knew that his audience would expect him to put new wine into old bottles. He had to dramatize the basic conflict between instinct and the moral law, and in this respect the play reveals the quintessential dilemma of the avenger. There were several variations on the basic theme. One of Tourneur's avengers left vengeance to God; one of Chapman's challenges his enemy to a duel and kills him in fair fight; Vindice in *The Revenger's Tragedy* becomes almost as evil as his victim. Shakespeare's solution was central in that he introduced four other avengers into his play (Laertes, Fortinbras, Pyrrhus, Lucianus) and his hero stands out as a civilized man among barbarians.

Apart from the relationship of *Hamlet* to the genre of revenge tragedy to which it belongs, there are other ways in which Freud's interpretation should be open to scrutiny. Two of these have been raised by other critics. First, it has been pointed out that readers and critics tend to identify with the hero, and when they analyse his character they ignore his particular situation and seem to be looking in a mirror. Coleridge, who attributed Hamlet's delay to his losing the

---

[1] For many years editors regarded a discussion of Hamlet's delay as an essential part of their task.
[2] These can all be explained away as symptoms of Hamlet's neurosis. As the Ghost is invisible to Gertrude, his words may be Hamlet's unconscious inventions.

power of action in the energy of resolve, confessed that he 'had a smack of Hamlet himself'.[3] Other critics saddle Hamlet with their own prepossessions, so that their theories are only too predictable. It would have been easy to forecast Freud's theory before he committed it to paper. This does not disprove it, but it should make us wary.

The second reason for caution is that any theory which claims to be exclusively true is bound to be limiting. There are many other explanations of Hamlet's delay, advanced by notable critics, which are believed by many to be true, and which may at least be partially true, or an aspect of truth.[4] Interpretations of any great play vary from one generation to another, even from one production to another. In the space of a few years after 1923 it was possible to see at the Old Vic three great Hamlets (Ernest Milton, Ion Swinley, John Gielgud). They were all different, but they were all based squarely on the texts, and all three gave convincing interpretations. What is true of performances is true of interpretations by critics. It is now universally agreed that there are several valid interpretations of most of Shakespeare's plays, and that the poet himself incorporated the conflicting impressions which rendered this inevitable. In some cases, indeed, he cut out passages which have been the cornerstone of some interpretations. Olivier's film was based on a speech that had been cut from the First Folio text. Albany's most important speech was dropped from the Folio *King Lear*. At least one performance of *Troilus and Cressida* in Shakespeare's time ended heroically with the line

Hope of revenge shall hide our inward woe.

Another version ended with Pandarus' obscene and satirical epilogue. It is obvious, therefore, that to take Oedipus Complex as the sole key to Hamlet's character is to undervalue the complexity of the play, as Freud himself partially realized, and to ignore the instability of Shakespeare's texts.

The third reason for caution is the fact that

another important Freudian concept, that of the superego, is also relevant to Hamlet, as I hope to show.[5] The superego is not merely the source of our finest thoughts, our idealisms and aspirations, but also of our profound feelings of guilt, our knowledge, in Scriptural terms, that we are all unprofitable servants. The superego is both 'High Priest and Police Agent', the image of the desirable and the propagator of taboos and prohibitions. It stands for inexorable law which condemns the cowering ego with such ferocity that it leads the victim to melancholia, and sometimes to suicide.[6]

Does not this remind us of the Prince of Denmark? He too is a man picked out of ten thousand for his honesty (2.2.178); 'a beautiful, pure and most moral nature';[7] one who asks his mother to forgive him his virtue (3.4.152–3); one who idolizes his father, despite the Ghost's confession of foul crimes (1.5.12);[8] one who eulogizes Horatio (3.2.56ff.), Laertes (5.1.217), and even the tough bandit, Fortinbras, as a 'delicate and tender prince' (4.4.48, omitted in F1). He has shared the view of Pico della Mirandola of man's godlike potentialities (4.2.203ff.), but is now utterly disillusioned. On his first appearance, the frailty of his mother makes him contemplate suicide, and reject it only because of the canon against self-slaughter (1.2.131–2). He longs for death, calling it a

---

3 C. S. Lewis, in his brilliant British Academy lecture, gave several examples of this tendency; but he did not realize that his own portrait of Hamlet as Everyman, burdened with Original Sin, was a reflection of his own theological views.

4 It would be absurd to dismiss the views of Coleridge, Bradley, Shaw, Alexander and Levin, to name no others; and more wayward interpretations have occasional insights.

5 This point may have been made before, but I have not yet found an example.

6 I have borrowed some phrases from Terry Eagleton's chapter on Freud in *The Ideology of the Aesthetic* (1990), published after this article was drafted.

7 Goethe's description in *Wilhelm Meister*.

8 Editors gloss the foul crimes as minor imperfections. This was not the Ghost's opinion.

consummation devoutly to be wished (3.1.63–4). He confesses that he has lost all his mirth, and that he regards the earth as a sterile promontory, the firmament as a foul and pestilent congregation of vapours (2.2.293ff.). He asks the girl he loves why she wishes to be a breeder of sinners, and tells her (3.1.121ff.)

I am myself indifferent honest, but yet I could accuse me of such things, that it were better my mother had not borne me . . . What should such fellows as I do crawling between earth and heaven? We are arrant knaves, all; believe none of us.

His love for Ophelia is tainted by his own sense of guilt, as well as by the frailty of women. He despises himself for not avenging his father's death and for 'the heroism of moral vacilla-tion'[9] which he stigmatizes as cowardice. Whether he kills Claudius or not he is doomed by his superego to blame himself. He is a classic example of the devastating effects on a sensitive spirit of the terrible cruelty of the superego.[10]

Freud regarded the superego as the result of Oedipus Complex, but it is surely plain that the superego is more important in the interpretation of *Hamlet*.[11]

---

[9] The phrase is Lascelles Abercrombie's.

[10] Less sensitive spirits (Laertes, Pyrrhus and Fortinbras) seem not to be troubled by the superego.

[11] Elio J. Frattaroli in a recent article (*Int. Rev. Psycho-Anal.* XVII (1990), 269–85) discusses the aesthetic response to *Hamlet*, based avowedly on R. Waelder's concept of the superego, but he does not relate it to the character of the hero.

'PRAY YOU, UNDO THIS BUTTON': IMPLICATIONS OF 'UN-' IN *KING LEAR*

LESLIE THOMSON

Perhaps no final scene of a play has had more attention than the end of *King Lear*.[1] Regardless of how any one critic interprets the play, an important element of that interpretation involves a response to the action from Lear's entrance with Cordelia in his arms to his death. And, however this scene is integrated into or used as justification for an overall interpretation, there is usually an acknowledgement of its inherent ambiguity: that we cannot be certain how to respond to these concentrated, intense moments. This has prompted everything from unqualified optimism to unrelieved pessimism – responses probably revealing more about the spectator or critic than the play. But the most perceptive attempts to understand the play allow for both joy and sorrow at its conclusion, a response signalled several times during the action.[2] As essentially tragic as the ending is, there also is, or should be, a sense of rightness about it that cannot be ignored in production and interpretation without lessening the impact by reducing the relationship between the conclusion and what has gone before. That things have come full circle is an idea voiced towards the end of the play. We are prompted to become aware of its complexity not so much by the rationalizing observations of Edgar and Edmund or the optimistic commentary of Albany and Kent as by signals in the language and action immediately before Lear's death suggesting a renewal of his essential roles of king and father for a few brief but significant moments. In this play built on visual and verbal paradoxes, in which appearance and speech obscure deeper truths, it should not be surprising that what is done and said at the protagonist's end contains and completes this motif. Nor is it uncharacteristic of Shakespeare to use language and action an audience should have come to recognize through the play to create the ironies and ambiguities that generate a mixed response to its conclusion.

Several critics, notably Rosalie Colie,[3] have studied the paradoxes of the play, especially their part in creating the sense of an inverted world where the two main characters, Lear and Gloucester, are deceived by what they see and hear. An audience watching the deceivers' actions and listening to their language should quickly become aware of these deceptions and thus attuned to other ambiguities not apparent

[1] William Shakespeare, *The Tragedy of King Lear*, ed. Gary Taylor, in *William Shakespeare: The Complete Works*, gen. eds. Stanley Wells and Gary Taylor (Oxford, 1986); henceforward, *Oxford Shakespeare*. All quotations are from this, the Folio text, unless otherwise noted. *King Lear* refers to this version except in quotations from other critics.

[2] As Stephen Booth says, 'The way of our escape and Lear's are one. We *want* Lear to die, just as, almost from the beginning, we have wanted the play to end. That does not mean that we are unfeeling toward Lear or that we dislike the play: watching *Lear* is not unlike waiting for the death of a dying friend; our eagerness for the end makes the friend no less dear.' ('*King Lear*', '*Macbeth*', *Indefinition, and Tragedy* (New Haven and London, 1983), pp. 16–17.

[3] In *Paradoxia Epidemica* (Princeton, 1966).

to the characters. What I want to suggest is that the audience is similarly prompted into a final acceptance of Lear's release from 'the rack of this tough world'. Any play is a series of verbal and visual signals, some consciously introduced, others a subconscious reflection of these. One of the elements giving Shakespeare's plays their lasting appeal is the integration of form and content produced by this creative process. Careful study of his plays reveals how the signals an audience sees – via action, gesture, costume, props – are completed by the signals it hears – via dialogue, imagery and iteration. For anyone concerned with the staging of a Shakespeare play, the words spoken provide, at the least, clues, at best, cues. In the case of *King Lear*, it is wholly typical of Shakespeare's methods that a play concerned with characters who need to see and hear better should, by its dramatic process, encourage the audience to do the same.

Almost at the end of that process comes Lear's final speech, with the request, 'Pray you, undo this button.' There is a variety of interpretations of these words, some depending on differences between the Quarto and Folio versions of the speech: in the Quarto, Lear's request and acknowledgement ('Thank you, sir') are followed only by his dying, 'O, O, O, O!', while in the Folio, before he dies Lear says, 'Do you see this? Look on her. Look, her lips. / Look there, look there.' In either case the undoing of the button seems to release what follows – it is, of course, the latter, more hopeful version with which readers and audiences are most familiar.[4] However, Lear makes the request in both versions and it seems no less unexpected in the one than in the other.[5] Why does Lear make this request at all and why is it phrased as it is? Is a signal being sent to the audience, and if so, what might it be?

Robert Heilman sees the request as part of the 'clothes pattern', and a 'synthesizing comment on [Lear's] career'. Lear's request, he says, is 'an indication, presumably, of the physical distress

which is death's messenger'. He continues,

But these unobtrusive words extend imaginatively way beyond the bare physiological fact which at the realistic level they denote: they are a means of pulling together a whole series of lines into an embracing system of meaning. Lear makes his last royal command, a very mild one, yet it takes us into the heart of the tragedy. For his words take us back to the *divest* of Act I, when he was preparing casually for retirement, for ease before the final sleep; to the frantic *unbutton here* of Act III, when he was attempting to make physical fact conform to the spiritual unprotectedness which he had brought about by his earlier disrobing; and to the *pull off my boots* of Act IV, when the fiercest travel in the hard world was over; and they tell us of a final freeing from clothes that can be followed by no new agony. Lear gives up prerogative and protection, throws away clothes which have no meaning, prepares to rest after a long struggle, and finally, a consequence of all that has gone before, gives up life. The king's only safe divestment is death.[6]

Maurice Charney, also tracing the clothing motif, says that in 4.6 the 'old king's return from madness is expressed by costume',

But the cure is never complete, and Lear can never take up his former status. He has gone too far in the pursuit of naked truth to return to the royal robes and crown of the opening scene. At the very end of the play, he is still thinking of the constriction of his clothes: 'Pray you, undo this button: Thank you, sir.' As in the scenes on the heath, Lear remains

---

[4] For a discussion of the differences between the Quarto and Folio versions of Lear's final speech and their implications see Thomas Clayton, '"Is this the promis'd end?": Revision in the Role of the King', in *The Division of the Kingdoms: Shakespeare's Two Versions of 'King Lear'*, ed. Gary Taylor and Michael Warren (Oxford, 1983), *passim*.

[5] William Matchett calls it an 'astonishing interruption' and 'as multivalenced a line as occurs in the play' ('Some Dramatic Techniques in *King Lear*' in *Shakespeare: The Theatrical Dimension*, ed. Philip C. McGuire and David A. Samuelson (New York, 1979), p. 202.

[6] *This Great Stage: Image and Structure in 'King Lear'* (Baton Rouge, 1948), pp. 82–3.

'unaccommodated', and his death seems the only possible fulfilment for him.[7]

Many interpreters see the line as another indication of Lear's physical and/or mental distress. Sidney Homan suggests that 'Lear's modest request . . . may indicate that since his heart is about to break, to ease the pain of death he needs more breathing room under his doublet.'[8] Judah Stampfer's similar but more complex analysis develops from his sense of 'the underlying tension in Lear until his death', which 'lies between an absolute knowledge that Cordelia is dead, and an absolute inability to accept it'. Thus when Lear makes his request,

Lear's life-blood rushes to his head. He chokes, and asks someone to undo the button of his collar. Then, against the undeniable pressure of reality, the counterbalancing illusion that Cordelia lives rushes forth once more.[9]

Inevitably certain elements of this or any dramatic speech are assumed in the development of an interpretation. In this case each critic cited, as well as most directors of the play, makes the same assumption, one that Rosalie Colie briefly calls into question:

From 'howl, howl, howl' to the pitifully courteous 'Pray you, undo this button', Lear recapitulates his violence and his conversion, as well as his capacity for immense feeling and gentleness: in the undoing of the button – his? Cordelia's? – he relives the reason, in a different mode altogether, of 'off, off you lendings!' to express himself, simply, as unaccommodated man seeking help from another: 'Thank you, Sir.' [my emphasis][10]

Philip McGuire has considered at length just whose button it is, whom Lear asks, and whether it is undone.[11] While we cannot, of course, ever be certain, the questions raised by the text(s) are nevertheless answered by assumption whether by scholars, directors, or actors. Usually it is Lear's button and Kent who undoes it, but there are numerous alternatives – as McGuire shows – including the possibility that 'no one acts in response to Lear's words, no button is undone, and Lear is in a world of his

own imagining'.[12] While this may make provocative theatre and cannot be disproved, if we are to speculate on the original purpose of the request it is important to keep in mind the quite remarkable degree to which dialogue was used to cue action on the very different stage for which Shakespeare was writing. That Lear not only asks for an action to be performed but also thanks the performer is persuasive evidence that one actor is cueing another.

Of those studies analysing the use of paradox and inversion in both the play's form and content, to my knowledge only one has examined what its author, Josephine Roberts, terms its 'prefixes of inversion': dis- and in- occasionally, but especially and most frequently un-. For Roberts the use of these terms 'mirror[s] the upheaval which Lear undergoes', and she shows how its use shifts from Lear to Edgar and Cordelia as they 'attempt to readjust the inverted condition of the King'.

Shakespeare's thematic use of the un- prefix may be most clearly shown by examining each of the three major scenes in which the terms cluster. In Lear's division of his kingdom at the beginning of the play the un- prefix plays a prominent role. The stripping of the King's royal powers prepares for the heath scene, in which Lear is to be reduced to the state of Edgar's disguise, a naked, raving madman. Yet Lear does not remain in the state of *unaccommodated* man, for in the closing scenes of the play he experiences the love and tenderness of Cordelia, who is able to 'redeem . . . nature from the general curse'

---

[7] '"We put fresh garments on him": nakedness and clothes in *King Lear*', in *Some Facets of 'King Lear'*, ed. Rosalie L. Colie and F. T. Flahiff (Toronto and Buffalo, 1974), p. 80.

[8] *Shakespeare's Theater of Presence* (London and Toronto, 1986), p. 192.

[9] 'The Catharsis of *King Lear*', *Shakespeare Survey* 13 (1960), 2–3.

[10] *Shakespeare's Living Art* (Princeton, 1974), p. 358.

[11] *Speechless Dialect: Shakespeare's Open Silences* (Berkeley and London, 1985), pp. 97–106.

[12] *Speechless Dialect*, p. 105. McGuire cites a suggestion to this effect by Michael Warren in 'The Diminution of Kent' (*The Division of the Kingdoms*), p. 71.

(IV.vi.207). It is through the hope that she provides him that he is able to die in peace: 'Pray you, *undo* this button.'[13]

This last cryptic sentence is unfortunately typical of Roberts's otherwise provocative and perceptive study. In part, what follows is a development of Roberts's ideas, but inevitably with a focus leading to somewhat different interpretations and conclusions, including but not only concerning that final 'undo'.

The un- prefix occurs sixty-three times in the Folio version of *King Lear*, and sixty-two times in the Quarto.[14] While it is most unlikely that each occurrence was deliberate, certainly the negating construction is in keeping with the overall impression of a chaotic world; indeed, the language, or the perceptions it signifies, is as much a cause as it is a result of the inversions of proper order in both the main and subplots. Frequently, as we shall see, the un- prefix is combined with another form of negation to further complicate both syntax and meaning so that an audience must puzzle out the implications of what is being said, and, as a consequence, hear what the characters do not.

If the purposes to which the un- construction is put in *King Lear* are particular to that play, its use by Shakespeare is not. He seems to have been well aware of the economy of the un- prefix for conveying complex ideas and uses it frequently in a variety of different contexts.[15] One way of gaining some insight into the purposes and effects of un- in *King Lear* is briefly to compare its use in three plays written at about the same time: *Macbeth, Antony and Cleopatra,* and *The Winter's Tale.*[16] To put it in terms of the word I have focused on so far, *Macbeth* dramatizes a man and a world undone, *Antony and Cleopatra* presents a virtually simultaneous doing and undoing, and *The Winter's Tale* offers an undoing that is a doing, a reparation that transcends Leontes's original sin. I suggest that while in *King Lear* the undoing surpasses that of *Macbeth*, there is also a doing analogous to that of *Antony and Cleopatra* and approaching that of *The Winter's Tale*. Shake-

speare's use of the un- prefix, especially in relation to the verb 'to do' in these plays supports, indeed invites, these admittedly rather vast but, I believe, applicable generalizations.

Lady Macbeth ('unsex me here'[17]), the woman of 'undaunted mettle' (1.7.72), worries her husband is 'too full o'th' milk of human kindness' (1.5.16) to be the opportunist she would have him:

> Thou'dst have, great Glamis,
> That which cries 'Thus thou must do' if thou
>   have it,
> And that which rather thou dost fear to do
> Than wishest should be undone.   (1.5.21–4)

Speaking in similar language, Macbeth proves her right: 'If it were done when 'tis done, then 'twere well / It were done quickly' (1.7.1–2). They finally do the deed 'upon / Th'unguarded Duncan' (1.7.69–70). Not surprisingly, the Porter has an unequivocal and apposite comment in his summary of the effects of drink: 'Lechery, sir, it provokes and unprovokes: it provokes the desire but it takes away the performance' (2.3.27–9). Malcolm accurately moralizes on the reactions we shall see: 'To show an unfelt sorrow is an office / Which the false

---

13 '*King Lear* and the Prefixes of Inversion', *Neuphilologische Mitteilungen* 79 (1978), 384–90; quotation, pp. 384–5.

14 See *The History of King Lear*, the Quarto, in *The Oxford Shakespeare*. Five occurrences are in the Folio only, four in the Quarto only.

15 See G. L. Brooke, *The Language of Shakespeare* (London, 1976): 'Shakespeare has more than six hundred words beginning with *un-*, half of them occurring only once. They often express concisely ideas that need a dozen words or so if they are paraphrased' (p. 132). Another study reveals that Shakespeare coined ninety-three 'un-words' (Bryan A. Garner, 'Shakespeare's Latinate Neologisms', *Shakespeare Studies*, 15 (1982), 149–70).

16 Dates for these plays in *William Shakespeare: A Textual Companion*, Stanley Wells and Gary Taylor with John Jowett and William Montgomery (Oxford, 1987): *Macbeth*, 1606, *Antony and Cleopatra*, 1606, *The Winter's Tale*, 1609, *The History of King Lear*, 1605–6, *The Tragedy of King Lear*, 1610.

17 *The Tragedy of Macbeth*, ed. Stanley Wells, *Oxford Shakespeare* (Oxford, 1986), 1.5.40.

man does easy' (2.3.135–6), and the comment of the Old Man to Ross is equally pertinent: ''Tis unnatural, / Even like the deed that's done' (2.4.10–11). Lady Macbeth advises her husband, 'Things without all remedy / Should be without regard. What's done is done' (3.2.13–14). But when Macbeth sees Banquo's ghost he is, as his wife says, 'quite unmanned in folly' (3.4.72). The doctor who attends Lady Macbeth is correct but ineffectual when he perceives that, 'Unnatural deeds / Do breed unnatural troubles' (5.1.68–9). After Lady Macbeth is dead and the prophecies continue to come true, Macbeth wishes 'th'estate o'th' world were now undone' (5.5.38). Whatever limited hope is present at the play's sombre end is embodied in Malcolm and made possible by Macduff, who vows to avenge his family's murder: 'Either thou, Macbeth, / Or else my sword, with an unbattered edge / I sheathe again undeeded' (5.8.5–7).[18] Inevitably Macbeth is defeated by this man who was 'from his mother's womb / Untimely ripped' (5.10.15–16).

The almost unrelieved bleakness of the world of *Macbeth* even unto its conclusion is in marked contrast to that created for Antony and Cleopatra; or perhaps more accurately the world of Cleopatra which transcends that of Caesar so that its appeal for Antony is understandable. It is in Enobarbus' oft-quoted speech that the key to the paradoxical appeal of Cleopatra and her world is conveyed:

On each side her
Stood pretty dimpled boys, like smiling Cupids,
With divers-coloured fans whose wind did seem
To glow the delicate cheeks which they did cool,
And what they undid did.[19]

After Antony is dead, Proculeius advises Cleopatra:

Do not abuse my master's bounty by
Th'undoing of yourself. Let the world see
His nobleness well acted, which your death
Will never let come forth.   (5.2.42–5)

But by this time we sense that what Proculeius calls Cleopatra's 'undoing' is just the opposite: a doing that undoes Caesar, however briefly, and that even he has to admire.

The un- prefix is used subtly to bear this out when Cleopatra says to the asp:

With thy sharp teeth this knot intrinsicate
Of life at once untie. Poor venomous fool,
Be angry, and dispatch. O, couldst thou speak,
That I might hear thee call great Caesar ass
Unpolicied!   (5.2.299–303)

And Charmian punningly confirms Cleopatra's triumph: 'Now boast thee, death, in thy possession lies / A lass unparalleled' (5.2.309–10).

If the use of the un- prefix in *Macbeth* and *Antony and Cleopatra* can be described as negative in the former and positive, if empty in real terms, in the latter, in *The Winter's Tale* the prefix conveys the actively positive quality of the progress of the action. In his jealousy, Leontes puts Camillo in a position where he agrees to 'do that / Which should undo more doing'[20] – murder Polixenes. But in this play, Time 'makes and unfolds error' (2.2.208–12). Thus when Perdita, echoed by the old Shepherd, says they are 'undone', Camillo advises 'A course more promising / Than a wild dedication of yourselves / To unpathed waters, undreamed shores' (4.4.441, 453, 565–7). The resolution of the play, which in effect removes the un- prefix, is prepared for by the acknowledgement of the inadequacy of how the reunion of Polixenes and Leontes is reported: 'I never heard of such another encounter, which lames report to follow it, and undoes description to do it' (5.2.56–8). Finally, as Paulina prepares to undo Hermione's seeming death she says, 'then, all stand still. / Or those that think it is unlawful business / I am about, let them depart', and Leontes, touching his wife, accepts that she is what she seems, 'O, she's warm! / If this be magic, let it be an art / Lawful as eating!'

---

[18] The *OED* attributes 'undeeded' to Shakespeare.
[19] *The Tragedy of Antony and Cleopatra*, ed. Stanley Wells, *Oxford Shakespeare*, 2.2.208–12.
[20] *The Winter's Tale*, ed. Stanley Wells, *Oxford Shakespeare*, 1.2.313–14.

(5.3.95–7, 109–11). In *King Lear*, the un- prefix can be seen as a means of both guiding an understanding of Lear's experience and prompting a response to the play's end that perhaps anticipates – albeit tragically – the end of *The Winter's Tale*.

The iteration of 'un-' words in *King Lear* begins when not only the prefix but the verb Lear uses at the end – undo – is used by Kent, who says of Edmund, 'I cannot wish the fault undone, the issue of it being so proper' (1.1.16–17). The convoluted syntax of 'cannot' and 'undone' creates an impression of negation that counters Kent's ostensible meaning, as if anticipating the revelation of Edmund's fault that we and Kent will wish undone as the action of both plots proceeds. Only at the play's end, when the two plots come together, is the undoing of both Gloucester and Lear, in which Edmund has played a key role, countered by the undoing of Edmund by Edgar – the truly 'proper issue'.

Rosalie Colie's discussion of the paradoxes in *King Lear* – an analysis that is itself replete with un- prefixes[21] – notes how 'the paradox itself is contradicted, the metaphor un-metaphored, as irony turns into truth', and how 'the paradoxes defy their boundaries . . . they flow together to draw the beholder into the experience of contradiction'. More specifically – and pertinently – Colie observes that '[Lear's] undoing is his recreation as a man'.[22] This ability of paradox to suggest the opposite of what is said is central to the dual responses engendered by the play; and more often than not at the heart of the many interrelated paradoxes is an un- prefix conveying an idea and its opposite, a duality of which we – unlike the speaker – should become aware. For example, a self-dramatizing Lear says,

> 'tis our fast intent
> To shake all cares and business from our age,
> Conferring them on younger strengths, while we
> Unburdened crawl toward death. (1.1.38–41)[23]

But the irony is that in doing so he acquires new burdens that will make the self-pitying image a reality. This dramatic contrast between what characters say and what we hear or see is epitomized the third time the un- prefix is used, when Goneril concludes her succession of superlatives describing 'A love that makes breath poor and speech unable' (1.1.60). It is as if Shakespeare is trying to condition the audience to 'look with [its] ears' long before the protagonists are able to.

Certainly in a scene and play ostensibly preoccupied with negation, a key event demonstrates how the un- prefix can convey positive values. Cordelia's 'Nothing, my lord', and Lear's threat that 'Nothing will come of nothing' (1.1.87, 90), are countered by the wholly positive intervention of France. Lear, having rejected Cordelia, calls her 'unfriended' (1.1.202), and Burgundy's refusal to marry her seems confirmation that this is so. But France, unable to comprehend the abrupt change says, 'Sure, her offence / Must be of such unnatural degree / That monsters it . . . which to believe of her / Must be a faith that reason without miracle / Should never plant in me' (1.1.217–19, 220–2). This prompts Cordelia to speak in her defence, insisting that Lear,

> make known
> It is no vicious blot, murder, or foulness,
> No unchaste action or dishonoured step
> That hath deprived me of your grace and favour,
> But even the want of that for which I am richer – (1.1.226–30)

France speaks her language: 'Is it but this – a tardiness in nature, / Which often leaves the history unspoke / That it intends to do?' The positive effect of the double negative, 'no unchaste', as well as of 'unspoke/do', is given its fullest articulation when France voices the

---

[21] Indeed, it is difficult to avoid using the un- formula, as this study also shows.

[22] *Paradoxia Epidemica*, pp. 470, 474, 480–1.

[23] 'Unburdened' is one of the un- words occurring only in the Folio text.

play's unequivocal standard of behaviour – a standard unpractised if not undone for much of the action to come: 'Love's not love / When it is mingled with regards that stands / Aloof from th'entire point' (1.1.235–7, 238–40). Belief in this wholly unparadoxical ideal allows France at least partly to undo what has been done to Cordelia. But as the episode concludes the paradoxes return even to France's speech, conveying that what has been done to Cordelia by her father is an undoing: to France she is, 'most rich, being poor; / Most choice, forsaken; and most loved, despised', an 'unprized precious maid' (1.1.250–1, 259).

France's accurate perception of the situation also results in his unambiguous use of the un-prefix to describe Regan and Goneril as 'unkind'. While 'unprized' suggests 'unpriced' and 'unpraised',[24] 'unkind' contains the idea of 'un-kinned', as Hamlet knew. In itself Shakespeare's use of 'unkind' in *King Lear* is not especially noteworthy – it occurs at least sixteen times in his main-plot source, *The True Chronicle Historie of King Leir*[25] – but he makes the most of its implications, bringing the pun to life when Lear unkins his 'unkind daughters'. By having France call attention to the 'unkindness' in relationships in the first scene, Shakespeare gives the audience a value against which to measure subsequent events and uses of the word. Similarly, when in the second scene the deceived Gloucester calls Edgar an 'unnatural, detested, brutish villain' (1.2.78–9), we know the truth: that it is the 'natural' son who is unnatural. This sad irony is again emphasized by the un- prefix when, after we have watched Edmund set up his brother and wound himself, we hear him deceive his father:

> Sir, in fine,
> Seeing how loathly opposite I stood
> To his unnatural purpose, in fell motion
> With his preparèd sword he charges home
> My unprovided body . . .　　　　(2.1.47–51)

Take away the 'uns' and you are closer to the truth.

The inability of the characters themselves – especially Gloucester and Lear – to see the truth, to be undeceived, is a blindness against which Shakespeare repeatedly sets our greater awareness, prompting us not only to perceive the deceptions but also to become conscious of the truths inherent in what the characters say. The role of truth in the inverted world of the play is repeatedly conveyed both by events and by use of the word 'true' and its variants. Although 'Time . . . unfold[s] what pleated cunning hides' (1.1.280), before that happens 'Truth's a dog must to kennel' (1.4.110). If Kent is 'the true blank of [Lear's] eye' who 'must speak truth' (1.1.159, 2.2.97), Edmund is his opposite. He tells Cornwall that he will serve him, 'Truly, however else' (2.1.116), but the hollowness of this is clear when the jealous Regan asks him: 'Tell me but truly – but then speak the truth – / Do you not love my sister?' (5.1.8–9). It is fitting that Edgar's challenge to Edmund is an accusation of deception – Edmund says he will 'maintain / [His] truth and honour firmly' (5.3.93–4). And if through the play we are prompted to judge for ourselves what is true, it is especially important that we do so when Edgar opines, 'The dark and vicious place where thee he got / Cost him his eyes', and Edmund concurs, 'Thou'st spoken right. 'Tis true. / The wheel is come full circle. I am here' (5.3.163–5). Our response to these sententious comments will largely determine how we hear and see Lear's final moments.

At the centre of the action for the characters and of the process of response and judgement for the audience are Act 3, Scenes 3 and 4. In a way opposite from what Gloucester intends,

---

24 On the uses and implications of 'praise', 'prize', and 'price' in another Shakespeare play, see C. C. Barfoot, '*Troilus and Cressida*: "Praise us as we are tasted"', *Shakespeare Quarterly*, 39 (1988), 45–57.

25 Anon. *The True Chronicle Historie of King Leir and his three daughters* (1605), in *Narrative and Dramatic Sources of Shakespeare*, VII, ed. Geoffrey Bullough (London, New York, 1973). Indeed, the un- prefix occurs at least fifty-three times in Shakespeare's source.

the turn begins with his confiding to Edmund about the letter he has received telling of support for the King, whom Gloucester has shut out of his castle. Thus, whether it is genuine regret or self-interest prompting Gloucester, he is right when he says, 'I like not this unnatural dealing', as is the dissembling Edmund, who replies, 'Most savage and unnatural' (3.3.1–2, 7). But Gloucester's limited perception of the true situation leads him to confide in Edmund who immediately betrays that trust, setting in motion the events to follow in both plots.

Perhaps the most often discussed un- word in the play is 'unaccommodated', which concentrates in itself the interrelated negative connotations of undo, unkind, and unnatural. Indeed, the OED does Shakespeare an injustice to cite his use of the word in King Lear with the definition, 'not possessed of, unprovided with'.[26] Certainly this is what Lear means, but as with other uses of the un- prefix in the play, the audience is encouraged to hear and see implications that the speaker cannot. Thus while on the most obvious level Lear's seeing Edgar as unaccommodated is an element of the clothing theme, as Lear's 'Come, unbutton here'[27] indicates, the insight made available to the spectator is gained if it is realized that in the most basic and important sense of the word, Edgar is *not* unaccommodated, as the later use of 'accommodate' suggests.[28] When Edgar, whom Lear has perceived as unaccommodated, says of the flower-bedecked Lear, 'The safer sense will ne'er accommodate / His master thus' (4.5.81–2), he verbally demonstrates the crucial difference between them: Lear is mad, Edgar is not and never was. Edgar as Poor Tom is physically unaccommodated but not mentally so as Lear is, and this difference goes to the heart of the play. From the moment Edgar dons his disguise, there is a series of soliloquies and asides to remind us that Edgar is both sane and good: humane. Furthermore, with Edgar as a standard, it should become apparent that it is the unnatural, unkind child, Edmund, who is unaccommodated in the truest sense: uncivilized, anti-social, inhumane – one of 'nature's bastards'.

If Edmund, the product of 'sport', a 'dark and vicious place', symbolizes the absence or negation of love, the other characters can be judged against him. Love or its absence is manifested in many forms through the play: ideally the relationship of parents and child, husband and wife, master and servant, lord and king, man and god, are all founded on reciprocal love, and we are repeatedly invited to judge them with that in mind. Depending on the degree to which self-love gets in the way, the characters are more or less successful in mounting the ladder from prudence to virtue, from cupiditas to caritas. By this standard, Edgar is far more than just the 'poor, bare, forked animal' Lear sees; as his help for his father demonstrates he is, like Cordelia, 'most rich being poor'.

Related to love and service in the play is the concern with justice. And again we are prompted to define the positive quality by seeing injustice – or, in the language of the play, the unjust. Shakespeare departed from the overt Christianity of King Leir to create the pagan world of his play. The result is a virtually neutral context for action that seems to set harsh, eye-for-an-eye justice against loving forgiveness. Conventionally these are Old Testament values against those of the New Testament, but given the times in which Shakespeare was writing it is also possible that the rigid views of the Puritans were a target. Certainly the doctrines and practices of Puritanism shared with those advocated in the Old Testament an

---

[26] OED, 2nd edn.

[27] This occurs in the Folio only. Clayton suggests it was introduced to anticipate 'Undo this button' ('"Is this the promised end"', pp. 126–8).

[28] According to the OED, 'accommodate' was used at this time to mean 'to fit' or 'to furnish' a person with something requisite. Thus Edgar literally means 'a sane man would not get himself up this way', but the association of the idea of accommodation with sanity suggests deeper implications. See also 'our mere defects / Prove our commodities' (4.1.19–21), cited later in this study.

unyielding quality that made little provision for forgiveness of human folly – blindness – and took little account of unequivocal love, human or divine. It is not enough to say that the suffering of especially Lear, but also Gloucester, is the stuff of tragedy; unlike Edgar, who seems satisfied that, 'The gods are just, and of our pleasant vices / Make instruments to plague us' (5.3.161–2), we on the outside are being brought to see how disproportionate the punishments of Gloucester and Lear are. The organization of *King Lear* has an anti-climactic effect, and one cause is that until the middle of the play we too want to see these foolish, blind, old men punished; but after the action turns toward Dover we are encouraged to agree to their release from the pain induced by what they have done. And by granting forgiveness, we too experience a release.

Just before the turn in the action is effected in the scene between Gloucester and Edmund (3.3), the beginning of a change in Lear is signalled when he says, 'My wits begin to turn.' His growing concern for others is indicative of his new perception that, 'The art of our necessities is strange, / And can make vile things precious' (3.2.67, 70–1). In his suffering he can pity others' 'unfed sides' and 'uncovered body' (3.4.30, 96). In the Folio the 'unaccommodated man' speech ends with Lear's 'Off, off, you lendings! Come, unbutton here' (3.4.102). If this is Shakespeare's emendation it can be contrasted with Lear's later 'Pray you, undo this button': in the first instance he tears at his clothes; in his last moments he quietly requests a service. The second half of the play dramatizes the process from one state to the other. This transitional segment ends with Kent echoing Lear's earlier diagnosis: 'His wits begin t'unsettle' (3.4.152), and the period of Lear's madness begins.

Concomitant with the sufferings of both Lear and Gloucester in the second half of the play is an undercurrent of positive signals countering but never overcoming the pervasive sense of tragedy. To convey this element the un- prefix is again put to use. Amid the graphic horror of Gloucester's blinding there is the action of the servant whose 'better service' results in what Cornwall calls an 'untimely' hurt (3.7.96). Similarly, when Oswald is defeated by Edgar he cries out 'O untimely death' (4.5.249). In both cases we perceive the oppposite: timely deaths; what these two have done cannot be undone but at least they can do no more.

Edgar voices the idea of better and worse being relative, and while his simplistic view is immediately undercut by the appearance of his blinded father, it is an idea that is not easily defeated. One wants to believe that some kind of balance is possible between evil and good, punishment and forgiveness.[29] On the heath the still self-dramatizing Lear says,

> Take physic, pomp,
> Expose thyself to feel what wretches feel,
> That thou mayst shake the superflux to them
> And show the Heavens more just. (3.4.33–6)

In the stocks, Kent speaks of 'seeking to give / Losses their remedies', and concludes optimistically, 'Fortune, good night; / Smile once more; turn thy wheel!' (2.2.160–1, 163–4). The blinded Gloucester can say, 'Full oft 'tis seen / Our means secure us, and our mere defects / Prove our commodities' (4.1.19–21). He elaborates on this even as he asks Edgar to lead him to Dover and death:

> That I am wretched
> Makes thee the happier. Heavens deal so still.
> Let the superfluous and lust-dieted man
> That slaves your ordinance, that will not see
> Because he does not feel, feel your power
>   quickly.
> So distribution should undo excess,
> And each man have enough. (4.1.59–65)

---

[29] It is perhaps worth noting that Edmund's plan to have Cordelia hanged and then 'lay the blame upon her own despair, / That she *fordid* herself' is echoed when Kent tells Lear that his 'eldest daughters have *fordone* themselves, / And desperately are dead' (5.3.229–30, 267–8; my emphasis).

This positive sense of 'undoing' – connoting reparation, restoration – is repeated often enough that it seems necessary to take it into account when assessing the play, especially the final scene when, in many ways, things have come full circle. In particular, to return to Lear's request – 'Pray you, undo this button' – perhaps it signals an action of release which, while not lessening the overall tragedy, allows his heart to 'burst smilingly'.

I would argue that the dying king's request can have the effect of implicating the audience in the last service performed for him.[30] If in experiencing the play we have come to understand that, 'Love's not love / When it is mingled with regards that stands / Aloof from th'entire point', we will release Lear even as the undoing of the button does; with those onstage, we will feel sympathy for this tyrannical, sad, old man. At the last he is once more a king and a father: what was done – by him and to Cordelia – has not, cannot be undone; but it can be countered for a brief moment. Perhaps part of the ambiguity of the play's painful end is created because as Lear bends over Cordelia's body and sees whatever he does, we *want* him to believe she is alive even if we know – or because we know – she is not. Lear's self-deception about Cordelia ironically echoes the initial one; but perhaps we should let him 'speak what [he] feel[s]', not what we might judge he 'ought to say'.

---

[30] William Matchett says he 'would have the button undone by the lowliest anonymous servant or soldier within reach. For Lear's "thank you, Sir" shows the distance he has come. They are not the words of a despot accustomed only to giving orders and having his own way . . . but the words of a man who has discovered human interdependence, a man who can now feel gratitude for the humblest service he would once have taken for granted' ('Some Dramatic Techniques in *King Lear*', p. 203).

MARX AND SHAKESPEARE

R. S. WHITE

The terminology and concepts used by Karl Marx in the field of political economy have entered virtually every intellectual field. In Shakespeare criticism there are numerous Marxist studies, there are Marxist critics such as Robert Weimann, Walter Cohen, Paul N. Seigel and Terry Eagleton. Behind such new movements as cultural materialism and new historicism the influence of Marx's thought is clearly discernible. However, there does not seem available a study of Marx's own views of Shakespeare, at least outside the Chinese language, where articles have appeared in publications which are inaccessible to this writer.[1] S. S. Prawer's splendid *Karl Marx and World Literature*,[2] while giving much information, does not specifically focus on Shakespeare and does not provide the kind of commentary that a Shakespearian may want. Other commentaries which consider the Shakespearian link do so in the context of the apparently more immediate influence on Marx of Hegel, who was himself steeped in German idealism and classical literature.

This article is a modest attempt to begin filling the need which exists for a study of Marx's use of Shakespeare, suggesting how it illuminates Shakespeare, and how Shakespeare may have influenced Marx's thinking. It is not in itself guided by Marxist ideology, but is fuelled by interests in how Shakespeare has profoundly entered and influenced the work of socialist intellectuals and in the general field of reader-response criticism. I do not deal with the

Note: I am grateful for a grant from the Australian Research Council while carrying out the research for this article, and I thank Jane Whiteley for her assistance in the task.

[1] A small number of quotations may be found in *Marx, Engels On Literature and Art* (Moscow, 1976). The following list excludes Marxist criticism in favour of criticism dealing with Marx on Shakespeare. Shamefully, the present author was unable to read many of the following items since many are in Chinese, Hindi, Japanese, Polish and Russian, but they are included for those who can. They are briefly summarized in earlier Bibliographies of *Shakespeare Quarterly*: Johanna Rudolph, 'Karl Marx und Shakespeare', *Shakespeare Jahrbuch* (Weimar), 105 (1969), 25–53; R. Riabov, 'The Favorite Writers of Marx', *Slovensky Pohlady*, 75 (1959), 1059ff.; G. Friedlander, 'Marx and Engels on Shakespeare', *Shekspirovski Sbornik* (1981), 9–42; Anne Paolucci, 'Marx, Money and Shakespeare: The Hegelian Core in Marxist Shakespeare Criticism', *Mosaic* 10 (1977), 139–56; Cheng Daixi, 'Marx and Engels on Shakespearization', *Guangming Ribao (The Guangming Daily)*, 10 June 1978, p. 4; Lalit Shukla, *Naya Kavya: Naye Moolya (New Poetry: New Values)* (Delhi, 1979); Sun Jiaxiu (ed.), *Makesi Engesi he Shashibiya Xiju [Marx, Engels and Shakespeare's Plays]*, (Beijing, 1981); Shi Zongshan, 'A Tentative Exposition of Shakespeare's Significance in the Development of the Theatre – Jottings from Studying "To Ferdinand Lasalle" by Marx and Engels', *Hebei Daxu Xuebao*, 3 (1981), 130–9; Lu Dazhong, 'Marx and the Theatre', *Xiju Yishu*, 1 (1983), 1–5; Jurgen Kaczynski, 'Marx and Shakespeare', *Jahrbuch für Wirtschaftsgeschichte* (1983), 9–24; Joel Kovel, 'Marx on the Jewish Question', *Dialectical Anthropology*, 8 (1983), 31–46; Zhang Siyang, 'Marx and Shakespeare', *Jilin Daxue Xuebo* (Journal of Jilin University), 3 (1983), 74–84; Ruan Shen, '*The Merchant of Venice* and "On the Jewish Question"', *Shashibiya Yanjiu*, 2 (1984), 128–38; Katsuhito Iwai, *The Capital of The Merchant of Venice* (Tokyo, 1985), esp. pp. 4–63; J. P. Brockbank, 'Jesus, Shakespeare and Karl Marx' in *On Shakespeare* (Oxford, 1989), esp. pp. 10–11.

[2] Oxford, 1976.

equally rich field of Shakespearian usage in 'the Marx circle', especially by Engels and Marx's wife and daughters, since there is enough material for another essay. The monumental, almost complete, translated *Collected Works* of Marx and Engels, published in fifty volumes since 1975, has provided the research base.[3]

The first and main point is that Marx was steeped in Shakespeare's works, and he placed Shakespeare with Aeschylus and Goethe as his favourite poets. His father-in-law to be, Ludwig von Westphalen, was his mentor in literary tastes, and Prawer opens his study with Eleanor Marx's comment on her father:

He never tired of telling us about old Baron von Westphalen and his wonderful knowledge of Shakespeare and Homer. He could recite whole cantos of Homer from beginning to end, and most of Shakespeare's plays he knew by heart in English and in German alike.

(Prawer, pp. 1–2, quoting from *Mohr und General. Erinnerungen an Marx und Engels* (Berlin, 1970), pp. 157–8)

Marx seems to have played the Baron's role in the education of his own children. He recounts an anecdote which turns on his daughters quoting from *Much Ado About Nothing*: 'Little Jenny called him 'BENEDICK THE MARRIED MAN', but little Laura said 'BENEDICK WAS A WIT, HE IS BUT "A CLOWN", AND "A CHEAP CLOWN TOO". The children are constantly reading Shakespeare.' (MEW, 40, 33). Daughter Jenny, when considerably older, was said by Marx to have 'had a *furibundus* success with a Shakespeare declamation' (MEW, 43, 466) at a London soirée in 1870. The letters of his wife (also Jenny) are peppered with quotations. She was to become a frequently published critic of Shakespeare on the London stage, and is described by Liebknecht in his memoirs as 'an excellent Shakespearian scholar' (Nicolaievsky, p. 258)[4]. More amusingly, Marx himself speaks of Edgar von Westphalen in Shakespearian terms:

Edgar has just recently caught a cold which has gone to his nose, which, as a result of this ACCIDENT, looks positively Bardolphian.   (MEW, 42, 177)

One of the delightful fringe benefits of the research undertaken for this essay is that time and again it shows Marx's irrepressible and infectious sense of humour, a side of his work and temperament that might not immediately come to mind when we hear his name. The pet-name by which Marx was known to his family and friends was Moor, and this may be a reference to Othello, since in a passionate letter to Jenny he says '. . . love you I do, with a love greater than was ever felt by the Moor of Venice' (MEW, 40, 55). Boris Nicolaievsky in his biography *Karl Marx: Man and Fighter*, without mentioning Shakespeare, tends to confirm this by suggesting that the name referred to Marx's dark complexion and black hair (p. 259).

Marx himself was thoroughly acquainted with Shakespeare's works, since we find scattered throughout his writings references to at least twenty-five plays. He can open an essay on 'The Coming Election in England' with a quotation from *Richard III* (MEW, 15, 219), and an essay on 'The Polemical Tactics of the Augsburg Newspaper' with words from *Othello*, 'It is merely a lust of the blood and a permission of the will' (MEW, 1, 288). A chapter in a book on European politics begins by eliding two Shakespearian references:

---

[3] Karl Marx and Frederick Engels, *Collected Works* (London, 1975–), a collaborative project between Lawrence and Wishart, International Publishers, New York, and the Institute of Marxism-Leninism, Moscow. This is the official, English translation of Karl Marx, Friedrich Engels, *Werke* (Herausgegeben vom Institut für Marxismus beim ZK der SED, Berlin, 1956–68). Referred to here as MEW.

[4] Boris Nicolaievsky and Otto Maenchen-Helfen, *Karl Marx: Man and Fighter* (translated Gwenda David and Eric Mosbacher, London 1936), revised edn Harmondsworth, 1973).

If the Prussia of the regency speaks as it writes, it is easy to explain its talent, newly proved in the European comedy of errors, not only to misunderstand but also to be misunderstood. In this it has a certain similarity with Falstaff, who not only was witty himself but was also the cause of other people's wit.   (MEW, 16, 450)

There is a reference in a letter to Engels that suggests Marx was a committee member of the Shakespeare Society when he was living in London in 1864 (MEW, 41, 517). A correspondent from the *Chicago Tribune*, when he interviewed Marx in his London 'villa', noticed on the bookshelves 'Shakespeare, Dickens, Thackeray, Molière, Racine, Montaigne, Bacon, Goethe, Voltaire, Paine . . .' (MEW, 24, 569). Marx shows that he is capable of sound Shakespeare criticism which could, if things had taken a different line, have led him into the profession of his wife:

A singularity of English tragedy, so repulsive to French feelings that Voltaire used to call Shakespeare a drunken savage, is its peculiar mixture of the sublime and the base, the terrible and the ridiculous, the heroic and the burlesque.   (MEW, 13, 132)

Instead of developing this line of discussion, however, he moves immediately into the political question of 'The War Debate in Parliament' in London, 1854, with a note of drily sarcastic irony that is characteristic:

But nowhere does Shakespeare devolve upon the Clown the task of speaking the prologue of a heroic drama. This invention was reserved for the Coalition Ministry. Mylord Aberdeen has performed, if not the English Clown, at least the Italian Pantaloon. All great historical movements appear, to the superficial observer, finally to subside into the farce, or at least the common-place . . .   (*ibid.*)

In another scathing passage, he describes the Poor Laws as devices to allow English farmers to depress wages to a point 'beneath that *mere physical minimum*', 'a glorious way to convert the wages labourer into a slave, and Shakespeare's proud yeoman into a pauper' (MEW, 20, 145). Of course, Marx is aware that there was poverty in Elizabethan England, but he is making a point about the representation of working men in Shakespeare.

Like von Westphalen, Marx evidently knew Shakespeare in German (in the edition of August Wilhelm von Schlegel (MEW, 5, fn)) and English (Johnson's edition). His perspective is sometimes unmistakably Goethe-inspired, since he cannot conceive Hamlet to be without melancholy (MEW, 14, 297). He is aware of some scholarly theories, such as that 'nunnery' in *Hamlet* may be a printing error for 'nonaria', a brothel. He is even capable of exercising the scholarly, philological interest of nineteenth-century Shakespearians, when in a letter to Engels he wrote

I am incapable of writing today, but must nevertheless ask you to clear up a philological doubt. In *Henry IV*, Shakespeare used the word 'hiren' for 'siren' and, according to a note made by that pedant, Johnson, the form 'hiren' also occurs in other early English writers. The substitution of h for s is QUITE in order, but might there not be some connection between 'hiren' and 'Hure', and hence also 'siren'? Or with 'hoeren', *auris*, etc.? You can see TO WHICH LOW STATE OF SPIRIT I AM DEPRESSED today from the great interest I show in this matter.
                                       (MEW, 40, 46)

Marx would no doubt take quiet satisfaction in the fact that modern editors reject Johnson's emendation and return Pistol's puzzling, repeated words as a fight brews, to its original 'Have we not Hiren here?' (*2 Henry IV*, 2.4.151 and 165). He might not be so happy with their reasoning, since they suggest the word is Pistol's grandiose way of saying 'iron', and the Arden editor at least finds support for the spirit of Johnson's emendation by finding that the phrase recurs in other Elizabethan works, recalling a courtesan called 'Hyrin' (Irene) in the title of a lost play by Peele.[5] These explanations

---

[5] A. R. Humphreys (ed.), *King Henry IV, Part II* (London, 1966), pp. 73–4. The references to Shakespeare in this article are from Peter Alexander (ed.), *The Complete Works of William Shakespeare* (London and Glasgow, 1951).

seem neither less nor more convincing than Marx's reading, which I take to be 'Have we not hearing here?' ('give me a hearing'), which arguably fits more easily into the context. I cannot find an edition which even inadvertently, let alone with acknowledgement, notices Marx's suggestion. The jokey tone of the comment does not disguise Marx's evident alertness to the *minutiae* of Shakespeare's language, and his intuitive understanding of some of the principles of textual emendation.

We can pass over as insignificant the many times when Marx uses the rhetorical phrase 'That is the question', clearly taken from *Hamlet* but not of much interest in itself. In the same category is his fondness for satirical variations on Richard III's 'A horse, a horse! my kingdom for a horse'. A little more conceptually functional is his great fondness for Hamlet's 'something is rotten in the state of Denmark' since it enables him to pinpoint state corruption: 'There must be something rotten in the very core of a social system which increases its wealth without diminishing its misery, and increases in crimes even more rapidly than in numbers' (MEW, 16, 489). While on the subject of crime, Marx with tongue in cheek invokes the example of Richard the Third to prove how productive, in the capitalist system, is the criminal (keeping in employment police, judges and criminologists), how he 'breaks the monotony and everyday security of bourgeois life', and gives a spur to the competitive edge of capitalism.[6] Another favourite with Marx is the controversy in *A Midsummer Night's Dream* over who is to play the Lion, Bottom or Snug the joiner, and the stage audience's appreciation of Snug's timid roaring. The references are employed in various ways, usually satirical:

Mr Hume was the man chosen to answer in the name of the country, just as Snug, the joiner, was chosen to play the lion's part in 'the most cruel death of Pyramus and Thisbe'. Mr Hume's whole Parliamentary life has been spent in making opposition pleasant.

(MEW, 13, 26)

May they, in particular, furnish Prussia with instructions that permit it, under high sovereign licence, so to speak *avec garantie du gouvernement*, to take over the role of mediating lion! Prussia, thus wants to play the European lion, but in the capacity of Snug the joiner.

LION Then know, that I, one Snug, the joiner, am
    A lion-fell, nor else no lion's dam:
    For if I should as lion come in strife
    Into this place, 'twere pity on my life.
THESEUS A very gentle beast, and of a good conscience.
LYSANDER This lion is a very fox for his valour.
THESEUS True; and a goose for his discretion.

(MEW, 16, 463)

he puts some London lackeys into French uniforms. They represent the army. In his Gang of December 10, he assembles 10,000 rogues who are to play the part of the people, as Nick Bottom that of the lion.

(MEW, 17, 35)

It is like the lion in *A Midsummer Night's Dream*, who shouts: 'I am lion and I am not lion, I am Snug the joiner.' Thus every extreme is here at one time the lion of contradiction, at another the Snug of mediation.

(MEW, 3, 87)

In the last example, Marx is speaking of contradictions in Hegel's view of sovereignty, but his comments inadvertently reveal a sophisticated understanding of what modern criticism describes as metatheatre, Shakespeare's simultaneous awareness of actor and role which sometimes becomes deliberately discrepant. In a speech delivered at the anniversary of *The People's Paper* in London on April 14, 1856, Marx seems to run together a memory of Robin Goodfellow in *A Midsummer Night's Dream* and the old mole of Hamlet's father's ghost that can 'work i'th'earth so fast' (*Hamlet*, 1.5.162), in a passage which stirringly sums up his view of social revolution:

---

[6] For an absorbing book which independently analyses the central part played by thieves in the insurance-dominated capitalist system, see Carl B. Klockars, *The Professional Fence* (London, 1975). The book deals with *The Beggar's Opera* which reminds us that Brecht's *The Threepenny Opera* is based on a similar idea.

In the signs that bewilder the middle class, the aristocracy and the poor prophets of regression, we do recognise our brave friend, Robin Goodfellow, the old mole that can work in the earth so fast, that worthy pioneer – the Revolution. The English working men are the first-born sons of modern industry. They will then, certainly, not be the last in aiding the social revolution produced by that industry, a revolution, which means the emancipation of their own class all over the world, which is as universal as capital-rule and wages-slavery.

(MEW, 14, 656)

We shall come to notice many occasions when Marx links up Shakespeare with his social analysis and his politics.

There are far too many occasions for quotation of examples of Marx using some apposite, sententious Shakespearian phrase such as Hamlet's 'Though this be madness, yet there is method in't!' (MEW, 1, 204), or '. . . to be honest, as this world goes, is to be one man picked out of ten thousand' (MEW, 1, 273), in order to cap an argument or ridicule an adversary's position.

Hamlet thought it disquieting that the dust of Alexander might have been used to stop a bunghole. What would Hamlet have said if he had seen the disintegrated head of Napoleon on the shoulders of the Plon-Plon? (MEW, 17, 190)

Early in Marx's writings, Cornwall's description of Kent as a plain-speaking knave, and Julius Caesar's 'Et tu Brute', both recur, as do 'such men are dangerous', and Antony's corrosive 'honourable men'. Napoleon III is advised to heed 'the remark of the "divine William"', to the effect that 'uneasy lies the head that wears a crown' (MEW, 16, 259). All these phrases, significantly, are used by Shakespeare in political contexts, and so they are by Marx. Speaking of Sir Robert Peel, Marx recalls the words in *Henry V*: 'He is what the English call "a chartered libertine"', a dashing madcap, a privileged eccentric, for whose impulses and outbursts, erratic manoeuvrings, words and deeds no Government is held responsible' (MEW, 14, 480). He describes the 'ludicrous pageantry'

devoted to the birth of a prince in the court of Bonaparte the Little in words from *Henry the Eighth*: 'all clinquant, all in gold, like heathen gods' (MEW, 14, 615). He quotes 'upon place and greatness many eyes are stuck' from *Measure for Measure* in speaking disparagingly again of the English administration (MEW, 14, 666), and he manages to place alongside each other two phrases from *King John*:

While the Low Church bishops, whom the veteran imposter allowed the Earl of Shaftesbury, his kinsman, to nominate, vouch his 'righteousness', the opium-smugglers, the dealers in 'sweet poison for the age's tooth', vouch his faithful service to 'commodity, the bias of the world'.   (MEW, 15, 219)

'A plague o'both their houses' from *Romeo and Juliet* seems ripe for appropriation in the context of party politics, and sure enough Marx seizes the opportunity (MEW, 16, 544 and 17, 378). Equally quotable in the context of a change of Ministries is Feste's 'The whirligig of time brings in his revenges' (MEW, 16, 101). Napoleon III is, Marx says, known as 'one who, having, like Macbeth, waded to a crown through human gore, finds it easier to go forward than to return to peace and innocence' (MEW, 16, 273). At other times Marx interprets politically incidents that are non-political in Shakespeare. Writing to Engels that he is 'reading Appian's Civil War of Rome in the original Greek', he recalls Shakespeare's parody portrayal of Pompey in the Masque of the Nine Worthies in Shakespeare: 'In *Love's Labour's Lost*, Shakespeare would seem to have had some inkling of what Pompey was really like' (MEW, 41, 265). Marx takes relish in using Jaques' 'seven ages' speech from *As You Like It* to describe the bourgeoisie: '– sans eyes, sans ears, sans teeth, sans everything – such was the *Prussian bourgeoisie* which found itself at the helm of the Prussian state after the March revolution' (MEW, 8, 163; again 11, 159 of the French *ancien régime* and at 12, 345 of the English public). The omission of 'sans taste' may be a mistake, but it might possibly be an ironic comment on the gustatory indulgence (or even the fastidious 'good taste' of the middle classes as Marx saw them).

The most frequent way in which Marx uses Shakespeare is to name a living politician or writer, usually negatively, as a character from the plays:

Shakespeare's poor devil, who wakes up as a lord after having gone to sleep as a tinker [Christopher Sly in *The Taming of the Shrew*], does not speak more movingly than Schleinitz, once he is overcome by the fixed idea of Prussia's calling to be the 'armed mediation power' of Europe. He is stung and disturbed, as if by a tarantula, by the 'uneasy conviction that he ought to act up to his newborn sublimity of character'. (MEW, 16, 457)

Faucher, foreign editor of the *Morning Star* in London, is 'a veritable Ancient Pistol of braggadocio, and once in six months it's amusing to listen to his boasting' (MEW, 40, 127). In systematically demolishing the argument of Heinzen's manifesto against communism, Marx likens the writer to the bombastic Ajax in *Troilus and Cressida*, quoting slabs from the play to hammer home the point (MEW, 6, 312–15), while in another essay the Whigs become 'as cunning as Ulysses' (MEW, 13, 602).

This habit of name-calling at times is irritating and at first sight meretricious. However, Marx does have a kind of theoretical substratum on which he is basing his practice. Something of its nature can be seen in an essay 'English' published in *Die Presse*, no. 39, 9 Feb. 1862:

'Eccentricity' or 'individuality' are the marks of insular John Bull in the minds of the continentals. On the whole, this notion confuses the Englishman of the past with the Englishman of the present. Intense class development, extreme division of labour and what is called 'public opinion', manipulated by the Brahmins of the press, have, on the contrary, produced a monotony of character that would make it impossible for a Shakespeare, for example, to recognise his own countrymen. The differences no longer belong to the individuals but to their 'profession' and class. Apart from his profession, in everyday life one 'respectable' Englishman

is so like another that even Leibniz could hardly discover a difference, a *differentia specifica*, between them. The individuality, so highly praised, is banished from every sphere of politics and society and finds its last refuge in the crotchets and whims of private life, asserting itself there now and then *sans-gene* and with unconscious humour. Hence it is chiefly in the *courts of justice* – those great public arenas in which private whims clash with one another – that the Englishman still appears as a being *sui generis*.

This is the preface to a diverting courtroom scene that took place a few days ago in the Court of Exchequer. The *dramatis personae* were . . . (MEW, 19, 163)

One could easily drive a horse and cart through Marx's logic here, since he is confusing Shakespeare's construction of character with the 'real life' of Shakespeare's England, and he is conveniently ignoring the many occasions Shakespeare himself equates character with class or profession. The theory is transparently created on Marx's own ideas about the negative effects of the class system, reinforced by the popular press. But more interesting are the underlying assumptions about connections between literature and life in the field of character presentation. Marx is strongly inclined throughout his writings to see the theatrical side of public occasions, and here he is quite explicit in regarding the judges as *dramatis personae* in a play. It is his basic justification for equating public figures with Shakespearian characters. Underlying this attitude is Marx's theory of 'alienation' to which we shall return, the idea that individuality becomes flattened and dehumanized by either money or occupation. Money, he says, dehumanizes, and he attributes this perception to Shakespeare:

How little connection there is between money, the most general form of property, and personal peculiarity, how much they are directly opposed to each other was already known to Shakespeare better than to our theorising petty bourgeois . . . (MEW, 5, 230)

and he quotes a passage from *Timon of Athens* (4.3) which we shall examine below. The irony is that Marx himself uses his Shakespeare references in an alienating way, often with the direct purpose of highlighting the sense in which a politician has himself alienated his humanity in his speeches. An English ministerial retainer, one Mr Milne, is dismissed with a quotation from *Julius Caesar*, 'Do not talk of him / But as a property' (MEW, 12, 272). The ploy is Marx's own ironic strategy for simultaneously emphasizing the merging of the person with the policy and also, paradoxically, suggesting the 'crotchets and whims' that lie behind the individual eccentricities of politicians. He justifies it in other terms when he sarcastically exclaims (in connection with the 'Beer Acts' which sought to close public houses on Sunday): 'This latest *ecclesiastical coup d'état* has caused much mirth and has proved that Shakespearean prototypes, etc., still flourish in the second half of the nineteenth century' (MEW, 13, 591).

In a letter to an aspiring playwright, Marx comments that he (Lassalle) does not '*Shakespearize*' his characters – 'I miss what is characteristic in the characters' – and instead like Schiller he uses 'individuals as mere mouthpieces for the spirit of the times' (MEW, 40, 420). Although Marx could be said to do the same in his quotations, he reveals here his assumption that Shakespearian characterization depends on generalizing or universalizing from the unique and particular. He seems to think it a mark of Shakespeare's own times, for he says 'And was there ever a time of more robust character traits than the sixteenth century?' (*ibid.*) The comments to Lassalle give more information about Marx's attitude to Shakespeare's characters. He deplores Lassalle's tendency to portray character 'much too abstractly' (implying the concreteness of Shakespeare's), and in censuring Lasalle's (and Schiller's) habit of creating characters who display 'the sometimes excessive preoccupation of individuals with themselves' he shows that he believes in the extrovertedness and social definition of Shakespeare's characters.

Falstaff is invoked to denote various negative qualities and attitudes. The references are particularly rich, commenting wittily as they do, on topical issues:

The troops that the 'Summing Up' puts into the field on its side resemble, with few exceptions, Falstaff's recruits: all they are good for is to fill the breach with the corpses of thoughts. (MEW, 1, 268)

. . . the slave-economy can exclaim, like John Falstaff, 'if reasons were as plenty as blackberries!'
(MEW, 6, 325. See also 17, 47; 43, 506)

If we compare the *corpus delicti*, the real body of the Government, with its echo, its constitutional declarations, appeasings, mediations and agreements in the Berlin Assembly, we can only use Falstaff's phrase: '*Lord, lord, how subject we old men are to this vice of lying!*' (MEW, 7, 466)

(Compare also 'You know Falstaff's opinion of old men. They are all of them cynics' (MEW, 43, 216) which is properly speaking an interpretation rather than a quotation).

The noble lord [Palmerston] is as uncertain of the day when the Porte implored his aid, as Falstaff was of the number of rogues in buckram suits, who came at his back, in Kendal green.
(MEW, 12, 373; see also 14, 12; 17, 29)

It is unnecessary to describe Mr Tite in detail. Shakespeare did so when he invented the immortal Shallow, compared by Falstaff to one of the little men made out of cheese-parings after supper.
(MEW, 14, 480)

Sir John Potter, for instance, the opponent of Bright, is only known as the fattest man of Manchester. He would go under the name of the Manchester Sir John Falstaff, if his small wit and his long purse did not protect him from being compared to that immortal knight. (MEW, 15, 240)

One particular writer, Herr Vogt, who coined the phrase 'The Brimstone Gang' to describe Marx's followers, came in for scathing criticism, much of it directed at his 'well-rounded character'. A 'spherical' man (MEW, 17, 28), Vogt inevitably calls to Marx's mind the corpulent Falstaff. Marx recalls a description of Vogt as 'the great vaulted belly from France' and adds: 'Thus all Falstaffian natures suffered from the sulphur disease in more than one sense' (MEW, 17, 33). And again, 'A peculiar characteristic of all Falstaffs is that as well as big bellies they also have big mouths' (MEW, 17, 59). In oblique parallel, he quotes from *Henry IV, Part One*, 3.3.153–6:

But, sirrah, there's no room for faith, truth, nor honesty in this bosom of thine; it is filled up with guts and midriff.   (MEW, 17, 38)

Marx mockingly hurls at Vogt phrases like 'Come, your proofs, Jack, your proofs' (MEW, 17, 48), and sustains to the end of the book a damning tirade against Vogt's 'Falstaffian travesty of justice'. If all these references taken together imply Marx's overall attitude to the Shakespearian character, it may strike one as curious that he did not appreciate Falstaff's subversive potential, but rather makes him a figure of fun and dwells on his lying. The reason for this may lie in the potential Marxist perception that Falstaff is a representative of the decadent aristocracy: he is, after all, a knight.

Shylock is just as important to Marx as Falstaff, and more than once Marx uses lines from *The Merchant of Venice* to make an important point which distinguishes the law from justice. This leads into a characteristic analysis of the way the law protects private interests and victimizes the poor, and it can be taken as an example of Shakespeare helping Marx to construct his model of social organization. The context which drew Marx's vehement indignation in articles published in *Rheinische Zeitung* in 1842, the so-called 'wood-theft' articles, needs explanation. A law was passed which criminalized the gathering of firewood from private landowners' woods. This in itself irked Marx, but what added insult to injury was that the 'offences' were considered grounds for civil action as well, whereby the poor wood-gatherers had to pay the landowners compensation. His argument is that this makes them into the landowners' serfs, and subjugates them still further. He sees the law as an act of tyranny over the disadvantaged. The trial scene in *The Merchant of Venice* is invoked:

But the acknowledged principle is 'the sense of right and fairness in protecting the interests of the forest owner', which is directly opposed to the sense of right and fairness in protecting the interests of those whose property consists of life, freedom, humanity, and citizenship of the state, who own nothing except themselves.

We have, however, reached a point where the forest owner, in exchange for his piece of wood, receives what was once a human being.

SHYLOCK Most learned judge! – A sentence come, prepare!
PORTIA Tarry a little; there is something else.
This bond doth give thee here no jot of blood;
The words expressly are 'a pound of flesh':
Take then thy bond, take thou thy pound of flesh;
But, in the cutting it, if thou dost shed
One drop of Christian blood, thy lands and goods
Are, by the laws of Venice, confiscate
Unto the state of Venice.
GRATIANO O upright judge! Mark, Jew. O learned judge!
SHYLOCK Is that the law?
PORTIA Thyself shalt see the act.
You, too, should see the act!   (MEW, 1, 256–7)

Marx goes on to argue that the basic reason behind the fine is not punishment for theft but compensation for the owner which is a confusion of the jurisdictions of criminal and civil laws. He argues that the state is not only punishing the thief for his criminal act, but also effectually enslaving him to the wood-owner. Indeed, the latter result is the one primarily intended, which sacrifices 'the immortality of the law' to a landowner's 'finite private interests'. The points are raised by the circumstance of Shylock's bond. The exchange between Shylock and Portia gives Marx a particularly neat example of the law actually protecting the 'rights' of one who seeks to take human life. It also shows the inherent contradictions in such laws, as Portia relentlessly drives home the point that those who invoke the law with such vehemence also must stick to the letter of it. Marx was to return, time and again, to Shylock as an example of the one who, hiding behind the law, dehumanizes others and alienates them into mere property. He uses Shylock also as the example of the creditor who terrifyingly turns his debtor 'into a martyr to exchange value', turning himself 'from religion to jurisprudence. "I STAY HERE ON MY BOND!"' (MEW, 29, 373). Marx also wrote an unsympathetic essay 'On the Jewish Question' where again he uses Shylock to make the point about the way in which money can turn human beings into commodity. S. S. Prawer may be right in making the general point that Marx shows here 'his ability to overlook facts which did not suit his argument' (p. 62), but in condemning Marx for seeing Shylock only from this point of view, he may not give enough justice to Marx's grasp of dramatic context. When Marx writes (quoted by Prawer in a different translation, p. 63), 'For every pound of flesh cut from the heart of the people the historical school of law – Shylock, *but Shylock the bondsman* – swears on its bonds, its historical bond, its Christian-Germanic bond' (MEW, 3, 177; my italics), the phrase 'but Shylock the bondsman' surely implies strongly that Marx could see other sides of the presentation of Shylock. He is choosing to dwell on the mercenary because he is making a more general point about the Hegelian account of German history. Moreover, he is not entirely unfaithful to Shakespeare, even if we need to emphasize that Shylock is what he is in Shakespeare mainly because of the way he has been treated in a dehumanized way by the Christians.

A couple of times Marx uses the bumbling constable of *Much Ado About Nothing* as his 'prototype' for a living person. Lord Malmesbury 'nods assent' several times in a sarcastic sentence before Marx reveals the reference: 'He nods assent in the same way that Dogberry nodded assent to the suggestions of the sexton' (MEW, 16, 523). In writing on 'Electoral Corruption in England' he refers to 'an outrageous Tory, Sir Robert Carden, of Dogberry memory' (MEW, 16, 526). Meanwhile, King George the Fourth is condemned as 'that royal Caliban' (MEW, 14, 670), publishers become 'THOSE CALIBANS' (MEW, 40, 81), and an inscrutable boy he plays chess with is inexplicably referred to as 'the strange Caliban boy' (MEW, 43, 10). In most of these uses of Shakespearian characters, Marx is partly constructing a literary context in which to place a living person, but more pertinently he is quite consciously, in his own word, 'alienating' (or 'estranging') people in order that they can be the more effectively mocked.

The most famous incursion of Marx into Shakespeare studies is his lengthy quotation from *Timon of Athens* in his discussion of money. Well-known as it is, the passage's importance has not been spelled out. It deserves quotation at length. It comes in a series of manuscript notes about the power of money:

[THE POWER OF MONEY]

‖XLI‖ If man's *feelings*, passions, etc., are not merely anthropological phenomena in the [narrower] sense, but truly *ontological* affirmations of being (of nature), and if they are only really affirmed because their *object* exists for them as a *sensual* object, then it is clear that:

(1) They have by no means merely one mode of affirmation, but rather that the distinct character of their existence, of their life, is constituted by the distinct mode of their affirmation. In what manner the object exists for them, is the characteristic mode of their *gratification*.

(2) Wherever the sensuous affirmation is the direct annulment of the object in its independent form (as in eating, drinking, working up of the object, etc.), this is the affirmation of the object.

(3) Insofar as man, and hence also his feeling, etc., is *human*, the affirmation of the object by another is likewise his own gratification.

(4) Only through developed industry – i.e., through the medium of private property – does the ontological essence of human passion come into being, in its totality as well as in its humanity; the science of man is therefore itself a product of man's own practical activity.

(5) The meaning of private property – apart from its estrangement – is the *existence of essential objects* for man, both as objects of enjoyment and as objects of activity.

By possessing the *property* of buying everything, by possessing the property of appropriating all objects, *money* is thus the *object* of eminent possession. The universality of its *property* is the omnipotence of its being. It is therefore regarded as omnipotent . . . Money is the *procurer* between man's

need and the object, between his life and his means of
life. But *that which* mediates *my* life for me, also
mediates the existence of other people for me. For me
it is the *other* person.

> What, man! confound it, hands and feet
> And head and backside, all are yours!
> And what we take while life is sweet,
> Is that to be declared not ours?
>> Six stallions, say, I can afford,
>> Is not their strength my property?
>> I tear along, a sporting lord,
>> As if their legs belonged to me.
>> Goethe: *Faust* (Mephistopheles)

Shakespeare in *Timon of Athens*:

> Gold? Yellow, glittering, precious gold? No,
> Gods,
> I am no idle votarist! . . .
> Thus much of this will make black white,
> foul fair,
> Wrong right, base noble, old young, coward
> valiant.
> . . . Why this
> Will lug your priests and servants from your
> sides,
> Pluck stout men's pillows from below their
> heads:
> This yellow slave
> Will knit and break religions, bless the
> accursed; Make the hoar leprosy adored,
> place thieves
> And give them title, knee and approbation
> With senators on the bench: This is it
> That makes the wappen'd widow wed again;
> She, whom the spital-house and ulcerous sores
> Would cast the gorge at, this embalms and
> spices
> To the April day again. Come, damned earth,
> Thou common whore of mankind, that put'st
> odds
> Among the rout of nations.

And also later:

> O thou sweet king-killer, and dear divorce
> 'Twixt natural son and sire! thou bright
> defiler
> Of Hymen's purest bed! thou valiant Mars!
> Thou ever young, fresh, loved and delicate
> wooer,

> Whose blush doth thaw the consecrated snow
> That lies on Dian's lap! Thou *visible God*!

> That solder'st *close impossibilities*,
> And makest them kiss! That speak'st with
> every tongue,
> ‖XLII‖ To every purpose! O thou touch of
> hearts!
> Think, thy slave man rebels, and by thy
> virtue
> Set them into confounding odds, that beasts
> May have the world in empire!

Shakespeare excellently depicts the real nature of
money. To understand him, let us begin, first of all,
by expounding the passage from Goethe.

That which is for me through the medium of
money – that for which I can pay (i.e., which money
can buy) – that am *I myself*, the possessor of the
money. The extent of the power of money is the
extent of my power. Money's properties are my –
the possessor's – properties and essential powers.
Thus, what I *am* and *am capable of* is by no means
determined by my individuality. I *am* ugly, but I can
buy for myself the *most beautiful* of women. Therefore I am not *ugly*, for the effect of *ugliness* – its
deterrent power – is nullified by money. I, according
to my individual characteristics, am *lame*, but money
furnishes me with twenty-four feet. Therefore I am
not lame. I am bad, dishonest, unscrupulous, stupid;
but money is honoured, and hence its possessor.
Money is the supreme good, therefore its possessor is
good. Money, besides, saves me the trouble of being
dishonest: I am therefore presumed honest. I am
brainless, but money is the *real brain* of all things and
how then should its possessor be brainless? Besides,
he can buy clever people for himself, and is he who
has power over the clever not more clever than the
clever? Do not I, who thanks to money am capable
of *all* that the human heart longs for, possess all
human capacities? Does not my money, therefore,
transform all my incapacities into their contrary?

If *money* is the bond binding me to *human* life,
binding society to me, connecting me with nature
and man, is not money the bond of all *bonds*? Can it
not dissolve and bind all ties? Is it not, therefore, also
the universal *agent of separation*? It is the *coin* that
really *separates* as well as the real *binding agent* – the
[. . .] *chemical* power of society.

Shakespeare stresses especially two properties of
money:

(1) It is the visible divinity – the transformation of all human and natural properties into their contraries, the universal confounding and distorting of things: impossibilities are soldered together by it.

(2) It is the common whore, the common procurer of people and nations.

The distorting and confounding of all human and natural qualities, the fraternisation of impossibilities – the *divine* power of money – lies in its *character* as men's estranged, alienating and self-disposing *species-nature*. Money is the alienated *ability of mankind*.

That which I am unable to do as a *man*, and of which therefore all my individual essential powers are incapable, I am able to do by means of *money*. Money thus turns each of these powers into something which in itself it is not – turns it, that is, into its *contrary*.   (MEW, 3, 323–4)

It seems inconceivable that any modern political or economic scientist would quote at such length from literary figures such as Goethe and Shakespeare, let alone giving their words virtually the status of primary *data*. (The habit was, however, more common in Marx's day, for an English Lord quotes from *Measure for Measure* at length (MEW, 15, 211) and Disraeli alludes to the opposition and government in England as being two Dromios, the identical twins from *The Comedy of Errors* (MEW, 14, 27)). That Marx does so emphatically exemplifies his profound respect for the insight into social processes of poets, especially Shakespeare. Moreover, the passage shows Marx using Shakespeare as primary source, advancing one of his own most central concepts, the alienating and dehumanizing power of money. In the satirical words of the misanthropic Timon, money surpasses the status of an instrument or agency and becomes a god which is universally worshipped. In an article published in 1946 which analyses the passage on *Timon*, Kenneth Muir points out that Marx wrote the piece in 1844 and that

it shows the mind of Marx at work at the turning point of his life, when he was finally converted to Communism. It provides the philosophical basis of Communism which he assumed in his more famous works.[7]

The context of the play as a whole is relevant to Marx's analysis, for Timon is the man who, when he had money, used it plenteously to effect the desires and needs of others, but who, when he is without money, discovers no reciprocal generosity from those he had helped. He grows bitter at the ingratitude of men and the hard power of money, retires to live in the forest, and dies on the margin of the beach. Timon has moved from a positive awareness that 'Money is the *procurer* between man's need and the object, between his life and his means of life' (which has strong implications for Marx's ideas of the commodity value of labour) to the position of seeing men dominated and governed by the '*divine* power' of money, 'its *character* as men's estranged, alienating and self-disposing *species-maker*. Money is the alienated *ability of mankind*'. A little later, Marx describes how money distorts individualities: 'Money, then, appears as this *distorting* power both against the individual and against the bonds of society'. Certainly, these are valid inferences to draw from the fate of Timon, since his own nature changes so drastically and destructively in the transition from wealth to poverty, and these distortions of his individuality inevitably destroy his position within 'the bonds of society'. From his initial popularity and social centrality, he turns to isolated misanthropy. For him, and in Marx's words again, money is the cause of 'self-estrangement', which interferes with and even prevents 'human relations to man' (MEW, 3, 214). Perhaps a revival of the play after the stock exchange crash on 'black Friday' in 1987 might have been timely.

If these manuscript notes are preparatory to a published work, Marx's great *Capital*, the next outcome seems to be the chapter on 'Money' in the original text of *A Contribution to the Critique*

---

[7] Kenneth Muir, '"Timon of Athens" and the Cash-Nexus', *Modern Quarterly Miscellany*, 1 (1946), 57–76.

of Political Economy (MEW, 29, 451–2). The same passage from *Timon* is quoted, accompanied by a brief commentary leading to the conclusion that money 'appears as the universal means of corruption and prostitution'. In another rough draft of the same work, *Outlines of the Critique of Political Economy*, the reference is more pithy:

in other words, the development of exchange values (and of monetary relationships) is identical with general venality, with corruption. General prostitution appears as a necessary phase in the development of the social character of personal inclinations, capacities, abilities, activities. More politely expressed: the universal relationship of utility and usefulness. Equating the incommensurate, as Shakespeare appropriately conceived of money . . .

(MEW, 28, 100)

The particular reference in *Timon* is 'thou visible god, / That sold'rest close impossibilities / And mak'st them kiss!' (4.3.385–6). Yet again Marx was to draw on the same passage in a collaborative work with Engels, *The German Ideology*, when he uses it to show that 'Private property alienates [*entfremdet*] the individuality not only of people but also of things' (MEW, 5, 230). Reference to the passage finally comes, even more briefly, in *Capital*.[8]

Marx developed these central positions which were established with reference to *Timon of Athens* and to *The Merchant of Venice* into his whole critique of capitalism. He came to take the argument along the line that money should be returned to its instrumental function, that labour is worth money, and that there should be a wholesale restructuring of the economic system whereby workers instead of capitalist speculators should directly own the means of production and share the profits. Thereafter, among workers, an egalitarian form of distributive economic justice should apply. It is perhaps curious in this context that Marx did not quote other lines in which a Shakespearian character advocates equal distribution of wealth, since he certainly read the plays in which they occur.[9] Of course, we cannot specu-late about the reasons for Marx's non-use of these lines, but it may be legitimate to make a more positive point about the value of allowing Marx to make us more alert in noticing some new potential in Shakespeare. The passage in *Timon* is clearly not isolated or aberrant in Shakespeare's work, but rather it clarifies at length one of the strains of radical challenge to the prevailing economic system that surfaces sporadically and briefly in a kind of guerrilla warfare in other plays. In this sense, whether he quotes all the available lines or not, Marx has recognized, absorbed and accommodated into his own thinking a form of social and political critique which is in Shakespeare's works. Elements of socialist theory are not imposed by Marx upon an unwilling Shakespearian text, but instead they are embedded in the material of the plays awaiting reconstruction by a reader alert to them.

The evidence I have amassed is the clearest sign we could have that, as with some of Freud's theories,[10] Shakespeare has directly influenced some of the most important, non-literary, theoretical models of the twentieth century. In particular, Marx's idea of alienation (like Brecht's related but different *verfremdungseffekt*) germinated in Shakespeare's presentation of characters guided by mercenary considerations. Kenneth Muir does not exaggerate when he argues that 'Shakespeare was one of the spiritual godparents of the *Communist Manifesto*.'[11]

---

8 Karl Marx, *Capital*, 2 vols. (London, 1930), I, pp. 113, 526, 824.

9 See, for example, *King Lear*, 3.4.26–36, *Coriolanus*, 1.1.14–24 and *passim*, and 4.1.68–72; *The Tempest*, 2.1.141–62. I shall be examining the occurrences in Shakespeare and his contemporaries of notions of distributive justice in a forthcoming book, *Justice: 1575–1625*.

10 See Ludger Lutkehaus, 'Hatte Marx einen Timon-Komplex? Literatur und Theoribildung', *Frankfurter Hefte*, 36 (1981). See also Marjorie Garber, *Shakespeare's Ghost Writers: Literature as Uncanny Causality* (London and New York, 1987).

11 Muir, 'Timon of Athens', p. 76.

PETER STREET, 1553–1609: BUILDER OF PLAYHOUSES

MARY EDMOND

In the sixteenth century the City of London, on the north bank of the Thames, was compassed by a wall 'on the land side, in forme of a bow', in the words of John Stow's *Survey* of 1598. Parts of the wall and the names of its great gates survive, and the modern street called London Wall runs alongside as it always did. At the heart of the City is its seat of government, Guildhall, and just to its east two streets – Basinghall and Coleman – still run north to London Wall. In the mid-sixteenth century this very small area was home for three families with names famous in Elizabethan stage history – Brayne, Burbage and Street.

Thomas Cromwell ordered parish registers to be kept in 1538, and the original paper books of St Michael Bassishaw and St Stephen Coleman Street survive from that date. 'Thomas Broyn and Alys Barlow', the future in-laws of James Burbage, builder of the Theatre in Shoreditch in 1576, were married at St Michael Bassishaw on 22 January 1540/1; and five years later, on 16 May 1546, John Street and Margaret Bullasse, the parents of Peter Street, builder of the Globe and Fortune, were married in the adjoining parish of St Stephen Coleman Street. The Braynes became parishioners of St Stephen's at some stage, and on 23 April 1559 James Burbage married their daughter Ellen – who cannot then have been more than seventeen years old – thus acquiring as brother-in-law the man who was to become his partner, and later sparring-partner, in the Theatre enterprise.[1]

The best-documented of the theatre families of Basinghall and Coleman Streets is undoubtedly that of Peter Street, Citizen of London, freeman of the Carpenters' Company and builder of playhouses. Trades and professions tended to run in families, and it is possible that the Streets had been carpenters and joiners for generations. Between 1389 and 1438 thirty-one wills of 'Citizens and Carpenters' were enrolled, including that of a William Strete dated 1417.[2] A Richard Strete was buried at St Michael Bassishaw on 21 July 1543. Whether these were relations or not, Peter Street had a solid London background: his father John was a Citizen of London and Joiner, and his maternal grandfather Thomas Bullasse a Citizen and Merchant Taylor, and thus a freeman of one of the Great Twelve livery companies. Bullasse died a month after his daughter's marriage to John Street, having bequeathed her two of his best gowns and a feather bed; she seems to have been his only child, which suggests that he died young. He left the rest of his goods to his wife Edith, who

---

[1] The first registers of St Michael's and St Stephen's are MSS 6986 and 4448 respectively. All MSS mentioned in this essay are in Guildhall Library unless otherwise stated. Thomas Brayne was buried at St Stephen's on 20 June 1562. In his original will, written on the 18th – Commissary Court, MS 9172/4B, fo. 91, unsigned – he leaves Alice all his goods to distribute 'as she shall thynke yt good'.

[2] See B. W. E. Alford and T. C. Barker, *A History of the Carpenters' Company* (London, 1968), p. 19.

was appointed executrix of the will, with John Street as supervisor; the principal witness was the 'Vicar perpetuall', Richard Kettell (who signs the register once a year), indicating that Bullasse was a valued parishioner.[3]

In the next fifteen years John and Margaret Street had eight children: Alice (1548–63); Robert (1549–51); William (baptized and buried in July 1552); Peter (1553–1609); Martha (1556–84); Nicholas (1558–9); Agnes (1561–3); and Elizabeth (May to September 1563). Peter's sisters Agnes, Alice and Elizabeth were buried on 17, 18 and 20 September 1563, a bad plague year in which the little parish suffered grievously.

Peter Street was baptized on 1 July 1553; the catholic Queen Mary came to the throne later in the month. Within a year, on 24 May 1554, his father John was involved in a bizarre episode in West Smithfield during a Corpus Christi day procession,[4] when he bumped into – or assaulted – the priest who was walking beneath a canopy and carrying the sacrament, and was haled off to Newgate gaol. With the accession of Queen Elizabeth in 1558, the catholic version of the incident – that the man was a dangerous criminal – was replaced by John Foxe's account, that he was John Street, a 'poor' and 'simple' joiner from Coleman Street, who had been caught up in the procession by mistake and then driven frantic by ill-treatment in prison. There is no need to take the martyrologist's version too seriously: he was telling an anti-catholic horror-story. John Street soon fathered four more children, and far from being 'simple' in the sense of 'simple-minded', was able, as the parish register confirms, to practise his skilled craft of joinery for the rest of his life, until he was carried off by plague in 1563. He was buried on 6 October in the month after his daughters Alice, Agnes and Elizabeth.

Thus Peter Street was left fatherless at the age of ten. On 15 August 1569 his mother married again: 'Willyam Marryt [a widower] and margeret Streete'. In the following year Peter was apprenticed in the Carpenters' Company, for an eight-year term beginning on Lady Day (25 March): his master was William Brittaine.[5] It is noticeable that the Carpenters' apprentices were usually a good deal older than those in other London companies, probably because the work was physically demanding and sometimes dangerous. Assuming that Street was baptized soon after birth, which was customary, he was not quite seventeen at the start of his service, rather young for his company. A good deal of transferring of apprentices – 'translating' or 'turning over' as they said then – went on among carpenters. The master paid 2s 2d on presenting his young man to the court, and if another master later took him over, he paid 12d; 3s 4d was paid at freedom, and the master was fined a further 3s 4d if, within a year and a day, he had not enrolled the new freeman at Guildhall if he intended to practise his craft in or near London. Those who practised elsewhere, or were not freemen, were called 'foreigners'.

In the year after the start of his apprenticeship, Peter Street was taken over by a leading member of the company, Robert Maskall, who freed him on 26 March 1577. (John Griggs, who in 1587 built the Rose for Philip Henslowe, was freed in the following year, on 8 July 1578.)[6]

---

3 Will, Commissary Court, MS 9172/1A, fo. 177, dated 16 June 1546 and proved on 21 June; Bullasse was buried on the 17th.

4 The tale is told in more detail by William Ingram, 'The Early Career of James Burbage', *The Elizabethan Theatre X* (Ontario, 1983), pp. 18–36. I am indebted to Professor Ingram for alerting me to the value of the first St Stephen Coleman Street register.

5 Carpenters' details in this essay are taken from the *Court Minute Books* (which date from 1533), MS 4329 series, and *Wardens' Account Books* (dating from 1438), MS 4326 series. See also *Records of the Worshipful Company of Carpenters* (Oxford and London, 1913–), transcribed and edited by Bower Marsh and others; seven volumes have so far appeared, taking the minutes to 1594 and the accounts to 1614, and more are planned. The introductions give useful general information about the company; the indexes are not always quite accurate.

6 See Mary Edmond, 'The Builder of the Rose Theatre', *Theatre Notebook*, 44 (London, 1990, no. 2), 50–4.

The question now arises: who actually built the Theatre in Shoreditch in 1576? James Burbage, the promoter, was a joiner, not a carpenter, and his brother-in-law and partner John Brayne a grocer; Street (and Griggs) were as yet too young to have been responsible. However, Street had nearly completed his apprenticeship, and Burbage had known him and his family for years, while they were all parishioners of St Stephen Coleman Street.[7] He might well have got Street to help build the Theatre. If he did, it was an obviously sensible decision by Cuthbert Burbage to engage him in 1598–9 to dismantle the playhouse and use the timber to build the Globe – as he did – since Street would have been familiar with the methods and details of the original construction. The most likely candidate for that construction in 1576 would seem to be James Burbage's brother Robert, who had completed his seven-year apprenticeship as a carpenter three years earlier – he was made free on 16 June 1573. Robert became a householder in the large parish of St Giles Cripplegate to the west of Coleman Street, and died in 1584.[8]

Peter Street's career seems to have progressed quickly and successfully. According to the regulations of his company (codified in 1607), a man was liable to be fined if he took an apprentice within three years of his freedom: Street kept to the rules, and took over his first youth (from another master) in 1580. This one seems to have dropped out, and later in the year he took a second. Piecing together details from various Carpenters' records, I conclude that during his career he had dealings, sometimes brief, with twenty-one apprentices in all, of whom he made six free of the City. The majority of apprentices in the company were not from London and its neighbourhood, but were sent up to the capital from more distant parts of the country; most did not complete their terms, but went home at some stage, armed with the prestige of a London training. Their fathers were generally husbandmen, labourers, or small tradesmen – of Street's collection, ten were the sons of husbandmen, from Buckinghamshire, Cambridgeshire, County Durham, Lancashire, Middlesex, Northamptonshire (two), Yorkshire and Wales (two); three the sons of carpenters, in Bedfordshire and Berkshire (two); one father was a Leicestershire shoemaker, and one a cook in County Durham; the callings of three others are unspecified. Only three were London men, a tiler, a merchant tailor, and a carpenter.

In May 1581 Peter Street's mother and stepfather made over to him a house in which they had been living, plus some other property in the parish of St Stephen Coleman Street, described in the standard Latin phraseology as consisting of 'shops, cellars, chambers, rooms' and so on: the stepfather is entered as 'William Marryot Civis et Pandoxator [brewer]'.[9] Street's company owned some houses and gardens adjoining their hall in the parish of Allhallows London Wall, and by 6 August 1581 he was already, at the age of twenty-eight, in a position to acquire a twenty-one year lease of the house previously occupied by his former master Robert Maskall, paying the company the substantial sum of £10. Thereafter, up to and including 1596–7 – the company's official year began in September – he paid an annual rent of forty shillings for the house (except in 1595–6, when he paid eleven shillings.)[10] He

---

[7] Burbage's last child baptized there was Ellen, in 1574, after which he moved to the parish of St Leonard Shoreditch, where his next child, Alice, was baptized in 1576.

[8] Will, MS 25,626/2, fos. 273–273v. He was buried at St Giles' on 17 August 1584, MSS 6418, 6419/1.

[9] Hustings Roll 265/18, Corporation of London Records Office.

[10] On 7 January 1585/6 he had been granted a lease in reversion for thirty years of a company house occupied by John Burton, a currier, but on 18 February he was permitted to give this up and remain in his present one. On the following 9 June it was stated that if he were to 'depart quietly' from it on Christmas Eve 1589, William Taylor, carpenter, could have the rest of the lease; this evidently did not happen, since Street continued to pay the rent until 1596–7.

also paid the company £6 13s 4d for a twenty-one-year lease of one of their gardens from midsummer 1584, and continued to pay annual rent of 9s 10d (19s 10d for two gardens in 1587-8 and 1588-9), until 1602-3. During 1603-4 the company bought back the lease from him for thirty-five shillings, with a further five shillings in the following year.[11]

Street married someone called Elizabeth – not at St Stephen's – in the early 1580s (probably in 1581, when his mother and stepfather transferred the properties to him), for his first son, John, was baptized on 22 March 1583/4. Although he was by then living in the parish of Allhallows London Wall, the baptism was at St Stephen's, the old family parish. (Another son, Peter, was buried there on 17 November 1594.) On 8 April 1584, very shortly after the baptism of Peter's first son, his unmarried sister Martha was buried at St Stephen's, leaving him the sole survivor of the original family of eight. A daughter Margaret was baptized at Allhallows on 2 February (Candlemas) 1585/6, and a daughter Elizabeth on 6 January (Twelfth Night) 1587/8 – she was buried 'in the church porche' on the 12th. Street's stepfather was buried at St Stephen's on the following 29 July.[12]

Within the Carpenters' Company, Street's career was still progressing; in June 1586 he was one of eight men elected to the livery ('clothing') – and although to begin with he declined to serve and was fined forty shillings, it was decided on 13 July that 'for certain considerations' (unspecified) the money should be returned to him, and he duly took up the position in September. His former master Robert Maskall served as Third Warden in 1588-9, as Second for part of 1591-2, and as First Warden from September 1592 until his death six months later. In September 1598 Peter Street became Second Warden, the First being a man of property called John Ansell who lived in the High Street of the parish of St Botolph Aldgate; he had been Third Warden in 1593-4 and Second in 1594-5, and went on to become

Master in 1601-2 and 1606-7.[13] There was no such progression for Peter Street. Unluckily, the company's court minute book for September 1594 to September 1600, covering the most momentous period of his life, is missing, but it can confidently be assumed that they did not take at all kindly to his preoccupation – from the end of 1598 until well into 1600 – with the demolition of the Theatre in Shoreditch, the building of the Globe on Bankside, and the building of the Fortune in the 'liberty' of Finsbury. In 1608, as will be explained later, they accused him (somewhat unfairly) of having persistently neglected company business for years and sought to 'take his ease'.

Andrew Gurr has recently told the intricate story of events in the mid-1590s which led up to the great Globe's being at first conceived as a 'second-best option', and built as a doubtfully legal last-minute gamble by a company facing financial disaster and the lack of any sort of playhouse for itself.[14] James Burbage had built the Theatre in Shoreditch in 1576 on land leased for twenty-one years. Under common law, a building put up on leasehold land belonged to the landowner, and as the date of expiry – 13 April 1597 – approached, Burbage faced daunting problems: the landowner, Giles Allen, refused to extend the lease; three open-air suburban playhouses – the Curtain, Rose, and Swan – now existed in addition to the Theatre, and Burbage may have felt that another would

---

11 MS 4326/5, fos. 81v, 95.

12 Allhallows London Wall register, MS 5083. At the stepfather's burial he is entered as 'Marrett': he died intestate, admon., Commissary Court, MS 9168/14, fo. 164.

13 Maskall was buried at St Peter Cornhill on 31 March 1593, aged fifty-nine, *Harleian Society*, I, p. 140; he died intestate, admon., Archdeaconry Court, MS 9050/2, fo. 108. Ansell's original will, Archdeaconry Court, MS 9052/3D; he was buried at St Botolph's – the entry is in especially prominent writing – on 23 August 1611, MS 9222/1.

14 Andrew Gurr, 'Money or Audiences: The Impact of Shakespeare's Globe', *Theatre Notebook*, 42 (London, 1988, no. 1), 3-14.

be one too many; and the Lord Mayor was firmly opposing playgoing in the City, which lured apprentices from their afternoon's work, so that the companies could no longer use large inns there in the winter.

Burbage conceived what seemed to be a brilliant solution: he laid out the large sum of £600 to buy the Blackfriars property – to avoid future leasehold problems; to evade the Lord Mayor's opposition (Blackfriars, although within the wall, was a 'liberty' exempt from City jurisdiction); and to provide an indoor playhouse, where everyone could be seated and higher prices charged, thus catering mainly for better-off patrons. He had the upper frater at Blackfriars expensively converted: work had begun by the middle of 1596, and the place was almost ready by November. It is reasonable to surmise that to carry out the conversion he engaged Peter Street. Persuasive evidence that both men moved down to the river to supervise can be found in three sets of manuscripts: a parish register, the accounts of the Carpenters' Company, and a lawsuit. Burbage must have moved into Blackfriars precinct itself, for his twenty-two year old daughter Ellen was buried at St Ann's parish church there on 13 December 1596.[15] As for Street: it will be remembered that in 1596–7 he left the house which he had rented from the Carpenters' Company for fifteen years; and a Court of Requests suit, also of 1596–7, clearly indicates that he moved to Bridewell precinct, on the west bank of the Fleet, and in those days linked to Blackfriars on the other side by a wooden footbridge.[16] (Bridewell, a royal palace built by Henry VIII, had been given to the City by Edward VI for use as a house of correction.)

The lawsuit consists mainly of a long Bill of Complaint, addressed to the Queen by Street, who describes himself as 'one of yor graces ordynary servants in yor ma^{ts} household'. He says that on about 6 March he had been 'desirous to take the Lease of some Woodwharf nere the Ryver of Thames and the rather for that yt would be a great ease for him to bringe his

Tymber and fframes which he bought and framed [prepared] in the Countrie by water to his owne house' – much better than carting them to the City on the notoriously bad Elizabethan roads. Accompanied by a middleman, William Dodd, Street went to see a woodmonger called Thomas Hill who rented a house and wharf near Bridewell stairs belonging to the masters of Bridewell. According to Street, Hill promised to secure for him a twenty-one year lease of the house, at the annual rent of £22 which he was paying himself, plus the wharf and a twenty-foot piece of waste ground adjoining it. Street in return would pay Hill £60, £40 at once and the remaining £20 when the transaction was completed. Next day he returned with the £40 – at which Hill 'presentlie went to his Chamber & sickened and wthin three or four daies died'. This must have been in June.[17] Street, 'perceiving himself to stand in a doubtful estate', immediately went to the widow, Margery, and urged her to carry out her husband's undertakings. Margery soon married a butcher called Simon Neale, and the couple tried (unsuccessfully) to sue Street in the Court of King's Bench for the £20 as yet unpaid (Street dates this attempt to the Michaelmas law term, and Neale to about fourteen days before Christmas).

It is clear that Street did take possession of the house, because he complains that if he 'contynewe' in possession, he will have to take a new lease from Bridewell, and pay a 'great fine' of £110, plus £15 more in rent than Hill had been doing. He also risks losing the £40 paid to Hill, and £3 to the middleman, Dodd.

---

[15] MS 4510/1: the page on which Ellen's burial entry appears is wrongly headed '1595' instead of 1596.

[16] Req. 2/91/57, Public Record Office. I am grateful to William Ingram for giving me the reference. For Bridewell, John Stow, *A Survey of London*, 2 vols., ed. C. L. Kingsford (Oxford, 1908), vol. 1, pp. 27, 40, 70; vol. 2, pp. 43–5.

[17] Hill died intestate, admon., Commissary Court, MS 9168/15, fo. 68v, relict Margery, dated 17 June 1596.

The Bill is accompanied by the 'joint and several Answers' of Neale and Margery, Margery's brother-in-law Robert Hill, and the middleman; Neale is the principal defendant, but confesses that he has no firsthand knowledge of the events in question. He pinpoints the house and woodwharf, described by Street as being near Bridewell stairs, as actually 'adioyning, & p[ar]-cell of the howse and scite of Bridewell' itself. (The present Bridewell Place covers the site, and the Fleet flows down underneath the roadway.) Having disputed at length the account in the Bill of what had gone on, he concedes that Margery (before he married her) had been afraid that she might break undertakings given by her late husband, and so had quickly yielded up the house to Street, 'wch he ev[er] sithens & yet inoiyeth as she thinketh'. The defendants end by accusing Street of having told two courts that he was the Queen's servant, and a third that he was servant to the Lord Chief Baron of the Exchequer, seeking under those titles 'lewdly to protect' his dishonest practices.[18]

At exactly this time James Burbage died, probably at the end of January: he was buried at his old parish church of St Leonard Shoreditch on 2 February[19] – the day after Simon Neale and his co-defendants put in their Answers to Peter Street's Bill of Complaint in the Court of Requests. Burbage's sons Cuthbert, aged thirty-one, and Richard, twenty-eight, now inherited all their father's problems. The Lord Chamberlain (the first Lord Hunsdon), a loyal and active patron of their company, had died on the previous 23 July, and his successor was less sympathetic; and in November the Blackfriars project had been finally blocked, by opposition from influential residents of the precinct who petitioned the Privy Council. The Theatre lease would expire in a matter of weeks, and the Burbages had to look urgently for another playing place.

In December 1598, they took out a thirty-one year lease on a vacant site across the river on Bankside, near the Rose and Swan, and determined to dismantle the Theatre and re-use its timber. The audacious deed was done by Peter Street, as 'Cheefe carpenter', and took place during the Christmas season of 1598–9, while everyone was preoccupied with the festivities and the ground landlord, Allen, was away at his house in Essex.[20] The Burbages had of course known Street all their lives (Cuthbert was baptized at St Stephen Coleman Street on 15 June 1565 – twelve years after Street – and Richard on 7 July 1568); and Cuthbert, the company's business manager, confirms that Street acted on his own 'direction and Comaundement'. There can be no doubt that he also commissioned Street to build the Globe (Griggs, builder of the Rose, had recently died, probably in the summer of 1598).[21] Half the

---

18 A lay subsidy entry of 1593 – on a single sheet – relating to the royal household, E115/349/87, PRO, refers to a Peter Street 'Servitor of Thawle', rated at £5 in goods and 'abyding here at the Courte' at taxation time. There is no way of telling whether this was the carpenter: if it was, he was perhaps lodging there while doing some special taskwork.

19 He is usually said to have died in February, but the end of January is much more likely – especially as the body had to be taken from Blackfriars to Shoreditch.

20 The timbers would have been transported on waggons by the direct route to the river (Shoreditch High Street, Bishopsgate and Gracechurch Street), but it seems unlikely that the waggons would have gone across the bridge, as is often assumed. Charlotte Carmichael Stopes, *Burbage and Shakespeare's Stage* (London, 1913), p. 75 (with a slightly inaccurate reference in f/n. 1), noted Street's Bill of Complaint about his woodwharf: she makes the point that the bridge gates would have been closed at night, and that there were heavy tolls for 'wheelage and poundage' at all times, which would have meant delays and questions. It is much more likely that the timbers were transferred to barges for the crossing to Bankside – but not from Street's own wharf at Bridewell upstream (as Mrs Stopes favours), but from another one engaged close to the bridge. Either Drinkwater Wharf or Fish Wharf, for which see Stow, *A Survey of London*, vol. 1, p. 215, is the most probable. The whole operation must have been complicated and time-consuming, and could not have gone unnoticed.

21 Edmond, 'The Builder of the Rose Theatre', p. 52 and p. 54, n12. His burial is noted first, St Margaret New Fish Street, *Churchwardens' accounts 1577–1678*, MS 1176/1, in a list for the year beginning 25 March 1598.

money for the enterprise was put up by the Burbages, and the other half in equal parts by Shakespeare, Will Kempe, John Heminges, Thomas Pope and Augustine Phillips (Kempe left the company at the end of 1599 and the other four took his share). The players now controlled policy for the operation of their playhouse.

Cuthbert Burbage would have conferred with his brother Richard the company's leading actor, their playwright Shakespeare, and their builder Street, on the precise design of the new theatre; and Street no doubt employed in his team some at least of the six apprentices whom he made freemen of the City during his career. From the Carpenters' records I have collected these names and details:

1 *George Bromley*: son of Robert, Citizen of London and freeman of the Tylers' and Bricklayers' Company; presented, aged twenty, for a seven-year term beginning on 30 November 1580; freed on 19 January 1587/8. (This family were neighbours: George was baptized at St Stephen Coleman Street on 23 March 1560/1 – in the same year as Peter Street's sister Agnes – and buried there on 29 October 1607, MS 4449/1; he died intestate, relict Margaret, admon., 3 November, Commissary Court, MS 9168/16, fo. 56.)

2 *Richard Radforth*: son of Robert, shoemaker of Hallaton in Leicestershire; presented, aged eighteen, for a seven-year term beginning on 25 March 1582, by John Fitzjohn (an important member of the company, Beadle and later Clerk); taken over by Street in the following February and freed on 14 May 1590.

3 *William Smyth*: son of George of Linton near Cambridge, husbandman; presented, aged seventeen, on 29 July 1589 for an eight-year term beginning on 1 August; freed, presumably by Street (the court minutes are lost) in 1597–8, when the accounts show that the required 3s 4d was paid.

4 *Ellis Curtis*: son of John of Basildon in Berkshire, carpenter; presented, aged twenty, by

John Hopkins senior on 27 November 1586 for a seven-year term beginning on 1 November; taken over by Street on 17 December 1590 and freed on 28 January 1593/4. (Parishioner of St Alphage London Wall near Carpenters' Hall, died intestate in 1600, relict Joyce, admon., 12 April, Archdeaconry Court, MS 9050/3, fo. 127v.)

5 *Austin/Augustine Drye*: son of Robert, a deceased husbandman of Hellidon in Northamptonshire; presented, aged twenty, by Street for a seven-year term beginning on 1 November 1590; freed, presumably by Street (court minutes lacking) in 1598–9, when the accounts show that the required 3s 4d was paid. (Parishioner of St Botolph Aldersgate, died intestate in 1626, admon., Archdeaconry Court, MS 9050/5, fo. 225v.)

6 *William Blackborne*: origin and age unknown, but presented by Henry Allen for a seven-year term on 23 April 1595; taken over by Street in 1595–6 (court minutes lacking), and freed on 19 October 1602. He appears in Henslowe's *Diary* as 'm^r stretes man'.[22]

Street completed the Globe during 1599 – it was open by 21 September, when the Swiss visitor Thomas Platter saw a performance of *Julius Caesar*, presumed to be Shakespeare's play.[23] By the end of the year, he was being employed by Philip Henslowe of the rival company, the Admiral's men, 'for bylldinge of my howsse vpon the banksyd wch was goodman deres'. His accounts for this work[24] include

---

[22] It was certainly William who was apprenticed by Henry Allen on St George's Day 1595 (accounts, MS 4326/5, fo. 11v – minutes lacking); by 1602, when he was freed by Peter Street, a new and less meticulous Clerk had taken over the court minute book, and Blackborne is entered as an otherwise unrecorded 'Christopher'. Some miscellaneous uncalendared court notes, relating to forthcoming meetings, MS 7784/2, fos. 3–9, confirm that the new freeman was indeed William.

[23] Gurr, 'Money or Audiences', p. 13, n12, notes that Platter's 'house with the thatched roof' might possibly mean the Rose rather than the Globe.

[24] *Henslowe's Diary*, ed. R. A. Foakes and R. T. Rickert (Cambridge, 1961), pp. 66–7.

seven entries about advances of money to Street himself, five to one of his employees 'goodman grimes', and two to his man Blackborne.

The Globe stood across Maiden Lane (now Park Street) from Henslowe's smaller Rose built twelve years earlier; its resident company the Chamberlain's men, with their leading actor Richard Burbage and playwright William Shakespeare, quite overshadowed Henslowe's Admiral's men. The Chamberlain's, debarred from acquiring a playing place in Blackfriars precinct, had moved across the river to the south bank: faced with this powerful competition, Alleyn and his father-in-law now moved from south to north, Alleyn leasing a plot of land (near our modern Barbican complex) in the parish of St Giles Cripplegate and liberty of Finsbury. By contract dated 8 January between Alleyn, Henslowe and Street,[25] the master carpenter undertook to build a theatre to be called the Fortune, supplying the men and materials and completing the work by 25 July: the cost was set at £440, and the building was to incorporate major features of the Globe, although this time to be square instead of round. Street is instructed to use 'good stronge and substancyall newe Tymber', implied criticism perhaps of the rival Globe's re-used wood.

Henslowe's accounts for the first part of 1600[26] – which supply the names of a number of the men taken on by Street – relate mostly to his activities in the country, where he spent about five months selecting and preparing his timber for the playhouse. He was presumably somewhere in Berkshire, since Maidenhead and Windsor are mentioned. In those days, builders in wood often did much of their preparatory work – involving a good deal of what we would call prefabrication – at a 'framing place': there timber could be dressed, cut, jointed and numbered, and joints tested for a good fit. The framing place might be some way away from the building site, and could provide better security for materials and tools and more room for manoeuvre.[27]

Street would have sent his prepared timber down-stream by barge – Henslowe mentions one bargeman called Richard Deller appointed by him – for unloading at his woodwharf at Bridewell acquired four years earlier. Edward Alleyn visited him at the framing place in mid-February, to see how things were going, and at the end of the month, Henslowe and his son-in-law both went down – £10 was paid 'when we wente into the contrey to mʳ strete hime sellfe'. A boy called Robert Wharton employed by Street, and later to be formally apprenticed, was evidently very reliable, for there are several references in the accounts to his taking a total of more than £44 from Henslowe to Street (on several trips), and one reference to Street's boy William Wharton, probably Robert's younger brother. Street's man Blackborne also appears once, taking £5. Towards the end of March Street makes his mark, 'P S', on the accounts to date, acknowledging receipt of the large sum of £180 18s 0d. The references to Robert and William Wharton suggest that promising boys were sometimes taken on unofficially by carpenters to do odd jobs until they were adjudged old and strong enough to be apprenticed.

An important day, when work in the country was nearing its end, was 8 May, when Henslowe paid £4 7s 0d to 'the carpenters wᶜʰ came from winser', £3 8s 0d to the labourers in London 'at the eand of the fowndations' of the playhouse in Finsbury, and ten shillings to Street. On 23 May £5 12s 8d was paid 'in yᵉ cuntrye to dyvers'; on Saturday the 24th Robert Wharton took down £6 14s 0d for wages; on Saturday the 31st Henslowe paid £8 for 'wages, sa[w]yers & carege & strete'; and finally on Saturday 7 June, a further £8 'for wagis & sawyers & cartes'. That presumably marked the end of the out-of-town operation.

---

[25] For the terms of the contract, *ibid.*, pp. 306–10.

[26] *Ibid.*, pp. 310–15.

[27] John Orrell, *The Human Stage: English Theatre Design 1567–1640* (Cambridge, 1988), pp. 24, 41–2 and 261–2, n45.

The accounts overlap slightly in date with the second batch,[28] which – in Henslowe's words – constitute 'A not[e] what I haue layd owte sence we went a bowt ower new howsse' as the Fortune rose above ground in Finsbury. An early undated entry, which seems in context to belong to the end of May, notes two shillings spent 'at the Rede crosse for brackfaste when we sowght strete' – perhaps the intended meeting-place on his return to the capital. From the beginning of June all the entries clearly relate to London. On 2, 3 and 4 June Henslowe and Street had dinner together, and on 5 June they were joined by Gilbert East, whom Henslowe calls 'my bayllefe'.[29] The earlier accounts show that on the 5th, Henslowe also lent Street £4 'to fetche his hores frome mr Ierlandes owt of pane [pawn]'. Next day he gave Street fifteen shillings to buy cartwheels – perhaps to transport timber from Bridewell to Finsbury; and a final entry in the first accounts, dated 10 June, notes payment of four shillings to Street 'to pasify hym'.

Henslowe and Street continued to have dinner together, usually in company with East, very often during June and July, and into August up to and including the 8th. These would have been midday meals, the equivalent of pub lunches, taken no doubt at inns or taverns near the theatre site. Street probably lodged in the parish for convenience during the Fortune period, for a son Edward (perhaps Alleyn was his godfather) was buried at St Giles Cripplegate on 29 November.[30]

After Street's playhouse activities were over, he resumed more regular company work, attending a few court meetings and presenting more apprentices. The first of these was Robert Wharton, presented (age not given) on 19 January 1601/2, for a seven-year term beginning at Candlemas (2 February); he is described as son of George, a deceased cook of County Durham. Street also presented a second youth from Durham (who seems not to have completed his term) in 1602, two from Wales in 1605, and the sons of two London men in 1606

and 1609. The Welshmen, both from Brecknock, were presented on the same day – 21 February 1604/5 – Griffith Morris, son of Thomas of St Clements, husbandman, and John Pryce, son of Ryce of Llanvihanell, deceased husbandman, both for seven-year terms. Some of these young men were probably employed by Street in 1606 on building a new gatehouse for the Beargarden on Bankside, commissioned by Henslowe and Alleyn at a total cost of £65.[31]

At this period, in the early years of James I's reign, there was much theatrical activity at court. In the reign of Elizabeth, professional companies had travelled upstream from the City from time to time by royal command to provide the principal entertainments, and this continued; but now a new form of show was developed – the masque in which members of the court themselves participated. The first, *The Masque of Blackness*, written and presented by Ben Jonson and Inigo Jones, was staged in August 1605, while Simon Basil was Comptroller of the Office of the Royal Works. The Office, then the most ambitious building

28 *Diary*, pp. 191–3.
29 Ibid., p. 245.
30 MS 6419/1.
31 Wharton's presentment, MS 4329/3, fo. 22; Thomas Browne, the other County Durham youth, had been presented on 20 January 1601/2 – apparently by another master – but was paid for by Street, 19 October 1602, fo. 41; for Morris and Pryce, fo. 90. A John *Price* was presented in the same year (by William Smith), and there is some confusion over the two in *Records*, VII, pp. 226, 231; Street's man is not indexed under his own name or his master's. The Welsh apprentices were freed by Street's widow Elizabeth in 1612 – Pryce on 20 May, William Kinge, carpenter, testifying his service, and Morris on 10 December, service testified by her son John, MS 4329/3, fos. 269v, 291v.

For the Beargarden gatehouse, see *Henslowe Papers: Being Documents Supplementary to Henslowe's Diary*, ed. Walter W. Greg (1907), pp. 102–3; and W. J. Lawrence and Walter H. Godfrey, 'The Bear Garden contract of 1606 and What it Implies', *The Architectural Review*, 47 (1920), 152–5. I am grateful to John Orrell for drawing my attention to this article.

organization in England, had its main centre in the building-yard at Whitehall: its head, the Surveyor – an office to which Basil was to succeed in April 1606 – was in supreme charge of all building operations; next came the Comptroller with his clerks, responsible for administration and finance, but by origin an artificer; the practising artificers worked to the Master Carpenter, Master Joiner, Serjeant Plumber and so on.[32]

In January 1605, a few months before *Blackness* was put on at Whitehall Palace, the Office had set up a temporary theatre in the Hall of Christ Church, for plays to be performed during a visit to Oxford by the King and his court: according to an anonymous Cambridge visitor, Basil and two of his senior carpenters travelled up for the occasion – as did Inigo Jones, who had as yet no formal connection with the Office of Works. The theatre is described by John Orrell as 'the first adequately documented neo-Roman theatre in England', and a surviving drawing shows that Basil had studied Sebastiano Serlio's *Architettura*. Orrell argues that the London builders of the Theatre, the Curtain, and the Rose, and James Burbage in his 1596 adaptation of the upper frater at Blackfriars, had been engaged – whether or not they too knew of Serlio – in a similar rediscovery of ancient classical forms suited to modern conditions. He writes at length about the pervasive influence of Serlio on English builders and surveyors generally, and suggests that Peter Street, as a major figure in the Carpenters' Company and accomplished London builder, may have been aware of Serlian designs.[33]

The year 1606 saw the start – probably in October – of a building project at Whitehall Palace marking a conspicuous departure from tradition, in which Street had a part. The King, always a lavish spender, ordered a banqueting house to replace the third and last Elizabethan one, dating from 1581; in the past such places had generally been used for serving light refreshments on special occasions in informal surroundings, but the first Jacobean version was to be a permanent building of brick and stone, to provide a fit setting for the splendid masques patronized by Queen Anne, and it was to incorporate classical features, columns in two orders, Doric and Ionic – something entirely new. The great majority of craftsmen, listed in the annual Works accounts, who were employed at the royal palaces and houses, remain anonymous; but a short list of special 'rewards' paid out in connection with the Banqueting House includes one to Peter Street. The ordinary carpenters presumably had neither the expertise nor the range of sophisticated tools to cope with large classical columns, so twenty shillings was paid to Street, at four shillings the piece, 'for the lone of v^e greate pumpaugurs for boringe the greate Collumbes'. That he was able to lend five of these is an indication of the size of his own business. The pump auger, as its name implies, was generally used for making pumps and hollowing out wooden water-pipes; it consisted of a long iron rod with a T-shaped handle at one end and the boring device (bit) at the other. The rod was propped horizontally on a forked post, and two men turned the handle while a third directed the bit into the centre of a log laid on trestles. Augers of ascending size were used to enlarge the initial hole – the object of their use being to bore out the core of the columns so that as they shrank they would not split. The columns of the Banqueting House were painted to look like stone or marble, by men working to the Serjeant-Painter, John de Critz.

The building was inaugurated on 10 January 1607/8, with a performance of Ben Jonson's *Masque of Beauty*, and the accounts include a long introductory passage describing the temporary structures erected for the occasion:

---

[32] Mark Girouard, *Robert Smythson & The Elizabethan Country House* (Yale, New Haven and London, 1983), p. 7.

[33] John Orrell, *The Human Stage*, pp. 119–29, 155, 157–63, 201.

these included 'a greate stage . . . wth a floore in the middle of the same . . . wth sondry devices [stage machinery] . . . sondry seates above for the Queene and Ladies to sett on . . . a halfepace [platform] vnder the Kings state [throne] and a greate nomber of Degrees [benches] on both sides of the saide house with railes before the same . . .'[34] The erection and dismantling of all this was under the direction of the Master Carpenter, William Portington; it is possible that the master builder of playhouses, Peter Street, was called in to assist, on this and other occasions, although evidence has yet to be found.

The two masques, *Blackness* and *Beauty*, were published together in 1608. Jonson, in the text, commends Jones for his work on the former, and Portington for the latter – 'The order of this *Scene* was carefully and ingeniously dispos'd; and as happily put in act (for the *Motions* [stage machinery]) by the *Kings Master Carpenter*.'[35]

Orrell believes that Simon Basil must have known Peter Street. By the seventeenth century the Carpenters' Company in the City of London had ceased to have any formal connection with the royal appointments of King's Carpenter and Surveyor of the Works at Westminster – although the Office staff would obviously have known about playhouse activities downstream in London; and the Carpenters' nineteenth-century historian specifically notes that they 'claim no connection' with Simon Basil. However, the company took great care to foster friendly and informal relations; the King's Carpenter, in particular, was 'regularly visited, consulted and dined'. Whenever the company exercised their powers of search beyond the City boundaries, they had to give notice to the King's Carpenter so that he could attend if he wished – which Mr Portington often did.[36] The company's accounts often mention dinners with him at places such as the Greyhound in the Strand and the Swan at Charing Cross, and there was boat-hire to fetch him and his wife to election dinners. The

inscription accompanying a contemporary portrait of Portington, still hanging at Carpenters' Hall, describes him as 'a well wisher in this Societe'. He and Peter Street, as a leading member of the company, would certainly have known each other well, and I think that the professional approach to Street for the loan of the pump augers would have come from Portington rather than Basil.

The first Jacobean Banqueting House had a life of only eleven years: it was burnt down in 1619 – to be rapidly succeeded by Inigo Jones's masterpiece, which still stands. Peter Street may well have been present at the inauguration of the first one in January 1608.

In the following July, and then in February and April 1609, he figures again in official documents: and at a time when such records usually tended to be impersonal, they provide welcome insight into his character, and suggest that he was a man of quick and forceful temper. He was now in his fifty-sixth year, and the last few months of his life, and it may be that the records also indicate a man in failing health.

On 26 July 1608, the court of the Carpenters' Company, meeting as usual at their hall, were in a state of high indignation: in one long, vehement, unpunctuated sentence, the Clerk

---

[34] Works accounts, E351/3242 (1 October 1606–30 September 1607) and E351/3243 (1 October 1607–31 March 1609); *The History of the King's Works*, ed. H. M. Colvin, 4 (1485–1660), Part 2 (HMSO, 1982), pp. 322–5, 339; and R. A. Salaman, *Dictionary of Tools used in the Woodworking and Allied Trades, c. 1700–1970* (London, 1975), pp. 38, 296–8 and Fig. 444a. The reference to the pump augers is quoted by John Orrell, *The Quest for Shakespeare's Globe* (Cambridge, 1983), p. 109, and *Human Stage*, p. 160.

[35] *The Characters of Two royall Masques* (London, 1608). The author's inscribed presentation copy for Queen Anne is in the British Library, c.34.d.4.

[36] E. B. Jupp (the then Clerk of the company), *An Historical Account of the Worshipful Company of Carpenters of the City of London* (London, second edn, 1887), pp. 170, 171 (the portrait), 180; and Alford and Barker, *A History of the Carpenters' Company*, at n2, pp. 89 and 248, n84. Portington was Master Carpenter for forty years.

recorded that Street had 'abused in words . . . at severall tymes' the Master and Wardens; had ignored orders to attend that day and gone away 'in contempt being commaunded to staye', and refused to come back when Mr Cockshutt (John Cockshutt, Third Warden) was sent after him; and was therefore being committed to prison, 'there to remayne vntill he submitt himself according to the ordinance of this howse'.[37]

On the same day – Tuesday 26 July – another meeting, of the Court of Aldermen, was taking place at Guildhall, and their minutes tell a very different story. They noted that Street had been admitted to the freedom of the City when he completed his apprenticeship in 1577, since when he had made 'six several apprentices free of this City', and had been Second Warden of the company, 'and of the Assistants and livery many years'. Yet he had been unable to find any record of his freedom in the City Chamberlain's office. The Aldermen conceded that there must have been 'negligence' by the then Clerk of the Chamber in 1577, and ordered that an appropriate entry be made in the books 'as it should have been at the first', and a copy given to Street, 'whereby the freedom to his son and servants may be confirmed'.[38]

The word of the Aldermen was law, and on 3 August Street's son John paid his 3s 4d and was made a freeman of the Carpenters' Company by patrimony. On the 9th the company's court, with rather ill grace, declared that since September 1598, when Peter Street became Second Warden (that is, shortly before he went off to dismantle the Theatre and build the Globe), 'he hath not made his appearance as other the assistants but hath heretofore requested to be forbourne & that he might take his ease'. (Attendance by assistants was voluntary, and the minutes show that he did in fact attend at least six court meetings between October 1602 and August 1607.) The court noted that he now 'desired to be admitted an assistant as in former time he had been and that he would make his appearance hereafter', and ordered

that he be admitted under the junior Warden, Mr Cockshutt.[39]

At a meeting on 8 February 1608/9, Street presented an apprentice called Robert Twentyman, son of a London carpenter, Richard of the parish of St Clement Danes, for a seven-year term.[40] The court also acted on a forceful complaint from Street about John Lipscombe, son of a Berkshire carpenter, who must have broken records for 'translations': having been first apprenticed in 1605, Street was his third master – and he was now punished 'for resisting and overthrowing his m^r at Sondry tymes when he offered him Correccion for his faultes, for Stealing his m^r his boordes and Conveying them awaye', for concealing stolen lead 'for wch Mr Street was fayne to paye', and for other offences. A terse entry in the accounts notes payment of eight pence to the Beadle 'for Carrying John Lipscomb to Bridewell' for punishment.[41] After Street's death, Richard Thomlinson took Lipscombe over from his widow, agreeing to pay her four shillings a month for the rest of his term, or if she should remarry, to pay the money to the company, for the relief of poor members. Lipscombe was finally freed in 1612 by yet another master.[42]

On 5 April 1609 Peter Street attended his last company meeting, and the court received due payment of 3s 4d for the freeing of his former

[37] MS 4329/3, fos. 167–167v.

[38] Aldermen's *Repertory 28*, fo. 258, Corporation of London Records Office.

[39] Minutes, MS 4329/3 – John's patrimony, fo. 169; court meeting, fos. 170–170v; Peter attending earlier meetings of the court, fos. 41v, 59, 64, 68v, 90, 134v.

[40] Presentment, MS 4329/3, fo. 181v. John Street paid 12d on 20 April 1614 to take him over, and freed him on 15 May 1616, MS 4329/3, fos. 322, 375v and MS 4326/7, fo. 19v.

[41] Lipscombe's presentment, *Records*, VII, p. 232; taking over by Street on 24 December 1606, MS 4329/3, fo. 127v; Street's complaint, *ibid.*, fo. 182 and payment to the Beadle, *Records*, VII, p. 367.

[42] Thomlinson's agreement with Mrs Street on 12 December 1609, MS 4329/3, fo. 205; Lipscombe's freedom on 23 September 1612, *ibid.*, fo. 287.

boy, Robert Wharton. But the Clerk squeezed in an extra note recording that 'Mr Streetes man was not enrolled [at Guildhall] and Mr Streete vtterlye refused to paye his suretye but required to have his other monney againe and his man should rem[ain] a fforrener'. The accounts confirm that Street did in fact pay 'nihil'. However, Wharton did become a freeman of the London company, and was still living in 1647 – when he had the misfortune to fall off a ladder.[43]

In August 1608 the Blackfriars playhouse had finally come into the possession of Shakespeare's company, now the King's Men. The Burbage brothers had been making some money from it since 1600 by leasing it to the managers of a boy company – who were in trouble by 1608; and this time the residents of Blackfriars precinct raised no objection. On 9 August Shakespeare, Heminges, Will Sly and Henry Condell joined the Burbages and a financier, Thomas Evans, to sign a co-partnership paper.[44] It must be more than probable that Peter Street was once again contracted to adapt the premises to the company's requirements, and the assumption is supported by the fact that he actually died in Blackfriars – in May 1609, a month after freeing Robert Wharton.[45] The body was carried across the Fleet to St Bride Fleet Street (the parish in which Bridewell stood) for burial on Saturday 13 May: the entry reads 'Peter Streat, Carpenter'. Quite a lot of the court minutes of Bridewell Royal Hospital are lost, but luckily not the ones for 1609, and they show that there was a meeting on the day of the funeral. One piece of business is minuted thus:

John Streete sonne of Peter Streete deceased late the Carpenter to this hospitall vpon his humble peticon in that behalfe exhibited, Is by a full Consent of this whole Court elected and admitted Carpenter to this hospitall in his fathers place: And by full consent it is ordered / That he (useinge his mother well and beinge helpefull vnto her) shall enioye the said place and have the ffees & p[ro]fittes of the same, in as ample manner as his said father or any other p[re]cedinge Carpenter to this hospitall hath had or enioyed.[46]

Shakespeare's company opened their new winter house in the autumn of 1609 – the first time that any adult company had been able to do such a thing. Thus Peter Street missed by a matter of weeks one of the most important events in English dramatic history – the move from the medieval open-air stage to the ancestor of all modern indoor theatres. His own two open-air houses, the first Globe and the first Fortune, were soon destroyed by fire – the Globe in 1613 and the Fortune in 1621.

His widow Elizabeth was buried at St Bride's on 7 April 1613: 'A wydowe, m^rs streete'. She is one of very few women parishioners there at this period to be accorded the title 'Mistress'.

Her son John, as we now know, had inherited valuable property and perquisites from his father at Bridewell Royal Hospital. He carried on his career within the Carpenters' Company, helping his mother to train Peter's late apprentices, freeing the last of them, Robert Twentyman, in 1616, and also taking two or three of his own. The most interesting case, illustrating as it does how closeknit was the world of the London theatre, is that of Richard Pennyale/ Peniall, son of Simon, Citizen and Saddler of London, whom Street took on for an eightyear term at Michaelmas (29 September) 1611. This youth was a brother-in-law of John

---

[43] For Wharton's presentment and freedom, MS 4329/3, fos. 22, 184v; for the accident, MS 4326/7, fo. 370v, where it is noted that on 30 July 1647 Wharton, 'a poore brother of this Company', was paid twenty shillings 'in Charity haveing gotten a fall of[f] a lather'; I am grateful to the present Beadle, Mr Dutton, for this reference.

[44] Gurr, 'Money or Audiences', pp. 8–9.

[45] St Bride's burial register, MS 6538; Street died intestate, admon., Commissary Court, MS 9168/16, fo. 87v.

[46] MS 513, vol. 5, fo. 347. One gap in the minutes is between November 1579 and February 1597/8, so there is no way of looking up Peter Street's acquisition of the house and woodwharf in 1596.

Webster – the dramatist had married his sister Sara in 1606.[47]

At this period the London companies were being required to contribute to the plantation of Ireland, and between March 1611 and September 1613 John Street made three payments totalling 13s 10d – an average amount. His last appearance in the Carpenters' records is in March 1620, when he paid 2s 2d to present an apprentice called John Willson, son of a Lincolnshire miller, for a seven-year term; he died intestate in the autumn, still a parishioner of St Bride's, leaving a widow Ann. A John Street had married Ann Agar at St Botolph Bishops-gate on 12 June 1608 (the year in which Peter's son secured his freedom by patrimony).[48]

---

[47] Richard Pennyale's baptism at St Bride's on 27 June 1594, MS 6536; presentment by John Street, MS 4329/3, fo. 261v and *Records*, VII, p. 412; freedom in 1619, MS 4329/4, fo. 25 and 4326/7, fo. 73. See also Mary Edmond, 'In Search of John Webster', *TLS*, 24 December 1976 and letter, 24 October 1980, and M. C. Bradbrook, *John Webster: Citizen and Dramatist* (London, 1980), pp. 1, 17 and pedigree, pp. 204–5.

[48] Plantation of Ireland, MS 4329/3, fos. 238, 309, 309v; presentment of John Willson, MS 4329/4, fo. 27v; admon., PRO, PCC Prob. 6/10, fo. 87, dated 4 October; possible marriage at St Botolph Bishopsgate, MS 4515/1. There is no burial entry in the St Bride's register.

SHAKESPEARE PERFORMANCES IN ENGLAND 1990–1

PETER HOLLAND

In 1933, reviewing a production of *Twelfth Night*, Virginia Woolf announced,

Shakespeareans are divided, it is well known, into three classes; those who prefer to read Shakespeare in the book; those who prefer to see him acted on the stage; and those who run perpetually from book to stage gathering plunder.[1]

Applied to the work of critics, her image of the last group of Shakespearians in ceaseless motion suggests a group of the damned in a circle of Dante's *Inferno*. Those of us committed to what is now labelled stage-centred or performance-oriented criticism scurry to and fro, risking finding, like most looters, that much of our booty turns out to be useless and worthless: as one of the soldiers curses, while plundering the battlefield in *Coriolanus*, 'A murrain on't, I took this for silver' (1.6.3).

Critics often complain about the taxonomic systems used for Shakespeare. Dissatisfied with F1's 'comedies, histories, tragedies', bored with divisions like 'the major tragedies', 'the problem plays' or 'the romances', we try to find new and invigorating sub-divisions of the canon, new juxtapositions designed to illuminate the perceived relationships of texts. My major piece of plunder from this year's stint of reviewing is a new system for grouping Shakespeare plays. If my system is, like any other ever offered, neither cast-iron nor water-tight, as plays seem to demand awkwardly to belong to more than one group, it is at least more likely to be silver than *Coriolanus*' soldier's booty. I have grouped the fourteen productions for review

into five new categories that I hereby commend to others' use: the dark tragedies, the unproblematic comedies, the analogue plays, the materialist dramas, and the triumphant histories.

There has to be, of course, as for any system, one condition for exclusion. My brief for this review is essentially Anglophone but two of the finest Shakespeare productions I have seen in the last year were not. Others will write – indeed must write – of Peter Brook's *La Tempête*, seen in the UK for only a week in Glasgow, a production of such brilliance it would require a whole lengthy review article to itself. Others may not write of Alexandru Darie's production of *A Midsummer Night's Dream* for the Comedy Theatre of Bucharest, seen in London and Cambridge as part of the London International Festival of Theatre, the best *Dream* I have seen since Peter Brook's. Both productions shared a celebration of acting skills and theatrical invention of an order English companies rarely aspire to; both freshly liberated their plays, making things work that had seemed almost impossible before (magic in *The Tempest* or the erotic comedy of the lovers in *A Midsummer Night's Dream*). Both reread the plays' politics, with Brook's attack on the traditional eurocentricity of *The Tempest* matched by Darie's astonishing use of *A Midsummer Night's Dream* to explore Romanian tyranny as Serban Ionescu's tripling of Theseus, Oberon

---

[1] Conveniently reprinted in Stanley Wells, ed., *'Twelfth Night': Critical Essays* (New York, 1986), p. 79.

and Quince showed the dictator's protean power. Both seemed to find it unnervingly easy to be so cleansingly new, refreshing this wearied critic with possibilities unimagined before. For the first time in my experience of the play, for instance, the workers performing 'Pyramus and Thisbe' understood only too well the courtiers' insults and, when Theseus threw them a bag of money at the end of their show, left the money lying there, staring back in a piece of passive resistance that was painfully resonant of the politics of the company's own country. It is not simply the lure of the foreign other that leads me to praise these productions so highly but rather that they tap into a rich European tradition of which English Shakespeare productions are almost always unaware.

THE DARK TRAGEDIES

What groups together Ron Daniels' *Richard II*, David Leveaux's *Romeo and Juliet* and Steven Pimlott's *Julius Caesar* (all for the RSC) has nothing to do with darkly cynical readings of the plays. Instead they share a literal darkness, a lighting plot so gloomy that by the interval in each my eyes were strained with the effort of peering into the murk to see what the actors were doing. When Coleridge described Kean's acting as 'like reading Shakspeare by flashes of lightning'[2] he was not being terribly complimentary. At the most extreme moment of darkness in these productions, Steven Pimlott left David Bradley's Cassius and Bernard Gallagher's Casca playing out their scene in 1.3 on a pitch-dark stage with occasional flashes of stage lighting. I know, of course, that they are meeting during a supernatural storm but there must be ways of suggesting that without forcing actors to deliver long speeches in circumstances which turn them into disembodied voices, denying them any use of their physical presence. The Royal Shakespeare Theatre is not the place to try out Shakespeare on radio. If these three productions show a new tendency in the RSC to try to economize on their electricity

bills, then it is one of the best arguments for increased subsidy the company has yet devised.

In *Richard II* the effect of the low level of lighting was intensified by the costumes. The ostentation of Richard's court was transformed into a world of blacks and dull greys. Only Richard himself in red velvets and blue cape had a showy extravagance. The costume aptly matched Alex Jennings' ostentatious physical presence. An extremely tall man, his head topped with cascading golden curls, there was nothing wimpish or limp and not a tinge of camp in his fiercely authoritative presence. This court of whisperers and muttered threats was in awe of their dictator whose presence at the lists in 1.3 was accompanied by sinister guards armed with crossbows ceaselessly scanning the stage for armed terrorists. There was no space here for intimating a lyrical, poetic Richard, only for the dictator's splendour and power. Throughout Mowbray's speech of accusation (1.1.47ff.) Richard did not take his eyes off Bolingbroke, trying to probe his face for a sign of weakness. It was of a piece with Richard's arrogant confidence in his tyranny that Jennings could deliver the council's decisions on banishment (1.3.123ff.) standing far downstage but facing upstage, turning his back on the audience.

If one expected this tyrant to make a journey in the play towards discovery of the poetry of Richard's language later, then it was a disappointed expectation. Jennings pursued his line rigorously to the end. Always a threat to Bolingbroke, as much by virtue of his vocal authority and physical power, as Jennings towered over Anton Lesser, Richard could burst disruptively into scenes that Bolingbroke was trying to control, introducing a wry, mocking tone that denied Bolingbroke any authority in, for example, 3.3.

In any case this extremely unlyrical Richard was opposed by an unambitious Bolingbroke

---

2 S. T. Coleridge, *Table Talk*, ed. H. N. Coleridge (1835), 27 April 1823.

of equally extreme degree. There was nothing subtextually hidden about this Bolingbroke's denial of desire for the throne; nervous and frightened, Bolingbroke seemed to put off the decision as long as possible and to regret it as soon as taken. The Duchess of York's praise of him as a 'god on earth' (5.3.134), praise Richard would have taken as his due, found King Henry extremely harsh in response out of sheer embarrassment. The pardon to the Bishop of Carlisle (5.6.24ff.) was a weary response to so much killing and Lesser's sharp emphasis on 'my head' (5.6.36) replying to Exton's news of Richard's murder made clear how much this King realized where responsibility would be seen as lying. Indeed so many of Lesser's most striking effects seemed to be reactions to others' lines that it marked this Bolingbroke as a passive pawn, pushed unwillingly into power, particularly by Paul Jesson's vicious machiavellian Northumberland.

Through the murky devious world of this production's politics wandered the central tragic figure, not Richard so much as Linus Roache's Aumerle, the political innocent destroyed. His touching concern for Richard in 3.2 was met only by being violently pushed aside. In the glove scene (4.1) the intervention of the Duke of Surrey made abundantly clear that Aumerle was being set up, the victim of an orchestrated campaign to smear him. By the time he returned to his parents in 5.2 Aumerle was traumatized into a state of near-catatonic shock, needing to be slapped hard into awareness by his father.

Antony McDonald's design was as unafraid of large gestures as the production's whole concept. As England's political system began to fall apart the steel walls were replaced by piles of industrial scrap and the back wall of an empty warehouse with grimy windows. The massive painting of Atalanta by Guido Reni that had backed the cosy princely domesticity of 1.4 was now to be seen in tattered decaying heaps on the floor. Such a production style carries its own predictability: inevitably

Richard in prison was to be found in grey prison garb, with a shaven head, curled up foetally on a bare iron bed; the murderers, of course, killed the groom as well as Richard to ensure there were no witnesses. Yet the production was as capable of small gestures of simple effectiveness: in 2.1, York's bedside dialogue with the dying Gaunt (Alan MacNaughton moving in his deep distress and shame at England's decline) hinting at a hospital visit, or Richard's genuine affection for his wife in 1.4 marked by caresses and closeness, or the sight of the Welsh departing across the back of the stage in 2.4 as Richard's power ebbs away.

Clear, consistent and as bleak as it could be, Daniels' production almost justified the eyestrain, even if it left the ear straining for a touch of Richard's imagination. Where Daniels made the darkness part of his argument about the play, Leveaux's transformation of the sharp Italian sunlight of Romeo and Juliet into a gloomy shadowy world was arrant nonsense, a meaningless rejection of the advantages of realism. But then the production was frequently nonsensical. Julian Glover's stylish Prologue, accompanied by two processional lines of torchlit Montagues and Capulets, promised 'the two-hours' traffic of our stage' (12) but I caught a wry apology in his delivery, fully aware that the production would last almost four hours.

Where Daniels nearly managed to compensate for the loss of poetry, Leveaux could not hope to compensate for the loss of passion. For this Romeo was the least passionate imaginable: these lovers seemed unable to touch each other, certainly incapable of desire. In 3.5, after making love, the two (Michael Maloney and Clare Holman) seemed only to have had a furtive cup of tea together. The balcony scene, with Romeo hideously over-theatrical and Juliet dully mundane, was blocked with the two so far apart as to dare them to try to act together. In any case it is surely no longer pedantic to complain that these actors were just too old. Neither looks nor can act convincingly

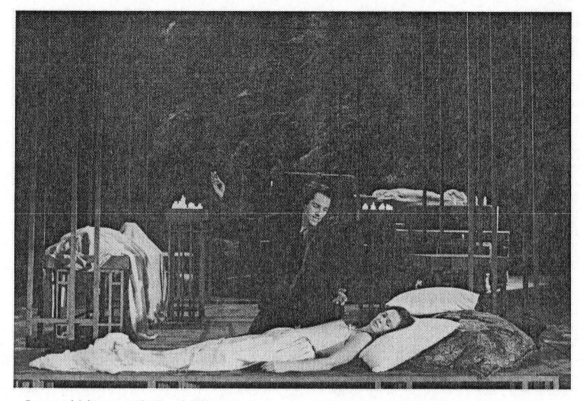

1 *Romeo and Juliet*, 1991. The Royal Shakespeare Company at The Royal Shakespeare Theatre. 5.3: Romeo (Michael Maloney) and the 'corpse' of Juliet (Clare Holman) in an open-plan tomb

adolescent and their childish passion became a rather mature affair.

Leveaux's interest was clearly much more in the macho world of young males. The fights became slow-motion cinematic explorations of violence as a series of tableaux, the young men out on the town more interested in each others' bodies than in any women. This homosocial world of prurient schoolboy sexuality was prone to have Mercutio trying to grab another young man by the balls but could not begin to suggest the fantastical world of his imagination, 'Queen Mab' becoming an unstoppable but uninteresting outpouring. Tybalt's fight with Mercutio was balletic and dancingly choreographed; Romeo's killing of Tybalt was the other side of the coin as he stabbed the unarmed man and then kicked him to death, the game of macho preening turned into a brutal street murder.

Such a view of the play's society was at least coherent but nothing prepared one for such oddities after the interval as Anthony Douse's weirdly insane Apothecary or the dance of death procession of plague victims weaving across the back of the stage or a tomb that Romeo struggled to break into but which everyone thereafter could enter from any direction. In the funereal pace of this production such bizarreries were all the more glaring and only Glover's Prince, a ruler easily capable of parting a fray single-handed, survived with honour.

Leveaux, whose production of *'Tis Pity She's a Whore* in the Swan Theatre earlier in the season showed him to be a talented and sensitive director, was left floundering on the main house stage, reducing his actors to a state of disordered incompetence. It is worth remarking here that Adrian Noble's first Stratford season as Artistic Director of the RSC had five productions in the main house of which three were by directors who had never directed on that stage before nor for the company before this season (the other two were by Noble himself). In a season in which Noble directed four productions himself (both parts of *Henry IV* and two evenings of Sophocles' *Thebans*) as well as shouldering new administrative responsibilities, I suspect he was simply too busy to give novice directors the support they deserve. Leveaux's *Romeo* was a conspicuous casualty.

Alison Chitty's design for Leveaux bisected the stage with a screen of quattrocento fragments, raised and lowered in panels as needed. Tobias Hoheisel's set for the first half of Steven Pimlott's *Julius Caesar* was a massive doorway of such complexity that when it needed to be removed for the second half the interval had to be extended to thirty-five minutes. Since the interval was taken inordinately late (after 4.1), that left a second half of only forty minutes, barely longer than the interval itself. This bizarre disregard for the play's architecture and the audience's ability to sustain attention seemed to me both operatic and European. At Covent Garden or when Peter Stein's production of *The Hairy Ape* visited the National Theatre such intervals seem conventional; at the Royal Shakespeare Theatre they seem self-indulgent and aberrant.

But Pimlott's grandly gestural style in such matters and extravagant operatic effects worked consistently against the play. Staging the forum scene with a crowd staring out at the audience on stage left while Mark Antony stares straight out at the audience on stage right makes good sense if both groups are singing but denies them any dramatic relationship; the sudden switch, midway through the sequence, to having Antony mobbed by a heaving mass of plebeians was peculiarly unmotivated. Similarly the strong colour coding of the second half with Octavius and Mark Antony associated

with red while Brutus and Cassius were linked to blue seemed more like a political statement (Octavius as Neil Kinnock?) than a simplistic device of differentiation. It was hardly surprising that the Soothsayer should double as the Poet of 4.2 and that both should be a clown-fool figure (Ken Wynne, the season's Feste) wandering in from an entirely different kind of play.

Pimlott began the evening with a joke on the audience's expectations, placing on centrestage an enigmatic cloaked figure who is revealed to be not the Soothsayer, as the audience has been lured into believing, but Mark Antony, leaping up when Caesar calls his name (1.2.6), ready for his race in leather cycling shorts. Such devices went with an Octavius played as a bald golden boy of brutal authority or a Ligarius whose sickness has made him dress up in grave-clothes more suited to a mummy. When from 5.2 onwards the stage slowly filled up with soldiers arranged around the walls like a frieze of death or exhaustion the effect was glib and distracting.

The gloom that left Cassius and Casca in the dark could be magnificently effective (as Brutus had to strike a match on a pitch-black stage to find Caesar's ghost confronting him) but was more often perverse: the quarrel scene was at least static and unfussy but, lit by a single overhead light, left Jonathan Hyde and David Bradley straining for vocal effects, Brutus' orotund language contrasted with a nasal mannered monotone for Cassius, the dynamics of the scene lost. Such visual tricks make life difficult for actors. I would have liked to have seen Bradley's neurotic Cassius or Hyde's intelligent Brutus properly but the lighting made it impossible. Only Robert Stephens' elderly Caesar, conspicuously deaf and physically frail, was consistently visible; I admired the controlled way in which he accompanied 'Et tu, Brute' by spitting into Brutus' face.

As with Leveaux's *Romeo*, the key-note was the stage's exploration of violence. Caesar was

stabbed over and over and over again till the blood ran over the stage floor and the conspirators were left weak and exhausted and hysterical. They really did 'bathe our hands in Caesar's blood / Up to the elbows' (3.1.107–8). The murder of Cinna the Poet was an exercise in stage violence of such extreme brutality and thuggery, such graphic detail, that I felt physically sick. The madness of violence has rarely been more exactly represented, connecting this murder with the neurotic fanaticism of Cassius. The confrontation of the two armies (5.1) seemed like rival hordes of football fans facing each other on the terraces, rhythmically chanting and beating their spears' ends on the ground. This violence, the production argued, was what lay all too near the surface of urbane or devious politics, a coarse brutality that denied political morality or individual dignity. In this setting, Owen Teale's beaming, open Antony, genuinely affectionate in his attachment to Caesar, came over, like Roache's Aumerle in Daniels' *Richard II*, as the innocent unable to cope with the demands of politics. At the end, as Octavius and Messala were sorting things out, Antony's final speech burst out, without preparation, across their distinctly unemotional dialogue. His praise of Brutus made no contact with Octavius' world and he seemed wrapped up so completely in his own grief as to leave no space for other contact. Discarding his sword he did not wait for a response but strode offstage, leaving Octavius enthroned on Caesar's golden chair. At such a moment the production's argument was both intriguing and justifiable but too often it had left its actors floundering in an operatic darkness.

THE UNPROBLEMATIC COMEDIES

If the dark tragedies left the audience straining to see what was happening then the unproblematic comedies have the reverse effect, making everything blindingly clear. This group of productions is made up of two contradictory subgroups. The first contains productions that simply ignore any problems in the text, passing over the play with an awe-inspiring simplicity. Where scholarship and previous productions have found complexity, doubt or irresolution, such productions find radiant joy and ease. Where others have found darkness, these find pure clear light. The second subgroup is made up of productions that recognize but surmount the problems, clarifying what had often seemed too obscure in production, renewing the texts as plays for the theatre through the consistent application of a theatrical and critical intelligence. It might be thought that it would be difficult to tell the two groups apart but that is not the case. The first induces intense disappointment and weary melancholia in the experienced critic, the second a lightness of heart that makes the dreariness of the other oddly bearable. Knowing that every so often one will experience the latter makes one prepared to put up with the former.

Two very different *Twelfth Night* productions belong firmly in the category of the bland refusal to recognize the problems. In a recent book, Michael Billington transcribed the conversations of recent RSC directors of the play about its difficulty. The four (Alexander, Barton, Caird and Hands) would probably have agreed with Billington's own assessment that Peter Hall's production of 1958 'solved many of the play's problems'.[3] The delicacy and intelligence that have so often been ascribed to that production were invisible in Hall's

2 *Julius Caesar*, 1991. The Royal Shakespeare Company at The Royal Shakespeare Theatre. 3.2: Brutus (Jonathan Hyde) addresses invisible plebeians

[3] Michael Billington, *RSC Directors' Shakespeare: Approaches to 'Twelfth Night'* (1990), p. xvii; compare Stanley Wells' praise of it as 'a classic' (in *Royal Shakespeare* (Manchester, 1977), p. 44).

return to the play with his own company at the Playhouse Theatre in London. Where many were prepared to find in it all the virtues of that mythic ideal of 'Shakespeare done straight', of 'traditional Shakespeare', of the director's humility before the wonders of Shakespeare's genius, I found only ordinariness and banality. It was also desperately unfunny, with barely a titter from the audience as the characters laughed away onstage to make up for our respectful silence. Seeing it on a night when Eric Porter (Malvolio) was ill and the production's highpoint admired in such rhapsodic terms by the theatre reviewers therefore given to an understudy, I was left with a bland and dull evening decked out in autumnal hues, a warning perhaps that one cannot and should not return to the scene of past triumphs. The piercing intelligence of 1958 had become either cliché, like the sea noises heard at oddly illogical moments throughout the evening, or straightforward error, like the Watteauesque swing on which Olivia sat in 1.5, denying her own mourning. The performances were mostly polished but too glossy by half, thereby circumventing anything that might be worth confronting. Martin Jarvis is too intelligent an actor to miss the opportunities of Sir Andrew but he is also not a natural comic fool, with the result that he offered not a fool but the performance of a fool, the actor's self-consciousness substituted for the character's self-confidence. Sir Toby (Dinsdale Landen) became a rather decrepit aristocrat, needing his walking-stick, but a relative neither endearing nor troublesome. Maria Miles, helped by the Caroline costumes, made a satisfyingly androgynous page-boy but her love was sentimentalized.

Of course there were nice touches: Malvolio, for instance, entering for 2.2 as Sebastian was leaving at the end of 2.1, had a neat doubletake as Viola entered from the 'wrong' side; the Priest in 4.3 was clearly the Sir Topas of Feste's disguise in 4.2; Feste tapping the drum which has been hanging at his belt for the raindrops of his final song. But such moments could not cover the perfunctory nature of 'doing it straight' or, perhaps, of actors unwilling to put much effort into a mid-week performance late in the run.

With this production I was, I must admit, out of line with most of the reviewers. With Griff Rhys Jones' production in Stratford the horror was more equally shared. The director, a gifted comic actor himself, would have been brilliant in any one of half a dozen different roles in the play but he seemed unable to conjure good performances from his actors. Only Tim McInnerny's Sir Andrew, his physique beautifully described by Peter Porter (*TLS*, 10 May 1991) as 'like a much-loved bendy toy', created a performance of density and thoughtfulness as well as fine comedy. Most of the others offered flashes of insight: Jane Gurnett's Olivia, struggling to keep her lunatic household in control, Linda Marlowe's Maria, a secret tippler, and Bill Wallis' seedy, sour Sir Toby, offering his brutal rejection of Aguecheek as a ghastly act of ingratiation to his niece. If there was a distinct and sharp view of the play, an argument or interpretation, perhaps what Peter Porter described in his review as the discovery that 'love is not moody but the occasion for a release of sexual energy', then it was comprehensively masked by the staging.

The problem was not entirely Jones' fault for most of the blame, if blame there must be, lay with Ultz's set. I do not think it matters greatly where or when one sets the play; almost any analogy can be made to work. If Illyria is the perfect romantic no-place, a place of disturbing connection with our world but equally disturbing distance, then the Gilbert and Sullivan style adopted by Ultz is a perfectly valid choice. It is not much of a leap from *HMS Pinafore* to Shakespeare: Orsino's court has lost contact with its function just as surely as Gilbert's sailors have never been to sea and I enjoyed the vision of Orsino in velvet knee-breeches as an early love-sick Bunthorne from *Patience*.

It was not the analogy but the scale of the set

3   *Twelfth Night*, 1991. The Royal Shakespeare Company at The Royal Shakespeare Theatre. 2.5: Malvolio (Freddie Jones) reads the letter in a William Morris garden

that caused the trouble; it was both overblown and flattening, its steps and levels forcing the actors into awkward lateral patterns that made interaction difficult or pushing the action far too far upstage, denying the actors the closeness to the audience that Hall's company, on a stage a quarter the size of the Stratford one, found it easy to enjoy. Actors were dwarfed by the William Morris sliding panels of Olivia's garden or lost on the flat planes of the stage. *Twelfth Night* is a tale of two households just as surely as *Romeo and Juliet* but the set militated against creating those households by putting characters into rooms in which they could not possibly live. Orsino and Cesario listened to Feste's song in 2.4 while seated at a mess-table (with much awkward nudging from the other officers as they became rather too pally – the production was surprisingly coy about homosexual desire) but the table was a device, not part of the daily rhythm of Orsino's court. The density of Illyria was replaced by a tawdry theatricality which made it impossible for the play's explorations of order and disturbance to flourish. When Malvolio came down to quell the late-night revelling he entered a set with a

4 *Love's Labour's Lost*, 1990. The Royal Shakespeare Company at The Royal Shakespeare Theatre. 5.2: The arrival of Mercadé

fireplace defined by a red footlight and vast hanging pots and pans but we had no sense that he came from somewhere else in the house, that there were other rooms contiguous. There was no sense of Olivia's house, of the noise of the knights stopping the rest of the household from getting to sleep.

What was left was a reminder of pantomime, with emotions simplified and gags broad. Characteristically, in the letter scene, the antics of the three hiding watchers were far more interesting than anything offered by Freddie Jones' Malvolio, as they restlessly crawled from one piece of scenery to another, leaving Sir Andrew at one point forced to pretend to be a statue in full sight of Malvolio and fainting from shock when he got away with it. Such gags have an honourable history but here they completely obscured the social tensions of

Malvolio's ambitions. Interest in character was replaced by the stock devices of comedy; the text was rendered unproblematic by the easy availability of comic business.

Adrian Noble had persuaded Griff Rhys Jones to be the actor turned director, entrusting a difficult play to a man with an apparently easy style of comedy. Terry Hands' last production as Artistic Director was *Love's Labour's Lost*, an odd choice for a director who has clearly never found comedy an easy option. This production marks the mid-point of my unproblematic comedies, by turns flattening and illuminating. If some of the problems were ignored, others were carefully laid out but the care was always a little too evident, our attention directed towards the production's hard work.

Surprisingly Hands managed to create a production that took no pleasure in the play's language, an odd parallel to Daniels' *Richard II*. When Dull replied to Holofernes' comment 'Thou hast spoken no word all this while' with 'Nor understand none neither, sir' (5.1.142–4), he raised the biggest laugh of the evening. The reason lay partly in Richard Ridings' fine comic performance, a Dull who moved with preternatural slowness so that, when playing boules, even the bowls themselves seemed to hang slowly in mid-air. But I suspect that the audience shared too readily Dull's incomprehension. The play's male world is bolstered by language but here it could find no support. Long speeches were scampered through in doublequick time, tossed off as so much verbiage. Biron's 'O, 'tis more than need' (4.3.287ff.) was a prime candidate with the rattle delivery brought to a sudden halt for a portentous intensity at 'It adds a precious seeing to the eye' (309). On the third night of the run, when I saw it, the production was a good twenty minutes faster than on the first, and it may well be that the slow relishing of language had been quickly rejected in a search to keep the audience's attention. But *Love's Labour's Lost* is not a play that any audience is going to enjoy for the pleasures of its plot. Only in the relishing of puns (e.g. Armado's swain/swine at 3.1.47 or Jaquenetta's grace/grease at 4.3.191) and in the language of Don Armado and Holofernes was the language savoured for its own sake.

Timothy O'Brien's set was French impressionism turned three-dimensional, its trees and hedges vivid splashes of colour. The lords sat for the first scene picnicking, reading, and sketching, in a tableau carefully arranged to remind the audience of Manet's *Déjeuner sur l'herbe*, though here with Manet's naked women conspicuous by their absence. By 2.1 the garden was cordoned off with a sign 'Interdit aux femmes', a pleasing if ponderous gag. At 1.1.158, once they have all signed to their oath (cue for another gag as the King disdained Longueville's offer of a pen, found his own would not work and had to ask Longueville to lend his), there was a long pause as the four realized they could think of nothing to do. A buzzing fly distracted them, eventually crushed by Longueville in his book, but Biron's enquiry 'But is there no quick recreation granted?' (1.1.159) was a welcome relief from the prospect of three years of unending tedium.

This heavy underlining of the men's naïvety in signing the oath in the first place contrasted rapidly with the confident sharpness and maturity of the Princess and her women (Amanda Root's Rosaline relaxed and inventive, Katrina Levon's Maria very much the winsome child and Caroline Loncq's Catherine all county and horsey in trousers). Gender confrontation was followed through to the end of the evening where the women were clearly embarrassed and ashamed at the men's vicious cynicism at the Pageant of the Nine Worthies, Simon Russell Beale's King sharing the women's distress. But such differentiation contrasted sharply with the clichéd treatment of Jaquenetta as a woman of rustic lasciviousness, close to orgasm as she listens to Nathaniel's dignified and sensitive reading of Biron's poem in 4.2 and so excited by the presence of Biron himself in 4.3 that, oblivious of what is going on around her, she unbuttons his shirt and starts nuzzling his stomach.

The production seemed more at ease with Armado and company. John Wood's fascination with the possibilities of voice was ideal for a very Spanish Don, matched by the excesses of pronunciation of David Troughton's Holofernes. From his first entrance collapsing onto a heap of cushions, Wood's Armado was madly illogical with a grasshoppering mind. Yet his devotion to Jaquenetta was deliciously obsessive, passionately excited by her easy display of sexuality, as he crawled around after her exit at 1.2.158 kissing the carpet wherever she had trod. By 5.1 the audience was in the presence of a mad gallery of eccentrics, each marked by odd tics, Armado's twitching, Dull's infinite slowness, Nathaniel's odd Japanese parasol and Holofernes' curious high giggle. The pageant was a logical outcome of such idiosyncrasies, but viewed so sympathetically that the hurt was all the more acute when, for instance, Nathaniel was reduced to tears. Only Don Armado's Hector, a performance unstoppably big, shamed the mockers with his panache and power.

By this point in the production the effort of the evening had been transformed into ease and confidence, the play doing what it wanted. As the song, turned for some reason into an inter-weaving of alternating verses of Spring and Winter, ended with Dull's basso profundo suddenly and surprisingly hitting a note at least three octaves higher than anything he had managed before, a note of poignant sweetness and beauty, the touching pleasures of art were complete. Armado's last lines were straight to the audience with a shrug: 'You that way, we this way' marking the division of the stage-world from us but also just emphasizing unportentously that this is how life and art are. When the stage cleared, Jaquenetta came on into the light previously occupied by Mercadé (here pronounced Marcadee) and Don Armado, happily ready for his three years' vow as a ploughman, kissed her, a tender act that the other nobles would never approach.

As the production moved from its effortful opening to its effortless conclusion, a rhythm that I wondered whether it might reasonably be seen as sharing with the play, so it moved from a blandness to a delicate recognition of the play's sensitivities, from one type of unproblematic comedy to the other.

Griff Rhys Jones' *Twelfth Night* was panned by the critics but played to full houses and huge ovations throughout the season, leaving the actors perplexed by their popular success in a critical catastrophe. David Thacker's production of *Two Gentlemen of Verona* in the Swan Theatre was that rare experience, a production both hugely popular and admired by Stratford's scholarly visitors. In David Lodge's novel *Small World* (1984), Persse McGarrigle proposes to write a book on the influence of

T. S. Eliot on Shakespeare; Thacker's production was surely about the influence of Denis Potter on Shakespeare. But where in Potter's work the Thirties songs function as a creative disjunction, marking the gap between the sordid and painful action of *Pennies from Heaven* and the language of lyric sentimental romance, in Thacker's *Two Gentlemen* the songs mediated and reassured, translated the action to a Thirties context in which the characters' obsession with love was validated. The audience needed to have no anxiety; there was no doubt that the disruptions of the action, its sharp pains, could and would be resolved within the terms of the discourse of this romance world. Gershwin and Cole Porter were offered as inhabitants of the same world as the play, sharing the same perceptions of love as an uncontrollable anthropomorphized force as the characters so often voice; Valentine could say with Gershwin 'Love walked in'. The play matched our yearning, that yearning that Potter's salesman so pathetically and unavailingly voiced, that the songs should turn out to be true.

The songs were also there as part of the play's visual – as well as aural – design. The band and chanteuse, placed upstage, made sure the audience could enjoy the scene-changes, covering the fairly laborious process of carrying on and carrying off rather a lot of furniture, turning the transformations into an entertainment. But they also belonged with the spring-blossom which decorated the stage, sharing with it the visual language of romantic springtime and the belief in the painful seriousness as well as the joyful immaturity of the play's view of love. One might want to say, with the wisdom supposedly born of age, that there is a great deal in the world that is more important than the concerns of the play but the production with immense efficiency and unflagging charm denied the space for such cynicism. One had to be feeling really curmudgeonly to dislike this production.

Only at one point did Thacker fall into the trap of treating this world as glib, in the final company song that misjudged and sentimentalized an ending that, up to that point, he had carefully and successfully refused to see as sentimental at all. Elsewhere the production proved capable of harsh pain and hard thinking. It was, in particular, remarkably successful at showing a character reconsidering himself or herself. Proteus' (Barry Lynch at his oleaginous best) extraordinary shift of tenses after first seeing Silvia was part of this: 'She is fair, and so is Julia that I love – / That I did love' (2.4.197–8), the actor's pause after 'that I love' creating the space for the character's awareness of the need to redefine the nature of the emotion and its temporal status.

When the Duke banished Valentine in 3.1, Richard Bonneville found in Valentine's soliloquy (3.1.170–87) a newly serious and wondering comprehension of the depth of Valentine's love for Silvia, at, for example, 'She is my essence' (3.1.182); Valentine was seen as puzzling out and thinking through the ramifications of a love that was proving to be far more profound than he had yet considered it to be. From being a string of romantic clichés the speech became a movement of the character into a new realm of feeling. I must admit that I am not entirely convinced that the speech will quite do all that; the language still seems to me to be caught up in the narrowness of feeling possible in the range of romantic simile, 'Except I be by Silvia in the night / There is no music in the nightingale' (178–9). But I respected the actor's attempt here, the ability to discard the slightly Woosterish silly-ass style of Valentine earlier in the play, a reasonable response there to his gullibility, magnified by the way that the 1930s setting inevitably suggested a tinge of P. G. Wodehouse.

Certainly the Duke's tricking of Valentine into a revelation of his elopement plot was beautifully handled, as the Duke prepared a picnic (obviously the staff's day off) with malign intent; I had never before taken the instruction in recipes to remove the seeds from a melon as an encouragement to mimic disembowelling. Significantly the audience was way

ahead of Valentine here and could be heard registering with a certain glee how innocently he strode into the trap. This was the Valentine that had become familiar in the production: young, handsome, innocent, good and very stupid. But the new access of the pain of love immediately afterwards, in the soliloquy, acted as a surprise, refusing the audience the right to patronize Valentine and forcing them to revalue their view of the rather naïve emotions and very naïve confidence that had driven the character thus far.

Something very similar happened in the remarkable playing of the scene between Silvia (Saskia Reeves) and Julia (Clare Holman) over Proteus' ring (4.4.106ff.). Again there was the transition between the audience's superiority to the action and its being surprised by the movement of the play. The audience's pain and sympathy for Julia when Proteus handed over the ring earlier in the scene was transformed into Silvia's pain and sympathy, a pain which was more than an expression of generalized sisterhood and was instead generated by what was apparent as a similarity of position for the two women, both vulnerable to the duplicity of Proteus. This scene, above all, managed to question and nearly to shatter the limits of romance, making of the women's vulnerability and the oppressive power of the man something that cut through the limited terms in which we are usually prepared to consider action in such a play. The transition was marked by the difference between Julia's comic tearing of Proteus' letter at 1.2.100 s.d. and the harsh truths that lay behind Silvia's pained tearing of another letter from him here (4.4.128 s.d.).

All problems in the play pale into insignificance beside Valentine's handing over the nearly raped Silvia to the rapist: 'All that was mine in Silvia I give thee' (5.4.83). Thacker's production, while not making the line unproblematic, offered it as a problem squarely confronted and tentatively solved. The production had, slowly and thoughtfully, allowed the significance of the women to grow as the play progressed, accepting their rights to decide what happens to them, their ability to initiate action and to express and actualize a form of friendship that the men talk of but cannot carry through into action. It seemed only logical and fully justifiable therefore to see Silvia resolving the play's crux. Anne Barton has argued that the moment is 'Shakespeare's blunder . . . when without warning he gives ideal friendship precedence over love', seeing the 'gift of Silvia to his friend' as 'an intolerable clumsiness' which 'has the effect here of negating the whole previous development of the comedy'.[4] Thacker's modest and highly intelligent solution reintegrated the moment into the development of the comedy as this production had explored it. After Proteus' 'My shame and guilt confounds me' (5.4.73) Barry Lynch left a colossal pause, showing Proteus considering the possibility of conning Valentine again, before finally resolving on genuine repentance. If the audience hesitated slightly as to the genuineness of the repentance – and Lynch's smirk was so beguiling that one had to have a moment's pause – it was Silvia's silent intercession, a calm gesture of moving towards Proteus, that reassured them. Her judgement that this man was worth forgiveness justified Valentine's generosity, a symbolic act of love and respect for Silvia as much as of friendship for Proteus, an act that re-established the male bonding through the pain of the scene as the earlier scenes had used emotional pain to unite the women. Such work, accepting the play's difficulty, was as honest and intelligent as one could wish for.

But the finest production of comedy in the year was well away from the RSC. Cheek by Jowl celebrated its tenth anniversary with a prolonged international tour of *As You Like It* directed, as usual, by Declan Donellan. It was like watching a much-loved picture restored, the colours bright and shining, unnoticed details newly apparent, the brilliance of the whole pristine and exhilarating.

Donellan used an all-male cast, defining his point by opening the evening with the beginning of 'All the world's a stage', using 'all the men and women' (2.7.140) as a means of dividing the cast. Where Clifford Williams' 1967 all-male production for the National Theatre had been coy and camp, Donellan rigorously resisted the trap. Gender became a construct of performance and sexuality was placed within the control of character, not actor. Adrian Lester's astonishing performance as Rosalind, sensuous and winning, was never simply a pretext for exploring the play's homosexuality, even though it enabled a subtle consideration of it. The play-acting of Rosalind-Ganymede was both more intriguing and simpler than it usually is when a woman plays Rosalind but the tremendous erotic charge between Rosalind and Orlando had nothing glibly homoerotic about it. Instead one enjoyed the gaps of gender action as when Orlando playfully punched Ganymede's arm and Rosalind awkwardly and tentatively returned the male gesture, though the actor could clearly have made the gesture with ease.

The problem of love and desire was defined as lying beyond gender, simply coming into being, irresistibly and unaccountably. Celia, irritated by the treachery of her friend in having fallen in love, wandered through the play waiting for Mr Right to come along, as he duly did in the person of Oliver. If Tom Hollander's outstanding Celia was inclined to the petulant flounce this was less a male comment on female behaviour than a response to the character's exceptionally long periods of time silently onstage, excluded by the rapt attention of Rosalind and Orlando in each other. This Celia proved the old adage that there are no small parts only small actors – and I do not intend the comment as a reflection on Hollander's height. Richard Cant's cheerily sexy Audrey, always ready to yodel summoning

---

[4] Anne Barton, Introduction to the play in *The Riverside Shakespeare*, ed. G. B. Evans (1974), p. 145.

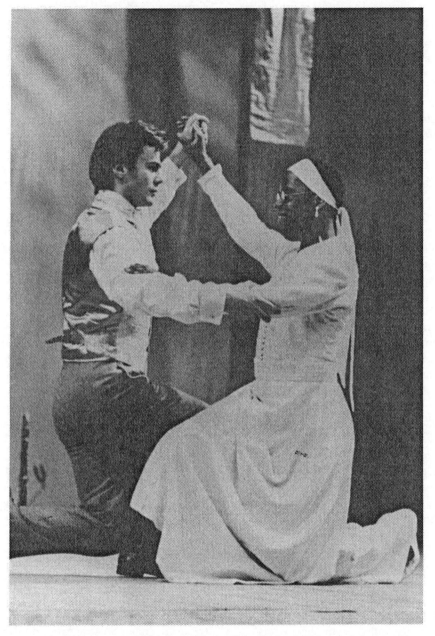

5 *As You Like It*, 1991. Cheek By Jowl. 5.4: Orlando (Patrick Toomey) dances with
Rosalind (Adrian Lester)

her goats, was innocently desirable without being mocked for it (unlike the RSC's Jaquenetta) and, for the first time in my experience, 'It was a lover and his lass' (5.3) became what it is obviously intended to be, a show-stopping chorus as Touchstone tried to keep Audrey away from the adult pages, while the four sat and cuddled under a blanket with their eight feet dancing to the tune.

Where Donellan at his worst (as in *The Tempest* in 1988) is excessive and mannered, this production was clear and controlled. Nick Ormerod's set of bare boards with hanging green strips of paper for Arden was all that was needed, a space on which the actors could work. The comic invention was always driven by the language, not by business. Mike Afford's Corin, whose words came out one by one as it took so long for messages from his slow brain to reach his mouth, driving a frustrated Touchstone to extremes of agony, sustained the device without strain to the very end. Only Joe Dixon's Jaques, played as a repressed homosexual who chose unaccountably to stay with Duke Senior at the end of the play, had difficulty avoiding being mannered.

The rethinking of the production allowed a sustained realism of reaction. When Rosalind lifted her bridal veil and offered herself to Orlando (5.4.115), Orlando turned on his heel and stormed to the back of the stage, shocked at the trick and shamed at his failure to have recognized her. It took time, covered with other action, before he could come downstage again, now back in control, fully accepting Rosalind, unashamed and unembarrassed and more in love than ever. This has a truth that far transcends the conventions of happy endings, finding an answer for the character in a realism of lived experience rather than the norms of comic endings and making the discovery all the more Shakespearian. Even the Epilogue, so often an awkwardness where the text's comments of gender are not matched by the performer's ('If I were a woman' (16–17) is gibberish if spoken by a woman), came over with

simplicity and limitless charm, Lester's natural easiness giving an engagement with the audience that I have rarely encountered.

In such a production there were no problems unresolved and no problems avoided, the play's joyousness fully accepted and expressed by the company. Unproblematic comedy needed no stronger advocate.

THE ANALOGUE PLAYS

Empires grow; success breeds expansionist policies. The English Shakespeare Company, after their extraordinary triumphs with the Histories, lovingly documented by Michael Bogdanov and Michael Pennington in *The English Shakespeare Company: The Story of 'The Wars of the Roses' 1986–89* (1991), decided that more meant better, subdivided the company into two and sent both out on tour. One, looking suspiciously like the B team, offered *The Merchant of Venice* and Jonson's *Volpone* both directed by Tim Luscombe to execrable reviews; the other, with Bogdanov directing and Pennington in the cast, offered *Coriolanus* and *The Winter's Tale* to reviews as excited as the others were despondent. I sampled one of each.

Both *The Merchant of Venice* and *Coriolanus* responded to the lure of the analogue, the precise historical analogy that would serve to illuminate the whole, relying on our knowledge of more recent history to explicate the Shakespearian text as if the play had no function in relation to its own time and, more significantly, could only be made popular by the recreation of the play as modern parable. The ESC is addicted to its own popularity, feeding off its own box-office figures as the justification for its existence. But at its worst its policy of trying to make Shakespeare popular makes the productions weakly populist, offering simple answers where the text is complex, failing to follow through the implications of analogy.

Luscombe's *Merchant* found its analogy in the rise of fascism in Italy in the 1930s. Pinpointing the production's date as 1938, the programme offered a helpful history lesson, documenting fascist anti-semitism. Venice, the city that invented the ghetto, has regularly been seen in recent productions of the play as structured on anti-semitism. Hence Luscombe could show more and more Venetians wearing fascist uniforms as the play progressed and follow Lorenzo's flight with Jessica (2.6) with a scene of an elderly Jew beaten up by black-shirted thugs.

The problem was that the more the production underlined the viciousness of the Christian community as equivalent to modern fascism, the more Shylock was consequently shorn of any villainy, standing only as the dignified representative of a beleaguered community. After arranging for Antonio's arrest with Tubal, Shylock (John Woodvine) did indeed head to 'our synagogue' (3.1.121) where he donned prayer-shawl and lit candles, joined by other Jews frightened by the growing fascist threat. As moving as such a moment was for the audience it denied any mercantilist motive for Shylock's pursuit of Antonio ('for were he out of Venice I can make what merchandise I will' 3.1.118–19), replacing it with the horror of threatened genocide. The modern anxiety of presenting a bad Jew was soothed: Shylock became a decent chap, a business man with barely a hint of a Jewish accent, seen at first working efficiently at his desk (1.3). In so far as the audience was anxious about Shylock's aims, they were excusable as the response of a desperate man to a vicious situation: his actions were nothing like as bad as those that the Venetian fascists had in store for his 'tribe', his 'sacred nation' (1.3.49, 46).

This is to make nonsense of the play but also to make nonsense of the chosen analogy. As Jonathan Steinberg has shown in *All or Nothing* (1990), Italian fascism was oddly lacking in anti-semitism and its government resisted Nazi pressure to hand over its Jewish community. If the analogy is not historically true it serves no purpose. It will not even work within the play. It is hardly credible that in 1938 Shylock could

have got a fair hearing or that the rule of law was such that the black-shirted guards would hold Antonio down for Shylock rather than taking the plaintiff out and beating him up. Even worse, the production could not defeat the inevitable rhythm of the scene so that, in spite of the fascist banners, uniforms and salutes, the audience still could be felt wishing that an answer to Shylock could be found, that this act of butchery, intensified by the sheer size of Shylock's carving-knife, could be prevented. The audience found itself siding with the fascists. The fears generated by the analogue were easily glossed over with relief and the consequent game of the rings.

Nothing in the production gave me any confidence that these paradoxes were within the director's awareness: too much else was equally inconsistent. Nerissa, told by Graziano to 'cheer yon stranger' (3.2.235), made much too much of her refusal to help a Jew; Belmont was as anti-semitic as Venice. To play Morocco in 2.7 as a parody of a westernized Arab was either risky or ignorant. In any case, the pleasures of Belmont were dulled by playing Portia (Lois Harvey) as a Jean Harlow lookalike addicted to her wind-up gramophone and a large heart-shaped box of chocolates; it was impossible to see what a Bassanio as sensible as Laurence Kennedy's could see in her.

At the end, with marital harmony comfortably restored and not the slightest hint of a problem left over Antonio, the couples danced out as an offstage crowd could be heard roaring as if at a Nuremberg rally. The play's fascination with the antithesis of place went for nothing.

Reports of productions of *The Merchant of Venice* are obliged to record Shylock's exit. John Woodvine's Shylock remained fiercely in control of himself until the bitter end. After hearing he would have to will his goods to Lorenzo and Jessica (4.1.387) he clearly suffered some sort of stroke and finally crawled offstage unaided as Graziano flipped off Shylock's skull-cap.

6 *Coriolanus*, 1991. English Shakespeare Company. 1.1: The plebeians perform an uprising

If this analogue over-reached itself, Bogdanov's *Coriolanus* worked hard at a parallel with Eastern Europe. I suggested last year, in reviewing Hands' *Coriolanus* for the RSC, that the collapse of the Soviet bloc seemed to lie behind the audience's perception if not the director's intentions.[5] Bogdanov made the analogy specific and explicit, not in terms of a precise historical moment but in terms of the tensions and potentials of popular movements overthrowing communist patricians. The plebeians' discovery of the power of the people was, in this production, the creation of a party, analogous to Solidarity of course but here called 'Democratie', identified by a large banner unfurled across the stage for the opening demonstration. The crowd, chanting 'Give us this day our daily bread', were broken up by sirens, tear gas, riot police and beatings – the weapons of the state – before reforming to be addressed by Bernard Lloyd's Menenius, a party apparatchik in an astrakhan hat, the sweetly reasonable face of Sovietism.

It is no disrespect to Michael Pennington's subtle and powerful performance as Coriolanus to suggest that this production displaced Coriolanus by placing the people at its centre. In its highly sympathetic treatment of the people and its not unsympathetic treatment of the tribunes, the ESC's production achieved what Brecht had suspected when, in a note in July 1955, he commented 'I again make an analysis of *Coriolanus*, and wonder if it would be possible

---

[5] *Shakespeare Survey 44* (1992), 163.

to stage it without additions (made by me two years ago) or with very few, just by skilful production.'[6] This was, in effect, Brecht's *Coriolanus* without Brecht's rewriting.

By intelligent individuating, the production turned the people into characters, not in terms of their trades and families but through identifying and sustaining a particular political position for each one. The crowd's discussions (for example in 2.3 and 3.3) became intense and complex political debates, conducted with the house lights up and with the people spread through the auditorium as well as on stage, debating through a microphone, prompted where necessary by the tribunes who saw their role as the creation of the new Party. In 2.3 the crowd's moderates attempted to oppose the direction in which the tribunes were taking the meeting but were soon silenced by the rational argument of the others, leaving a fairly united group to exit chanting 'Democratie'. This examination of the hijacking of a popular movement by ideologues whose personal ambition was balanced by their genuine belief in the role the people's party should play was consistently thoughtful, helped by the fine work of Michael Cronin (Sicinius) and Robert Demeger (Brutus). Demeger's performance was, as usual, so fine indeed that I wonder whether there is a more underrated actor in the country; he deserves to be seen in major Shakespearian roles. In this context of workers' politics, it was fitting that the gown of humility for Coriolanus should be a dirty boiler-suit, a symbol of the plebeians' workclothes.

Bogdanov has often been accused of using rather cheap theatrical tricks but in *Coriolanus* the logic of the production was consistent in its use of the apparatus of modern media. The news of Coriolanus' league with Aufidius arrived over the telephone in 4.6 in an office, obviously the editorial hub of the Democratie newspaper, where Sicinius was dictating to a worker-typist; the scene of the triumphant return of the 'ladies' (5.5) was watched on television by Sicinius and Menenius in the middle of 5.4. But the production was equally capable of achieving its effects by the simplest means: Volumnia's humiliation after Coriolanus' banishment was pinpointed by highlighting her extraordinary arrogance in the image of herself as 'Juno-like' (4.2.56), the phrase mockingly echoed by a woman in the crowd who could not this time be stared down by Volumnia's withering gaze.

Even the treatment of the battle redirected attention away from Coriolanus. The sequence was narrated by Aufidius, reading large chunks of, I presumed, Plutarch, while groups of exhausted soldiers lay around; slowly, as the sequence unfolded, a succession of mourning women came on and placed wreaths at the foot of a huge statue on an upper level. Each miniature battle was fought in dumb-show by the soldiers, forming a brief tableau and then, as another soldier was killed, relapsing back into their waiting groups.

This rebalancing of the play did not diminish the central struggle but made it more equal, Coriolanus never being allowed unquestioned dominance, the sharpness of his wit and his vocal brilliance always offset by the dogged reasonableness of the people and their politically astute tribunes. It did, however, marginalize Andrew Jarvis' Aufidius, a bizarrely alien figure with his crossed bandoliers, *four* swords and headband, a man for whom the political realities of Rome could have no meaning. At the end Aufidius moved from standing triumphantly on Coriolanus' corpse to a horror at the strength of his own emotion, stroking the corpse with love and despair. Volscian militarism was no longer a response to sophisticated urban politics and this rejection of war was neatly evidenced in the soldier's kitbag which Coriolanus carried into exile or the presentation of his son in 1.3 charging around playing soldiers, a ghastly ironic parody of his father.

---

[6] Quoted in John Willett, ed., *Brecht on Theatre: The Development of an Aesthetic* (1964), p. 265.

In this context Volumnia's plea (5.3) was a serious attempt to reconcile two sides, a genuine argument for compromise but with a strong awareness, shared by Coriolanus, of the price he will have to pay. The silence of his acceding to her (5.3.183) was sad, almost tragic, precisely because his subsequent outlining of its danger ('Most dangerously you have with him prevailed, / If not most mortal to him' 5.3.189–90) only made explicit what both already knew.

It was part of the success of the production that it could turn theatrical clichés into potent meaning. Productions of the Roman plays have used statues on stage for many, many years. Here the statue's decapitated head, wheeled forward in 3.1 and looking sufficiently like Coriolanus', suggested the panoply of Soviet representations of its deities. For an audience, seeing the production when statues of Lenin were being decapitated throughout Eastern Europe only gave the image a genuine, unforced potency.

An English company's view of Eastern European politics cannot possibly have the same emotional charge as an Eastern European company's view. Bodganov's work was not as charged as Darie's *A Midsummer Night's Dream*. But it was as intelligent and considered as one could hope. To claim, as Lachlan MacKinnon did (*TLS* 19 April 1991), that the production made 'a political nonsense of Shakespeare's most overtly political play' was grotesquely wide of the mark. This production made the analogue a means of redefining the play in ways that Brecht would certainly have approved without going against the grain of the text.

THE MATERIALIST DRAMAS

Reviewing Trevor Nunn's production of *Othello* for the RSC in 1989, Stanley Wells commented on its 'wealth of social detail'. He identified its technique as 'rooted in naturalism; indeed, a fully written account of this production would read like a Victorian novel'.[7] In

1991 Nunn directed two Shakespeare productions, *Timon of Athens*[8] at the Young Vic in London (the theatre to which his *Othello* had transferred) and an RSC touring production of *Measure for Measure* which opened in the new Other Place (less draughty than of old but still with the same exhilarating atmosphere). What had seemed experimental in *Othello* was now becoming a recognizably fixed style: emphatically naturalistic acting as if the plays were Ibsenite social dramas, consequently a phenomenal density of detail, a certain literalism with the text and above all a belief in the plays' explicability. Nothing now could be left enigmatic or inexplicit and the process of explication was doggedly rooted in the material reality of the design and the style – hence my label for this group. Pudovkin recognized that 'the playing of an actor which is connected with an object and is built around it . . . is always one of the strongest methods of cinematic construction'[9] but this proof that 'films can be an excellent means of materialistic representation'[10] will not necessarily hold true for theatre.

The opening of the two productions exemplified the approach. *Timon* began with the after-effects of an armed robbery. Two masked gunmen rushed onstage carrying the loot; one was shot by a plain-clothes policeman on a stake-out, while the other escaped. I was quite happy to put this down as a symbol of a dangerous materialist world in which this very modern Timon lived, the violent under-belly of the Thatcherite consumer capitalism which the rest of the production delineated in all its horror. But at the opening of the second half, with the whole stage now transformed into a scrap-yard with the wrecks of six cars and a

---

7 *Shakespeare Survey* 43 (1991), 195–6.
8 My first responses to this production appeared in a lengthy review in *TLS* 15 March 1991.
9 Quoted in Walter Benjamin, *Illuminations*, ed. Hannah Arendt (1970), p. 249.
10 Benjamin, ibid., p. 249.

heavy layer of sand and rubble, the escaped bank-robber reappeared, dug a hole in the sand and buried the loot so that, a few scenes later, it was conveniently in place for Timon (David Suchet) to uncover it (4.3.25). This is explication with a vengeance. It had never occurred to me that the gold was other than a symbolic entity, there because it is there, not something that needed its source exactly depicted. Such a narrative gave it a social reality and a history, drastically reducing its emblematic potency.

Measure opened to the strains of Strauss' Emperor Waltz and with the Duke (Philip Madoc) seated on a couch which looked (quite deliberately) uncannily like Freud's. He read from a well-thumbed book the first few lines of 'He who the sword of heaven would bear' (3.1.516ff. – the rest of the speech would be read at various other points during the performance). He also looked at and carefully pocketed some newspaper cuttings and a photograph. These, again, seemed easy to interpret, objects defining his own life, mementoes he wanted to carry with him; again, the explanation was shown to be inadequate. In 3.1, explaining the history of Mariana to Isabella, the Duke produced the cuttings as verification of his story; the photograph, needless to say, proved to be of Mariana. What in Shakespeare is troublingly discontinuous – when after all *does* the Duke know about Angelo's treatment of Mariana and should that have affected his

7   *Timon of Athens*, 1991. The Young Vic. 4.3: Timon (David Suchet) and Apemantus (Barry Foster), two tramps in an inner-city scrapyard

decision to leave Angelo as his deputy? – was now in Nunn's version completely apparent. The entire feigned disappearance had no cause other than the need to test out Angelo. In 1.3 none of the other reasons offered, least of all the Duke's own slack government, was remotely as important as the heavy emphasis placed on the last: 'Lord Angelo is precise' (1.3.50).

In both productions the careful, over-deliberate placement of detailing functioned both as novelistic realism but also as laying bare cause and reason for every line. Nunn's stuffing of the plays with material detail so emphatically underscored the lines that every word seemed to need its accompanying point, indeed until the business justified the existence of the line rather than the line justifying the business. Out of dozens and dozens of examples I offer a few. The First Gentleman's comment to Mistress Overdone, 'How now, which of your hips has the most profound sciatica?' (*Measure* 1.2.56–7), was a direct question about her health and she walked through the play in acute need of her walking-stick, rather viciously removed from her when she was in prison later. The Duke could think of death as 'an after-dinner's sleep' (3.1.33) because the Provost could be seen asleep on a chair. The 'stuff' at which the Duke wonders ('Oh heavens, what stuff is here?' 3.1.274) turned out to be a stock of dirty postcards which were revealed when Pompey turned out his pockets on going to prison; Elbow's comment that Pompey 'will needs buy and sell men and women like beasts' (3.1.272) became a comment on pornography, not prostitution. Lucullus proved it was 'no time to lend money' (*Timon* 3.1.40–1) by calling up some account displays on his computer-screen. When the Poet and the Painter came to 'offer you our service' (5.1.70) they offered Timon a camping stove and toothbrush, gifts which they had brought in their backpacks; their entry had already been a cue for unpacking of Evian water and packets of biscuits and much massaging of weary feet.

Sometimes this emphasis on the visible reality denied what the play's language is clearly saying: Timon's comment on 'Twinned brothers of one womb' became not a thought on sun and earth but, bizarrely, a comment on two halves of the parsnip he was eating. Sometimes it was so glibly underscored as to be parodic: Timon's jewels handed out at the first banquet (1.2.166ff.) were car-keys, cheaply emphasized by the sound of the new cars hooting offstage; Sempronius was found for 3.3 changing after a game of squash, writing out a cheque and then tearing it up – the change of mind cued by 'No' (19) – before grabbing his shampoo and heading off for his shower.

While *Measure* was played unaltered (apart from the treatment of 'He who the sword of heaven'), *Timon* was extensively rewritten. At its simplest this tidied up the problems of the talents so that 'five talents' (1.1.97) became 'fifty thousand' (suggesting pounds), 'A thousand talents' (2.2.195) became 'A million'. But speeches and entire scenes were added wholesale to make the movement of the action absolutely clear. To ensure that no one in the audience could imagine that Timon was the friend for whom Alcibiades was pleading in 3.6, Alcibiades asked for the case to be delayed until Timon could arrive. A new scene between a senator and one of Alcibiades' men, dressed as a motorcycle messenger, made explicit the progress of the strategic manoeuvring in Act 4. Other sections were re-ordered: the scene with Apemantus (Barry Foster in filthy raincoat, old boots, old school-tie knotted over a string vest and a woolly hat making him a parodic labourer) in 4.3 was moved to follow 5.1, a decision that made a natural dramatic progression from what is inconsequential in the text. Other characters were substantially developed, particularly Timandra; far from making only a brief appearance in 4.3, her role was built until she became a major figure. Starting as one of the Amazons in 1.2 (who changed midway through their routine from figures from a baroque opera into frilly-knickered prostitutes) Timandra was named in Timon's thanks and clearly took up with Alcibiades. By the end of the play she had become his second-in-command and political adviser, negotiating with Athens on his behalf in another series of newly added speeches.

Nunn is, of course, perfectly entitled to his view, in his programme-note, that the play is unfinished; he saw it as his task in the production 'to clarify what is impossibly obscure, to expand what is impenetrably telescoped and to make dramatic what is inert in the story'. But he and I obviously have different views on what is obscure or inert. To have Timon tell Alcibiades at the climax of their dialogue in 4.3 'I despise myself' was to spell out what Shakespeare deliberately left a vague possibility, as well as crediting Timon with a degree of self-awareness hardly apparent in Shakespeare's text; what had been simple and rich in the playing of the scene became simplistic. To have the dying Timon – he had shot himself in the back of a van – brought back onto the stage, so that the evening could close on a spotlit weeping Flavius kneeling beside the corpse while Apemantus stands behind it, was to make the magnificent casualness of Shakespeare's deliberately perfunctory exit and offstage death ('Timon hath done his reign' 5.2.108) into a sentimentalized cliché, to turn what was unquestionably dramatic, a prime moment of the play's 'extraordinary originality and urgency' (Nunn's note again) into something inert, rather than the other way round.

There was never any doubt in the production that one was watching the work of a virtuoso director but the virtuosity seemed misplaced. The materiality of this play-world seemed less a representation of a fiercely materialist culture and more a slightly self-regarding tribute to the director's own imagination. I did not find that the brief scene 2.1 played better for being set in an airport departure lounge or that Lucullus' aside about what Flaminius might be bringing (3.1.5ff.) was sharper for being spoken over a telephone intercom to his secretary or that the Second Senator's offer of 'such heaps and sums

of love and wealth' (5.2.37) is helped by his brandishing a blank cheque drawn on Coutts.

But equally there was never any doubt that whenever Nunn's largesse, which at times risked rivalling Timon's, was capable of being restrained the results could be extraordinarily worthwhile: the Apemantus-Timon scene (4.3.198ff.) took on the collocations of Beckett's tramps, the Shakespearian waste-land and inner-city decay in the 1990s without any difficulty, adding historical precision to what might otherwise sound like a recapitulation of Peter Brook's treatment of Lear and Gloucester in the 1960s and creating a precisely imaged material and social reality of desperate emptiness.

Nunn's *Measure for Measure* was distinctly more restrained than his *Timon* but for one highly visible quirk. Concerned to underline the time-sequence of the play, its rapid movement through day and night towards the moment fixed for Claudio's execution, Maria Bjørnson fixed a large clock dominantly over the set. Walter Benjamin warned that 'a clock that is working will always be a disturbance on the stage'[11] but the warning was not heeded this time. Sometimes the clock moved in real time but sometimes it had to move faster so that it would, for instance, hit the time with appropriate precision for the Justice's reply to Escalus' 'What's o'clock, think you?': 'Eleven, sir' (2.1.264–5). It jumped hours between scenes, forcing the audience to watch it: 8.45 p.m. for 4.1, 11.55 p.m. for 4.2, 4 a.m. for 4.3, 8 a.m. for 4.4 and 11 a.m. for the Duke's arrival back (by train) in 4.5. What it never managed to manifest was the play's temporal pressure: that is present in the play's language, not its material design.

Set in Freud's Vienna and touring in tandem with Pam Gems' new version of *The Blue Angel*, *Measure* was bound to be about sexuality and repression. Given the fascination in recent productions with the Duke, Nunn's interest

---

[11] Ibid., p. 249.

was fresh, clearly much more firmly focused on Angelo (David Haig). The Duke may judge Angelo as someone who 'scarce confesses / That his blood flows' (1.3.51–2) but here the blood became specific: Angelo's reaction to his first meeting with Isabella ('What's this? What's this?' 2.2.168) was his awareness that he had an erection, his body reacting without the conscious control of his repressing mind. The physical response to her – by 141 he had been close enough to find himself sniffing at her hair – turned in 2.4 first into a quivering sexual fantasy as he imaged her body lying over him during his opening soliloquy and then a violence close to rape when she fails to fulfil the fantasy, throwing her on the couch and, during 'Who will believe thee, Isabel?' (2.4.154ff.) holding her firmly, almost viciously, from behind with his hands clamped on her breasts. With an Isabella as much the fair young English rose as Claire Skinner's the vulnerability was intensified frighteningly. Haig pursued every twist and turn of Angelo's psychology with an intelligence and power that was quite extra-ordinary, far outplaying Skinner's limitations and Madoc's dull Duke. Haig was only really

8   *Measure for Measure*, 1991. The Royal Shakespeare Company at The Other Place. 5.1: Reunited under the clock, Isabella (Claire Skinner) kneels to embrace Juliet (Teresa Banham) and Claudio (Jason Durr), watched by the Duke (Philip Madoc, right)

matched, in an uneven company, by the quiet, benevolent authority of Allan Mitchell's magnificent Escalus and Peter Hugo-Daly's Pompey, the confident wide-boy, violently angry at Lucio's contempt for him (3.1.340ff.) and gleefully delighted at Lucio's discomfiture at the end (5.1.506ff.).

Haig's Angelo, as a study in sexuality and repression, was matched throughout by parallel examples of neuroses and sudden emotional excess: Isabella's hysterical outbreak when Angelo announced that Claudio 'must die tomorrow' (2.2.84), Juliet's grief when the Duke revealed his inadequacy as a psychologist in telling her the same news (2.3.39) and Mariana, barefoot but clad in her wedding-dress as if she were some prototype for Miss Havisham and the moated grange really Satis House.

I have suggested that Nunn's treatment of the end of *Timon* was surprisingly sentimental. He was certainly content in *Measure* to see the play reaching a conclusively happy ending, with Claudio and Angelo shaking hands, Isabella accepting the Duke's proposal and all dancing offstage. Other critics found this fully justified by the detailing of the production, achieving the emotional intensity of the re-united family. I was much more struck by the naturalistic truth of Angelo's shocked faint when Claudio was brought in or the grotesque arrival onstage of a fat prostitute, presumably Kate Keepdown, to claim Lucio. Fairy-tale endings do not belong in materialist settings. Yet, if finally unsatisfying, Nunn's productions had been as freshly provocative to the traditions of English Shakespeare production as one might have expected. It would be a pity, though, if such a style became a new orthodoxy.

THE TRIUMPHANT HISTORIES

The last production at Stratford during Terry Hands' reign was *Richard II*; the first under the new king, Adrian Noble, was *Henry IV Part 1*. One could, in the summer, see Anton Lesser's Bolingbroke being crowned King Henry IV at the Barbican while Julian Glover's King Henry IV ruled in Stratford. In some ways the disconnection symbolized the gaps in the RSC change-over, a deliberate discontinuity, a touch of the new broom. Where one might have expected a link between the two productions the change of Artistic Directors denied any. It was hardly surprising that Noble should choose to begin his reign with the two parts of *Henry IV*: Trevor Nunn had directed them to open the Barbican. I have dubbed Noble's productions 'the triumphant histories' for the simplest of reasons, for they were a triumph, a coherent, sophisticated and, above all, jubilantly theatrical exploration of the two parts.

In an interview in 1988, Ralph Berry, noting the 'exciting and vivid theatrical moments, which [Noble had] found for the characters and the world of the characters' in his *Macbeth* asked 'Is that what you are consciously working for, much of the time, this eliciting of metaphors and vivid theatrical images?' Noble replied,

That's the easy bit of directing. I find it very stimulating to create exciting pictures on the stage. I can do that. The real grind of rehearsals takes place with the actors trying to make a text 400 years old alive with meaning, now, that it should have the right rate, the right phrasing, that it should penetrate our dull ears.[12]

Creating exciting stage pictures may be easy for Noble but I was awestruck by the visual and theatrical imagination that created the battle of Shrewsbury in Part 1, when a backstage panel lifted to disclose a huge battery of percussion thundering away and through the stage-floor there came, rising further and further, an extraordinary seething, writhing tableau, figures struggling in slow motion for the throne with a woman screaming silently at the horror of war to one side. It is not simply that battles are notoriously difficult to stage – Shakespeare knew that as well as any modern director – but that

---

[12] Ralph Berry, *On Directing Shakespeare* (1989), p. 164.

9 *Henry IV Part 1*, 1991. The Royal Shakespeare Company at The Royal Shakespeare Theatre. 5.4: Prince Henry (Michael Maloney) kills Hotspur (Owen Teale)

the icon complexly imaged the war, bringing together so much that the production had been exploring. The incorporation of the throne itself as the focus made manifest the aims and ambitions of the rebellion, satisfyingly concretizing the notion of kingship and rule. The mass of bodies was terrifying but the woman, dissociated but reacting, brought together all the production's thinking about the place of women in this society, connecting back, for instance, to 3.1, where Lady Percy and Mortimer's Welsh wife appeared with a female harpist behind a gauze scrim, plaintively separated from the political debate and masculine posing of the rebels in their debate at the front of the stage.

One of the major achievements of Noble and his designer, Bob Crowley, was precisely this

sense of interconnectedness, forcing the audience to link together events across vast tracts of stage time through a visual device that echoed and resonated. The stage lift that rose so slowly and threateningly for this emblem of war in Part 1 was used once again – and only once – for Part 2 5.3, now bringing up not the perfect image of political disturbance and disorder but the perfect emblem of English rusticity, Shallow's house, a world of peace and drinking and singing, its warm glowing reds and browns suggesting an idyll, the utopic space it wants to define, a world one might want to patronize but cannot for its charm is not sentimental, its comedy too fulfillingly gentle. The song that accompanied that scene fed back to the other songs in the production, the raucous songs of the Boar's Head Tavern, the violent urban sexy world of London, the other side of Englishness, and a different form of comedy, the thrilling energies of Albie Woodington's mad biker Pistol and Joanne Pearce's dangerous loving Doll. The songs encouraged comparison, the difference of rural and city England, the calmness of the one and the hysteria of the other but also the comedy of both.

But such echoes were everywhere. To take a much smaller but equally resonant example, Henry IV violently and mockingly crowned Prince Henry with a cushion and the crown during his great tirade in Part 2 (4.3.221ff.), offering the audience an echo of the cushion Falstaff used as his crown in the play-acting of Part 1 (2.5.382), a similar mockery of kingship, a dense part of the production's consideration of the two kings, Henry IV and Henry V, and the two fathers, Henry and Falstaff, and the same son. Did those cushions make their last appearance as the ones stuffed up Doll's dress to feign pregnancy in Part 2 (5.4.14), the plays' last visual image of the child?

Let me take a third, even smaller object, the tale of two ribbons in Part 1, the one taken by Lady Percy from her girdle to give to her husband as he leaves for the rebellion in 2.4, the other given by Mrs Quickly to Prince Henry when he arrives at the tavern in 3.3, transformed in his magnificent armour and on his way to Shrewsbury. That Prince Henry has no other woman, no wife, mother or lover to give him her favour is touching, a mark of his isolation in the play, and the simple sincerity and emotion behind Mrs Quickly's gesture is equally moving. But it becomes potently poignant when it is this ribbon that Henry uses at Shrewsbury to 'let my favours hide thy mangled face' (5.4.95), inadequately covering the face of Hotspur's corpse.

Noble's control over the architecture of the whole structure was magnificently assured. I noted dozens of examples of such parallels and links traversing the expanse of the two plays, articulating the movement of the action, the changing relationships of the characters, the development of dramatic meaning. Noble adds to it a rather different effect, what I want to call cinematic theatricality. Elizabethan theatre thrived on the fluidity of space, the empty stage metamorphosing with a few words from one location to another. But Noble used a theatrical version of the dissolve in film, the slow fading from one scene to another, to great effect.

When, for instance, King Henry entered onto the set of the tavern in Part 2 at the end of 2.4, the space both was and was not still there; the King was obviously not in the tavern – this was not realist theatre – but the tavern was an echo of so many things for him: a version of the England that he rules, a representation of the anxiety focused on his son that was preventing sleeping and a perspective and commentary on the political concerns with a philosophy of history in 3.1, all of which justified the simultaneity of space. This particular transition made for great difficulty for the actors in 3.1: after the boisterous energy and endless chasing of Pistol across the set almost any actor delivering a long, slow agonized speech would have struggled to keep the audience's attention and even Julian Glover, who spoke the verse with an intensity and clarity that made it a privilege to listen to him, had to work hard. But such a moment combines a vivid theatrical image, the exciting stage-picture, with an actor triumphant at finding what Noble described in that interview, that 'right rate' and 'right phrasing' to 'penetrate our dull ears'.

There were some moments that did not animate the language in that way: the dirty politics of Gaultree Forest in Part 2 (4.1) was neither clear nor interesting, the scene marking time till the production could move on to something more important. I had reservations too about moments where animation was taken in the wrong sense: Michael Maloney's Prince Henry was generating restlessness in the tavern scene of Part 1 (2.5) but not energy, the result of the actor's insecurity rather than the character's lines. He needed to have learned the lesson Kenneth Tynan once offered: 'Don't just do something – stand there'. I exempt from this stricture Woodington's Pistol, a glorious performance that explained exactly why the title-page of the 1600 quarto made sure it announced that this was the play with 'swaggering Pistol' in it.

In the same interview, Noble offered this view of Shakespeare's method:

[He] worked in a theatre and explored an aesthetic in which each play created its own imaginative world, its own cosmology, if you like, its own earth, heaven and hell. Which are different from play to play. And which indeed are sometimes different within the plays themselves. For example, you will go on a journey in a Shakespeare play and you may well *en route* visit paradise, briefly. You may well visit Dante's purgatory. The world changes in the course of the evening and has its own rules.[13]

The *Henry IV* plays are clearly a journey, a strange and disconcerting one in which the heavens and hells are not quite what one would expect. I had never quite thought of heaven as populated by ghostly beekeepers but I was moved by the cinematic dissolve that took Henry IV's funeral procession through a ghostly Gloucestershire, underlining the rustic activities that throughout the Shallow scenes were offered not as intense realism but instead as emblems of rustic rhythm, cycles that continue irrespective of the activities of kings and that are more important than kings' temporary and temporal concerns.

The religious side of this cosmology was

[13] Ibid., p. 165.

10 *Henry IV Part 2*, 1991. The Royal Shakespeare Company at The Royal Shakespeare Theatre. 2.4: Pistol (Albie Woodington) makes his escape from the tavern by rope

fixed from the very beginning of Part 1 by the churchy effect of candles flickering in pillars on either side of the stage, the cross into which the massive mobile panels of the back wall had been arranged and by the reliquary, shaped like a model of a Jerusalem church, lowered downstage and then suspended over the stage throughout the performance. But it is an ironic religion: Henry's reaction to realizing that the Jerusalem he will die in is a room, not a city, was mocking laughter (Part 2, 4.3.364).

Noble realized, as too few directors ever do, that stages are vertical as well as horizontal spaces. The tavern scenes had upstage rooms with musicians or prostitutes and their clients, adding new perspectives to the scenes' rich blend of the medieval, Hogarth and Brecht. But a play's cosmology has to be vertical. Noble used ladders often in the production, as the way down to the cellars of the inn in the cold dawn as the carriers prepared to make their journey in Part 1 (2.1), on the battlefield of Shrewsbury where Prince Henry perched on one to mock Falstaff (4.2), and for the apple-picking in Shallow's orchard (3.2), suggesting the complexity of Noble's view of the two plays' cosmology, the different English places on their journey, the ambiguities of place.

More than any other production of these plays I have seen, Noble's was able to allow for those ambiguities, the delights as well as the stupidities of Gloucestershire, the viciousness and sleaziness as well as the energies of Eastcheap, the shallowness as well as the honesty of rebellion. It was there in the knife Doll kept concealed in her hair, in Owen Teale's naïve Hotspur, by turns charming and brutal, a Welsh rugby-player with the physical energy of Henry IV, his would-be father, in David Bradley's Shallow, an old fool but also a man at peace with himself and his community, in Philip Voss' brilliant double, marking the change between the two parts as he was transformed from a wickedly machiavellian Worcester to a Lord Chief Justice benignly tolerant of Falstaff, epitomized in his final generous

handshake with him as Falstaff and his companions were forced from the stage at 5.4.94.

It was there above all in Robert Stephens' Falstaff, the most intelligent of Falstaffs, witty and charming of course but also delicate and almost fastidious rather than gross and gluttonous. But the intelligence, the foresight and perceptiveness induce melancholy. Falstaff's clear thinking, in, for instance, the cold, hard logic of the catechism on honour, only confirmed his belief that the end will be melancholy. Desperately pained by his isolation and the self-awareness that went with it, his goodbye to Doll split the conventional word, 'farewell' (2.4.385), into an emphatic and regretful parting and hope for her health, 'fare well', stating both his concern for her and his sharp awareness that they will not meet again.

This awareness of his isolation meant that the whole of Part 1 seemed to hinge on the search for an embrace, the gesture that his Hal found it so difficult to give him, for instance as he lay asleep at the end of the tavern scene (2.5), just as Prince Henry so desperately wanted the same embrace from *his* father but was in turn refused it when Blunt entered (3.3.161). Falstaff's childlessness was an acute pain, there in the hollow boast of 'if I had a thousand sons' in Part 2 (4.2.118). But it was registered most powerfully at the end of Part 1 in Falstaff's lamenting embrace of the dead Hotspur, the man whose true father, Northumberland, had left him to his fate. Only at such a moment, in the recognition of his own grief, could this Falstaff be surprised. Certainly King Henry V's rejection came as no surprise at all; he had read the signs clearly enough even before Henry's 'I do; I will' in Part 1 (2.5.486). Confronting the crowned Henry V he knew what the response would be; everything he had learned about people had taught him to expect it.

If this clear-sighted Falstaff induced our sympathy – as well as that of the Lord Chief Justice – the intelligence revealed a callousness as well. It was funny before the battle of Shrewsbury when Bardolph waved a tatty banner after the swirling multiplying banners had thrillingly filled the back of the stage. But during the battle Falstaff was surrounded by corpses and wounded men, a visual reminder both of the truth of his discourse on honour but also of the practice to which he had put his theory, leading his men 'where they are peppered' (5.3.36), while Bardolph looted the corpses. In Part 2 the conning of Mrs Quickly out of yet more money was heartless. The mustering of men in Gloucestershire was plain nasty. Wart, a little too much like an early Smike, a refugee from the RSC's *Nicholas Nickleby*,[14] was humiliated by the drill (3.2.268ff.) and Feeble, for all his courageous statements, was reduced to tears. There was a sneering contempt for people in Falstaff here as well as a cunning streak, a contempt that only mellowed as the good humour and benign good will of Shallow's world began to affect him. Falstaff's intelligence was hurtful and cruel as well as melancholic. In the sharp and disturbing oscillations of audience response, the ambiguities of Falstaff's earth, heaven and hell were perfectly registered.

It is pleasant to end after my strictures on the gloomy work of other lighting designers – whose names I have left as covered in obscurity as their work left the plays – with praise for Alan Burrett's brilliant lighting for these productions, subtle and, dare I say it, illuminating. Noble himself, praising Burrett's work in a talk at Stratford, has suggested that his understanding of the broader canvas of Part 2 was intensified by Burrett's comment that he could light Part 1 with two follow-spots but would need three for Part 2, a marvellous perception of the structure of the dialogue in the plays. But then the productions were consistently perceptive, offering this critic rich plunder to take back from the stage to the study in a way that Virginia Woolf might have approved.

---

[14] That production seemed also to lie behind the playing of Rumour's prologue to Part 2 as an exercise in choric speaking, even as the device showed the shift to the broadest canvas of England that Noble found to be characteristic of Part 2 in general, the stage always far fuller than it had been in Part 1.

PROFESSIONAL SHAKESPEARE PRODUCTIONS IN THE BRITISH ISLES, JANUARY–DECEMBER 1990

compiled by

NIKY RATHBONE

Most of the productions listed are by professional companies, but some amateur productions and adaptations are included. Information is taken from programmes supplemented by reviews held in the Birmingham Shakespeare Library. Details have been verified wherever possible, but the nature of the material prevents corroboration in every case.

ALL'S WELL THAT ENDS WELL

The RSC at the Barbican, London: 24 March 1990–
Transfer from Stratford. See *Shakespeare Survey* 44, pp. 191, 158–61

Theatre Set Up, Forty Hall, Enfield and tour: 14 June 1990–
Director: Wendy McPhee
Helena: Jennifer Draper

AS YOU LIKE IT

The RSC at the Barbican, London: 5 April 1990–
Transfer from Stratford. See *Shakespeare Survey* 44, pp. 192, 161–3

Next Stage Company, St Augustine's Hall, London: 24 April–5 May 1990
Director: Valerie Doulton
Designers: Katie Beresford and Jane Davies
Benefit at the Garrick, 13 May.

Polesden Lacey Open Air Theatre: June 1990
Producer: Joan Macalpine

Designer: Tim Shortall
Music: Chris Parry
Rosalind: Sandra Berkin
A semi-professional production.

The Everyman Theatre, Liverpool: 27 September–27 October 1990
Director: John Doyle
Designer: Elizabeth Ascroft
Music, Duke Senior, Duke Frederick: Graeme du Fresne
Rosalind: Susan Curnow
Celia: Phillida Hancock
Jaques: Susan Jane Tanner
Touchstone: Peter Russell
A modern-dress production with some rather idiosyncratic casting, but good reviews. The seating in the auditorium was removed, and the audience sat in groups among the trees of the Forest of Arden.
Graeme du Fresne played both Dukes and provided the music.

THE COMEDY OF ERRORS

The English Shakespeare Company, British and foreign tour: University of Warwick Arts Centre 29 January 1990–
Director: Glen Walford
Designer: Rodney Ford
Antipholus of Ephesus: Mark Anstee
Antipholus of Syracuse: John Elmes
Dromio of Ephesus: Charles Dale
Dromio of Syracuse: Stephen Jameson
Adriana: Jill Brassington

The RSC at the Royal Shakespeare Theatre, Stratford: 19 April 1990–
Director: Ian Judge
Designer: Mark Thompson
Music: Nigel Hess
Antipholus of Syracuse/Ephesus: Desmond Barrit
Dromio of Syracuse/Ephesus: Graham Turner
Adriana: Estelle Kohler

Adaptation

The Boys from Syracuse by Richard Rodgers and Lorenz Hart
The Crucible, Sheffield: April 1990
Director: Claire Venables
Designer: Simon Higlett

CORIOLANUS

The RSC at the Barbican, London: 26 April 1990–
Transfer from Stratford. See *Shakespeare Survey 44*, pp. 192, 163–6

The English Shakespeare Company, The Grand, Swansea: 24 September 1990– and national and world tour, with *The Winter's Tale*
Directors: Michael Bogdanov and Michael Pennington
Designer: Chris Dyer
Music: Terry Mortimer
Coriolanus: Michael Pennington
Aufidius: Andrew Jarvis
Volumnia: June Watson
Modern dress, East European setting.

HAMLET

Compass Theatre Company (Sheffield) Tour continues
See *Shakespeare Survey 43*, p. 206

Salisbury Playhouse and Forest Forge co-production: 23 February–17 March 1990 and tour

Director: Karl Hibbert
Designer: Bill Crutcher
Hamlet: Colin Wyatt
Originally produced in the Studio Theatre, 1989.

Outrageous Fortune, Brixton Assembly Rooms, Pentameters and the Shaw Theatre, London: 20 July 1990–
Director: Max Jacobson-Gonzalez
Hamlet: Stephen Haynes
Ophelia: Francesca Gonshaw
Voice of the Ghost: Timothy West (recording)
Modern dress with some anachronistic details.

Bulandra Theatre Company, Romania at the National Theatre, London, and Dublin Theatre Festival: 20 September, 1990–
Director: Alexandru Tocilescu
Designer: Dan Jitianu
Music: Dan Grigore
Hamlet: Ion Caramitru
Claudius: Ion Cocieru
Gertrude: Gina Patrichi
Ophelia: Mariana Buruiană
Polonius: Ion Besoiu
In Romanian. First performed Bucharest, 1985. A tense, political interpretation, set around 1900.

Cheek by Jowl, Theatre Royal, Bury St. Edmunds; Lyric, Hammersmith and tour: 4 September, 1990–
Director: Declan Donnellan
Designer: Nick Ormerod
Music: Paddy Cunneen
Hamlet: Timothy Walker
Claudius: Scott Cherry
Gertrude: Natasha Parry
Ophelia: Cathryn Bradshaw
Polonius: Peter Needham
King Hamlet/Player King: Daniel Thorndike

Harrogate Theatre: 25 October–10 November 1990
Director: Andrew Manley
Designer: Michael Spencer
Hamlet: Crispin Redman

Modern dress, with television screens used to suggest that the whole court was under constant surveillance.

Adaptations

Carnal, Bloody and Unnatural Acts
Custard Factory at the Allardyce Nicoll Studio, Birmingham and Edinburgh Fringe and Midlands tour with 9 × 9 (Macbeth)
Director: Julie-Ann Robinson
Hamlet: Jez Thomas
A ninety-minute deconstruction using five actors, with some rather confusing cross-gender casting; the Ghost was played by a woman.

Hamlet goes business, a film based on *Hamlet*, Electric Pictures.
London: 23 February 1990–
Director: Aki Kaurismaki
Hamlet: Pirkka Pekka Petelius
First released Finland 1987.
A farcical comedy set in a modern Finnish timber company.

HENRY IV

Extracts from *Richard II*, *Henry IV* and *Henry V*
Theatreaction, Farnham, schools tour: November 1990
Director: Bill Bankes-Jones

HENRY V

Henry V, A Shakespeare Scenario
The Walton music for Olivier's film of *Henry V* arranged by Christopher Palmer, with speeches spoken by Christopher Plummer. Played by the Academy of St Martin in the Fields, Festival Hall, London 11 May 1990.

JULIUS CAESAR

Compass Theatre Company (London) Buxton Opera House and tour: 12 March 1990–
Director: Michael Joyce

Designer: Rod Langsford
Music: Stephen Warbeck
Brutus: Tim Pigott-Smith
Mark Antony: John Duttine
Cassius: Peter Blythe

Commonweal Company, Paisley Arts Centre and tour of the North West: 16 March 1990–
Director: Tony Hegarty
Designer: Kathy Pogson
Brutus: Max Hafler
Mark Antony: Jo L.A. Jones
Inspired by Greek theatre. The set consisted of scaffolding hung with drapes and tragic masks.

The New Shakespeare Company, Regent's Park Open Air Theatre: 13 June–6 September 1990
Director: Caroline Smith
Designer: Michael Holt
Music: Mark Emney
Brutus: Pip Donaghy
Mark Antony: Martin Clunes

KING LEAR

Renaissance Theatre Company, world tour, with *A Midsummer Night's Dream*, Theatre Royal, Newcastle: 25 June 1990–
Director: Kenneth Branagh
Designer: Jenny Tiramani
Music: Patrick Doyle
Lear: Richard Briers
Fool: Emma Thompson
Edgar: Kenneth Branagh
Edmund: Simon Roberts
Regan: Francine Morgan
Goneril: Siobhan Redmond
Kent: Jimmy Yuill
Opened at the Mark Taper Auditorium, Los Angeles, January 1990.

The RSC at the Royal Shakespeare Theatre, Stratford, 28 June 1990–
Director: Nicholas Hytner
Designer: David Fielding
Lighting: Chris Parry
Music: Peter Hayward

Lear: John Wood
Fool: Linda Kerr Scott
Cordelia: Alex Kingston
Goneril: Estelle Kohler
Regan: Sally Dexter
Edmund: Ralph Fiennes
Edgar: Linus Roache
Kent: David Troughton
Gloucester: Norman Rodway

The Lyttleton Theatre, National Theatre and world tour: 26 July 1990–
Director: Deborah Warner
Designer: Hildegard Bechtler
Music: Dominic Muldowney
Lear: Brian Cox
Fool: David Bradley
Cordelia: Eve Matheson
Edmund: Hakeem Kae-Kazim
Edgar: Derek Hutchinson
Goneril: Susan Engel
Regan: Clare Higgins
Kent: Ian McKellen
Gloucester: Peter Jeffrey

King Lear adapted for the Kathakali Theatre, India, by David McRuvie; Royal Lyceum Theatre, Edinburgh: 15–18 August 1990
Directors: David McRuvie and Annette Leday
Lear: Keezhapadam Kumaran Nair and Kalamandalam Padmanabhan Nair
Fool: Kalamandalam Manoj Kumar
Cordelia: Sadanam Annette Leday
Regan: Kalamandalam Unnikrishnan Nair
Goneril: Nelliyode Vasudevan Namboodiri
King of France: Sadanam Krishnankutty
Kathakali is traditionally an all-male art form. Musicians recite and sing the text, while fantastically masked dancers depict the action. The costumes and make-up symbolize the essential qualities of the characters presented according to Kathakali tradition. In this version the Gloucester sub-plot was omitted.

LOVE'S LABOUR'S LOST

Argonaut Theatre Company at the Rheingold Theatre Club, London: 29 May–30 June 1990
Director/Designer: Dee Hart
Producer: John Greco
Berowne: Geoffrey Towers
The Princess of France: Camille Evans
Rosaline: Hilary Derritt
A very fast production, set in the Wild West.

The RSC at the Royal Shakespeare Theatre, Stratford: 30 August 1990–
Director: Terry Hands
Designer: Timothy O'Brien
Music: Guy Woolfenden
King of Navarre: Simon Russell Beale
Longaville: Bernard Wright
Dumaine: Paterson Joseph
Berowne: Ralph Fiennes
Princess of France: Carol Royle
Maria: Katarina Levon
Rosaline: Amanda Root
Boyet: David Killick
Holofernes: David Troughton

MACBETH

Full Company, continuation of 1989 tour. See *Shakespeare Survey 44*, p. 196 for details.

Faction Theatre Company, tour of Leicestershire colleges
Directors: Daniel Buckroyd and Peter Smith
Designers: Rachael Gorton and Kaz Williams
Macbeth: Alastair Leith
Lady Macbeth: Leisa Rea
Modern-dress adaptation with workshops and discussion groups.

The London Shakespeare Group at the Warehouse, Croydon: and foreign tour 30 January–18 February 1990
Director: Delena Kidd
Macbeth: Frank Barrie
Lady Macbeth: Elizabeth Bell
Much doubling of parts, a simple set, and slightly cut text.

Great Eastern Stage, a schools production of scenes and themes from *Macbeth* and other Shakespeare plays, touring with *Richard III*: February–March 1990
Director: Maria Pattinson
Designer: Neil Richardson

Theatre Foundry, Darlaston and local tour: 21 April–June 1990
Director: Jonathan Chadwick
Designer: Purvin
Macbeth/Murderer: Tony Turner
Lady Macbeth/Seyton/Witch: Janys Chambers
Played by a cast of seven doubling on a stage hung with nets entangled with toys.

Vanessa Ford Productions, touring with *Rosencrantz and Guildenstern are Dead*, King's Theatre Southsea: 18 September 1990–
Director/Designer: Ron Pember
Macbeth: Colin McCormack
Lady Macbeth: Angela Phillips

Birmingham Repertory Theatre: 29 September–27 October 1990
Director: Anthony Clark
Designer: Kate Burnett
Macbeth: Jack Klaff
Lady Macbeth: Sara Mair-Thomas
Music: Mark Vibrans
The second witches' scene was dominated by a huge model of Hecate in an otherwise traditional production on a blood-spattered set.

New Triad Theatre Company, Forum 88 Barrow-in-Furness and tour: 9 October 1990
Lady Macbeth: Debbie Radcliffe

Traffic of the Stage at Pentameters Theatre Club, London: 13 October–22 December 1990
Director/Designer: Tom Leatherbarrow
Music: Henry March
Macbeth: James Reynard
Lady Macbeth: Karen Cooper
Set to heavy metal music.

Red and Gold Theatre Company at the Riverside Studios, Hammersmith: 12 November–15 December 1990

Producer: Jane L'Epine-Smith
Director: Malcolm Ranson
Designer: Demetra Hersey
Lighting: David Hersey
Music: Brian May
Macbeth: Roy Marsden
Lady Macbeth: Polly Hemingway
A slightly adapted version, in a Ruritanian setting.

Third Theatre, touring: December 1990–
Director: Phillip Knight
Macbeth: Graham Alexander
Set in modern Latin America.

Adaptations

Macbeth by Marks and Gram
Volcano Theatre, Swansea and tour: January 1990–
A lampoon on the government of Margaret Thatcher, loosely based on *Macbeth*.

9 × 9
Custard Factory, Birmingham, tour of the Midlands and Edinburgh Fringe Festival, with *Hamlet*: March 1990–

The Kingdom of Desire, adapted from *Macbeth* by Lee Huei-min
Contemporary Legend Theatre, Taiwan at the Lyttleton, National Theatre, London: 14–17 November 1990
Designer and Au-Shu Cheng, Lord of Chi (Macbeth) Wu Hsing-Kuo
Lady Au-Shu (Lady Macbeth) Wei Hai-Ming
Set in third-century China and performed in the style of Chinese opera, with acting, dancing and singing. The plot was simplified and the witches reduced to one. Contemporary Legend Theatre was formed in Taipei in 1984 by a group of Peking opera actors and actresses, led by Wu Hsing-Kuo.

MEASURE FOR MEASURE

Barebones Theatre tour continues: see *Shakespeare Survey 44*, p. 197

Pentameters Theatre Club, London; and tour:
17 January 1990–
Director/Angelo/Pompey: Tom Leather-
barrow
Isabella: Sarah Carpenter
A modern-dress production set somewhere in
Europe.

Rendezvous Theatre Company, Queen's Hall
Arts Centre, Hexham and tour: 14 February
1990–
Produced and designed by Susanna Martin and
James Brining
Director: James Brining
Designers: James Brining, Susanna Martin,
Alexander Smith
Isabella: Susanna Martin
Angelo: James Barham

Oxford Stage Company at the Rose Theatre,
Oxford and tour: 27 June–11 August 1990
Director: John Retallack
Designer: Kenny Miller
Music: Howard Goodall
Isabella: Carla Mendonca
Angelo: Terry McGinity
The Duke/Vincentio: John Michie
Lucio: David Solomon
Claudio/Froth: Derek Riddell
Played in the round and set in Mussolini's Italy.
Excellent reviews.

Regeneration, Finborough Arms, London:
7–23 August 1990
Director: Richard Syms
Angelo: Rob Swinton
The costuming was drawn from a mixture of
periods in a rather haphazard way.

THE MERCHANT OF VENICE

Compass Theatre Company (Sheffield) tour of
Britain and the Far East with *The Alchemist* and
Waiting for Godot: May 1990–
Director: Neil Sissons
Costumes: Jenny Neville
Portia: Mary Bullen
Antonio: David Westbrook

Shylock/Lorenzo: Nick Chadwin
A modern-dress production.

D.P. Productions, (Nottingham) Theatre
Royal, Hanley and tour: 21 May 1990–
Director/Bassanio: Ian Dickens
Costumes: Norma Samuel, Trish Woodhouse
Antonio: Glynn Dilley
Shylock: Phil Rose
Portia: Lara Marland
Set in the 1930s, the production emphasized
social and cultural differences.

Ludlow Festival: 23 June–7 July and the Hol-
land Park Theatre, London 10–16 July 1990
Director: Michael Napier Brown
Designer: Ray Lett
Antonio: Eric Carte
Shylock: James Ellis
Portia: Doran Godwin
Set in the eighteenth century; racism contrasted
with the Age of Enlightenment for comic
effect.

Argonaut Company at the Rheingold Theatre
Club, London: 17 July–18 August 1990
Director: Daniel Evans Rees
Shylock: David Zoob
With Meryle Anderson, Joanna Dadd, Naomi
Sachs, Duncan Piney, Anthony Keetch and
Anthony Styles
A modern-dress production.

The English Shakespeare Company, Warwick
Arts Centre and tour, with *Volpone*: 13
November 1990–
Director: Tim Luscombe
Designer: Paul Farnsworth
Music: Corin Buckeridge
Antonio: Gary Raymond
Shylock: John Woodvine
Portia: Lois Harvey
Bassanio: Laurence Kennedy
With Richard Attlee, Guy Burgess, Julian
Gartside, Piers Gibbon, etc.

THE MERRY WIVES OF WINDSOR

Chichester Festival Theatre: 2 May–30 June 1990
Director: Michael Rudman
Designer: High Durrant
Falstaff: Bill Maynard
Mistress Ford: Penelope Keith
Mistress Page: Phyllida Law
Music: Matthew Scott
Queen Elizabeth as a spectator: Pamela Wickington
A traditional period setting.

A MIDSUMMER NIGHT'S DREAM

Factotum Theatre Company, Sussex tour: February–April 1990
Director: Alastair Palmer
Oberon: David Stevens
Titania: Teresa Mangan
Bottom: Jack Power
Set in the 1930s, to popular music. A cast of seven actors, with the fairy attendants treated, according to a review, as figments of the imagination.

Theatre Podol, Kiev at Hampton Court Theatre: 13–17 March 1990
Director: Vital Malakov
Designer: Jean Godwin to Malakov's design
Oberon/Theseus: Alexander Ruboshkin
Titania/Hippolyta: Tamora Plashenko
Puck: Igor Krikunov
Bottom: Alexander Krizanovski
A surrealist production set in a mobile iron frame with ropes, bells and loose drapes suspended from it, as in a gym. The lovers gradually shed costumes resembling tin foil and put on the loose drapes. The bergomask was transposed to the middle of the action, becoming a dream within a dream sequence, and the play ended with Titania/Hippolyta weeping over Bottom's lifeless corpse. The fairy attendants were cut, and Bottom became a four-legged centaur; Bottom with Snout as the back half of a pantomime creature. Performed mainly in Russian. The production has been in the repertoire for about twelve years.

Renaissance Theatre Company, world tour, with *King Lear*. Theatre Royal, Newcastle: 25 June 1990–
Director: Kenneth Branagh
Designer: Jenny Tiramani
Oberon/Theseus: Simon Roberts
Titania/Hippolyta: Siobhan Redmond
Bottom: Richard Briers
Demetrius: Max Gold
Lysander: James Larkin
Hermia: Francine Morgan
Helena: Emma Thompson
Peter Quince: Kenneth Branagh
First performed at the Mark Taper Forum, Los Angeles, January 1990.

Moving Being at St Stephen's Theatre space, Cardiff: August 1990
Director: Geoff Moore
Oberon: Robert McKern
Titania: Ella Hood
Bottom: James Miller
The walls were hung with huge paintings in the style of Chagall. A local amateur rock band played the Mechanicals in this modern-dress production which emphasized ecological themes.

Chester Gateway Theatre: November 1990
Director: Hettie Macdonald
Designer: Judith Croft
Music: Pat Whymark
Theseus/Oberon: Neil Phillips

Adaptations

Roar Material at the Roman Fort site, Castlefield: 27–30 June 1990
Director: Camden McDonald
Designer: Lesley Martin
Music: Steve Howe
Theseus/Fairy: Bill Hopkinson
Hippolyta/Titania: Philippa Coslett
A semi-professional adaptation of *A Midsummer Night's Dream* and Purcell's *The Fairy Queen*, performed with masks.

SNAP Theatre Company and Aklowa at The Hawth, Crawley and tour: 18 September–9 November 1990
Director: Michael Wicherek
Designer: Carl Stevenson
Cast: Edward Brittain, Elizabeth Uter, Ian Henderson, Lisa Hopkins, Tanya Franks, Tom Skipping
Aklowa are a West African music and dance company from Ghana. In this multi-cultural adaptation all the characters were, according to the programme note, personified by Puck, who in turn was played by the whole company. A narrator acted as puppeteer and director of the rest of the actors.

MUCH ADO ABOUT NOTHING

The Royal Shakespeare Company at the Royal Shakespeare Theatre, Stratford: 5th April 1990–
Director: Bill Alexander
Designer: Kit Surrey
Music: Ilona Sekacz
Beatrice: Susan Fleetwood
Benedick: Roger Allam
Hero: Alex Kingston
Claudio: John McAndrew
Don Pedro: John Carlisle
Don John: Vincent Regan
Leonato: Paul Webster
Dogberry: George Raistrick

The New Shakespeare Company at the Regent's Park Open Air Theatre: 29 May–8 September 1990
Director: Lindsay Posner
Designer: Julian McGowan
Beatrice: Susan Tracy
Benedick: Carl Johnson
A Victorian period production with overtones of Gilbert and Sullivan.

OTHELLO

Second Stage at the Tivoli Theatre Dublin: 1 February 1990–
Director: Derek Chapman

Designers: Monica Frawley and Gabby Dowling
Othello: Trevor Laird
Iago: Alan Stanford
Desdemona: Orla Charlton

Bristol Old Vic: 8 February–10 March 1990
Director: Paul Unwin
Designer: Tim Reed
Othello: Jeffery Kissoon
Iago: Jack Klaff
Desdemona: Melanie Thaw
Emilia: Maureen O'Brien
Cassio: Sean Murray
Reviews mentioned that Jeffery Kissoon is an Indian from Trinidad and Jack Klaff is a South African in exile. The production was seen as a series of personal confrontations between the two.

The Stephen Joseph Theatre, Scarborough: 26 September–27 October 1990
Director: Alan Ayckbourn
Designer: Michael Holt
Music: John Pattison
Othello: Michael Gambon
Iago: Ken Stott
Desdemona: Claire Skinner
Emilia: Elizabeth Bell
Cassio: Simon Dormandy

PERICLES

Leicester Haymarket: 5–31 March 1990
Director: Simon Usher
Designer: Anthony Lamble
Music: Corin Buckeridge
Pericles: Kevin Costello
Marina: Sarah Winman
A modern-dress production.

The RSC at the Barbican, London, transfer from Stratford. See *Shakespeare Survey 44*, pp. 199, 166–170
Pericles: Rob Edwards took over from Nigel Terry

Show of Strength Theatre Company at the Hen and Chickens, Bristol: 28 November–22

December 1990
Director: Nick Bamford
Designer: Peter Milner
Music: David Ogden
Pericles: Donald MacNeil
Gower: Esmond Rideout
Marina: Emma Healey

RICHARD II

The Coliseum, Oldham: 11–20 October 1990
Director: Paul Kerryson
Designer: Craig Hewitt
Richard: Alan Perrin
Bolingbroke: Paul Rider
An indeterminate period setting. A huge circle suspended over the set suggested a crown or the grill of a dungeon.

The RSC at the Royal Shakespeare Theatre, Stratford: 1 November 1990–
Director: Ron Daniels
Designer: Antony McDonald
Music: Orlando Gough
Richard: Alex Jennings
Bolingbroke: Anton Lesser
John of Gaunt: Alan MacNaughton
Aumerle: Linus Roache
Duke of York: David Waller
Duchess of York: Marjorie Yates
Isabella: Yolanda Vazquez

Richard II, Henry IV and Henry V
Theatreaction, the Redgrave Theatre, Farnham, touring local schools: November 1990
Director: Bill Bankes-Jones
Extracts from all three plays.

RICHARD III

Great Eastern Stage, Stamford Arts Centre and tour of the Midlands: 7 February–20 March 1990
Director: Michael Fry
Designer: Neil Richardson
Music: Duncan Chapman
Richard: Jonathan Oliver

Co-produced with the Theatre Royal, Lincoln and sponsored by Central Television. Performed by an all-male cast of six. The production toured with workshops on Shakespeare in performance and *Stage Shakespeare*.

The Royal National Theatre at the Lyttleton, London and world tour with *King Lear*: 25 July 1990–
Director: Richard Eyre
Designer: Bob Crowley
Music: Dominic Muldowny
Richard: Ian McKellen
Buckingham: Brian Cox
Queen Elizabeth: Clare Higgins
Queen Margaret: Susan Engel
Lady Anne: Eve Matheson
Lord Hastings: David Bradley
Henry, Earl of Richmond: Colin Hurley

Adaptation

Richard III
The Hyacinth Girl, Covent Garden Drama Centre, Cambridge: August 1990
Director: Ben Hall
Richard: Mark Jamieson
An adaptation of *Richard III* played by a cast of nine in T-shirts and leggings on a black-walled stage in a production which developed the theme of the upheavals of war and the emergence of a strong personality.

ROMEO AND JULIET

Hull Truck, Spring Street Theatre, Hull and tour: 3 April 1990–
Director: Bill Homewood
Designer: Andrea Carr
Romeo: Roland Gift
Juliet: Daahne Nayar
The Nurse: Claire Benedict
A modern-dress production with an ethnically mixed cast. The set was a series of large moveable blocks.

Aberystwyth Arts Centre: November 1990

Director: Richard Cheshire
Designer: Meri Wells
Romeo: Paul Manuel
Juliet: Michelle Hughes
An Italianate 1950s set.

Adaptation

Romeo and Juliet

The Custard Factory, Birmingham, tour of Midlands schools. October 1990
Nick and Sharon from the TV serial *Neighbours* in a modern farce ending in a custard fight.

THE TAMING OF THE SHREW

Bradford Playhouse: March 1990
Director/Designer: Chris Ambler
Petruchio: Richard Cole
Katherine: Julie Armstrong

Merry Go Round at Floral Hall, Southport: April 1990
Director: Wendy Welton
A mixed amateur and professional cast. The production was played in the round, in a Carnival setting with jugglers and fire eaters.

Questors Theatre, Ealing: 23–30 June 1990
Director: Pat Gowman
Designer: Ray Dunning
Petruchio: Michael Langridge
Katherine: Gillian Kerswell
The production included the Christopher Sly scenes.

The RSC/British Telecom tour, Marina Centre, Great Yarmouth and tour: 25 September 1990–
Director: Bill Alexander
Designer: Tim Goodchild
Music: Jonathan Goldstein
Petruchio: Gerard Murphy
Katherine: Amanda Harris
Bianca: Sally George
Tranio: Brian Parr
Baptista: Michael Loughnan
Christopher Sly: Jim Hooper

The Christopher Sly scenes were played as a modern-dress huntin' shootin' and fishin' set joke, the main play was set in the Regency period, with actors from the 'audience' occasionally being drawn into the action.

Leicester Haymarket: 10 October–3 November 1990
Director: Alison Sutcliffe
Designer: Paul Farnsworth
Petruchio: Ian Gelder
Katherine: Kate Nicholls
Sly was portrayed as a contemporary tramp dragged off to the theatre. The main play was then set in Elizabethan Padua, presented in simple story-book designs. Good reviews.

The Cambridge Theatre Company, Malvern Festival and tour: 10 July–1 September 1990
Director: Robin Midgley
Designer: Martin Johns
Petruchio: John Labanowski
Katherine: Toyah Wilcox
Played in knockabout Commedia dell'arte style. Christopher Sly became Grumio. There was some re-writing and redistributing of text.

The Crucible, Sheffield: 8 November 1990–
Director: Mark Brickman
Designer: Tim Hatley
Petruchio: Bruce White
Katherine: Maureen Beattie
Set in an invented modern world, drawing on the theme of the ugly duckling becoming a swan.

Adaptation

Pushkala Gopal and Unnikrishnan: The Palace Theatre, London: autumn 1990
Music: L. Subramaniam
Ten actors performing a Bharata Natyan and Kathakali Indian dance adaptation.

THE TEMPEST

Wales Actors' Company, tour of Welsh castles: 12 July–18 August 1990

Director: Ruth Garnault
Prospero: Paul Garnault
Caliban: Tim May
Ariel: Richard Santhiri
Miranda: Rachel Atkins
A company of eight actors in a production which incorporated Burmese Buddhist music and dance.

Outreach Theatre Company tour of North Wales: July 1990
Designers: Rita Hogben and Stuart Seller
With Kevin Lewis, David Lloyd Skillern, Bernadette O'Brien and Alison Wynne

Kent Repertory Company, Hever Castle: Summer 1990
Director: Richard Palmer
Designer: Michael Coghlan
Prospero: Peter Sowerbutts
Caliban: David Bromley
Ariel: Dominic Kemp

The Duke's Playhouse, Lancaster, promenade production in Williamson Park: 7 June–31 July 1990
Director: Ian Forrest
Designer: Paul Kondras
Prospero: Stephen Ley
Caliban: Jim Findlay
Ariel: Ian Poitier
Miranda: Kate Paul
Set in the 1920s with West Indian spirits in white-face clown make-up.

Manchester Royal Exchange: 13 September–27 October 1990
Director: Brabham Murray
Designer: Johanna Bryant
Prospero: David Horovitch
Caliban: Dan Hildenbrand
Ariel: Emil Wolk
Miranda: Emily Raymond
Music: Chris Monks
A modern-dress production set on a mirror floor.

La Tempête
Centre International des Créations Théâtricales at the Tramway, Glasgow: 30 October–3

November 1990
Director: Peter Brook
Designer: Chloé Obolensky
Translation: Jean-Claude Carrière
Ariel's songs: Harué Momoyama
Prospero: Sotigui Kouyaté
Caliban: David Bennent
Ariel: Bakery Sangaré
Miranda: Romane Bohringer or Shantala Malhar-Shivalingappa
A production which made imaginative use of racial casting. Prospero was played by an African of great height and presence, Caliban by a small white man, Ariel was black, the other actors black, oriental and white. The set was a sand pit which faded back into darkness; ships, spirits, and the feast were suggested by the use of stylized props and mime. Peter Brook saw the play as a meditation on the meaning of 'freedom'. First produced Zurich Schauspielhaus 14 September 1990.

Barebones Theatre, Bristol and tour: October 1990
Director: Nick Benson
Adapted for seven actors by Tim Clark. Ariel was played by a group of actors.

Argonaut Theatre Company at the Rheingold Theatre Club, London: October 1990
Producer: John Greco
Director: David Evans Reese
Designer: Chris Roupe
Music: Simon Packman
Prospero: Don McCorkindale
Caliban: Grant Cottrell
Ariel: Anthony Styles
Miranda: Naomi Sachs

TROILUS AND CRESSIDA

The RSC at the Swan Theatre, Stratford: 18 April 1990–
Director: Sam Mendes
Designer: Anthony Ward
Music: Shaun Davey
Troilus: Ralph Fiennes

Cressida: Amanda Root
Thersites: Simon Russell Beale
Pandarus: Norman Rodway
Hector: David Troughton
Helen: Sally Dexter
Ulysses: Paul Jesson
Ajax: Richard Ridings
Achilles: Ciaran Hinds

TWELFTH NIGHT

Traffic of the Stage, tour continues. See *Shakespeare Survey 44*, p. 202

Leeds Playhouse, run continued to 20 January 1990. See *Shakespeare Survey 44*, p. 202.

The Pocket Shakespeare Company, Royal Spa, Brighton: 14–26 May 1990
An open-air production.

Oracle Productions, Holland Park Theatre, London: June 1990
Director/Malvolio: Peter Benedict
Designers: Michael Baldwin and Peter Collins
Music: William Hetherington
Viola/Sebastian: William Conacher
A production which emphasized the sexual ambiguities in the play, set in a 1930s film studio set.

TAG, Glasgow, tour of Scotland: 25 August–3 November 1990
Director: Alan Lyddiard
Designer: Neil Murray
Music: Iain Johnston
Viola: Caroline Paterson
Malvolio: Robert Carlyle
Feste: Malcolm Shield
The players doubled as a band of modern travelling actors and switched constantly from their roles as performers, in white Elizabethan costumes, to black modern dress to act as stage hands, musicians etc.

THE TWO GENTLEMEN OF VERONA

Four Corners, the New End Theatre, London: January 1990
Director: John Abulafia
Designer: Kit Line
Valentine: Jonathan Coyne
Proteus: Vincenzo Nicoli
Set in Italy in the 1950s.

THE WINTER'S TALE

Manchester Royal Exchange, tour with their 'tent': 8 February 1990–
Director: Phyllida Lloyd
Designer: Anthony Ward
Leontes: Sean Barker
Hermione: Barbara Marten
Music: Gary Yershon
Autolycus/Emilia: Myra McFadyen
Perdita/Gaoler: Claire Hackett
Paulina: Ellie Haddington
An excellent production, in a near-contemporary setting with Autolycus played as a vagabond woman.

Deal Theatre Project, Walmer Castle, Kent: 3–18 August 1990
Directed and designed by Luke Dixon and Paul Dart
A mixed cast of amateur and professional actors.

The English Shakespeare Company, Swansea Grand Theatre, Swansea, British and foreign tour, with *Coriolanus*: 24 September 1990–
Director: Michael Bogdanov
Sets: Chris Dyer
Costumes: Claire Lyth
Music: Terry Mortimer
Leontes: Michael Pennington
Hermione: Lynn Farleigh
Perdita/Mamillius: Trilby James
Paulina: June Watson
Autolycus: James Hayes
A Victorian setting was used as a 'frame' for the main play, which then became the tale told by a

boy to his mother. Leontes' jealousy was manifest from the beginning. The roles of Mamilius and Perdita were doubled in a very well thought-out production which received excellent reviews.

Adaptation

Etcetera Theatre/Canopy Theatre Company, Oxford Arms, Camden, London and Edinburgh: 9–28 January 1990–
Director: Nicholas Cohen
An adaptation.

SHAKESPEARE APOCRYPHA

ARDEN OF FAVERSHAM

Classics on a Shoestring at the Old Red Lion, London: August 1990
Director: Katie Mitchell
Designers: Vickie Mortimer, Mark Ager and Dave Ludlan
Arden: Ian Reddington
Alice Arden: Valerie Gogan
Mosbie: Peter Lindford
Played as a black comedy.

SIR THOMAS MORE, William Shakespeare and Anthony Munday etc.

Stage One Theatre Company at the Shaw Theatre, London: September 1990
Director: Michael Walling
Acting script by Michael Walling
Thomas More: Ken Bones
Billed (inaccurately) as the first professional performance.

MISCELLANEOUS

Stage Shakespeare

Great Eastern Stage, tour of Midlands schools with *Richard III* and *Shakespeare in Performance* workshops: February–March 1990
An all-female workshop production of scenes from *Macbeth* and other Shakespearian plays.

Shakespeare As He Liked It

The Rose Theatre Trust in association with the British Actors' Theatre, the Theatre Royal, London: 13 May 1990
Director: Patrick Tucker
With James Fox and Kate O'Mara
Scenes from the plays, played directed but unrehearsed, in an attempt to re-create the conditions of Shakespeare's theatre.

The Fantasticks by Tom Jones and Harvey Schmidt

The New Shakespeare Company at Regent's Park Open Air Theatre and tour: August 1990–
1950s American musical based on *Romeo and Juliet* and other Shakespearian plays.

Two Shakespearian Actors by Richard Nelson

The RSC at the Swan Theatre, Stratford: 29 August 1990–
Director: Roger Michell
Designer: Alexandra Byrne
Music: Jeremy Sams
Edwin Forrest: Anton Lesser
William Charles Macready: John Carlisle
A staging of the confrontation between the two Shakespearian actors in New York, 1849.

The Battle for the Bard

The Medieval Hall, Salisbury: 11 September 1990
Jill Nott-Bower and Robert Spencer in a programme of songs and extracts from Shakespeare and the critics.

SONNETS

The Sonnets

South Bank Centre, London: Spring 1990
The complete sonnets read in aid of CRUSAID
Judi Dench, Derek Jacobi, Dorothy Tutin, Timothy West

The Sonnets, a speculation

The QEII theatre, Woking and Edinburgh Festival: 27 May 1990
Mark Kingston one-man show.

The Dark Lady reads the Sonnets

Lyric Theatre Hammersmith and tour: September 1990
Faith Kent reading.

THE YEAR'S CONTRIBUTIONS TO SHAKESPEARE STUDIES

1. CRITICAL STUDIES
reviewed by DAVID LINDLEY

GENERAL STUDIES AND COLLECTIONS

Three contributions to the study of Shakespeare's reception begin this year's survey. A special issue of *Michigan Germanic Studies* (15, 1989) is devoted to eighteenth-century France and Germany. Among other essays, Kenneth E. Larson points out how limited was the range of Shakespeare plays to which reference was made (the major tragedies plus *Julius Caesar*) (pp. 114–35). Byron R. Wells sees Le Tourneur's (comparatively) literal translation of Shakespeare marking a shift of attitude from the earlier part of the century, where a translator's duty had been to rework and improve the original (pp. 160–70). Judith P. Aikin gives an account of the intertextual dialogue between Lessing's *Minna von Barnhelm* and Shakespeare's *Othello* and *Merchant of Venice* (pp. 171–89), noting the ways in which Lessing's text comments upon and revises the originals by locating struggle within the individual consciousness, and giving a more central place to female self-determination.

Rajiva Verma considers one branch of Shakespeare criticism in *Myth, Ritual and Shakespeare* (New Delhi: Spantech, 1990). Bearing the marks of its doctoral thesis origins, the book surveys in a rather undifferentiated fashion studies of the plays from the mid-nineteenth century onwards which can (some-times with some effort) be accommodated to the categories of myth and ritual.

Much more ambitious and rewarding is Hugh Grady's *The Modernist Shakespeare* (Oxford: Oxford University Press, 1990). He sees the story of Shakespeare criticism in this century as one of an 'interplay between the forces of modernization (economic, scientific, and technical) and of modernism (cultural and aesthetic in relation to the former)'. Beginning with the scientism of the disintegrators of the late nineteenth and early twentieth centuries and continuing through to the diverse voices which are making the 'postmodern Shakespeare', he charts the tensions and accommodations between these two impulses that have characterized the Shakespeare industry. He sets out clearly the coincidence between the political conservatism of the New Criticism and modernism, and offers a useful discussion of G. Wilson Knight as a modernist and a perceptive account of the rise and fall of E. M. W. Tillyard amongst his considerations of individual critics. Throughout he is aware of the ways in which the professionalization of Shakespeare criticism has been at war with a desire to give it an address to the world outside the academy. This leads him in his final chapter to celebrate the achievement of feminist criticism as that which most resists these institutionalizing pressures.

Grady's opinion is conveniently to be tested by the anthology *The Matter of Difference: Materialist Feminist Criticism of Shakespeare*, edited by Valerie Wayne (New York and London: Harvester Wheatsheaf, 1991), which grows explicitly out of professional in-fighting between new historicists and feminists, but claims a wider contemporary political agenda. Its ten essays (not all on Shakespeare, despite the title) are of a very high standard, demonstrating the range and suppleness of contemporary feminist criticism. Three essays I found particularly stimulating. Cristina Malcolmson's discussion of the relationship between social mobility and gender in *Twelfth Night*, charted through consideration of the functions of Viola and Malvolio is convincing in its demonstration of the negotiation the play makes between 'individual interests and those of traditional society' (pp. 29–58). Valerie Traub attempts to break the identification of gender with sexuality that is habitual in our culture and to test her thesis against the configurations of homoerotic desire in *As You Like It*, in a challenging, if sometimes obscure essay (pp. 81–114). Marion Wynne-Davis sets her discussion of the ambivalent functions of the women in *Titus Andronicus* in the framework of Elizabethan attitudes to rape, which she sees as undergoing significant change (pp. 129–53).

Two other feminist essays may be noticed here. Abbe Blum's '"Strike All That Look Upon With Mar[b]le": Monumentalizing Women in Shakespeare's Plays', in *The Renaissance Englishwoman in Print* edited by Anne M. Haselkorn and Betty S. Travitsky (Amherst: University of Massachusetts Press, 1990, pp. 99–118) arrives at a detailed consideration of the statue scene in *The Winter's Tale* after a survey of sundry ways in which other plays monumentalize women, usually as a means of silencing them and displacing male anxieties. Jeanne Addison Roberts deals with Shakespeare's and his male society's fears about women in 'Birth Traumas in Shakespeare', *Renaissance Papers* (1990), 55–66, by pointing to the ways in which all births in the plays are in some way problematic, or the rituals that appertain to them maimed.

The various general books I have received locate themselves across the spectrum of current approaches. Graham Holderness, Nick Potter and John Turner's *Shakespeare: Out of Court* (Macmillan: London, 1990) is the most 'historicist' of them. Recognizing the complexity of relationships between the court and society at large and taking account of the competitive and contradictory demands upon courtiers themselves the authors embark upon detailed analysis of six plays – *Love's Labour's Lost*, *Hamlet*, *As You Like It*, *Twelfth Night*, *The Tempest* and *The Winter's Tale*. John Turner approaches the first two using perspectives deriving from psychoanalysis; Nick Turner deploys a 'philosophical mythology' for the second pairing; Graham Holderness takes a semiotic approach to the last two. There are persuasive details in all the chapters, especially perhaps in the analysis of courtly competition in *Love's Labour's Lost*, and in the discussion of *Hamlet* as a deconstruction of the two Renaissance systems of platonism and machiavellism. Though I am not entirely convinced that the different perspectives of the authors work together coherently, nor that the various ways they identify 'the court' are entirely compatible, the book succeeds in widening the terms of the current debate about the relationship of the theatre to the systems of power.

Though Alan Hager in his *Shakespeare's Political Animal: Schema and Schemata in the Canon* (London and Toronto: Associated University Presses, 1990) gestures in his preface towards Greenblatt and Dollimore, his work is founded upon a humanism which sees Shakespeare's plays as finally concerned with delineating an essential 'human nature'. Beginning with a study of Sonnet 94, which he sees as a dramatization of the Machiavellian principle of necessary deception in a ruler, he proceeds in a series of short chapters to lay before us a somewhat conservative Shakespeare, pragmatic in politics (*The Taming of the Shrew, Henry V*), fearful of the dangers of 'levelling' (*Julius Caesar*), intent on the preservation of a necessary hierarchy in human affairs (*Much Ado, Macbeth*) and suspicious of idealism (*As You Like It, The Winter's Tale*). Each of the chapters is short, and in their brevity they often seem rather oversimplified. None the less the undergraduate will find some of the chapters (especially perhaps those on *Julius Caesar*) useful starting points, even if the overall thesis of the book is less than clear.

Charles and Michelle Martindale's *Shakespeare and the Uses of Antiquity* (London and New York: Routledge, 1990) surveys Shakespeare's relationship to classical literature in a traditional fashion. They assume that Shakespeare was not enormously learned, but argue that he was uniquely capable of representing the ancient world. General chapters on Shakespeare's Ovid and his Stoicism frame a short chapter on *Troilus and Cressida* and Homer and a more extended discussion of features of the Roman plays. Though the student will find useful material here, the book is curiously unfocused. Concentration on detailed connections between texts (which often seems to be giving Shakespeare marks for his accuracy or lack of it) alternates with some very generalized assertions about the plays' truthfulness as recreations of the Roman world. The total effect is rather fragmentary.

John Alvis's *Shakespeare's Understanding of Honor* (Durham, North Carolina: Carolina Academic Press, 1990) is avowedly 'reactionary in intent'. His work is intended, he says, to rouse American youth to 'recover their founders' sense of the choice-worthiness of honor'. In analyses of the Roman plays, together with *Lucrece, Hamlet* and the histories, he suggests that Shakespeare negotiates between a Roman, republican honour and the Christian celebration of a passive virtue. It is clear that Alvis's own emotional investment is much more in the former than the latter, but he does try to chart the way in which Shakespeare in his Roman sequence traces the rise and fall of the republican ideal, and gives a more ambiguous reading of *Henry V* than one might have anticipated. It is symptomatic of the book's politics that though Lucrece is the most unambiguously praised figure in his book, yet the disparity between male and female honour is barely considered.

For a generation or more teachers at all levels have been trying to make their students consider plays as plays, rather than novelistic texts. Analysis of the theatrical design of Shakespeare's plays has traditionally centred on the scene, but Charles A. Hallett and Elaine S. Hallett in their *Analyzing Shakespeare's Action* (Cambridge: Cambridge University Press, 1991) suggest that the 'sequence', defined as 'a unit of action which raises a single dramatic question and answers it', offers a more valuable point of departure. These sequences, they argue, are built up of 'beats', small building blocks defined as 'units of motivation'. In the course of the book a complex taxonomy of beats and scenes is established. All analytical study of this kind runs the risk of claiming empirical status for subjective constructs and, crucially, of being more interested in the naming of parts than in the effect or purpose of the whole. The Halletts' study doesn't entirely avoid these dangers, but because they have a clear sense of the consequence of their theory for the ways in which actors and directors might work upon the scenes of the play, many of their observations are useful and stimulating. If one could persuade students to invest the time in learning the vocabulary, then one would, I am sure, obtain valuable results in terms of their understanding of the plays.

The collection of essays *Reading Plays: Interpretation and Reception*, edited by Hanna Scolnicov and Peter Holland (Cambridge: Cambridge University Press, 1991) addresses the problems of discussing theatrical texts from a variety of perspectives. Among the Shakespearian chapters is a succinct and eminently sensible discussion by Stanley Wells of 'the problem of editorial intervention' in the making of the texts we read (pp. 30–55). James Redmond surveys the long history of a preference for reading plays over seeing them, and concludes that the two activities should be acknowledged in their complementary difference (pp. 56–80). Manfred Pfister writes on the 'corporeality of Shakespeare's text' (pp. 110–22); Ruth von Ledebur contributes an interesting account of finding teaching strategies for dealing with *The Merchant of Venice* in the context of recent German performances, which have tended to de-emphasize Shylock's Jewishness (pp. 123–39), and Hanna Scolnicov mediates on Chekov's 'impressionistic reworking' of *Hamlet* in *The Seagull* (pp. 192–205).

The nature of the audience Shakespeare addressed has been a lively area of controversy in recent years. Leo Salingar's Shakespeare Lecture, 'Jacobean Playwrights and "Judicious" spectators' in *Proceedings of the British Academy*, 75 (1989), pp. 1–23, contributes little new information, but points to the ways in which appeals to (or condemnations of) the audience increase in plays written after 1600, suggesting both a growth in the number of the educated amongst the theatre audience and a heightened uncertainty amongst dramatists (especially Jonson) about their relationship to that audience.

The volume of essays dedicated to Philip Edwards, *Literature and Nationalism*, edited by Vincent Newey and Ann Thompson (Liverpool: Liverpool University Press, 1991), contains amongst its Shakespearian offerings an amiable excursus by Joan Rees on Shakespeare's Welshmen (pp. 22–40), Arthur F. Kinney's situation of *Macbeth* in the context of ambiguous attitudes to the Scots (pp. 56–75), Inga-Stina Ewbank's elegant pairing of Shakespeare's *Richard III* with Strindberg's *Gustav III* (pp. 98–110), and Ruth Nevo's 'Yeats, Shakespeare and Ireland' (pp. 182–97).

There are two essays on music to remark. In 'Shakespeare's Provoking Music', in *The Well Enchanting Skill*, edited by John Caldwell, Edward Olleson and Susan Wollenberg (Oxford: Oxford University Press, 1990), pp. 79–90, I take the Duke's comments on Mariana's attachment to music as a starting point for consideration of the ways in which the ambiguous status of music in the period generates complex thematic and emotional effects upon the audience. Jeffrey P. Beck's essay 'Pulled from the Melodious Lay: A World Elsewhere and the Songs of *As You Like It* and *Hamlet*' in *Hamlet Studies*, 12 (1990), 9–28, draws out the contrast between songs which elaborate the promise of fulfilment in the comedy, but which, mangled and fragmented, image the dislocation of the tragic world.

By way of coda to this section one notes that amongst the reprints of already available material this year is *Learning to Curse* (London, New York: Routledge, 1990) where Stephen Greenblatt, the doyen of the recycled essay, re-presents the title essay on linguistic colonialism in *The Tempest*, and his discussion of King Lear's family problems in relation to a nineteenth-century tale of love-compulsion. Charles R. Forker's collection of essays entitled *Fancy's Images* (Carbondale and Edwardsville: Southern Illinois University Press, 1990) reprints work ranging from his early piece on theatrical symbolism in *Hamlet* to a recent essay on incest in the drama. It does include one new essay, an extended discussion of Perdita's 'flower speech', arguing that though it functions like a lyrical inset, it is more fully integrated into the whole pattern of its play than earlier such set-pieces. In the posthumous collection of Philip Brockbank's essays, *The Creativity of Perception* (Oxford: Blackwell, 1991) his freewheeling 'Urban Mysteries of the Renaissance: Shakespeare and the Carpaccio' is reprinted together with his poetic 're-creation' of the painting of The Martyrdom of Saint Ursula.

HISTORIES

The ghost of Tillyard seems to be still a necessary 'other' to accounts of the history plays. Larry Champion, in his school-book version of the new orthodoxy '*The Noise of Threatening Drum*' (Newark: University of Delaware Press; London and Toronto: Associated University Presses, 1990) structures each of his chapters round a routine invocation of the old 'conservative' view of the plays, and its replacement by a reading which argues that Shakespeare satisfied his heterogeneous audience with plays that asked questions about the nature of kingly and aristocratic power. The novelty in the book is the consideration of a number of non-Shakespearian plays (*The Famous Victories of Henry V, The Reign of Edward III, Sir John Oldcastle, Thomas, Lord Cromwell* and *Edmund Ironside*). But the brevity of each of the chapters generates a clumping oversimplification of argument, one which structurally privileges the subversive over any other reading. Though Champion suggests that different members of the audience might have had different reactions to the plays, it seems as if each section of that audience is allowed only one response.

By contrast Phyllis Rackin has produced a richly argued, clearly written account of the English chronicles in her *Stages of History* (London: Routledge, 1991). The introductory chapter offers a sensible account of the developing state of Renaissance historiography which rendered the ideological capture of historical narrative increasingly problematic. To this account she adds both an awareness of the compromised relationship of 'official' history to the marginal theatres in which it was staged, and a self-awareness of the position of the modern historian investigating the past. The second chapter discusses the consequence of tensions between providential and secular notions of causation; the third, 'Anachronism and Nostalgia' is especially valuable in its insistence that anachronism is consciously used in the plays to stage the contrary pull of a nostalgic idealism and the desire to make history speak directly to present needs. These ideas are developed in a persuasive and detailed analysis of different temporal perspectives in *Richard II*. The two concluding chapters deal with the marginalized figures of history, women and commoners. Rackin is especially good on the subversive function of the female characters in *King John*, and more generally on the ways in which patriarchal history requires the continuous suppression of the women who alone could guarantee its genealogy. She charts the sundry forms in which women, excluded from patriarchal history, represented 'the material physical life that patriarchal discourse could never completely capture or control'. In its careful analysis of the plays and its evocation of the multi-valent possibilities of history in the late sixteenth century, this is likely to be an influential book.

Sherman Hawkins considers the two tetralogies in his 'Structural Pattern in Shakespeare's Histories', *Studies in Philology*, 78 (1991), 16–45. He suggests that considering them in the order of their composition, rather than the historical order of the events they record, enables one to perceive diptychal organization in which the first, negative tetralogy is answered by a second, positive one. He complicates the architectonic model by positing in addition a chiastic, ABCD:DCBA relationship between the groups of plays. Many simplifications of the plays seem necessary to sustain the scheme, though some such architectonic ambition is by no means impossible.

Randall Martin's 'Elizabethan Civic Pageantry in *Henry VI*', *University of Toronto Quarterly*, 60 (1990/1), 244–63, suggests that the three plays draw on the scenic choreography and moralizing didacticism of pageants, processions, triumphs, and popular shaming rituals. Many of the parallels he notes seem to me to be rather a drawing upon common stock than purposeful intertextuality, though there is clearly a general case for such influence upon the ritual action of the histories. Craig A.

Bernthal focuses on one incident in *2 Henry VI* in his 'Treason in the Family: The Trial of Thumpe v. Horner', *Shakespeare Quarterly*, 42 (1991), 44–54. He contends that this episode challenges the 'subversion-containment' model of New Historicism in its provocation of a split reaction in the audience, satisfied about the victory of a loyal subject, but made anxious by the fact that such a victory is achieved by a servant against his master.

In the context of a symposium on 'desacralization' in *Deutsche Shakespeare-Gesellschaft West Jahrbuch* (1991), William C. Carroll's 'Desacralization and Succession in *Richard III*' (82–96) discusses the way in which *Richard III* systematically empties out the significance of all rituals. But, he notes, Richard never questions the principle of hereditary succession on which he relies absolutely. In the end, however, Carroll suggests that 'the more strongly Richard depends on it and Richmond reaffirms it, the more doubtful it becomes'.

Anthony Miller's approachable essay '*Henry IV Part I* and Renaissance Ideologies', *Sydney Studies in English*, 16 (1990–91), 35–53, points to the anxieties about nationhood implicit in the play, and discusses its treatment of female characters in the context of the uncertain succession to Elizabeth.

In recent years *Henry V* has become increasingly the site of theoretical battles. The anxieties that attend our response to Hal's ambiguous conduct in his apprenticeship, and to his kingly warfare are considered in Joel B. Altman's '"Vile Participation": The Amplification of Violence in the Theater of *Henry V*', *Shakespeare Quarterly*, 42 (1991), 1–32. He first discusses Hal's preparation for his kingly role, noting its obsessive concern with the problematic nature of the relationship between monarch and people. Altman argues that Shakespeare constructs through the narrative of Hal's life and the rhetoric which surrounds him in *Henry V* an illusory but potent sense of mutual participation between monarch and subject, play and audience. Most interestingly he sets this discuss-

ion in the context of contemporary anxieties about the conduct of the Irish campaigns of the 1590s and concludes that the play works to displace both that uneasiness, and uncertainty about Henry's conduct in battle, on to the foreign enemy. It is a subtle and persuasive article.

TRAGEDIES

In the studies of the tragedies, perhaps even more markedly than elsewhere, the context between old and new critical styles is foregrounded. T. McAlindon's *Shakespeare's Tragic Cosmos* (Cambridge: Cambridge University Press, 1991) sets its stall clearly in an older marketplace, the 'history of ideas'. He places the major tragedies within a world-view, not one which stresses hierarchical order, but an Empedoclean vision of nature as 'a system of concordant discord or "harmonious contrarietie", moved incessantly by the forces of love and strife'. McAlindon is not hostile to the idea that the plays may have had specific contemporary reference – his discussion of *Othello*, for example, depends upon the implications for an Elizabethan audience of their knowledge of the fate of Cyprus at the hand of the Turks – but he insists throughout that Shakespeare 'consciously and systematically referred the contradiction which troubled him most to a transhistorical model of human and universal nature'. For some readers this statement no doubt puts the book beyond the pale; but many others will find in this committed, scholarly and humane study much to appreciate. Instructive, for example, is his highlighting of the importance of the ways in which characters' perception of time functions with varying effect in each of the plays. The discussion of the image of the heart in *King Lear* is especially forceful, as is the way in which he lays out the multilayered references to myths of Mars and Venus, Isis and Osiris, and to Ovid and Plutarch in *Antony and Cleopatra* in support of his contention that these mythological sets inform the play's assertion of 'the underlying unity of East and West and point to the notion of *discordia concors* as essential to the understanding of the protagonists'. McAlindon is prepared even to resuscitate numerology in his readings of several plays, and if this (as he himself recognizes) runs the risk of seeming merely quaint in the current critical universe, his book as a whole reminds one of what is valuable in that which is under threat of expulsion.

Arthur Kirsch's *The Passions of Shakespeare's Tragic Heroes* (Charlottesville and London: University Press of Virginia, 1990) rather more aggressively identifies its enterprise as belonging to an older mode of criticism. Kirsch focuses on the four heroes of the 'great tragedies', in the conviction that the effect of the plays depends primarily upon the psychological richness with which these characters are explored. He invokes a Christian context and makes some reference to contemporaries, especially to Montaigne, but his use of Freud as guide and commentator emphasizes the fundamentally ahistorical, individualist perspective from which the book operates. So Hamlet, for example, is considered in terms of the psychopathology of mourning and melancholia, and his readiness to act in the conclusion of the play is construed as a symptom of his psychic recovery. Similarly founded analyses of Othello, who 'enacts for us the primitive energies that are the substance of our own erotic lives', of Lear as a man confronting death, and of Macbeth and Lady Macbeth as 'disunited parts of a single psychic identity' are offered with a clear sense of purpose. The concluding chapter of the book swats at the demons of New Historicism and cultural materialism, without much argumentative rigour, but with a deal of bad temper.

Analysis of character is the basis also of Bernard J. Paris's *Bargains with Fate: Psychological Crises and Conflicts in Shakespeare and his Plays* (New York and London: Plenum Press, 1991). His exegesis derives from the psychoanalytic work of Karen Horney, who identified three possible strategies through which human beings overcome their sense of weakness: the 'self-effacing', the 'aggressive' and the 'resigned' (with subdivisions to each). In adulthood, she suggests, we adopt one strategy and repress the others. Paris develops the theory by suggesting that characters in the tragedies make a 'bargain with fate' demanding that obedience to the dictate of their chosen defence strategy should be rewarded. Tragedy comes about when that bargain is unfulfilled, unpicking the self's ideal image and precipitating psychological conflict. Paris considers the main characters of the four major tragedies in the first part of the book; in the shorter second part Shakespeare himself is analysed and his career seen as an attempt to come to some accommodation between these various defensive strategies. Whether this book contributes to psychoanalytic theory I am not competent to judge, but even those literary critics sympathetic to such approaches may well find some of Paris's fitting of characters to prescribed labels rather simplistic.

Much trendier is Molly Smith's *The Darker World Within: Evil in the Tragedies of Shakespeare and His Successors* (Newark: University of Delaware Press; London and Toronto: Associated University Presses, 1991). She says: 'seventeenth-century stage drama in its concern with evil contributed much to the social drama (sociopolitical events) of the period'. Unexceptional statement, one might think, but in execution this carelessly printed book presents such a jumble of material in the service of such a simplified notion of the relationship of texts to their ambient culture that one cannot recommend it.

A rather different new perspective is offered by H. W. Fawkner in two books published concurrently, *Deconstructing Macbeth: The Hyperontological View*, and *Shakespeare's Hyperontology: Antony and Cleopatra*, (Rutherford, Madison, Teaneck: Farleigh Dickinson University Press; London and Toronto: Associated University Presses, 1990). Even with the glossary of terms provided in the first of the books, and the experience of both of them, I'm still not sure I understand what 'hyperontological' really means. For though the books are placed within the terrain of a deconstructive approach, the most interesting parts seem very like close readings of a much more traditional kind, with the goals of interpretation being a celebration of the collapse of definition rather than a triumphant organic wholeness. The discussion of Macbeth's murderous intent, for example, draws heavily on John Bayley, but explores further the way in which 'the idea of murder is stronger for Macbeth than the murder, and he therefore in a strange way has to perform the murder in order to murder the idea of it'. The highlighting of the significance of patterns of leaving and following in *Antony and Cleopatra* engenders suggestive readings of a number of episodes. But throughout both books the reliance on a very unproblematized notion of the genius of a Shakespeare who perceived the truths of deconstruction and intended to convey them in the plays, suggests that behind the insistent teasing of terms in approved deconstructive fashion, lies an interpretative position that is not so significantly different from the 'essentialist' critics he so often berates.

Titus Andronicus is given a straightforward scene by scene reading in Maurice Charney's volume in the New Critical Introductions series (London: Harvester Wheatsheaf, 1990). He discusses the play's dramatization of Rome in decline, sees Titus' rage as a precursor of Lear, and claims that the rhetorical, emblematic nature of the language is not at odds with dramatic effectiveness on the stage. It is a sensible, if rather ponderous account of the play.

Romeo and Juliet is the subject of two articles in *Studies in Philology*, 78 (1991). Joan Ozark Holmes focuses upon the function of Mercutio in her '"Myself Condemned and Myself Excus'd": Tragic Effects in *Romeo and Juliet*' (345–62) suggesting complex motivation for his fighting. Nathaniel Wallace dusts off the linguistic categories of metonymy and metaphor, standing here for 'the principle of tran-

sition' and 'the principle of dissolution' respectively, suggesting that they might provide a way of explaining the complex relationship of the central figure to the culture of Verona. ('Cultural Tropology in *Romeo and Juliet*', 329–44).

Of the essays I've encountered on *Hamlet*, Karin S. Codden's '"Such Strange Desygns": Madness, Subjectivity and Treason in *Hamlet* and Elizabethan Culture', *Renaissance Drama*, 20 (1989), 51–75 seems to me the most stimulating. It usefully sets Hamlet's madness in the context of reports of the career of the melancholic (or mad) Earl of Essex, which, she argues, demonstrate the way in which madness was seen both as cause and as symptom of politically threatening behaviour. Hamlet's undecidable madness, she suggests, is therefore to be read both as a crisis of subjectivity to the Prince, and a crisis of authority for the political world he inhabits.

Alan Fisher revalues Polonius in 'Shakespeare's Last Humanist', *Renaissance and Reformation*, 26 (1990), 37–47. Placing Polonius' fondness for maxims within humanist educational tradition, Fisher suggests that he is not merely a fool, but a figure symptomatic of humanist confidence in modes of understanding by maxim and oratorical expression that are shown to be inadequate by the world of the play. David Thatcher in *Hamlet Studies*, 12 (1990), 59–74, suggests that the killing of Polonius is an unresolvably ambiguous episode, and that its imponderability is paradigmatic of the imponderability of the play as a whole. Sandra K. Fischer's feminist account of Ophelia in 'Hearing Ophelia: Gender and Tragic Discourse in *Hamlet*', *Renaissance and Reformation*, 26 (1990), 1–10, follows a now fairly familiar course in arguing that 'the politics of Ophelia's rhetoric offers a feminine counterpart to Hamlet's tragedy' – though not all will be convinced that it is also 'a devastating commentary on it'.

King Lear generates readings from very different critical perspectives, though most are variations on the fundamental question of the play's ultimate optimism or pessimism. Jagannath Chakravorty's *King Lear, Shakespeare's Existentialist Hero* (Calcutta: Avantgarde Press, 1990) is perhaps the oddest. He sees Lear's renunciation of the kingship as the first stage of an heroic existential quest in which the Fool is Bad Faith seeking to impede his progress, and Cordelia a model of autonomous self-determination. For Edward Taylor, in '*King Lear* and Negation', *ELR*, 20 (1990), 17–39, the insistent repetition of 'nothing' and related words at the play's opening is what prepares us to understand the full force of its ending. Meditating on the 'no'/'know' pun, using Freud as well as classical and Christian discussions of negativity, he draws a map of Lear's movement to the moment when he 'comes to know No, to know naught and nothing no longer through a glass darkly'. A different approach to the play's preoccupation with 'nothing' is offered by Paul Hammond's thoughtful and substantial essay 'The Play of Quotation and Commonplace in *King Lear*' in *Toward a Definition of Topos*, edited by Lynette Hunter (London: Macmillan, 1991), pp. 78–129. In his view Shakespeare subjects the rhetorical and generic commonplaces which sustained his sources to a fundamental dislocation. The uses Erasmus and Montaigne made of adage and quotation are examined as analogues to Shakespeare's procedures in the play. After detailed close analysis of the rhetoric of the opening scenes and the fragmented quotations of the Fool and Edgar, Hammond concludes that 'Shakespeare's *King Lear* reveals to us the structure of our thinking by means of the intricate and destabilizing play of commonplace against commonplace'. Where Hammond emphasizes the instability of point of view implicit in humanist rhetoric, Erasmus is invoked to quite opposite ends in John X. Evans's essay 'Erasmian Folly and *King Lear*', *Moreana* 27 (1990), 17–39, where Cordelia is a type of Christian folly and the final scene a reworking of the Pietà with its promise of victory in defeat. Folly is the subject also of R. A. Zimbardo's 'The King and the Fool: King Lear

as Self-Deconstructing Text', *Criticism*, 23 (1990), 1–30. Though I am not convinced by the framing argument of this essay it is valuable for its illustrated investigation of versions of the King/Fool antithesis and synthesis from the Hebrew legend of Solomon and Marcolf through medieval representations to Armin's works.

Macbeth has a rather dull time of it this year. S. Schoenbaum's collection of essays on *Macbeth* (New York and London: Garland, 1991) concentrates on old favourites, with only Marvin Rosenberg and Carolyn Asp representing more recent approaches. Sarah Wintle and René Weis consider the functioning of the image and actuality of childlessness in '*Macbeth* and the Barren Sceptre', *Essays in Criticism*, 41 (1991), 128–46, without coming up with very much that is novel. Rachel Trubowitz sets Shakespeare alongside Milton in '"The Single State of Man": Androgyny in *Macbeth* and *Paradise Lost*', *Papers in Language and Literature*, 26 (1990), 305–33. She suggests that the play legitimates an imperial and masculinist ideology where the 'only good androgyne is a male androgyne' since Duncan and Banquo are positive versions, while Lady Macbeth and the witches are negative ones.

Julia Genster's 'Lieutenancy, Standing In and *Othello*', in *ELH*, 57 (1990), 785–805, opens up interesting possibilities by considering the ways in which the fixed structures of military rank may be 'mapped on to the structures of personal identity, of social and sexual governance' in the play. Especially useful is her meditation on the significance of a lieutenant (a rank only recently codified in the period) as deputy, substitute and potential usurper, though the extension of this image to the audience's relationship to the play seems rather overstretched.

Wayne A. Rebhorn parallels the conduct of the Romans with the situation of the Elizabethan aristocracy in his 'The Crisis of the Aristocracy in *Julius Caesar*', *Renaissance Quarterly*, 43 (1990), 75–111. He focuses usefully on the way both the play and contemporary society were preoccupied with 'emulation', a quality which may either promote intense rivalry and hostility or, on the other hand, foster fellow-feeling. His suggestion that the suicidal ends of the Romans is a warning of the likely future of the nobility, however, seems excessively crude.

Similarly blunt is Larry R. Clarke's '"Mars his heart inflam'd with Venus": Ideology and Eros in Shakespeare's *Troilus and Cressida*', *Modern Language Quarterly*, 50 (1990), 209–26. Here the Trojans are the old aristocracy and the Greeks the new men of the bourgeoisie, and the play a warning to aristocrats to curb their licentious behaviour. A much more productive approach to this play is to be found in Barbara Hodgdon's 'He do Cressida in Different Voices', *ELR*, 20 (1990), 254–86. She concentrates on the way in which Cressida is represented, especially in her opening and closing scenes, as a female figure who at first might seem to be able to own her 'gaze', but who, at the end, is enclosed within the fetishizing male gaze of those who watch her scene with Diomedes. Her essay gains enormously from detailed consideration of a number of prompt copies for recent productions. She finds in Howard Davies' 1985 performance an attempt to interrogate the familiar Cressida, always already marked out as whore. The ambivalent reaction to that performance becomes a symptom of cultural resistance to the unpicking of the stereotype that, in Hodgdon's view, the play text seems to permit. If sometimes tangled in expression (and, I think, underplaying the degree to which the male gaze is itself rendered problematic in the mutual eyeing up of male opponents) this is a stimulating piece.

Sakae Yoshitomi's 'The Influence of Robert Ashley on Coriolanus', *Scientific Reports of the Kyoto Prefectural University, Humanities*, 42 (1990), 13–25, suggests that a brief comment on Coriolanus in Robert Ashley's *Of Honour* may have prompted Shakespeare's insistence upon his hero's honourable integrity.

A brief but pointed essay by Clare Kinney, 'The Queen's Two Bodies and the Divided Emperor: Some Problems of Identity in *Antony and Cleopatra*' in *The Renaissance Englishwoman in Print*, pp. 178–86, contrasts the inclusiveness of Cleopatra as an Egyptian sovereign who fuses private and public, male and female, with the Roman world, predicated upon male competition, where Octavius grows great by severing the part of him that is Antony. A similar celebration of Cleopatra as a positive transgressive figure is offered by Jyotsna Singh in 'Renaissance Antitheatricality, Antifeminism and Shakespeare's *Antony and Cleopatra*', in *Renaissance Drama*, 20 (1989), 99–121. She points out the ways in which opposition to the theatres was characteristically linked with fear of effeminacy and femininity, and argues that this same association is embodied in Cleopatra both to reveal and subvert the existing ideology.

COMEDIES AND ROMANCES

The only full-length study of the comedies to have come my way is David Richman's *Laughter, Pain, and Wonder: Shakespeare's Comedies and the Audience in the Theater* (Newark: University of Delaware Press; London and Toronto: Associated University Presses, 1990). In the opening chapters he isolates and exemplifies the three comic attributes of his title, then discusses their combination, with a chapter on 'Endings' to round things off. What gives the often conventional readings of the plays their life and their usefulness is the way problems of tone and response are continuously discussed in terms of theatrical solutions in the records of past performances. This gives a focus, for example, to discussion of comic cruxes like the imprisonment of Malvolio, or the trial of Shylock. It is not the most demanding of books, but will be useful for undergraduate teaching and provide some stimulus to producers and actors.

Foucault provides the under-text for Richard Wilson's heavyweight article 'The Quality of Mercy: Discipline and Punishment in Shakespearian Comedy', in *The Seventeenth Century*, 5 (1990), 1–42. Through detailed study of *Measure for Measure, The Merchant of Venice* and *The Tempest* Wilson argues that these plays reflect the movement of English society away from the theatre of execution and towards a carceral society at a much earlier historical moment than Foucault suggested. Mercy in this dispensation becomes a way of enforcing obedience; Vincentio's surveillance becomes a prototype of Prospero's panoptic control. There is much else in this dense piece about the ways in which the comedies stage the transformations of the machineries of power in the transition from Elizabeth to James. If the effect is to make comedy seem unduly dark and threatening, there is a subtler deployment of the Foucauldian paradigm than one often encounters in New Historicist work.

The relationship of plays to sources features in three articles, the first Laurie Osborne's 'Dramatic Play in *Much Ado About Nothing*: Wedding the Italian Novella and English Comedy', *Philological Quarterly*, 69 (1990), 178–88, which suggests that the structurally emphatic opposition of the brothers Don John and Don Pedro as malign and comic manipulators figures the way the play struggles to combine the melodrama of the novella with the comic impulse. Shakespeare's modification of Lodge's conventional figure of Coridon into a Corin who brings *As You Like It* closer to the economic and social realities of the 1590s is A. Stuart Daley's subject in 'Shakespeare's Corin, Almsgiver and Faithful Feeder', in *English Language Notes*, 27, 4 (1990), 4–21. He suggests that Corin's generosity mobilizes resonances of Christ's command to show hospitality to strangers. Margaret Lael Mikesell, in '"Love Wrought these Miracles": Marriage and Genre in *The Taming of the Shrew*', *Renaissance Drama*, 20 (1989), 141–67, argues that Shakespeare purposefully modifies the nature of both his main source-types, the New Comedy of the Bianca plot and the shrew-taming stories of the main plot, in order systematically to bring the play into conformity with the Protestant view of companionate marriage.

A much less benign view of the play is taken in Lynda E. Boose's 'Scolding Brides and Bridling Scolds: Taming the Woman's Unruly Member', *Shakespeare Quarterly*, 42 (1991), 179–213, though commentary on the play itself quickly gives way to discussion of the cucking-stool and the scold's bridle as symptoms and symbols of a patriarchal culture.

Dorothea Kehler also takes a feminist approach in her brief but punchy piece 'Jaquenetta's Baby's Father: Recovering Paternity in *Love's Labour's Lost*', *Renaissance Papers*, (1990), 45–54, suggesting that the uncertainty as to whether Costard or Don Armado is actually the father allows for the articulation in the 'lower-class' subplot of anxieties about hierarchy, heredity and cuckoldry which are present but foreclosed in the main plot. Jaquenetta, unchaste but unpunished, figures a challenge to male fears, and emerges even as a proto-feminist in her ability to claim sexual freedom.

Michael Ferber's long and complex essay 'The Ideology of *The Merchant of Venice*', ELR, 20 (1990), 431–64, suggests that the play combines three different ideological matrices in a provocative, but unstable way. The first is the ideology of aristocratic friendship and generosity, the second a mercantilism which privileges risk-taking and denigrates usury, and the third a Christian contempt for worldly things. He argues, moreover, that Venice was a locale particularly pertinent to England, which saw itself as taking over from the declining republic, and he sees Shylock as in part a version of Puritan usurers in London. In his reading the Venetian world is not so simply the undesirable opposite to Belmont it is often taken to be. It's a heady brew, stimulating if not altogether lucidly presented. (The abstract is necessary preliminary reading.) Equally fashionable, but rather less exciting, is Lawrence Normand's 'Reading the Body in *The Merchant of Venice*' in *Textual Practice*, 5 (1991), 53–73. In both the casket scene and, of course, the trial scene, he points to the ways in which 'textuality and the body are overlaid' and asserts that the final act attempts to escape from the problematics of the earlier part of the play in its assertion of a transcendental unity of body and soul.

Cynthia Lewis adopts a theological perspective in '"Derived Honesty and Achieved Goodness": Doctrines of Grace in *All's Well that Ends Well*', *Renaissance and Reformation*, 26 (1990), 147–70. She suggests that the play stages a conflict between free will and Calvinist doctrine. The problem of our response to Bertram, therefore, is one of deciding whether some reformation in his character means that at the end he has merited reward, or of accepting that despite his lack of moral progress he receives the free gift of divine grace. She concludes that the play comes to no conclusion on the matter.

Maurice Hunt's approach in *Shakespeare's Romance of the Word* (Lewisburg: Bucknell University Press; London and Toronto: Associated University Presses, 1990) is to focus on language, in particular on the ways in which 'rare acts of expression and ways of knowing supersede and occasionally rectify earlier disasters of speech and understanding'. So, for example, Pericles is redeemed from passivity when he is able to speak that which the 'uncreative word' of Antiochus' riddle had locked up; the narrative of Cymbeline requires the liberating perspective of Jupiter's riddle, when 'the divine word provides the key for interpreting earthly happenings'. Though there are many local insights into the workings of language in the plays, the book is curiously elusive in its total effect, complicated but not illuminated by reference to some (relatively) modern theories of language. A similar concern with language and interpretation forms the basis of David M. Bergeron's study of the reading of letters in 'Reading and Writing in Shakespeare's Romances', *Criticism*, 23 (1991), 91–114.

The Winter's Tale receives two substantial exegeses of determinedly theoretical cast.

William R. Morse attacks the New Historicist overstatement of the power of the dominant ideology in 'Metacriticism and Materiality: The Case of Shakespeare's *The Winter's Tale*', *ELH*, 58 (1991), 283–304. Shakespeare, Morse suggests, 'produces a disengagement with his audience that works towards the demystification of authority through the deconstruction of the transcendent conceptions of metaphysics and rationality that privilege and sustain it'. The somewhat opaque style is fairly typical of the article as a whole, which in many ways seems to be saying rather unexceptional things about the irrationality of Leontes and the self-conscious 'staginess' of the final act but making them demonstrate Shakespeare's ideological fluidity. Michael D. Bristol's 'In Search of the Bear: Spatiotemporal Form and the Heterogeneity of Economies in *The Winter's Tale*', *Shakespeare Quarterly*, 42 (1991), 145–67, opens with a discussion of the perception of time, which he sees as much more multilayered in the Renaissance than standard oppositions of 'cyclical' and 'linear' temporality allow. He then sets up the play's structure in terms of an opposition between the feasts of winter and summer. The action in Leontes' court is persuasively characterized as 'a type of spatiotemporal derangement of the ethos of gift, hospitality and expenditure mandated by the Winter festival'. The bear who marks the moment of transition is an appropriately liminal figure, connected both with Candlemas (the end of the winter), with tyranny and aggressive sexuality but also with the nature and creativity that is anticipated at this point. The second half of the play jumps past the penitence of Lent to a summer feast. It's at this point that I confess to losing the thread. For Bristol argues that the sheep-shearing feast is predicated upon the shepherd's gold, and upon a new, market economy quite unlike the gift-giving principles abused in the first half of the play. The ambition of the article seems to exceed its space, and in the process it loses clarity of direction.

That *The Tempest* draws upon Virgil and is

implicated in the discourses of colonialism has long been agreed. In her valuable and stimulating study, *Virgil and "The Tempest": The Politics of Imitation* (Columbus: Ohio State University Press, 1990) Donna B. Hamilton maps both of these on to contemporary debates about the limits of monarchical power to argue that '*The Tempest* is not a transcendent, indifferent text and that Shakespeare was not an apologist for monarchy'. She sets her consideration of Virgilian influence within Renaissance theories of imitation, and goes on to explore the rich and varied relationships of the play to its pre-text. Because the *Aeneid* was read as a poem about imperial power and colonization it was a model which enabled Shakespeare to encode discussion of contemporary concerns about these issues within his drama. She investigates the relationships of the play to the language and assumptions which underpinned Parliament's opposition to the Great Contract, demonstrating that the construction of the play, its focus on reciprocality and its articulation of questions about the limits of power permit Shakespeare to articulate a contractual view of sovereignty. Though not all the resemblances claimed with Virgil's text or Parliamentary debates seem equally compelling, this study moves discussion of *The Tempest* emphatically forward from the now rather stale reiteration of its duplicitous colonialism.

Stephen Rupp arrives at similar conclusions about the political message of the play via a comparison with Calderón, in his 'Reason of State and Repetition' in '*The Tempest* and *la vida es sueño*' in *Comparative Literature*, 42 (1990), 289–318. Both playwrights, he suggests, are responding to the debate over Machiavellian statecraft. The frequent repetitions to be found in the plays indicate that the ruler who proceeds only by secular reasons of state will induce a repetitive cycle of intrigues which will only be ended when he learns to accept the traditional limits of sovereignty.

A SHAKESPEARE MUSIC CATALOGUE

Ours is the age of information gathering. It is also the period of the substantial grant-funded research project. *A Shakespeare Music Catalogue*[1] is an outstanding product of a marriage between the two. Its first three volumes record 20,000 musical items composed before the cut-off date of 31 December 1987 (seven times more than Phyllis Hartnoll's 1964 catalogue in *Shakespeare in Music*). They are organized in play-by-play listings, each prefaced by a summary of music cues in the text. Entries are subdivided into lists of incidental music, operas and related music, non-theatrical vocal settings and non-theatrical instrumental music, with further sections of settings of combined texts and 'obliquely related works'. A final section clears away works mistakenly thought to be of Shakespearian inspiration, such as Beethoven's *Coriolan*, or Bellini's *I Capuleti e i Montecchi* amongst many lesser pieces. The fourth volume indexes the music; the fifth is a bibliography of criticism.

As the editors acknowledge in the preface, their labours do not alter our global sense of the plays which have prompted most music, nor of the songs which have been most frequently set. It is rather the sheer quantity of music that overwhelms. 'It was a lover' and 'O mistress mine' each have over 250 settings; *Romeo and Juliet* has prompted about thirty-five operas. Vaughan Williams's wonderful 1938 setting of 'How Sweet the Moonlight' in the *Serenade To Music* is preceded by twenty-eight settings of some of the same words, and its success has not deterred a further twenty-five composers from attempting the same text since. The *Catalogue* is witness to the ever-growing cultural pre-eminence of Shakespeare as it traces the exponential growth from a thin trickle in the

[1] Bryan N. S. Gooch and David Thatcher, eds. *A Shakespeare Music Catalogue*, 5 vols. (Oxford: Oxford University Press), 1991 (pp. xcv; 2847, vol. 1 £70; vol. 2 £70; vol. 3 £60; vol. 4 £45; vol. 5 £40).

eighteenth century to the flood of composition in the last half-century. It can scarcely be the inherent quality of Shakespeare's lyrics that has attracted composers in such quantity; nor does the conspicuous failure of most attempts to convert the plays into operas suggest that they are the most natural fodder for librettists. Indeed, as one follows the course of Shakespearian adaptations from the seventeenth century (where most of the finest music was produced to non-Shakespearian texts – Purcell only set a single line of Shakespeare, and that was in a lyric by another poet) through the nineteenth-century career of Henry R. Bishop (the 'deranger' of Shakespeare as Winton Dean called him) to modern musical versions such as *Kiss Me Kate*, *West Side Story* or the profusion of 'rock' operas such as *Rockbeth* or the work variously entitled *Kronberg: 1582*, *Rockabye Hamlet* or *Something's Rockin' in Denmark*, one becomes aware of how much of this music is but tangentially related to the play texts themselves. Shakespeare's words have been varied, fragmented and travestied by composers and their librettists. One composer has even attempted to dramatize the proposition that monkeys left alone for long enough could by chance type the Complete Works in his *The Monkey Opera*, whose climax is the performance by Monkey 3 of the vowels only of the 'O that this too too solid flesh' soliloquy.

The plays have, of course, been the source of inspiration for serious musical works such as Elgar's *Falstaff* or Prokofiev's *Romeo and Juliet*, but the *Catalogue* also enables one to see ways in which Shakespeare functions as a cultural icon, prompting a *Shakespeare Hymn Tune Book*, making endless series of piano pieces marketable, and registering as jocular point of reference for pieces such as *Tuba or not Tuba*, or *Rumba-Fortinbras*.

The geographical scope of the compilers' searches is one reason for the *Catalogue*'s bulk. Eastern Europe and America are fully represented – as are two Chinese operatic versions of *Much Ado About Nothing* and *The Taming of the Shrew*. But perhaps the most significant factor in overgoing any previous catalogue is the decision to list incidental music composed for actual performances. Not surprisingly resident theatre musicians figure strongly in this category, from Robert Johnson, the chief composer for The King's Men, some of whose settings might have been used at the first performance, to contemporaries like David Amram, Juriaan Andriessen (whose third set for *Hamlet* is his Opus 642!), Guy Woolfenden, who has composed music for more plays than any other, and, champion of them all, Conrad Susa, whose eighty-five sets of incidental music make him the most prolific of all. Represented in this category are musicologists from Charles Burney to Jack Westrup. Academics such as John Wilders and John Hollander have also tried their hand, as have actors, including Dudley Moore in his organ-scholar days, Ben Kingsley and Laurence Olivier, who composed his own entrance music for a performance of *Romeo* in San Francisco in 1940.

The *Catalogue* also makes one aware of those composers for whom Shakespeare has had an almost obsessive fascination. Berlioz's infatuation with Shakespeare is well known and fully documented, as is the wide-ranging effort of Castelnuovo-Tedesco, whose ninety-one compositions include incidental music, operas, song-settings and instrumental music inspired by the plays. Others seem to have been taken over by individual texts. Between 1917 and 1962 Carl Orff made six attempts at getting his music for *A Midsummer Night's Dream* right; Frank Martin not only composed an opera on *The Tempest* from which he adapted a set of choral songs, but three of his orchestral works are recorded as being inspired by the text. But perhaps the most remarkable recorded obsession is that of the amateur Richard Simpson (d. 1876), whose Herculean labour in setting every one of the sonnets (and some of them twice) still doesn't get him into the company of the elect in the latest *Grove*.

Most of the *Catalogue*'s entries are strictly

functional (though the indication of the scoring of musical works gives rise to some surprises — why on earth did Gabriel Charpentier need a 'food processor' in his score for *I Henry IV*, and what kind of effect did the 'crackle paper from chocolate boxes' have in Helen Gifford's music for *Merchant of Venice*, one wonders?) Occasionally however the contributors allow more expansive entries, which sometimes give a human touch to the material. Edmund Kean apparently relaxed by composing music, though ignorant of notation, and Jean-Jacques Rousseau sang of an evening in 'a weak, cracked voice' his settings of Desdemona's 'Willow song'.

As one contemplates the *Catalogue* further, however, one is struck by the way in which its monumental solidity barely masks the degree to which it is in no small measure a record of ghosts. The names of thousands of composers have been rescued from oblivion, but their works remain hidden in Time's chest. Especially is this the case in the listings of incidental music. A quick count of the music for *Julius Caesar*, for example, reveals that almost two-thirds of the two hundred or so items are no longer extant, while just under a third are available in manuscript (provided one can contact the composer of many of them), and only a tiny handful have achieved print in whole or in part. It is not surprising that this should be so. Where the expansive musical provision in nineteenth-century theatres enabled composers to create substantial overtures and entr'actes which might then be published in full or issued for the domestic market in pianoforte arrangements, modern theatrical habit reduces the scale of a composer's intervention. Furthermore, as the presence of three or more musically unrelated sets of music for a play by a single composer indicates, contemporary theatre insists upon novelty and upon the integration of music with a particular vision of the play. (In a manner quite unlike the continued life of settings of Middleton and Davenant's Hecate scenes known as 'The Famous Music'

for *Macbeth*, which occupied the stage continuously from about 1702 to the late nineteenth-century.) Contemplating these recorded absences one regrets, for example, the loss of Manuel de Falla's music for *Othello* — but then perhaps he felt, as we are told Menotti felt about his music for *Romeo*, that even if the score were found he would not wish it to be performed. One wonders whether the disappearance of Lennox Berkeley's music for *The Tempest* prevented the production of a work analogous to his *Suite: A [sic] Winter's Tale*, derived from incidental music to a 1960 production, or whether the composer simply saw no good musical reason to preserve his earlier score.

The ghosts which hover over the other sections of the *Catalogue* are rather different. Here one is struck not so much by the loss of works known to have existed (though it would have been pleasant to have known a little more about Leoncavallo's *Dream* opera, apparently privately performed in Paris in 1899, though not recorded at all in *Grove*). It is rather the *Catalogue*'s listing of operas contemplated but never achieved that provokes a wistful sense of what might have been. Balfe, Berlioz, Bizet, Glinka, Mendelssohn, Schumann, Prokofiev and Verdi all seem to have contemplated a *Hamlet*. It is cause for sadness that Bloch, Britten, Mascagni and Verdi failed to bring projects for *King Lear* to completion (though one might be less distressed that Elton John's project for a rock *Hamlet* was apparently nothing more than a rumour). Sometimes reasons are given for the failure of compositions to materialize, ranging from Verdi's comment that *Lear*'s heath scenes 'terrified him' down to Hamish McCunn's refusal to compose music for *Macbeth* because he 'declined to introduce the bagpipe' for the hero's entrance. But much more often one is simply left to meditate on what has been lost, and on what might have been achieved.

The ghosts are not just musical. Theatre programmes for performances in major cities and universities are one of the major sources of information. These persuade the compilers to offer, where known, details of the director, some of the actors and musicians – information which might possibly have its own kind of interest, but which seems less than central to a music catalogue. Contemporary composers have been solicited for information, producing notes of compositions not yet completed (ghosts *in potentia*, as it were).

The overwhelming desire for comprehensiveness also generates lists of transcriptions and arrangements of Shakespearian pieces. This on occasion gives an interesting sidelight on the popularity of certain works – items from Ambroise Thomas's *Hamlet*, or Nicolai's *Merry Wives* have much more often been rearranged than anything from the operas of Verdi, for example. (It also gives weary church organists someone to blame for institutionalizing 'The Wedding March' – a couple in Tiverton in 1847 – and offers wedding parties the chance of choosing a version for six hands at one piano, or even for concertina or mandolin should the organist want a day off.) But sometimes the effort seems unduly conscientious. Do we really need the names of performers and recordings of Elgar's *Introduction and Allegro*, because it contains a motto from *Cymbeline* on the MS (but not the printed) score, or ninety pieces arranged from Weber's *Oberon*, which the compilers admit has little connection with Shakespeare, let alone five piano pieces entitled 'Silvia' which we are assured have nothing to indicate they were inspired by Shakespeare at all?

The real test for these volumes, however, will be how productively and how easily they might be employed by a wide variety of potential users. For many *Survey* readers the self-contained fifth volume of criticism may well be the most immediately valuable. It is selective, say the editors, but in its listing of over 3,000 items I can see no obvious omissions. The volume contains its own comprehensive index. Indeed readers should perhaps be warned that the index knows more than the text – looking up a play, for example, provides references to

items in the catalogue which give no indication of concentration on particular texts.

Whether those mounting productions of the plays will choose to consult the *Catalogue* must be a matter of doubt – for reasons already given they might find the effort of tracking down the material rather daunting. (Though anyone contemplating, say, a nineteenth-century setting for their performance could find interesting matter to achieve an authentic flavour.)

Undoubtedly the existence of this resource will of itself help to generate masses more material for future updating of the bibliography. Theses on theatre history, on musical and performance style, or on the chronological and geographical popularity of the plays will become more possible, and be more securely founded. So too, it is likely that singers and conductors will be inspired to search out items for concerts. (Expect an even stronger rash of Shakespeare Birthday events in the next few years.) But whatever their interest, students will have to do a great deal of digging around in the *Catalogue*.

Even the simplest of tasks – counting the most popular plays in terms of settings of the songs, generation of operas or incidental music – is made more difficult by the way that all items, whether new or arrangements, are numbered sequentially. (Might it not have been better to sub-classify such arrangements numerically as well as typographically?) Matters are complicated further by some uncertainties in the placing of material within the compilers' categories. While decisions must often have been difficult, the criteria by which some musical arrangements appear in the incidental music section, as 'operas', or are demoted to the 'obliquely related' category are not always clear. Some individual settings of songs occur only as incidental music while other pieces, like Peter Maxwell Davies's *Fool's Fanfare*, appear wrongly placed in this category. Some further sub-categorization would certainly have helped one to enumerate different genres of music much more easily.

A minor niggle concerns the way that some items frequently recur in full for no apparent reason, where others are dealt with more appropriately by brief cross-reference. An identical page of information about Verdi's *Falstaff* appears under *1 Henry IV, 2 Henry IV* and *Merry Wives*, for example, and it is surely excessive to offer under every play six lines on Johnny Dankworth's 'The Compleat Works', because it sets all Shakespeare's titles.

More importantly, though the index runs to more than 300 pages it inevitably cannot give access to the *Catalogue's* information by date, by country, by genre, instrumentation or vocal requirements. As an experiment I tried to construct programmes of music for choir, with and without instruments. Though I look forward to investigating a wide variety of pieces of which I hitherto knew nothing, I wonder how ready others will be to undertake the play-by-play, section-by-section trawl that was necessary to produce my reading list. Since the *Catalogue* itself was computer generated, one would welcome an index on disk that would greatly facilitate searches other than those by play, composer, or title of musical works.

In the end, however, such reservations as one might have about the *Catalogue* derive principally from the excess of its virtues. Its 2,847 pages are a monument of a particularly late twentieth-century kind, fearsome in its determination that nothing shall be lost; but it must surely be one of the most important reference works to have appeared in the last quarter-century.

2. SHAKESPEARE'S LIFE, TIMES, AND STAGE
reviewed by MARTIN WIGGINS

I

It is a courageous scholar who publishes a book with the professed aim of adding to the sum of human ignorance; but in Shakespeare studies we need such books. If the first age of the discipline saw figures like Fleay, Chambers, and Greg create a model of English Renaissance drama that was part scholarship, part hypothesis and guesswork, the second was an age of credulity, of critics in awe of dead giants whose authority lived on. As we enter the third age, the old certainties topple, and we aim for a state, to misquote John Ford's Friar Bonaventure, of knowledge in ignorance. One of the books helping us on our way is Margreta de Grazia's subtle and persuasive analysis of the birth of Shakespeare scholarship, *Shakespeare Verbatim* (Oxford, 1991).

The giant whom de Grazia has set out to bury goes back further than most: Edmond Malone, arguably Shakespeare's first truly scholarly commentator, whose assumptions, aims, and methodology remain the foundation of modern Shakespeare studies. De Grazia shakes those foundations:

To recognize the synthetic and contingent nature of the Shakespearean apparatus is to allow for the possibility of its being otherwise. Once the apparatus is situated in relation to historical exigency, its conceptual grip begins to weaken.　　(p. 13)

By showing scholarship to be the product of a precise set of historical and cultural circumstances in the late eighteenth century, she calls into question the view that it contributes to a positivist, evolutionary movement towards truth and understanding – such claims are still informed by the values of Malone's time.

Malone's centrality, for de Grazia, lies in the importance he gave to authenticity: as an editor, he sought to determine the exact words which Shakespeare wrote, and as a biographer to record the verifiable facts about his life. These aims, which seem so natural to modern scholars, and which inform so many of the questions we ask, were radical in their day. Before Malone, Shakespeare's life was more *bildungsroman* than biography, a collection of anecdotes which gave a narrative focus to the key turning-points in the writer's early development, but paid scant regard to the accuracy of such traditions: Shakespeare had the same reality which is today attributed to figures like Sherlock Holmes, their 'mythical' existence independent of conventional distinctions between historical personages and fictional characters. The words of the texts, too, were determined by what Shakespeare should have written rather than what he actually wrote: the Shakespeare plays were seen as an instrument in cultural projects such as purifying standards of taste or rectifying the English language, so each successive editor took as his copy-text the most recent edition, because it was the one most free from the sixteenth-century barbarisms of the original. Like Winston Smith rewriting *The Times*, their aim was to transcend that original text, not restore it: thus might Shakespeare, in time, be canonized as a fit work of Augustan literature.

Against this background, Malone's innovations look like a significant step towards a scholarship which seeks to understand Shakespeare in his own cultural context rather than assimilate him to ours. For de Grazia, however, the historicizing of Shakespeare was for Malone simply a more devious technique of assimilation:

Malone's sense of what was customary in Shakespeare's time was a convenient and commodious cache for what could not conform to Malone's standards, enabling him to countenance and condone what would formerly have been corrected or condemned. The strange particulars of the past could thereby coexist with the self-evident absolutes of the present. (p. 125)

Malone's methodology was different from his predecessors' not because he effaced his own cultural concerns, but because the concerns themselves changed. The rise of Romanticism in the late eighteenth century brought a sense of historical period into vogue, for instance: Malone's scholarly imperatives reflect the same interests that lie behind, say, the novels of Walter Scott. At the same time, aesthetic theory came to interpret works of art in personal terms as the product of the individual artist's imagination. This assumption permeates Malone's work: an accurate biography, correct assignment of authorship, the establishment of Shakespeare's chronological development, and the clarification of obscurity with reference to Shakespeare's usage elsewhere, all are underpinned by the Romantic concept of the artist. Such scholarship laid the foundations for the view of Shakespeare's works as a spiritual biography of their author: epigrammatically, Malone begat Dowden. It is suggestive that Malone's life of the artist ends at the point when he began to write plays: from there, it seems, the plays take over the story.

II

Malone's tutelage, according to *Shakespeare Verbatim*, delimited the ways in which subsequent scholarship was able to produce meaning in texts: it became not only an interpretative but an associative process. Admit, with Malone, that the plays are not works of contemporary literature, and you can no longer rely solely on their content to understand them: context – historical, cultural, biographical – becomes the determinant of interpretation, and investigative activity turns from the texts themselves to the appurtenant areas of life, times, and stage. A classic example of this procedure is Anne Jennalie Cook's study, *Making a Match* (Princeton, NJ, 1991), which discusses the plays in the light of a reconsideration of ideas about the wooing and wedding practices of Shakespeare's England.

We are told what to make of *Making a Match* in its last chapter, where Cook takes it upon herself to review her own book, and rewards herself with glowing praise. Regrettable though this may be as a lapse of taste, it is a fair account of this important study, which presents a vast collection of evidence covering most social ranks – though, as might be expected, the gentry provide the lion's share. The result is that the details of the plays take on new colours: Othello's jealousy of Cassio, for instance, seems more reasonable (though no less mistaken) when one learns of the suspicion in which proxy wooers were often held – a suspicion that lies behind other Shakespearian characters such as the Earl of Suffolk in *1 Henry VI*. Equally, many popular ideas about Elizabethan marriages are contradicted by much of the available historical evidence. In particular, the belief that Elizabethan women always married young – the *Romeo and Juliet* syndrome – turns out to derive from the naïve view that Shakespeare's plays invariably represented the common practice of his time. For the original playgoers, Cook demonstrates, a woman would and should usually marry in her twenties; so the play's emphasis on Juliet's age is a sign that she is atypical. Ironically, the most normal set of marital negotiations in English Renaissance drama appear to be those represented by John Ford in *'Tis Pity She's a Whore*.

Instead of the world of tyrannical parents and under-age brides of academic folklore, Shakespeare's seems to have been a time that was eminently sensible about marriage. Cook stresses that the financial arrangements so often despised by modern critics were both pragmatic and proper: fathers did not sell their daughters to the highest bidder (a charge often levelled at Baptista Minola), so much as ensure that the couple were adequately provided for. One reason why the charge of money-grubbing cynicism doesn't stick is that the heart as well as the wallet had its part to play: it was also expected that the prospective partners would meet and consent to the match. In theory, no one could be married against their will.

In practice, however, Cook's evidence shows that many people *were* forced into marriage – and this exposes a weakness of the book. As an attempt to make sense of Elizabethan and Jacobean practices and attitudes relating to the bonding process, it is excellent; but as a reconstruction of actual social behaviour, it presents only an intellectualized ideal. The specific examples often give an impression that runs counter to the expressed case: for instance, having laboured the point that dowry and dower were quite distinct concepts at the time, Cook then ignores the fact that Lear speaks of Cordelia's 'dower' when, inescapably, he means her dowry. Cook is clear and convincing when she explains the logic underlying opinions and customs which might seem unreasonable to us today; what she does not mention, and what her evidence demonstrates in abundance, is that many people none the less held those opinions and followed those customs out of blind prejudice.

This is a criticism less of Cook's fine study in particular than of the Malone methodology in general: Shakespeare scholars see history primarily in relation to the canon ('background', it used to be called), and that makes it all too easy to simplify the past. In fact, history is not smooth: it is not reducible to convenient homogeneity, which is what we can make of it if we are impatient to get on with reading Shakespeare. That is where historians come in, providing books like Michael MacDonald and Terence R. Murphy's *Sleepless Souls: Suicide in Early Modern England* (Oxford, 1990). This offers a fascinating and meticulously researched social history of attitudes and practices relating to suicide in the period: readers of Rowland Wymer's *Suicide and Despair in Jacobean Drama* (Brighton, 1986) will find that MacDonald and Murphy have little to add about the treatment of the act in plays, but their findings are most valuable in helping to establish a firmer period context for Wymer's conclusions.

The authors identify the sixteenth and early seventeenth centuries as an 'era of severity' in the treatment of suicides, during which the act was understood as a heinous crime, a category of murder and instigated by the devil: the corpse of a suicide was afforded only maimed rites of burial, and the forfeiture of the person's goods was effectively a financial penalty for the surviving family. These are values strikingly discontinuous with the respectful treatments of suicide in contemporary plays: only in the eighteenth century did opinions liberalize in a way that might tolerate Othello's self-destruction. In Malone's terms of reference, it would *therefore* not have been tolerated in 1604, irrespective of the emotional pull of the text itself; but MacDonald and Murphy resist this easy option. They see drama instead as a record of 'opposition and ambivalence' to the dominant attitudes to suicide.

Unfortunately they are not content with this reasonable generalization, as Wymer was with remarking on the difference between art and life.[1] When they attempt to pin text more firmly to context, the result is a simplification reminiscent of the 'privileged playgoers' era of Shakespearian scholarship. Evidently there were cultural traditions more favourable to suicide, and evidently some of these were most accessible to the educated classes, but it is reductive to assimilate the plays to these discourses, and so interpret them solely as carriers of élite values. It is hard to maintain such an assumption in the light of recent work showing how drama was infused with the popular culture of the time, such as Lynda Boose's feminist analysis of the scold in relation to *The Taming of the Shrew*, or Frederick Jonassen's discussion of the folk scapegoat 'Jack-a-Lent', alluded to by Falstaff in *The Merry Wives of Windsor*.[2] In particular, Sandra Billington's *Mock Kings in Medieval Society and Renaissance Drama* (Oxford, 1991) makes popular social customs a major factor in the contemporary appeal of the Elizabethan theatre.

Billington's thesis concerns the English folk tradition of the lord of misrule and its relevance to treatments of power and authority on the Elizabethan and Jacobean stage. Drawing on material from medieval times up to 1649, she analyses the practice of enthroning commoners as mock kings, which took place at winter festivities and summer games, but with different implications in each case. Winter kings, such as the Prince of Purpoole in the Gray's Inn revels of 1594, were treated with respect, and ruled over a world which inverted the norms of ordinary life; they served the valuable social function of reminding the powerful of the limitations of their own authority. In contrast, summer kings were more likely to be derided – which may well explain (though Billington misses this) why Malvolio's gulling is called 'midsummer madness' (3.4.54) in a play entitled *Twelfth Night*. Midsummer games, played out on hilltops, had different symbolic values from their winter counterparts: whereas the reign of a Christmas monarch celebrated a liminal, alternative world, the election of a summer king represented 'the ascent and superiority of a man at his physical peak' (p. 65), with the implication of decline to come; the association of hilltops with Fortune only added to that sense of the future, and this served to subvert the summer king's pomp, making it look instead like the pride that comes before a fall. In short, winter kings were honoured for their licence; but summer kings were Fortune's fools.

The crux of Billington's argument is that the assumption of kingly qualities by men who were not born to them was not only a social practice but a pervasive idea which informed the discourses of politics and literature in the medieval and Renaissance periods. The association of mock kings with the organization of rebel or outlaw groups seems to have fallen into abeyance by the sixteenth century, but the concept remained useful in less drastic forms of dissent. Actual monarchs who failed to live up

---

[1] Wymer, *Suicide and Despair*, pp. 157–8.

[2] Lynda E. Boose, 'Scolding Brides and Bridling Scolds: Taming the Woman's Unruly Member', *Shakespeare Quarterly*, 42 (1991), 179–213; Frederick B. Jonassen, 'The Meaning of Falstaff's Allusion to the Jack-a-Lent in *The Merry Wives of Windsor*', *Studies in Philology*, 88 (1991), 46–68.

to the ideal of kingship could be satirized as lords of misrule – in effect, mock kings could be used to mock kings. Such manifestations are the book's route from medieval society to Renaissance drama.

From the late 1580s, Billington contends, a theatre dependent on the custom of a popular audience began to incorporate popular forms in its play-texts, and duly achieved mass success: from Marlowe's shepherd-ruler in *Tamburlaine* to Beaumont and Fletcher's unknowing usurper in *A King and No King*, king games are a recurrent structure underlying some of the greatest plays of the period. Numerous ideas and issues prominent in the English Renaissance mind, from Fortune to the *mundus inversus*, were associated in one way or another with representations of unconventional or inadequate kingship, and Billington offers a stimulating analysis of the ways in which the drama engaged with such matters in a wide range of plays.

The book's drawback is a general conservatism in its foundations. Though Billington deals, in an admirably lucid way, with critical issues raised by some of the more recent schools of thought – by post-structuralists with their interest in the repressed 'other' as well as by new historicists – her scholarly assumptions are all too often time-dishonoured ones. She is, for instance, one of that thought-to-be-extinct species who believe that *The Troublesome Reign of King John* is a two-part play rather than a single work divided by a publisher hoping to cash in on the success of *Tamburlaine*, as J. W. Sider has demonstrated in the most recent edition.[3] Moreover, there is an understandable attachment to the exploded idea of court premières, which serves to centre interpretations on the king-games associated with festive occasions.[4]

The fundamental problem with the argument lies in the priority which is given to the folk rituals which occupy the first half of the book: it is apparent that *any* undermining or satirizing treatment of an authority-figure is taken to be a form of king game, however minimal the evidence for direct association (though it is true that such association would be hard to prove at the best of times). Moreover, Billington has a habit of making connections without properly articulating her criteria: for instance, she sees hilltops in several pictures where (without an explanation of the iconographical signals informing her interpretation) methinks the ground is even. In the absence of specific parallels, one wonders whether king games might better be regarded not as a source for the plays but as an analogous cultural form dealing with some of the same issues. If we can conceive of significant relationships between texts or cultural practices only in terms of the diachronic link of source and influence, are we not making evolutionism too much of a fetish? This is a limitation encoded in the very structure of Billington's book: it offers a fascinating insight into an aspect of social and intellectual history, and an interesting study of a wide range of Elizabethan and Jacobean plays; its weakness lies in its attempt to draw a direct link between the two.

In Margreta de Grazia's terms, this is a case of Malone's interpretative structures serving to determine interpretative conclusions: it is all too easy to allow our interest in the plays of the period to generate arguments which, unconsciously or otherwise, locate drama as the terminus into which all other Renaissance culture flows. In the present state of criticism, the most visible alternative is the radical one offered by new historicism and cultural materialism, to see plays as interventions in history rather than works standing outside and feeding

---

[3] J. W. Sider (ed.), *The Troublesome Raigne of John, King of England* (New York and London, 1979), p. xiv.

[4] See Richard Levin, *New Readings Versus Old Plays* (Chicago and London, 1979), pp. 167–71. However, see also Leah Marcus, 'Levelling Shakespeare: Local Customs and Local Texts', *Shakespeare Quarterly*, 42 (1991), 168–78 for a sophisticated, pluralist version of 'occasionalism'.

upon it; but is this any less naïve? The political readings produced by these schools of thought are challenged in Paul Yachnin's essay 'The Powerless Theater'.[5]

Yachnin contends that during the later sixteenth century the English theatre became increasingly apolitical, at least in its perceived effect on reality; and that, paradoxically, this powerlessness made it easier for plays to address topical issues, albeit indirectly, and so to generate political discussion amongst its audience. This disempowerment was fostered by the literary theory of the period: with Sir Philip Sidney in the vanguard, it developed the view that poetry was a discourse representing a golden world of Platonic ideals, and so was unrelated to the concerns of real life. Yachnin shows how even overtly political plays like *A Game at Chess* promulgated such views, for example in epilogues which treat the events of the foregoing play as a dream, innocuous because unreal.

So far, so convincing: it may not be a golden world that we find in plays like *Titus Andronicus* and *Edward II*, but theory reflected practice at least in so far as, from the 1580s onwards, plays began to abandon the morality-style abstractions that translated easily into contemporary concerns, and represent instead particular social and political environments that were demonstrably not Elizabethan England. However, Yachnin's argument founders when he proposes that the authorities accepted the disclaimer. He draws on two cases to suggest that official reactions to literary and non-literary discourses were different: John Hayward was imprisoned for his *Henry IV* in 1600, but Shakespeare and the Lord Chamberlain's Men were forgiven for their *Richard II* the following year; there is the same differentiation in the treatment of those responsible for *A Game at Chess* and that of Thomas Scot, the author of its non-literary sources. But this evidence, though suggestive, is also selective: Yachnin nowhere mentions *The Isle of Dogs*, *Eastward Ho*, or *The Isle of Gulls*, for which playwrights and others

were imprisoned; and though he makes a point of mentioning that 'not a single prominent poet or playwright ... was prosecuted for libel' (p. 73) in the period, he ignores evidence (such as the Prologue to *The Woman Hater*) that dramatists did not consider themselves, as artists, immune from such prosecutions.

A knee-jerk reaction to Yachnin's argument would be to object that he posits a theatre that sits on the fence and rakes in the profits; but such a theatre is not impossible, however ill it suits our contemporary taste for 'committed' drama, a taste which informs the new historicist readings Yachnin seeks to rebut. A more considered response might question the breadth of the political indeterminacy he assumes in his suggestion that rebels might suck rebellion from the same play that would bolster the loyalty of the obedient subjects among the playgoers. It is a singularly unreceptive audience that comes out of a play simply having had its prejudices confirmed,[6] but it is salutary to be reminded that the covert subversion seen in the plays by many new historicists would normally be invisible to all but the like-minded radicals in the auditorium. Such readings sublimate literature to historical process, and so, in Yachnin's view, over-simplify the relationship between content and context. Aware as we are of the textuality of history, we run the risk of neglecting the literariness of literature, if only as perceived in the period: by stressing the distinctness of the literary discourse, Yachnin draws attention to the possibility that English Renaissance drama could have been 'only plays' to its contemporaries (and therefore harmless). If he is right, the theatre could be a stalking-horse for politics only by very oblique means: fiction might raise political awareness if the

---

[5] *English Literary Renaissance*, 21 (1991), 49–74.

[6] I have argued the contrary, for the ability of drama to expand cultural horizons of expectation, in my article '*Macbeth* and Premeditation', in Arthur Marwick (ed.), *The Arts, Literature, and Society* (London, 1990), pp. 23–47.

diverse playgoers were stimulated to compare notes, but a dramatist could scarcely hope to determine the ensuing opinions by what he wrote in his play. The ways of policy are winding and indirect indeed!

III

When Sir John Harington visited Queen Elizabeth late in 1602, she told the translator of Ariosto and metamorphoser of the jakes, 'When thou doste feele creepinge tyme at thye gate, these fooleries will please thee lesse.'[7] The 42-year-old poet duly recorded the visit in a letter to his wife, as if grimly aware of the truth of the dying Queen's prediction, and indeed the Jacobean Harington approached life with a new mood of seriousness; his resolution was only strengthened by a spell in a London debtors' prison in 1603. Simon Cauchi has made available the first fruits of this middle-aged sobriety in his edition of Harington's translation of Book VI of Virgil's *Aeneid* (Oxford, 1991).

Harington originally prepared the translation to help his son with his Latin, but revised it in 1604 for presentation to the ten-year-old Prince Henry. Besides the translation itself, Harington gave the Prince extensive annotation, explanatory and moral, and a concluding commentary which discusses some of the theological issues raised by the poem, as well as the moral benefits of reading poetry. If this seems a surprise in a poet with Harington's rakish reputation, we should remember that the translation was not prepared as a private *jeu d'esprit*, but as an instrument in the education of a ten-year-old prince: the bad boy of the Elizabethan court had to adjust his image if he was to find favour in the new and different world of Jacobean politics.

It is attractive to take Harington's Virgil as evidence of the early development of a literary circle around Prince Henry, a circle which would take in important figures like Ralegh, and would ultimately result in the unprecedented outburst of elegies on the Prince's early

death in 1612, which included contributions from many of the playwrights of the time. But perhaps this *post hoc* reading places too much emphasis on the subsequent disintegration of the Jacobean court: Prince Henry had yet to achieve his later independence, and Harington's offering went first to his father the King, to whom the epistle is addressed; Cauchi speculates that some of Harington's revisions of the text used by his son were made to cater for James's literary prejudices, although the original version has not survived, and we can only guess at the nature of most of these changes.

Harington's translation has many interests, then: it is one of the earliest bids for literary patronage in the Jacobean court; it contains Harington's mature statement of his literary theory; it is another example of a Christian Renaissance response to a classic of pagan antiquity. Cauchi's critical edition of the presentation manuscript (now in the Berkshire Record Office) makes the text available in print for the first time, along with a considered introduction, helpful notes, and an excellent index. This is a work that will be of value to Renaissance scholars for many years to come.

For Shakespearians in particular, its principal importance is the raw material it feeds into the associative matrix which cocoons the plays: whether disintegrated by the disciples of Malone or swallowed whole by those of Stephen Greenblatt, it makes available a little more evidence about the intellectual and literary culture of Shakespeare's period, one more text with which to constellate the Globe. Two other texts freshly edited from manuscript bear more directly on the study of English Renaissance drama. As the author of a Latin play during his Cambridge days, Abraham Fraunce is a figure on the peripheries of dramatic history who went on to write under the patronage of members of the Sidney family. Among his less literary contributions was a

---

7 Harington, *Nugae Antiquae*, ed. H. Harington (London, 1804), vol. I, p. 323.

discussion of emblem theory, *Symbolicae Philosophiae*, published in 1588, which has been available for some years in a Garland reprint (New York, 1979). This can now be usefully supplemented by John Manning's new edition (New York, 1991) of the manuscript version, a presentation copy dedicated to Robert Sidney. Manning gives in appendices the additional material included in the 1588 printed edition, and provides a handy facing-page translation of the Latin text.

Two passages in particular will catch the drama scholar's eye, both references to the application of *imprese* to theatrical practice (pp. 15, 17). It is a little disappointing to find in Manning's helpful annotation that Fraunce adapted both allusions from Girolamo Ruscelli's 1566 treatise on *imprese*. All the more tantalizingly, the first of the two passages is not an exact translation: where Fraunce refers to 'comedies and tragedies when actors' faces are concealed by masks and are, as it were, veiled by some allegorical dress' (p. 15), Ruscelli's original spoke not of tragedies but tournaments and masques. Could the change reflect Fraunce's memories of the tragedies staged at his Cambridge college, St John's?

In most respects the academic stage is just a siding in the theatrical history of this period; and perhaps the court stage is no more than a branch line, but it is a key document in its early development which Gordon Kipling has made available in his admirable Early English Text Society edition of *The Receyt of the Ladie Kateryne* (Oxford, 1990). Cast in the form of a prose romance, the *Receyt* describes in detail the entertainments laid on to welcome Katharine of Aragon to England in November, 1501, entertainments which Sydney Anglo has called 'the supreme masterpiece of English civic pageantry' and 'the pinnacle of display at the court of Henry VII'.[8] That may not be saying much, given the first Tudor's popular reputation as a miser, but Kipling's account casts a different light on Henry and his early Renaissance court: the expense of such an enter-

tainment could only have been considered with the sanction of the King. Henry's personal interest in the Revels (which forced a later Master of the Revels to ship all the 'disguising stuff' up to Richmond for his inspection) probably reflects the diplomatic significance of such occasions: 'Henry clearly wanted to stage a festival that would present his court as the equal in magnificence and status to any court in Europe' (p. xxv). The lavish spectacle of the celebrations did honour to the Spanish princess, but also asserted England's glory.

For historians of the drama, it was the disguisings devised for the royal wedding itself which were, in several respects, a landmark. For the first time in the history of the Revels, the Children of the Chapel Royal appeared as performers, singing in two of the four disguisings – a first tentative step on the path that led to the organization of the boys as an acting company. For Kipling, however, the event's formal innovations were more important than this symbolic first: the dramatic elements that traditionally preceded the disguising itself became more extensive and more spectacular, with pageant cars introduced as settings in the shape of ships, castles, mountains, and the like. Spectacle continued to be the fashion in subsequent court entertainments. In the 1501 Revels, Kipling suggests, we see the first separation of drama from dance that was to grow into the court masque. The *Receyt* was the fullest contemporary account of the festival, and Kipling's valuable edition replaces the unreliable text of 1808, hitherto the only version available to scholars.

The less literary manuscripts of the period continue to be sifted for information, and Mark Eccles's investigations in London record offices have yielded a fine crop of new data about Elizabethan actors, the first instalment of which has appeared in *Notes and Queries*, covering

---

[8] Sydney Anglo, *Spectacle, Pageantry, and Early Tudor Policy* (Oxford, 1969), pp. 97, 103.

surnames from A to D.[9] It is a fascinating collection of trivia that puts our knowledge of well-known theatrical figures into better perspective: among the bullies and cheats whom Eccles has unearthed, Shakespeare's record of tax evasion seems venial, and even the roaring-boy activities of Marlowe and Jonson are no longer extraordinary. More important, it contains a heap of new material about the London theatre: here is information about the hiring of costumes and props, about players on tour and the support they gave to their wives at home, and – most interesting of all – about James Burbage's arrangements to supply refreshments to playgoers at the Theatre in the 1580s, and the legal trouble he got into as a result. Scholars will eagerly await further collections of pickings from the Guildhall Library, from E onwards.

Meanwhile, the mysteries of Henslowe's diary continue to attract attention. Winifred Frazer's attempt to banish the obscurities of 'ne' contains nothing about how 'ne' a play so designated might be: she rejects altogether the traditional understanding of the word as meaning 'new', and offers instead the hypothesis that 'ne' is an abbreviation used by Henslowe to indicate the company's irregular performances at the Newington Butts playhouse outside London.[10] It is true that the established view has minor inconsistencies – there are a few plays marked 'ne' which had been acted before – but Frazer's idea eliminates these at the cost of major implausibilities. All the evidence indicates that Newington Butts was not the company's favoured venue: when required to play there by the Privy Council, probably in 1594, they petitioned for the reopening of the Rose because, owing to 'the tediousnes of the waie', their usual patrons were not making the journey out to Newington village.[11] Yet Henslowe's 'ne' takings were high, usually the highest in any given week: if Frazer's theory is right, one might have expected the players to increase the number of Newington shows, not complain about dwindling audiences there.

Perhaps the culture-starved Newingtonians flocked to the theatre whenever the players made one of their irregular visits, and perhaps, more often than not, the out-of-town playhouse was used as the venue for a pre-London 'try-out' of a new play. Neither seems a particularly likely scenario.

At the other end of the academic food chain are two new overviews of English Renaissance drama. Jennifer Goodman's *British Drama before 1660* (Boston, Mass., 1991), the first volume of Twayne's Critical History of British Drama, is intended for the general reader, but its broad approach gives it some interest for the scholar too. Goodman follows much recent criticism in rejecting earlier evolutionary interpretations of the development of drama: the book engages with previous historiography in a combative and constructive way. Much of the first of the four main chapters, for instance, is devoted to what happened before British drama's traditional point of origin, the '*Quem quaeritis*' trope: there is much speculation about Roman drama and strolling players, but inevitably, without texts to discuss, a purely critical account of drama diffuses into fields such as archaeology and anthropology. More importantly for students of Renaissance drama, the book also seeks to break down the clear dividing line that segregates the plays of the later sixteenth century from their medieval forebears.

Seeing Shakespeare's time from this long perspective has its interest and value. Goodman offers a useful reminder of how long-standing were theatrical issues such as popular prejudice against players; she also makes a suggestive association between the two-tier system developed by Elizabethan legislation for licensing

[9] Mark Eccles, 'Elizabethan Actors I: A–D', *Notes and Queries*, 236 (1991), 38–49.

[10] Winifred Frazer, 'Henslowe's "Ne"', *Notes and Queries*, 236 (1991), 34–5.

[11] *Henslowe's Diary*, ed. R. A. Foakes and R. T. Rickert (Cambridge, 1961), pp. 283–5.

acting companies and a similar division in the fourteenth-century Statute of Labourers (p. 34). Moreover, the traditionally asserted predominance of the amphitheatres becomes less obvious when there is no cut-off at 1567 (or 1576): indoor theatre was thoroughly established before the opening of the Red Lion, and touring companies generally preferred hall venues to innyards. Instead of the clear development from amphitheatres to halls that we see when we start in 1567, the London outdoor theatre seems more the aberration than the rule.

The down-side is that, as a medievalist, Goodman has had to 'get up' the Renaissance material. Unfortunately, in too many cases she has got it wrong to boot: as the sixteenth century wears on, the book's error content increases alarmingly. The Curtain is said to have opened in 1576 rather than 1577 (p. 157). Heywood's court prologue to *The Jew of Malta* is attributed to Marlowe (p. 172). Goodman shows undue conviction in attributing *Soliman and Perseda* to Peele, but dates it, mysteriously and incredibly, *c.* 1609, thirteen years after Peele's death (p. 174). Painter's *Palace of Pleasure* is said to be an English translation of Cinthio (p. 178), who accordingly supplants Bandello as the original Italian source of the Romeo and Juliet story (p. 181). Francis Beaumont acquires a knighthood (p. 195), and the paragraph on Massinger (p. 198) makes particularly astonishing reading as (among other things) Goodman cites 'Shakespeare's *Henry VIII* and *The Two Noble Kinsmen*' as Fletcher-Massinger collaborations!

In some respects, the book is up-to-date with recent scholarly work, but there are also major blindspots: the Rose excavation offers its quota of information, but Goodman makes no mention of the Red Lion, the commercial playhouse that was in operation in 1567, nine years before the opening of the Theatre. It is tiresome, too, to find crackpots getting a share of the attention: was it really necessary, in a book of this nature and scope, to spend a paragraph on the alternative claimants to the authorship of Shakespeare?

A safer book to leave in undergraduate hands is *The Cambridge Companion to English Renaissance Drama* (Cambridge, 1990), in which A. R. Braunmuller and Michael Hattaway have gathered much useful and distinguished material to produce a volume that should, in most cases, be the first port of call for the enquiring student. Ten chapters cover the principal dramatic genres of the period and other important topics, though the logic of the arrangement is not always clear: it is odd to find Lee Bliss's piece on tragicomedy placed before those on the component genres of comedy and tragedy. Most of the authors do a fine job in producing readable, informative short accounts of their respective subjects: in particular, Martin Butler brings to life the difficult, strongly occasional genre of the Elizabethan royal entertainment, and Michael Hattaway provides a judicious summary of the complex and controversial issues which inform the interpretation of the relationship between drama and society.

The greatest disappointment of the book is the chapter that should have been its centrepiece, Robert Watson's account of English Renaissance tragedy. It is, of course, no small undertaking to produce a fresh and critical overview of such a well-worked field, but Watson scarcely attempts the task: the chapter does little more than string together pedestrian studies of six individual plays. As a result, the volume has some blindspots: it has very little to say, for example, about Elizabethan academic tragedy, which Martin Butler skims over as if in deference to coverage elsewhere, coverage which Watson's chapter does not deliver. Perhaps it was compiled in a hurry to replace Kathleen McLuskie's essay on the same topic, pre-announced by McLuskie herself but mysteriously absent from the published volume; one cannot help but feel it would have made racier reading than Robert Watson's anodyne contribution.[12]

---

[12] Kathleen McLuskie, *Renaissance Dramatists* (Hemel Hempstead, 1989), p. 230 n9.

The supplementary material prepared by the editors is excellent. A set of potted biographies, covering even the most minor of dramatists, will save a lot of people wading through Chambers and Bentley for basic information, and there is a helpful general bibliography. The chronological table of plays is the fullest to be found outside Harbage and Schoenbaum's *Annals of English Drama*, and it rightly rejects some of the more eccentric datings in Sylvia Wagonheim's unreliable third edition (London, 1989). That said, the list's blanket exclusion of lost plays limits its usefulness, and there is no index to help the inexperienced find their way about. A few errors have also crept in – Thomas Legge's *Solymitana Clades* (1583) is included despite the stated intention to omit Latin academic plays; the entry for 1600 lists both *Lust's Dominion* and *The Spanish Moor's Tragedy*, the latter a possibly lost play whose only claim to inclusion is the hypothesis that it is one and the same as the former; Francis Verney's play *Antipoe* (1604) is given as *Antiope* – which might usefully be corrected when the book goes into a well-deserved reprint.

By then, we may have to acknowledge a few more uncertainties. Several recent contributions to the dating game have attempted to reassess the accepted chronology of Shakespeare's works. In *Notes and Queries*, Elizabeth Schafer has convincingly demonstrated that the 1597 date of *The Merry Wives of Windsor* is no more than a weak hypothesis.[13] The underlying assumption is that the Windsor setting in general and the 'garter passage' (5.5.54–75) in particular relate to Lord Hunsdon's inauguration in 1597 as a member of the Order of the Garter. But there are dramatic rather than occasional reasons for the play to be set at Windsor: in the 1590s, the small towns close to London were associated with adultery, for Londoners used places like Ware, Brentford, and Windsor as venues for their sexual day-trips; the 'Garter passage' in turn could be interpreted as just another piece of Windsor local colour. Schafer goes on to argue for a date closer to *Henry V*:

the two plays share similar joke structures, and it is attractive to see them as companion sequels to *Henry IV*, enforcing Falstaff's exile by keeping him apart from Hal in a separate text of a different genre. This new hypothesis may be as unprovable as the old, but at least it treats the play as a play, and not a political acrostic.

A more vexed question is the dating of the Sonnets, partly because we still cannot agree whether to see the text in Malone's Romantic terms as the poetical expression of internal pressure, or as a literary exercise in a popular 1590s genre. Each view carries different implications for the methodology of dating: should we look for the specific biographical events which prompted composition, or should we instead see a text continually in process? A new rare-word test adds fuel to the latter view: though it locates the original composition of the main body of the sequence in the early 1590s, it also indicates that one group (nos. 104–26) was not written until the turn of the century, and, most important of all, the first sixty sonnets are Jacobean revisions of an earlier original.[14] This may not be the earth-shattering new direction for sonnet scholarship which its authors claim, but, if their mathematics are correct, it makes the 1609 volume more of a constructed literary artefact than the biography-hunters would like to imagine.

Perhaps the most startling piece of chronological revisionism comes in Sandra Billington's *Mock Kings* (pp. 176–9). She argues for a much earlier date for *Timon of Athens*, on the strength of a clutch of possible allusions in Marston's *Jack Drum's Entertainment*. As well as a direct reference to Timon, Marston's play includes a character, Sir John Fortune, whose house stands atop Highgate Hill and who is upbraided, like Timon, for the prodigality of

---

[13] Elizabeth Schafer, 'The Date of *The Merry Wives of Windsor, Notes and Queries*', 236 (1991), 57–60.

[14] A. Kent Hieatt, Charles W. Hieatt, and Anne Lake Prescott, 'When Did Shakespeare Write *Sonnets* 1609?', *Studies in Philology*, 88 (1991), 69–109.

his largesse. *Jack Drum* is an immovable object: firmly dated 1600 by other allusions in the text, the play was in print the following year, so Shakespeare's *Timon of Athens*, if these are indeed references to it, must have been on the stage several years earlier than hitherto thought.[15] The problem, as with many such arguments, is that an allusion to an historical figure, especially one as written about as Timon of Athens, need not suggest a play on the subject, and even if it does, the play need not be one whose text is extant. Billington tries to link the Marston passages to a theatrical representation of Timon, and to Shakespeare's in particular, but it makes a puny, wire-drawn case when set against the weight of stylistic evidence for an early Jacobean *Timon*.[16]

All this scholarly activity, suggests *Shakespeare Verbatim*, is part of the fetishizing of authenticity which Malone initiated: the more we know of the literary context, the better able we shall be to reconstruct the moment of authorship and understand its mystery. Working at the summit of this critical project is James Shapiro, whose *Rival Playwrights: Marlowe, Jonson, Shakespeare* (New York, 1991) synthesizes a good deal of scholarship and theory in its investigation of the literary relations between the Trinity of late Elizabethan drama. The book interprets those relations in terms of a rivalry in which Marlowe had the signal advantage of being a Dead Poet: Harold Bloom is rarely out of sight as Shapiro theorizes about the processes, conscious and unconscious, which fashioned the artistic careers of Shakespeare and Jonson.

Perhaps Jonson's greatest work was 'Ben Jonson': few men have authored themselves so thoroughly. In his iron control of his published output he sought to dictate the interpretation of his own development: the sequence of the texts and dedications in his First Folio is such a work of self-fashioning, as W. H. Herendeen shows in the highlight of an otherwise unexciting collection of essays, *Ben Jonson's 1616 Folio*;[17] and in the Induction to *The Magnetic Lady* he

looked back on his career as a movement from *Every Man in His Humour* to *Humours Reconciled*, an attractive circularity achieved at the expense of suppressing most of his early work. For Shapiro, that suppression is the key: enough is recoverable in scraps and through hearsay to establish a far more diverse and Marlovian Jonson, whose hand may then be traced in the surviving plays. It is his need to re-create himself out of Marlowe's image that betrays in Jonson the anxiety of influence.

Rival Playwrights contributes valuably to our understanding of Ben Jonson; Shapiro's attempt to apply the same theory to the more elusive figure of Shakespeare is rather more undistinguished. The result is no upstart crow but a playwright who pussy-foots around Marlowe's achievement, who reacts to his rival obliquely rather than head-on: an uncertain young Shakespeare establishing his own artistic territory by working around the areas already claimed by Marlowe. It is not just bardolatry that would find such awkward self-consciousness less credible in Shakespeare than in Jonson: Shapiro's case itself is far more strained. Here is a Shakespeare whose response to *The Massacre at Paris* is to write the same characters into *Love's Labour's Lost*, who counters the heroical history of *Tamburlaine* with the anti-heroics of the *Contention* plays, and who, most astonishingly, avoids meeting Marlowe on his own ground by writing no tragedies between *Titus Andronicus* and *Julius Caesar* (save, *via* romantic comedy, *Romeo and Juliet*)! Direct engagement comes later, with maturity and confidence, when Shakespeare transcends Marlowe by guying his style in Pistol and in *The Murder of Gonzago*, but for much of the 1590s his work is the product not of mastery but neurotic

---

[15] E. K. Chambers, *The Elizabethan Stage* (Oxford, 1923), vol. 4, p. 21.

[16] Stanley Wells and Gary Taylor, *William Shakespeare: A Textual Companion* (Oxford, 1987), pp. 127–8.

[17] Ed. Jennifer Brady and W. H. Herendeen (Newark, 1991).

anxiety: Shapiro reads *The Merchant of Venice*, for instance, as a record of the dramatist's struggle to contain the influence of *The Jew of Malta* and keep his artistic identity as 'Shakespeare'.

The quest for a play's point of origin at which dramatist flowed meaningfully into text is never more convincingly discredited than by this sort of Romantic, unverifiable psychobiography. Throughout his argument, Shapiro never gives us reason to suppose that Shakespeare's anxieties are any less mythical than his sorrows, or any more relevant to an understanding of his plays. Shakespeare, he silently assumes, is like Jonson; but Shakespeare left little evidence outside his work of a strong, distinct personality, nor did Shakespeare visibly intervene in his own canon as Jonson did. Attempts to penetrate the private world of his mind can therefore be no more than the amusing speculations of a parlour game; it is an activity that tells us nothing about the public concerns of the plays as plays.

IV

The Verdi Falstaff who beams contentedly from the jacket of Gary Schmidgall's *Shakespeare and Opera* (New York and Oxford, 1990) could not have been better chosen. This gargantuan book contains the material for at least two shorter studies, one dealing with the many operas derived from Shakespeare's plays, the other a defence of opera as a medium which shares many characteristics of style and dramaturgy with Shakespearian drama. But this is a single, formless bulk of a book, made readable by Schmidgall's engaging enthusiasm for his subject, but none the less, like Falstaff, defying all reasonable compass.

In fact, Falstaff makes an apt emblem for an important area of Shakespeare studies which is excluded by Malone-inspired habits of thought. If authenticity, which was so important to Malone, derives from Shakespearian authorship, then later versions of the plays, whether

authored by Verdi or by Terry Hands, can have no claim on our attention; if it is only in the Globe that we will find the texts' authentic meaning, then we can safely ignore what has happened in the theatre since. Performance criticism and studies of Shakespeare's reception after 1642 are commonly banished to the Eastcheap of academic criticism – a tempting resort for stagestruck young scholars, but a pernicious distraction from the real academic business of understanding the plays themselves.

This does not seem to have bothered Manchester University Press, which has brought out three new volumes in its 'Shakespeare in Performance' series: James C. Bulman on *The Merchant of Venice*, Alexander Leggatt on *King Lear*, and Scott McMillin on *Henry IV, Part 1* (all Manchester and New York, 1991).[18] Leggatt's and Bulman's volumes offer the usual consideration of productions from a wide historical range, Leggatt concentrating especially on the problems and choices imposed on a director by the storm and battle scenes, and Bulman, perhaps inevitably, on the question of attitudes to Shylock; McMillin's, however, is a more unusual contribution to the series. His book foreshadows a study of the institutional development of the post-war British theatre, and accordingly he limits himself to productions from 1945 onwards, and concentrates on some of the broader interpretative issues raised by theatre history. The strengths of this approach are most evident early on: each production is seen with a firm sense of context, which brings out how criticism and theatrical conditions can determine how the history plays are perceived and also how other plays in a company's repertory can affect interpretation and business. The central interpretative change which he documents is from single-play to cycle staging, under influences ranging from

---

[18] The volumes on *Richard III* and *The Taming of the Shrew*, by Hugh M. Richmond and Graham Holderness respectively (both Manchester and New York, 1989), have also been reissued in paperback.

Tillyard to Festival-of-Britain ebullience. This is excellent cultural history, but it peters out as the book continues. Partly this is because it is hard to bring adequate historical perspective to bear on the more recent productions, but also partly because the material outruns the argument: once Henriad cycles have entered theatrical tradition, there is nowhere for McMillin to go except into detail, and for all its competence the end of the book lacks the clear sense of direction which made for such a promising start.

Leggatt's volume demands comparison with another new book on *Lear*, *Reading Shakespeare in Performance* (Rutherford, Madison, and Teaneck, 1991), by James P. Lusardi and June Schlueter. Both books approach the play as a performance text by focusing on the realization of specific incidents in production; but Lusardi and Schlueter are more basic in every way. They work the reader through the methodology of performance analysis, assuming no prior experience, except in the more conventional methods of literary criticism. Their selection of performances, too, is narrower than Leggatt's: the discussion concentrates almost exclusively on the 1982 Miller-Hordern and 1983 Elliott-Olivier television versions, and a substantial appendix serves as a useful sourcebook on these productions. *Reading Shakespeare in Performance* would make a good textbook for a foundation course on text and performance, not least because the two productions in question are easily accessible on video – and this illuminates, obliquely, a weakness of the Manchester series.

You don't have to read very much performance analysis to see how often visual and vocal effects elude description: if CD-ROM technology ever enables us to abandon print and publish books on videodisc, theatre history will be among the disciplines most blessed in the change. In the meantime, and in the absence of generally available videos of the productions under discussion, such studies require substantial photographic illustration. Each volume

of the 'Shakespeare in Performance' series is allocated a meagre eight stills, too few to meet the reader's needs, however skilfully they may be chosen. Reading Scott McMillin's account of Anthony Quayle's bizarre, 'metallic' make-up for Falstaff (p. 46), for instance, you long to see a photograph, and must make do with squinting at a full-stage shot of the first tavern scene. What modern publisher would even contemplate a book on architecture or painting without illustrations of the objects discussed? Economics, like physicians, may brook no contradiction, but in the case of the 'Shakespeare in Performance' series they have made theatre the poor relation of the other visual media.

Lusardi and Schlueter's book testifies obliquely to the increasing use of videotape in the teaching of Shakespeare, and in particular of the Cedric Messina – Jonathan Miller – Shaun Sutton series produced between 1978 and 1985. Thanks to BBC empire-building, these productions have entered many classrooms as a canon in their own right, and offer some students their only chance to see the less popular plays in production. In her book *The BBC Shakespeare Plays: Making the Televised Canon* (Chapel Hill and London, 1991), Susan Willis has provided an excellent history of the series, based on personal observation as well as background research: there is a good deal of unique interview material included, as well as interesting production diaries for *Troilus and Cressida*, *The Comedy of Errors*, and *Titus Andronicus*. The book will not serve teachers as a *vade mecum* to the productions, nor does it aim to be one (a single-volume collection of the Henry Fenwick production guides in the BBC editions might usefully fulfil that function), but it is essential reading for its account of the circumstances in which the series came into being, and which determined the sort of Shakespeare it gave us. It may not be altogether surprising to learn that the BBC's American commercial backers had a conservative artistic policy written into the contract, but the knowledge valuably equips us to approach the series and its claims to canonicity and authoritativeness with the same critical scepticism that *Shakespeare Verbatim* invokes against traditional methodology.

Perhaps the most persuasive *sic disprobo* to that methodology's marginalizing of performance criticism is Roger Warren's account of *Staging Shakespeare's Late Plays* (Oxford, 1990) at the National Theatre in 1988 and at the Canadian Shakespeare Festival two years earlier. These institutions transcended the usual separation (or even antagonism) between the theatre and the academy in having Warren present at rehearsals as an observer and adviser; Peter Hall in particular emerges as a director who uses academic criticism as a basis for his productions. For instance, the theory that *Cymbeline*, *The Winter's Tale*, and *The Tempest* were plays specifically tailored to the Blackfriars led Hall to begin their run in the National's studio theatre, the Cottesloe. One of Warren's recurrent points, however, is that the plays always came into their own when they transferred to the larger space of the Olivier Theatre; the implicit conclusion is that we must reconsider our belief in their suitability for a small playhouse. For Warren, any staging of a play is an experiment in interpretation: the theatre can be a crucible in which the views of academic critics are tested. His book is an elegant report of the experimental results from the five productions he observed.

It is fair to say that Warren is not always as scientifically deductive as his method might require. Though he constantly speaks of surprises as the actors worked on the text in rehearsal, there is a sense in which he is unwilling to be surprised about some things: preconceptions which should be laid on the line in the experimental process can instead dictate the conduct of that process. For instance, *Henry VIII* is summarily excluded from consideration not, as one might expect, because Warren has had no opportunity to attend rehearsals for a production, but because he thinks it uneven, and also because it is not wholly by Shakespeare

(as if that made a play somehow less deserving of attention). Reverence for academic conclusions can also lead him to misrepresent theatrical fact: that well-known extended misprint Imogen is banished from the book, as it was from Peter Hall's production; but even if one accepts the Oxford editors' arguments in favour of Innogen, it seems curiously ahistorical of Warren to impose their correction retrospectively, as he also did in his 'Shakespeare in Performance' volume on *Cymbeline* (Manchester and New York, 1989), on productions which used the traditional name. If he speaks of Peggy Ashcroft's Innogen, would he also insist on, say, Anthony Quayle's Sir John Oldcastle?

Even so, these are mere quibbles about a book which is admirable in its use of performance criticism to blow away academic cobwebs. Warren's central contention is that we should pay much more attention to what is actually happening in the plays – even if doing so forces us to empathize with extreme or unpleasant situations. Taking the story seriously is something which critics of the late plays have tended, in one way or another, not to do: the Wilson Knight approach has sired a host of abstract, thematic interpretations, while others have taken the plays' theatricality as a form of self-consciousness which serves as a Brechtian alienation effect. Warren's experience of rehearsals gives the lie to such notions: because a play must be communicated by actors, he insists, its themes, 'however apparently central, can only be expressed in terms of the attitudes and responses of characters in particular situations' (p. 135); and the most theatrical moments, especially in *Cymbeline*, worked to sharpen, not distance, the audience's awareness of the characters' predicament.

The greater particularity of interpretation which Warren advocates is a necessary feature of any theatrical performance, a point made by several of the contributors to G. K. Hunter's *festschrift*, *The Arts of Performance in Elizabethan and Early Stuart Drama* (Edinburgh,

1991).[19] The best of the essays exemplify that quality from a variety of angles of approach. Eugene M. Waith draws on critical and theatre history in an attempt to explain the inconsistent fortunes of *King John* and *Henry VIII*. The possibilities for the performance and reception of *Coriolanus* at the Globe are painstakingly investigated by Marion Trousdale, while Stanley Wells brings a mass of historical evidence to bear on the question of how Shakespeare's ghosts might have been staged.[20] Textual scholarship underlies Ernst Honigmann's genial consideration of the problems and uncertainties raised by the surviving versions of *Dr Faustus*; freed by textual inadequacy from the normal rules of evidence, he engages in imaginative, fascinating, and wholly unprovable speculation about missing elements that might make better sense of the ruined greatness that remains. A. D. Nuttall is more conventionally critical as he ruminates in an unstructured but sometimes brilliant way about the difficult transition from life to art with which actors and audience are faced at the opening of a play, and suggests some of the ways in which Shakespeare helped his colleagues to overcome the problem in the first moments of *Hamlet*, *Twelfth Night*, and *The Tempest*; and Inga-Stina Ewbank makes some perceptive comments about Thomas Middleton's tragicomic manner in one of the less investigated periods of Jacobean drama, the later 1610s, a period important not least for the progressive absorption of Shakespeare by his successors, as her essay brings out.

That a *festschrift* should take performance as its organizing theme shows how far we have moved on from the days when scholarly consensus held that 'the nearer we get to the stage, the further we are getting from Shakespeare', as one recent editor of *Hamlet* has put it.[21] Roger Warren's book makes it clear that theatrical experience has a contribution to make to the traditional mainstream of literary studies; and such experience informs most of the essays presented to G. K. Hunter in *The Arts of Performance*. If Falstaff is an emblem for performance criticism, marginalized by eighteenth-century contributions to editorial tradition and to methodology, then today, it seems, the court has moved to Eastcheap.

V

The bullishness of performance-orientated criticism, like new historicism's questioning of assumptions about the relationship between history and text, raises the issue of how radical is *Shakespeare Verbatim* as a contribution to modern Shakespeare studies. It would be hard to overrate the book's importance in advancing our understanding of the eighteenth-century origins of the discipline, and it is to be welcomed, too, in making us more aware of the invisible implications of our scholarly and critical method. But for all that they can still lead us astray on occasion, we are clearly no longer in thrall to Malone's ways of thinking – even if, reading yet another dutiful account of class, race, or gender in Shakespeare, one may sometimes feel that this is not the liberation of a new methodological openness so much as, after Caliban, a simple change of masters. In today's academy, de Grazia's deconstructions may seem more belated than timely.

Perhaps it is unfair to place the book in so narrow a context: a look at the Shakespearian issues which interest the modern press shows the public mind caught in a crude version of the Malone epistemology which de Grazia identifies. Its essential feature is a superstitious concentration on the relationship between the plays and the person of their author; the ever

---

[19] Ed. Murray Biggs, Philip Edwards, Inga-Stina Ewbank, and Eugene M. Waith.

[20] Reconstruction of the original performances is also Michael Mooney's aim in his competent but dull book, *Shakespeare's Dramatic Transactions* (Durham, NC and London, 1990), which applies Robert Weimann's theories of staging to the texts of seven tragedies.

[21] Philip Edwards, in his New Cambridge edition (Cambridge, 1985), p. 32.

more bizarre candidates put forward for that honour are only one symptom. Malone sought to establish facts about William Shakespeare, but in an age when conspiracy makes good copy, journalists are more concerned to disestablish them: every so often there is a minor flurry as the name of Anne Whateley is 'discovered' in the Worcester Episcopal Register, and most recently a computer graphics analyst has declared the Droeshout engraving in the first Folio to be a thinly disguised portrait of Queen Elizabeth I.[22] For whatever reason, the authenticity so important to Malone has become an end in itself for many people; so who knows what other Malonery we shall find in their books?

With this in mind, the concept behind *Shakespeare: The Living Record* (Basingstoke, 1991), a recent 'freelance' contribution from Irvin Leigh Matus, sounds refreshingly up-to-date. The 'living record' which Matus takes as his subject is the surviving buildings and local traditions of Warwickshire, London, and other places that Shakespeare might have visited on tour with his acting company; the book seeks to explore the points of contact between such cultural artefacts and Shakespeare's plays.

In fact, *Shakespeare: The Living Record* is not the first amateur work of cultural materialism, however promising the subject might be for exponents of that school of criticism. Matus is resolutely biographical in his approach, aiming (or so it seems) to bring his readers 'closer to Shakespeare': to record all the sights and the associated traditions which Shakespeare might have known. This makes for some interesting imaginative leaps from local detail to specific points in the plays, but without the rigour to take the ideas beyond speculation. The central weakness of Matus's arguments is evident in the curious discontinuity between the passages recording what we know of Shakespeare's movements and those dealing with the local history through which he is presumed to have passed. The unstated principle of construction is that, as Shakespeare entered the towns on his itinerary, he was bombarded with all the local information that Matus has been able to collect, much of it no doubt from eighteenth-century antiquarians and their successors. Matus never considers whether the information he presents so engagingly was available in Shakespeare's time – let alone how much might have been purveyed to the players as they passed through towns on tour.

The book's usefulness is diminished by its lack of footnotes or other references, and there is a certain amount of basic misinformation: the ghost of Nathaniel Field the actor walks again, for instance, and Matus even manages to back-date decimal currency to the seventeenth century! In the final analysis, *Shakespeare: The Living Record* is an anecdotal tourist guide, which may help in the planning of many a literary pilgrimage, but leaves its subject still open for serious academic consideration.

The risk in reviewing the offerings of amateur scholars like Matus is that one will either patronize or condescend. Fortunately no such restraint is necessary in the reviewer of Facts On File's *Shakespeare: A to Z* (New York and Oxford, 1990), a curious mixture of the accurate, the erroneous, and the dated, which the publishers advertise as 'authoritative and definitive information'. It is a book which illustrates the process by which guesswork hardens into plausibility, plausibility into probability, and by this declension 'scholarly consensus' is reached: thus Thomas Kyd is named, with unwarranted assurance, as scholarship's favoured candidate for the authorship of *Arden of Faversham*, while Webster and Marston (new-christened Thomas for the nonce) enter the running for *The Revenger's Tragedy* and *The London Prodigal* respectively. Much of this reflects the fantastic academic speculation of the last age, and repeatedly the book exemplifies the time-lag between amateur scholarship and its professional counterpart: every departure

---

[22] Roger Lewin, 'Did Queen Bess have a head for Shakespeare?', *New Scientist*, 16 November 1991.

from verifiable fact seems to be a journey into the scholarly and critical past, where we encounter such exploded notions as *The Troublesome Reign*'s being a bad quarto of *King John*, the 'decadence' of Jacobean drama, and Marlowe's death in a tavern.[23] It is reassuring, at least, to read, under 'Authorship controversy', that 'Scholars of the period know beyond doubt that Shakespeare wrote Shakespeare' (p. 44).

A good deal of space is taken up by entries for plays and characters, which offer such detailed summaries of the action that one wonders whether the book's users will ever need to read Shakespeare again. This scrupulous detail extends, absurdly, to multiple entries for generic characters, so that, for instance, there are ten different characters called 'Boy', thirteen Soldiers, thirty-two Messengers, and even three 'Ones!' 'Murderer', incidentally, cross-refers us to 'First', 'Second', and 'Third Murderer' (though not to Leonine), each with virtually identical write-ups. Perhaps we should count ourselves lucky that the eleven ghosts of *Richard III* are grouped in a single entry.

The coverage is most conspicuously weak in the field of twentieth-century theatre, with no entries for Richard Burton, Alec Guinness, Michael Hordern, Derek Jacobi, Antony Sher, and many others; it is symptomatic that the entry for a sixteenth-century bit-part player, John Sincklo, is twice the length of the one for Trevor Nunn. This weakness is reflected in the collection of off-puttingly ancient theatrical photographs which (along with the usual portraits and sketches) serve for illustration: only two seem to date later than the mid-1950s (though it is hard to be certain about this, since most of the illustrations are inadequately captioned). One would never guess from this book that, as the jacket blurb tells us, Shakespeare's drama 'is as alive and relevant today as it was at the time of the early performances at the Globe'.

Puffed by its publishers as the first ever Shakespeare encyclopaedia, *Shakespeare A to Z* will not replace its predecessors in the field. The reader seeking a reliable one-volume reference book on Shakespeare would be best advised to stick to Campbell and Quinn's *Shakespeare Encyclopaedia*, which, if it too is not quite up-to-date, at least has the excuse of having been published in 1966.[24]

Amongst amateurs, their views seemingly freeze-dried from some earlier epoch of criticism, Margreta de Grazia's strictures become all the more pertinent. The issue which remains, however, is how far she means to go with them. Having shown Malone's methodology to be the product of a specific period in British cultural history, her argument questions the extent of its subsequent influence. The danger is that, in burying Malone or any other titan, we will inter some good scholarship with his bones: his approach has produced facts about the plays, their author, and his times (irrespective of the critical uses to which we then put those facts), and this begs the question, can the contingency of the methodology be reconciled with the absolute truth of the results? Malone may also be father to a line of *canards*, but few scholars take such ideas seriously any more. We have already thrown out much of the bathwater: does de Grazia really want to dispose of the baby too? Or, to put it another way, should *Shakespeare Survey* ever again review the year's work on Shakespeare's life, times, and stage?

---

[23] On the last point, cf. William Urry, *Christopher Marlowe and Canterbury* (London, 1988), pp. 83–4.

[24] O. J. Campbell and E. G. Quinn, *A Shakespeare Encyclopaedia* (London, 1966).

3. EDITIONS AND TEXTUAL STUDIES
reviewed by H. R. WOUDHUYSEN

There is a passage in *Antony and Cleopatra* (4.16) where confused composition has been suspected. In the Folio, Cleopatra greets her mortally wounded lover:

CLEO
Oh Sunne,
Burne the great Sphere thou mou'st in, darkling stand
The varrying shore o'th'world. O *Antony, Antony, Antony,*
Helpe *Charmian,* helpe *Iras* helpe: helpe Friends
Below, let's draw him hither. (TLN 3011–15)

The fact that twenty lines later (3035–6) Cleopatra is still urging her women to draw Antony up, as well as the repetition of Antony's 'I am dying Egypt, dying' (3022 and 3050), have caused some division among editors and scholars. John Dover Wilson sought to explain the confusion by arguing that Shakespeare's manuscript (from which most scholars think the play was set), was marked here for a cut either by the author or by the book-holder in advance of preparing the promptbook. On the other hand, Greg (who found Wilson's explanation of the causes of the confusion 'not very clear') took the apparent difficulty as a confirmation that the play was set from foul papers. He also noted the unusual spelling in the passage of Antony's name, which here almost uniquely appears without the medial h. While aware that there may be something odd about this passage, most recent editors reject theories about a false start and might well agree with Emrys Jones that since 'this is a play uncommonly concerned to render – in some of its scenes, at least – the feel of life as it is lived and especially its tendency to untidiness and anti-climax', if the passage 'seems confused and repetitive, that may be exactly what Shakespeare intended'.[1]

The episode has also attracted much attention because of the stage directions which specify that Cleopatra and her maids enter '*aloft*' and that they eventually '*heaue Anthony aloft to Cleopatra*'.

What exactly 'aloft' means in this context, and how Antony was to be heaved, remain difficult questions in respect both of theatrical practice and the nature of the copy behind the Folio text, the play's only authoritative witness.

The evidence of spelling, of compositorial errors and of stage directions in F have all led to the belief that the play was set from an authorial manuscript, either 'from Shakespeare's papers in a late stage of composition or from his own fair copy'.[2] Two compositors, B and E, are supposed to have worked on the play, the first generally described as well experienced and particularly cavalier in his treatment of proper nouns, the second, on both counts, less so. There are, however, problems with these theories. Three main areas of difficulty have been pointed out by the play's latest editors.[3] The speech prefix '*Omnes*' occurs six times in *Antony and Cleopatra* but only four times elsewhere in all substantive editions of Shakespeare's other plays. In as much as the manuscript's punctuation can be reconstructed from F it does not appear to be Shakespearian. Finally, F's preference of 'oh' for 'o' goes strongly against the practice in other plays believed to have been set from authorial manuscripts.[4]

---

[1] *Antony and Cleopatra*, ed. John Dover Wilson (Cambridge, 1950), pp. 128–30; W. W. Greg, *The Shakespeare First Folio* (Oxford, 1955), pp. 402–3 and 403 n9. *Antony and Cleopatra*, ed. Emrys Jones (Harmondsworth, 1977), p. 270. At TLN 1978 there is the form '*Thantoniad*'.

[2] Stanley Wells and Gary Taylor, *William Shakespeare: A Textual Companion* (Oxford, 1987), p. 549.

[3] *Antony and Cleopatra*, ed. David Bevington (Cambridge, 1990), in the New Cambridge Shakespeare Series; *A New Variorum Edition of Shakespeare: Antony and Cleopatra*, ed. Marvin Spevack (The Modern Language Association of America, 1990).

[4] Until Jowett's and Taylor's promised piece '"With New Additions"', *Textual Companion*, p. 142, is published, Spevack's figures (p. 378) on o/oh occurrences in three plays allegedly set from foul papers must suffice; they are striking: *MND* Q1 60:3; *MV* Q1 33:0 and *Hamlet* Q2 103:5.

Neither of the play's most recent editors comes to any conclusion about the nature of the manuscript underlying F firmer than the Oxford Shakespeare's summary 'Holograph (foul papers) or a scribal transcript of it'.[5] What, however, does it mean when editors talk about 'foul papers' and authorial transcripts? Shakespeare may have composed *Antony and Cleopatra* and then made his own fair copy of the play, but running to over three thousand lines this would have been quite an undertaking for such a busy man. In this period, authors often did make fair copies of their own works, but – in as much as a generalization can be made about a vast and disparate practice – these were generally prepared for presentation to patrons, or for the press. Perhaps Shakespeare's first editors were telling the truth and the first drafts of his plays could be used without difficulty as printers' copy. Yet doubts inevitably remain: while *Antony and Cleopatra* shows some definite marks of being set from autograph material of one kind or another, other marks suggest this was not necessarily the case.

The spelling of the thrice-repeated '*Antony*' (on which neither Spevack nor Bevington comments) might be taken as a token of these doubts. The passage was set in F by compositor B who was careless with the spelling and presentation of names. His change of practice from his usual *Anthony* might simply be chance. Equally, in a play with much mislining of verse, he may have been anxious to keep the line (already on the full side) in TLN 3013 and so left the h's out; but there was room in both 3011 and 3015 for some rearrangement to be made, even if it were not to accord with modern editorial practice. However, if B was following his copy, why should the copy suddenly change from Anthony to Antony here? Greg hinted that Wilson's theories about a false start might gain some support from the variant spelling, in other words, that some disturbance occurred in the copy at this point; this is an attractive hypothesis. Of course, there is no certain way of knowing exactly what happened, but some

possibilities – whose further investigation could raise larger questions about the nature of the texts from which the early editions of Shakespeare's plays were printed – might be worth considering.

The reaction against Bowers's belief in the importance of intermediate transcripts, of scribal copies of Shakespeare's manuscript – a reaction conveniently summed up in the editorial thrust of the Oxford *Textual Companion* – has placed pressure on the concept of foul papers. These are generally agreed to represent the author's original draft of a play corrected or much corrected, not least in the light of its production on the stage; they are therefore taken to be in a state which substantially reflected the author's final intentions. From these foul papers, the theatrical company would prepare a promptbook. In time, when a play came to be sent to the printing house, it was the authorial foul papers, retained by the company, not its valuable and useful promptbook, which would be sent to produce 'good' quartos and some Folio texts.

The economy and textual optimism of this theory have been seriously challenged by Paul Werstine, who argues that in fact no examples of authorial foul papers, as traditionally understood as 'first-and-final authorial drafts' (p. 72), have survived, not even in the recently discovered Melbourne Hall fragment (p. 74).[6] The

---

[5] *Textual Companion*, p. 147; this does not quite accord with what is said later in the volume on p. 549.

[6] 'Narratives About Printed Shakespeare Texts: "Foul Papers" and "Bad" Quartos', *Shakespeare Quarterly*, 41 (1990), 65–86; his scepticism is complemented by the next article in the same issue of the journal, Marion Trousdale 'A Second Look at Critical Bibliography and the Acting of Plays', 87–96, who questions the modern desire to find method and orderliness in promptbooks. Her discussion is more theoretically based than Werstine's and is marred by an apparent – and general – confusion (p. 88) between a scrivener as a name for a scribe and as the name for a class of notaries, legal copyists and money-lenders who acted in effect as solicitors. In 'The Texts of *Twelfth Night*', *English Literary History*, 57 (1990), 37–61, Laurie E. Osborne looks at

burden of Werstine's argument is that since no foul papers can be identified, scholarship has proceeded in a circular fashion: scholars guess at what foul papers were like by reconstructing their features from printed texts they believe were set from foul papers. Yet the supposedly characteristic features of foul papers are to be found in texts which have been positively identified as theatrical promptbooks. Werstine associates the desire to find foul papers behind 'good' texts with the theory that memorial reconstruction lies behind the so-called 'bad' quartos. 'Memorial reconstruction by an actor or actors identified with specific parts', he writes (p. 81), 'has never proved an adequate explanation for the genesis of any "bad" quarto: the case for such reconstruction has always broken down and has needed to be supplemented by secondary hypotheses'.

Werstine's argument is dense and not easy to summarize in a brief account: his questioning of these two categories is certainly valuable. He points out that they are of comparatively recent invention, and that they reveal something about the scholarly desire for neat alternatives and certainties. He is not the only scholar recently to have questioned assumptions behind 'bad' quartos or memorial texts.[7] Traditionally, scholars have wondered why even 'good' quartos appear to be so badly printed in comparison with other literary texts of the period. Yet not all 'good' quartos were badly printed (Q1 of *A Midsummer Night's Dream* is an example of a carefully printed text), and it might be the case that printers simply considered plays less worthy of their attention than other literary texts. However, the traditional conclusion — that even 'good' quartos must have been set from the sort of disorganized copy represented by authorial foul papers — is one that Werstine, following Blayney, rejects.

Instead, he suggests that other narratives behind the production of printed texts deserve to be given consideration. One of these, based on Moseley's preface to the Beaumont and Fletcher folio of 1647, can be taken to imply a role for theatrical transcripts prepared for private presentation. Greg sought to show that this was a practice brought into fashion by the scandal of *A Game at Chess* in 1624 and so not applicable to the development of Shakespeare's texts.[8] As Werstine points out, the manuscripts of Middleton's play derive largely from the author himself or from his collaboration with Ralph Crane. Moseley, on the other hand, bears witness to a different, more immediately theatrical origin, 'a transcript of the stage adaptation of a play by an actor' (p. 86). Furthermore, since Crane's extant manuscripts of plays were prepared for individual presentation, it is worth considering that the plays in the Folio for which he supplied the copy may also derive from such private transcripts.

They may turn out to be a red herring: if no contemporary manuscript can be found to fit the modern conception of foul papers, scholars are on equally weak, perhaps even weaker, ground with private, theatrical transcripts. If a group of these could be positively identified as extant, it would be interesting to know what they looked like, as well as for whom and under what circumstances they were made.

Yet, this questioning of categories might help to accommodate some of the unusual features in *Antony and Cleopatra*. Scholarly disagreement as to whether it was set from foul papers or from a transcript of them of some

---

eighteenth-century 'performance' editions of the play and proposes that (since all copies of the Folio are different) all texts of the play are equally valuable. Her article might prompt the question of why quartos were produced in the first place.

7 Eric Sams returns to a favourite theme (that Q1 of *Hamlet* is not a memorial text, but an early version of the play) in 'Assays of Bias', *Notes and Queries*, NS 38 (1991), 60–3.

8 *A Game at Chess by Thomas Middleton 1624*, ed. T. H. Howard-Hill, John Creaser, H. R. Woudhuysen and John Pitcher, Malone Society Reprints, 1990. The Malone Society has also reprinted its edition of *The Book of Sir Thomas More*, 1990, incorporating Greg's original edition of the play and the supplement prepared by Harold Jenkins and first issued in 1961.

kind, might suggest a degree of uncertainty about the very nature of foul papers and the play's textual history. One possibility might be that it was set from some sort of private transcript – since there is no evidence to show that there was a contemporary production of the play, a copy of such a private transcript might well have been particularly sought after by early enthusiasts of Shakespeare's work. But there does also appear to be a case for questioning the unitary nature of its textual origins. A fair copy deriving from foul papers need not necessarily be in one hand only: the Huntingdon manuscript of *A Game at Chess* was made by two scribes, with a title-page and two sections of text and some corrections in Middleton's own hand. Equally, a fair copy might be produced by mixing scribal transcripts of passages of the author's draft too foul for easy reading with more legible passages in the author's hand. In the case of *Antony and Cleopatra*, more than one hand, authorial and scribal, may have been present in the manuscript which was sent to the press.

Whatever manuscript was used, both recent editors of the play adopt very conservative textual approaches. As one might expect from David Bevington (for whom this is the third time he has edited the play), his text is accurate and carefully prepared. He allows himself minor emendations at 2.1.22 and 2.6.16, but rejects emendations by others of 'arm-gaunt steed' (1.5.50), 'That art not what thou'rt sure of' (2.5.105), 'Yon ribaudred nag' (3.10.10: 'Perhaps a way of spelling "ribald-rid"'), 'The mered question' (3.13.10), 'The rack dislimns' (4.14.10), 'The round world' (5.1.15), 'this wild world' (5.2.308). At the famous crux in 5.2.85–6, he rejects bold attempts to follow F's powerful '*Anthony* it was' by letting his bounty be described as having 'no winter in't; an autumn 'twas / That grew the more by reaping.' Generally, he keeps his text as close as possible to the Folio, to the extent of often following its lineation, especially its lack of indentation of half-lines. The result, which

seeks to avoid 'hypermetrical and unconvincing' verse (p. 72), is very attractive, especially with a difficult passage such as 2.2.9–19. As with other volumes in the Cambridge series, details of relined verse are not given. Most of his emendations concern stage directions, which become much fuller than they are in the Folio (it is only in this area that Bevington adopts any of Oxford's emendations).

Bevington's introduction is full and generous, proceeding subtly to illuminate a carefully mediated view of the play, influenced most by the accounts of Janet Adelman, Maynard Mack and Rosalie Colie. Instead of simply declaring his own hand, by selective quotation from a wide range of those who have written about the play, Bevington builds up a picture of its wonderful complexity and rich diverseness. He deals with its mythopoeic power, its contrarieties and its sense of transcendence, as well as with more familiar features such as sources, genre, style and stagecraft in such a way as constantly to bring out the play's imaginative suggestiveness. His account of the play's history on the stage convincingly shows how directors have had more and more difficulty in responding to this aspect of it. Productions have moved from a consideration of the nature of its protagonists and their relationship to concentrating on its depiction of the world of politics. Bevington's annotation rarely seeks to close possibilities off, but maintains a constantly sharp linguistic and theatrical sense of what is reasonable. This is an excellent edition that will repay prolonged reading and use.

Of course, Marvin Spevack's New Variorum edition is conceived on a different scale and with a different purpose from Bevington's New Cambridge. Sometimes, however, it is hard to see quite what Spevack's massive editorial labours and the MLA's elaborate publishing project are seeking to achieve. The first third of the book is taken up with a modified diplomatic reprint of the text of the play in the Folio, with textual notes based on a collation of fifty-two editions and a commentary summarizing what has been said about individual words and passages by previous editors and commentators. The next forty or so pages are given over to a list of emendations of accidentals in F, rejected conjectural emendations and accounts of the play's text (with valuable material on compositorial practices) and date. Over two hundred pages are then filled by dealing with the play's sources, influences and analogues, in which substantial old-spelling extracts are reprinted from Plutarch, Mary Sidney and Daniel among others. Almost all of the rest of the book is devoted to summarizing criticism of the play under the headings of 'Genre', 'Themes and Significance', 'Technique' and 'Characters'. Finally there is a section about the play on the stage, a long bibliography and a full index.

The scope of the edition is enormous, but whether it represents the best way of transmitting all the information it contains is by no means certain. It also deliberately excludes material which a user might reasonably expect to find. A collation of Bevington's textual commentary against Spevack's reveals features which Spevack chose to exclude. Bevington records some punctuation variants not in the Variorum (for example, 'Thou, eunuch / Thou eunuch', at 1.5.9, TLN 533). Variant spellings have often been ignored, so that Bevington (2.7.11) notes 'lief' as Capell's rendering of Folio's 'liue' ('lieve' in F3), but Variorum (TLN 1346) only notes that 'liue' is a 'spelling variant' of 'lief' in the commentary, without reference to Capell; Bevington's treatment of 'we do launch / Diseases in our bodies' (5.1.36–7) records Pope's 'launce' and Theobald's 'lance', where Variorum (TLN 3153–4) is less informative. As might be expected, there are differences in the historical collations (for example with 'brows' bent' at 1.3.36 and TLN 346), even in the record of Folio variants (Bevington notes Folio's 'chapsn o more' at 3.5.11 which the Variorum (TLN 1738) does not include in its list of accidentals emended in F).[9]

Given the amount of detail Spevack includes in his collations from fifty-two editions and the arbitrary way in which they often treated stage directions there is no doubt a good reason for omitting such material. But in itself this might make the user wonder what value there is in collating so many editions, manuscript notes and letters in the first place: they cannot all be of equal value and significance. The collations in the textual notes end with the Riverside edition of 1974, and consequently readings from Emrys Jones's edition and the Oxford texts of the play are only occasionally noted in the commentary and elsewhere. Against this editorial decision might be set the inclusion of a long list of unadopted conjectural emendations (pp. 346–60), which – if of little other value – supplies some amusing moments. Yet, too often, the Variorum seems pulled apart by contrary desires to exclude and to include: it would certainly be foolish to ignore what the volume has to offer, but its limitations need constantly to be borne in mind.

Among these might be the value of having a near-diplomatic transcript of the Folio's text of the play. It appears that the user is getting an unmediated version of Folio's text, but while i/j and u/v have not been modernized, the long s has been dropped. Except for a few minor typographic corrections, the Folio's punctuation has been retained throughout, a practice to which Fredson Bowers turns his attention in relation to *All is True*.[10] He is mainly concerned to examine the punctuation as it appears in R. A. Foakes's Arden edition of the play, of which he generally approves. In the course of the article he comes to the not unexpected

9 In 'A Curious Press-Variant in Folio *Antony and Cleopatra*', *The Library* 6th ser., 12 (1990), 132, Paul R. Sternberg draws attention to an uncorrected variant (sig.xx6 b31; TLN 1489) 'heere a,' in addition to Hinman's 'heare a,', later corrected to 'heare,'. The Variorum edition (p. 370) rejects Hinman's reading as an error.

10 'The Problem of Semi-Substantive Variants: An Example from the Shakespeare-Fletcher *Henry VIII*', *Studies in Bibliography*, 43 (1990), 80–95.

conclusion that 'faulty punctuation can affect meaning in a substantive manner on the same level as verbal signs' and goes on, with 'some hesitation', to call these signs 'semi-substantives' (p. 85). This development in Bowers's consideration of accidentals and substantives may excite bibliographers and textual theorists, and his conclusions offer sound practical advice: 'Editors of modernized texts – influenced to follow tradition by the custom of marking up some previous text with their own alterations – have paid too little attention to the necessity to paraphrase every line of an Elizabethan dramatist . . . Editors truly need to raise the level of their consciousness when dealing with Elizabethan dramatic punctuation whether they are producing unmodernized or modernized texts' (p. 89).

Spevack's text is a curious hybrid, unmodernized, but not edited and not, so to speak, the thing itself. He might have considered the possibility of presenting his text in facsimile and rejected it on grounds of format, but it hardly needs to be said that editions in which the text is reproduced in facsimile have great advantages for editor and reader alike. The business of reproducing Shakespeare's texts in photographic facsimile is by no means over, as the latest quarto facsimile published by the Malone Society shows.[11] This reproduces the Huntington copy of Q(b) of 2 Henry IV as well as the two uncancelled and uncorrected leaves from sig.E preserved in the British Library copy of Q(a). The facsimiles are actual size: the quarto is given its own TLNs and those of the Folio have been supplied to allow differences between the texts to be easily identified; there is also a table of correspondences between Q and the Riverside edition. The Introduction provides a list of copies collated and their press variants, accounts of the differences between the two issues of the quarto, and its relationship with the Folio text of the play. No detailed textual theories are put forward but Jowett's and Taylor's and Melchiori's theories about the texts of the play and about the cancel affecting 3.1 are challenged.

There is as yet no modern facsimile of the second quarto of Othello: in the light of Thomas L. Berger's article on it, there should be one.[12] He argues that since editors are more or less bound to produce a text of the play which conflates the first quarto and the first Folio, attention should be paid to Q2 since it represents, in Berger's view, the beginnings of editorial work on the play. Indeed, some of its 'readings demonstrate an active, alert editorial intelligence at work' (p. 147) and as an early witness to the play Q2 'merits attention and repays scrutiny' (p. 152) – surprisingly M. R. Ridley's Arden edition is the only modern, substantial edition to include readings from the second quarto in its collations. Berger's piece begs some questions about the usefulness of early witnesses, but he defends himself by invoking the long series of theatrical quartos which derive from the second. These early quartos are certainly of some interest for their proximity to Shakespeare's language and playhouse practice, but still need to be treated with caution. Berger looks briefly at examples where Q2 provides a more satisfactory reading than F (where Q1 is silent) and where it mediates between the two witnesses.

In an essay by Kathleen Irace, Gary Taylor's textual theories about another play come under scrutiny.[13] She argues that the quarto of Henry V 'was reconstructed from the reporters' recollections of a version similar to the Folio, which they apparently abridged as part of a single process of reconstruction and adaptation' (p. 228). She attempts to refute Taylor's theory

---

[11] *The Second Part of King Henry the Fourth 1600*, ed. Thomas L. Berger, G. R. Proudfoot and John Pitcher (Malone Society Reprints, 1990).

[12] 'The Second Quarto of *Othello* and the Question of Textual "Authority"', *Analytical and Enumerative Bibliography*, NS 2 (1988), 141–59. Berger also adds some slight evidence (pp. 152–3) that in preparing his 1709 edition Rowe consulted early quartos of the play rather than just F4, as is usually stated.

[13] 'Reconstruction and Adaptation in Q *Henry V*', *Studies in Bibliography*, 44 (1991), 228–53.

that Q was reconstructed from an intermediate theatrical abridgement by a computer-aided analysis of the texts. Beginning with the question of memorial reconstruction in Q, she looks for the likely reporters by analysing lines entirely, mostly and partially found in Q as against those found in F; she then does the same for paraphrased and 'unique' lines. These are then divided between lines spoken by individual characters and those they could be said to have witnessed. Her findings point to the primary role of Exeter in the process of reconstructing the text from memory; he was assisted by the actors playing Pistol and Gower who doubled the parts of Nym, Scrope and possibly the Governor and York (p. 233). Since the suspected reporters consistently reproduce, according to her figures, such a high proportion in Q of their F parts (Exeter, the highest, retains eighty-four per cent of his F part in Q), Irace argues that Q was linked to F not to an intermediate abridgement of it — if an abridgement had intervened, the reporters' roles would have been cut in proportion with those of the rest of the cast.

The second section of her article is given over to showing that the eighty or so lines in Q which have different speech prefixes from those in F were reattributed 'by the reporter/adapters when they reconstructed the text' (p. 234). Most of these lines occur in two groups of scenes, involving the French and the English nobles, and seem to show that most of the reattributions were made deliberately in the course of the play's memorial reconstruction. Finally, Irace turns to examine the omissions and alterations 'that shape the Quarto as well as simply abridging it' (p. 239). Her main conclusion is that the text of the play as represented in the Folio was essentially the same (including the Choruses) as that from which the quarto derives.

Since Taylor believed that the abridgement which the reconstructors of Q drew on was a theatrical one, possibly even prepared in parts by Shakespeare himself, he felt free to draw on

it as a witness in his two Oxford editions of the play. Irace is more sceptical: since Q represents an abridgement of F reconstructed by 'actor/adapters' (p. 249), its use 'may be inappropriate in the text of an edition of *Henry V* that seeks to communicate Shakespeare's intentions'.

As Irace is aware, there are some problems with her studies, not least those revolving around questions of doubling, the nature of the copy underlying the Folio text, and recent doubts about 'bad' quartos (she refers to Werstine's article discussed above). On the one hand she suggests that the quarto (about half the length of, and with seven fewer speaking parts than, the Folio) was 'probably the first deliberate abridgment of Henry V [sic], designed, perhaps, as a promptbook for use in performances outside London' (p. 249), on the other that uncertainty is growing among theatre historians that '"bad" quartos were adapted for a reduced company, presumably for touring' (p. 243 n24). Her most powerful piece of evidence is the high percentage of Exeter's identical and near-identical lines in both the quarto and the Folio, but the conclusions that can be drawn from this fact may well deserve to be challenged. Irace's valuable article assembles interesting evidence about the play, but the implications she draws from it deserve further scrutiny. In particular, it is hard to gain a firm sense of why and how the memorial abridgement was made. Perhaps while on tour, within a year or so of its first performance, the reduced company decided to perform *Henry V* for which they had no script; they reconstructed as much as they could from memory, wrote that version out (?), and then abridged it; after the performance they sold their version to a stationer.

Computers, which played an important part in Irace's essay, also feature in two areas of investigation which have recently received further attention. Sceptics of the value of stylometry will find some ammunition to fortify their doubts when arguments about the accuracy of the data and about the methodology of the subject still seem to rage. At a very basic but still important level, Thomas Merriam points out two typographical errors in one of the tables supplied by Taylor in the Oxford *Textual Companion* and an underlying error in another table; he also observes inconsistencies in the presentation of material elsewhere. Turning to function words, Merriam suggests that 'Size as well as genre could be a factor in causing a systematic divergence, if indeed it is such' between what he perceives may be a difference in their behaviour in the poems and in the plays. He finally calls attention to an inconsistency in Taylor's Table 6 of function words in disputed works: for *1 Henry VI* and *All is True*, Taylor supplies statistics for the whole plays as well as for each of the disputed parts, but does not do so for *Titus*, *Timon*, *Kinsmen* or *Pericles*. Merriam supplies such figures for the last of these, but concludes that 'the overall picture is inconclusive', and then calls for smaller samples with which 'to establish the pattern of variation'.[14]

The Oxford *Textual Companion* comes in for further scrutiny in an article by M. W. A. Smith which argues that a 'closer technical examination unfortunately reveals fundamental flaws which seriously undermine the validity of Taylor's study'.[15] Smith's objections to Taylor's methodology centre on his limited choice of function words, exclusion of contracted forms from the statistics and most of all his adoption of a percentage rate of use of words, which 'is not an accepted starting point from which to embark on a statistical description: a regularity of use is implied which is not reflected in the plays themselves'. He challenges Taylor's calculations concerning standard deviations and his interpretation of the results, not least Taylor's confident assertion that he has conclusively shown that Marlowe could not have written Shakespeare's works. Smith presents revised versions of Taylor's tables 3 to 7, which yield some interesting results (both parts of *Tamburlaine* are like each other, but different from the rest of Marlowe's works apart from *Massacre* which may be a corrupt

abridgement; of the suspected memorial texts *Romeo* and *Hamlet* alone are likely to be Shakespearian). He concludes that 'the revised procedure is no more able to provide reliable information on authorship than Taylor's original flawed approach'. The problem is, he argues, that 'while function words can distinguish authors, their occurrences in texts are frequently more erratic than the statistical description of a random variable would allow'. Far from suggesting that these tests are a waste of time, Smith argues that they could be made more useful by analysing larger samples in a more precise way.

Function words – whether analysed in large or small samples – may have appeared at one time to offer a reliable and convenient approach for stylometrists, but the work of Eliot Slater pointed to the value of word-links. With the help of Hugh Calvert, Smith has also turned his attention to these. Applying Slater's methodology to *The Spanish Tragedy* and *James IV*, Smith and Calvert show that the plays are linked most strongly with early works by Shakespeare and appear 'as Shakespearian as any Shakespeare play'. At the same time they conclude that Slater's method could be generally useful in dating works.[16] In a later article,[17] Smith returns to word-links and chronology, once more examining Slater's methodology and proposing in its place one 'which relies more on trends over groups of plays rather than on the sporadic excesses of word-links in individual plays'. When the canon is divided into six sets of play-ranges varying from two to nine groups the number of observed, consistent

[14] 'Taylor's Statistics in *A Textual Companion*', *Notes and Queries*, NS 36 (1989), 341–2.

[15] 'Statistical Inference in *A Textual Companion* to the Oxford Shakespeare', *Notes and Queries*, NS 38 (1991), 73–8.

[16] 'Word-Links as a General Indicator of Chronology of Composition', *Notes and Queries*, NS 36 (1989), 338–41.

[17] 'Shakespearian Chronology: A New Approach to the Method of Word-Links', *Notes and Queries*, NS 37 (1990), 198–204.

word-links between *Venus and Adonis* and the rest of the canon can be charted to show that the poem belongs to the period after the *Henry VI* trilogy, *Richard III* and *The Comedy of Errors*. Smith suggests some refinements of Slater's system of identifying and listing word-links and considers how this should be done mechanically rather than manually: he is well aware of the problems of mixing different genres in these tests.

This is only one of the difficulties which sceptics might raise about stylometry: others must involve the nature of the texts on which these investigations are based in the first place. On the one hand, the treatment of some function words can be used allegedly to determine compositors, on the other the same function words are supposed to identify authorship or chronology. Similarly, word-links between works are thought to be able to perform the same role as function words, yet editors will emend one text on the basis of comparable usage elsewhere in the canon.

If the proof of the pudding is in the eating, some mouthfuls prove harder to swallow than others. *Pericles* provides a good example of this, as questions about its authorship continue to attract scholarly attention. M. W. A. Smith continues his investigation of what he regards as the split authorship of the play by returning to function words in it.[18] Summarizing previous work on function words (including his own), Smith reports that he gathered a pool of forty-six such words which he then traced through seventeen plays by Shakespeare and by his contemporaries. The result, he reports, was that the last three acts of *Pericles* 'were found to be more likely to be the work of Shakespeare than that of any of the other six writers' of the plays which formed the test group. When Acts I and II of *Pericles* were compared with the works of all the other playwrights apart from Wilkins, they were found to be more like Shakespeare's work than anyone else's. However, when the acts were compared between Wilkins and Shakespeare they were closer to the former

than the latter, 'but the closeness of the result encourages speculation that Shakespeare also had a hand in this part of the text'. A similar result showed the possibility that Wilkins had a hand in the rest of the play and leads Smith to speculate that he 'wrote his novel *The Painful Adventures of Pericles* in disappointment at having his play passed to Shakespeare for revision and perhaps completion, and in doing so hoped to retain some of the credit he thought was due to him'.

In the event, these function words hardly take the argument much further, except into the psychology which may lie behind Wilkins's still puzzling production of a novel based on memory of a play in which he is supposed to have had a hand. MacD. P. Jackson, in a powerful piece,[19] draws on E. A. J. Honigmann's observation of George Wilkins's fondness for the use of a latinate 'resumptive which'. He classifies these into three kinds, observing that there are twenty such usages in the first two acts and none at all in the rest of the play. He then notes that in the rest of the canon Shakespeare's use of the different varieties of this formula is rare; it is equally unusual in twenty contemporary plays by nineteen other dramatists and in a further ten plays. The same fondness for it is, however, found in Wilkins's known work. Jackson concedes it is possible that the feature occurs in the first two acts of *Pericles* because Wilkins was in fact the reporter rather than the part-author of the play, but he regards this as unlikely. Instead, he praises the cohesiveness of the play, finding more evidence

---

[18] 'Function Words and the Authorship of *Pericles*', *Notes and Queries*, NS 36 (1989), 333–6. Smith contributes 'A Note on the Authorship of *Pericles*' to *Computers and the Humanities*, 24 (1990), 295–300, in which he reports on comparisons of the two parts of the play against six dramatists based on first words of speeches, all other words and collocations; the new tests reinforce his conclusion that 'Wilkins is more likely be the (main) author of *Pericles* 1, 2 than the mature Shakespeare'.

[19] '*Pericles*, Acts I and II: New Evidence for George Wilkins', *Notes and Queries*, NS 37 (1990), 192–6.

of 'imaginative unity' in Shakespeare's work with the disreputable hack, Wilkins, than with the better dramatist and more experienced collaborator, John Fletcher.

This last observation might give pause for thought: Jackson supplies a striking piece of further evidence for the usual division of *Pericles*, but in so doing poses other questions about it which still await answer. It would, for example, be interesting to know what a historian of grammar and language thinks of his approach. As a socio-historical linguist, Jonathan Hope might be the man to ask about this sort of methodology. In a piece on the authorship of *All is True*, he presents arguments for the traditional division of the play between Shakespeare and Fletcher, countering Cyrus Hoy's theory that in some scenes Fletcher was merely revising or touching up Shakespeare's work.[20] His discriminator is the use of the auxiliary 'do' in its regulated (that is, now standard) and unregulated (now non-standard) forms in sentences.

When applied to ten of each dramatist's plays, this shows that Shakespeare (the older, lower class, less well-educated, more provincial writer) used the regulated form less often than Fletcher. When refined, the test produces similar results where the sample is large enough on a scene by scene analysis. Refined further, Shakespeare's preference for unregulated positive declarative sentences ('I did go home' as opposed to 'I went home') in *All is True* is marked against Fletcher's rare use of them. Unlike some discriminators, this one is not prone to scribal or compositorial interference and because of the metrical awkwardness of turning unregulated into regulated lines the possibility of a second author's revising hand can be discounted. Hope is aware that authors might write in a consciously antiquated style: the question of deliberate imitation remains to be considered. While Hope's article may strike some readers as over-simplifying the historical and sociological side, it presents interesting new material on the linguistic.

It is only one test, of course, and others, even of the same kind, may well present different results. This is no reason for ignoring tests, but rather a motive for thinking about what sort of tests and results would definitively prove a play, or part of a play, was by one hand rather than by another. Eric Sams is certainly the man to go to for definite answers. In a characteristically lively and iconoclastic piece, he has turned his attention to *Pericles* in the belief that contemporary witnesses were right not to question Shakespeare's authorship of the whole play.[21] Wilkins, he argues, never claimed to have written the play and the idea of his collaborating with Shakespeare strikes Sams as unlikely. Since Wilkins was a plagiarist, he goes on, looking for parallels between his work and the first two acts of *Pericles* is pointless. Believing that the play was an early work which Shakespeare later revised, Sams calls for a stylometric study of the 'garbled text' of the 1609 quarto to be made against Shakespeare's other early works. This conveniently takes the question back to the dangers of making bibliographical or critical judgements of texts whose origins are still disputed.[22]

[20] 'Applied Historical Linguistics: Socio-Historical Linguistic Evidence for the Authorship of Renaissance Plays', *Transactions of the Philological Society*, 88 (1990), 201–26.

[21] 'The Painful Misadventures of *Pericles* Acts I–II', *Notes and Queries*, NS 38 (1991), 67–70. Sams (p. 68 and n5) brings Thomas Warton as a witness that *Pimlyco. Or, runne red-cap*, which contains an allusion to *Pericles*, can be dated to 1596; the only extant edition is dated 1609 and was entered and transferred in the Stationers' Register in the spring of that year. There is a very impressionistic and subjective account, arguing for 'William Shakespeare, Sole Author of *Pericles*', by Karen Csengeri in *English Studies*, 71 (1990), 230–43; Csengeri's article takes no account of work on the play published since 1986.

[22] These dangers are rather clearly exposed in Thomas Merriam's examination of four sets of collocations in *Sir Thomas More*, Shakespeare's First Folio plays, and parts of plays ascribed to Anthony Munday ('Did Munday Compose *Sir Thomas More*?', *Notes and Queries*, NS 37 (1990), 175–8): the results provide Merriam with addi-

Shakespeare's Sonnets provide an example of one of the few texts about which disagreement may be said to have lessened rather than grown during recent years. This is partly due to the work of MacDonald P. Jackson who has analysed the respective shares and habits of the quarto's two compositors. He has now turned to a crux in Sonnet 51 (set by the inaccurate compositor B), in which according to the quarto since no desire can 'with my desire keepe pace, / Therefore desire . . . / Shall naigh noe dull flesh in his fiery race . . .'[23] Almost all editors modernize 'naigh' to 'neigh', but Jackson argues that 'naigh' represents a simple minim error and the sense is better served by 'waigh', meaning to disregard, take no account of, something. He also points out that 'naigh' as a variant form of 'neigh' is not in OED, nor is it found in Shakespeare's works; he adds that he has never come across it in contemporary texts.

The point at issue is fundamentally a theoretical as well as a practical one. There are those who recognize the need to emend texts (Jackson approves of, but does not accept, the Oxford edition's 'raign' or 'rein' in the Sonnet) and those who are reluctant to: among the latter are, he says, critics who prefer complexity and perplexity to 'coherence and completeness'. Unfortunately, emendators are by no means always free of the desire to make meaning more rather than less complicated.[24] However, this could not, generally, be said to apply to a final batch of shorter notes on texts.

Anthony Brian Taylor properly defends the usual modernization of Folio's 'Tyke' to 'tike' in *Henry V* 2.1.29 rather than Gary Taylor's 'tick', by noting Pistol's strain of canine abuse directed at Nim in the scene and a contemporary 'opprobrious' usage of the word in reference to Cerberus.[25] Another emendation, to *2 Henry VI* 1.3.150, adopted by Oxford is strongly challenged by N. F. Blake. In the Folio, Buckingham says of Eleanor 'Shee's tickled now, her Fume needs no spurres', which is metrically unsatisfactory and has led editors to emend 'Fume' to 'furie' and modernize to

'fury'. Blake suggests that the passage in Buckingham's speech does not, as is usually supposed, refer to Eleanor's anger but to her 'readiness to resort to witchcraft which will lead to her downfall'. The language Buckingham uses is the language – 'part of the cant register' – of drink: 'tickled' means 'befuddled' and Folio's 'Fume', the correct reading, refers to the fumes of alcohol which rise from the stomach. The line's metrical irregularity may mean it is 'when heightened emotion needs to be expressed that a different stress pattern is used' – but then, it may be objected, 'heightened emotion' could be invoked to allow characters to speak any amount of metrical or unmetrical nonsense.[26]

In 'More on "The Base Judean"' Peter Milward supports his reading by arguing that *Othello* is 'charged with a recurring vein of implicit reference to the betraying of Christ by

---

tional evidence for his belief that Shakespeare was sole author of *Sir Thomas More*. In a more pertinent article, 'Shakespeare's Handwriting', *Shakespeare Survey* 42 (1990), 119–28, Giles E. Dawson re-examines the palaeographical evidence for identifying Shakespeare's writing with that of Hand D in *Sir Thomas More*; in the course of his article, he defends Theobald's emendation 'and a babled of greene fields' in *Henry V* and considers Shakespeare's use of dialectal 'a' for 'he' against that of contemporary playwrights.

[23] 'How Many Horses Has Sonnet 51? Textual and Literary Criticism in Shakespeare's Sonnets', *English Language Notes*, 27 (1990), 10–19. In '*Titus Andronicus*: Play, Ballad, and Prose History', *Notes and Queries*, NS 36 (1989), 315–17, Jackson rebuts G. Harold Metz's rebuttal of his theory (shared with Marco Mincoff and G. K. Hunter) that the line of descent of the story follows the chronological order of its three extant witnesses.

[24] The life and works of one of the princes of emendation are considered in Peter Seary's *Lewis Theobald and the Editing of Shakespeare* (Oxford, Clarendon Press, 1990). Marvin Spevack briefly considers the history, motives, theory and practice of emendation in 'The Other Shakespeare: Some Observations on the Vocabulary and Text', *Analytical and Enumerative Bibliography*, NS 3 (1989), 41–65.

[25] 'The Case for Pistol's 'Base *Tike*', *Notes and Queries*, NS 36 (1989), 324–5.

[26] 'Fume/Fury in *2 Henry VI*', *Notes and Queries*, NS 38 (1991), 49–51.

Judas'.[27] Finally, John Pafford proposes that where Sly in the Induction to *The Taming of the Shrew* refers apparently to the Hostess as 'boy', the correct reading may be the dialectal 'bor' (as in 'neighbour') used as a familiar form of address.[28] Sly, however, may not necessarily be addressing the Hostess, but anticipating what he will say to the Headborough (or thirdborough) she has gone to fetch: if not in a state of 'heightened emotion' he is certainly 'tired and emotional'.[29]

Notes and Queries, NS 36 (1989), 329–31. Berger (see n12, above) observes that Q2, like Q1, of *Othello* prints '*Indian*'.

[28] '*Shrew*, Induction, 12. For *Boy* ?Read *Bor*', *Notes and Queries*, NS 37 (1990), 172–3.

[29] Among other books which have been received are a new edition of *Shakespeare: A Select Bibliographical Guide*, ed. Stanley Wells (Oxford, 1990) and a revised third edition of Brownell Salomon's *Critical Analyses in English Renaissance Drama: A Bibliographic Guide* (New York and London, 1991).

BOOKS RECEIVED

This list includes all books received between 1 September 1990 and 31 August 1991 which are not reviewed in this volume of *Shakespeare Survey*. The appearance of a book in this list does not preclude its review in a subsequent volume.

Annali XXXI, 3, *Rivisitazioni Shakespeariane*. Napoli, 1988.

Bache, William B. *Design and Closure in Shakespeare's Major Plays: The Nature of Recapitulation*. New York: Peter Lang Publishing Inc., 1991.

Bloom, Harold, ed. *Major Literary Characters: Cleopatra*. New York: Chelsea House Publishers, 1990.

Cohen, Robert. *Acting in Shakespeare*. California, London, Toronto: Mayfield Publishing Company, 1991.

Edwards, Viv, and Thomas J. Sienkewicz, eds. *Oral Cultures Past and Present: Rappin and Homer*. Oxford: Basil Blackwell Ltd, 1990.

Jorgens, Jack J. *Shakespeare on Film*. New York and London: University Press of America, reprinted 1991.

Kinney, Arthur F. *Elizabethan Backgrounds: Historical Documents in the Age of Elizabeth I*. Hamden, Conn.: Archon Books, newly edited 1990.

Lamb, Mary Ellen. *Gender and Authorship in the Sydney Circle*. Madison and London: Eurospan. University Press Group, 1991.

Livi-Bacci, Massimo. *Population and Nutrition. An Essay on European Demographic History*. Cambridge: Cambridge University Press, 1991.

Martin, Jacqueline. *Voice in Modern Theatre*. London and New York: Routledge, 1991.

Schlueter, Kurt, ed. *The Two Gentlemen of Verona*, The New Cambridge Shakespeare. Cambridge: Cambridge University Press, 1990.

Taylor, Barry. *Vagrant Writing: Social and Semiotic Disorder in the English Renaissance*. Hemel Hempstead: Harvester Wheatsheaf, 1991.

INDEX

INDEX

INDEX

INDEX

INDEX

7952

Printed in the United Kingdom
by Lightning Source UK Ltd.
93508